D1825060

47 Billion Years of Evolution:
A Case Report

Physical and Spiritual Development of Humankind

Martha J. Barham, R.N., Ph.D.
Edited by
Elaine M. Heiby, Ph.D.

Memoria

"God is Awesome"

James Thomas (Tom) Greene, Ph.D. assisted in an early draft of this book. His old beat-up automobile had the quote above on a bumper sticker. He transitioned on September 4, 2008 in Honolulu, Hawaii. Tom was a clinical psychologist who practiced in Honolulu for over 30 years. He contributed to four other books by Marti Barham: *Bridging Two Worlds* (1981), *Silver Cord: Lifeline to the Unobstructed* (1986), *Yesterday's Children* (1993), and *Our Spiritual Connection* (1994).

Jay Barham served as a channel for over 30 years without hesitation or financial gain. His only qualifier was that he would not take responsibility for any action to which a participant agreed or for any information relayed by materialized entities (i.e., spirits). He was always appreciative of the positive experiences people shared. He was humble in accepting his gift of serving as a reliable physical medium. He transitioned on October 31, 2009.

Copyright

ISBN e-book: 978-0-9892484-0-2
ISBN paperback print on demand: 978-0-9892484-1-9

About the Author and Editor

Biography of the Author Martha (Marti) J. Barham, R.N., Ph.D.

Dr. Marti Barham, as she is known in Honolulu, is a Registered Nurse and Licensed Psychologist. She has practiced as a therapist for over 40 years. She has published papers and numerous books. Her experiences reflect many circumstances recorded in this and her previous books. She may be contacted at marti@drbarham.com.

Biography of the Editor Elaine M. Heiby, Ph.D.

Elaine M. Heiby has been a professor of clinical psychology and a licensed psychologist for over 30 years in Honolulu. She has over 100 scholarly publications. In recent years, her research interests have included the integration of quantum physics as an explanatory mechanism for human experiences that are generally labeled as spiritual or psychic. She may be contacted at heiby@hawaii.edu.

Note to the Reader

This book *47 Billion Years of Evolution: A Case Report* contains direct quotes from materialized entities (discarnate spirits who temporarily assume a physical human body). Quotes are in ***bold italics***. This font is used to emphasize that this information is not a summary or commentary by the Author or Editor.

To place this book in context, the Reader is encouraged to attend to the Preface and the Appendices. Some Readers may find it useful to begin with the Preface and then peruse Appendix A on how materialization was accomplished and Appendix B for additional background teachings of the entities. Appendix C contains additional information on how to use physical, psychic, and spiritual energies for healing.

When the term "we" is used, it refers to Marti Barham and Tom Greene unless otherwise indicated by the context. Both Marti and Tom attended the lectures by the entities that are quoted in this book.

Citations used in the Preface and Chapters are indicated in the text by putting the authors' last name and year of publication in parentheses. The full citations are listed under References. There is also a list of Additional Suggested Readings related to the material presented in this book. The References and Additional Suggested Readings are not meant to be comprehensive.

The e-book version of this book will appear somewhat differently depending on the e-reader. For example, the size and style of the font may change throughout the book. This does not reflect errors in the uploaded manuscript, but technical differences among various types of e-reader devices.

Table of Contents

Foreword

The Energy That Creates Energy
By John Turner, M.D.

I became interested in psychic phenomena after reading about the American psychic Edgar Cayce. At the time I was a graduate student in physics and the Cayce winds blew my sails toward medical school and eventually, neurological surgery. My goal was to find the meaning and existence of the spiritual world. With that said, years passed, the last 33 of which were spent in Hawaii as a practicing brain surgeon while at the same time, researching the subject of an afterlife. This culminated in meeting one of the authors of *47 Billion Years of Evolution: A Case Report,* the result of years of dedicated exploration into this very topic.

Starting with the automatic writing with the *Ouija* board, and culminating with a long series of discourses by materialized entities who took shape from ectoplasm during the Darkroom sessions, I found that the entities' teachings were commensurate with the conclusions described in my book, *Medicine, Miracles and Manifestations: A Doctor's Journey Through the Worlds of Divine Intervention, Near-Death Experiences, and Universal Energy.* I was pleasantly surprised to read the entity's accounts of perfecting the spirit in multiple incarnations in preparation to once again return to and meld with the Source.

With an understanding that there are no coincidences, I now realize that there was a deeper purpose to my being kindly invited by the authors to write a foreword for this *47 Billion Years of Evolution: A Case Report.* After study of this book, I feel that I am finally on the way to completing my task of answering the question, from *whence we came?*

With an open mind, and with the certainty that the truth needs no defense, you will be gently steered into deeper study about the meaning of life and the mechanisms of what the entities call the *obstructed* and *unobstructed* universes, concepts that I heretofore labeled the physical and

1

spiritual worlds. Most importantly, you will learn (as did I), that as part of our spiritual evolution, we must, and will, reach a point where each of us openly accepts that there is a meaning to our existence and behind it all, a divine guiding force. We can think of this One Supreme Power as an energy that can create energy. You might feel guided to review the work of physicist Lawrence Krauss (2012) to see how this concept is plausible under the laws of physics as we know them . . . that is, the creation of *something from nothing.* You may be surprised to know that it will all end in the creation of *nothing from something.* I don't mean to confuse you with this, but in time, two-trillion years or so, any remaining astrophysicist or astronomer will only be able to examine his/her own 100-billion star Milky Way galaxy, everything else long gone behind a relativistic curtain that prohibits any other light from detection. That is to say, what was once *something,* the observable universe as we know it now, will end up as *nothing.* . . absolutely nothing at all.

   47 Billion Years of Evolution explains the plausible concept of a 47 million year history of human life on this planet. You will find it helpful to incorporate a meaningful look at the cited work of Cremo and Thompson (1996), as their work is crucial to understanding how such a concept can hold water as it runs contrary to mainstream science's teaching of a mere 100,000 year history of human life. Enjoy your read of this wonderful book as it addresses cosmology, cosmogony, and religion. As cogently stated by the channel Jay Barham, "The Entities exist, they are just as real as we are and they are awaiting their opportunity to communicate with us in whatever way they can."

   This wonderful book gives them that very opportunity and allows us to learn from their wisdom.

Foreword

Messages from Higher Realms
By Michael Tymn

Had I come upon this book 25 years ago, before I became
interested in mediumship, I'm sure that I wouldn't have gone
beyond the front and back covers before tossing it aside with
a scoff. Even 10 years ago, after I had done extensive
reading in the subject matter and had come to accept that
genuine mediumship exists, I likely would not have gone
beyond the Introduction, though my scoff would have then
been more of a curious smirk.

  I believe in spirits and spirit communication through
mediums. It took much studying, comparing and discerning
before I became convinced of the reality of mediumship, but
even after I accepted certain types of mediumship as genuine
I remained skeptical as to much of it. It was one thing for a
deceased loved one or close friend to obtain some small
piece of evidential information through a medium, quite
another thing for some "high spirit" or famous name from
history to communicate. Until a few years ago, I was highly
skeptical when the spirit communicator claimed to be Jesus,
St. Michael, Socrates, Plato, St. Augustine, Swedenborg, or
some other historical figure held in high regard by many.
The skeptic in me said, "And, yes, Cleopatra, too."

  And then there were names like Patience Worth,
Seth, White Eagle, Silver Birch, Ramtha, Imperator, and
others in which there was no way to confirm that such a
person ever existed. Nevertheless, there was so much
wisdom coming from these entities, Silver Birch being my
favorite, I figured there must be something to it. I couldn't
believe that a charlatan posing as a medium could
spontaneously produce such sustained profound verbiage.
Nor could I accept that the subconscious mind of an
uneducated person could offer such deep and insightful
information. As an example, Pearl Curran, the medium for
Patience Worth, had no more than an eighth grade education

3

and had never traveled more than a few hundred miles from her home in St. Louis, and yet the writings of Patience Worth were compared with Shakespeare, Chaucer, and Spenser. She was called a wit, a poet, a dramatist, and a philosopher. Today, some skeptical psychologist might say that the child's subconscious absorbed it all from the television next to her playpen, but Pearl Curran lived before television and even for the most part before radio. Even if she had a photographic mind and had spent the better part of her life in a library, which she didn't, it would have been extremely difficult to account for the spontaneous creativity and the immediate answers given to questions by researchers.

And in this book we meet entities named Aenka and Mario offering us information about the history of the universe and the meaning of life. My first reaction was, "Mario? Come on, no advanced spirit would have a name like Mario. Aenka, maybe; but not Mario. How ridiculous!"

During the early 1850s, Victor Hugo, the renowned French author, was supposedly receiving messages from Socrates, Moses, Jesus, Mohammed, Martin Luther, Galileo, and others. One communicating spirit identified "itself" to Hugo as 'Death,' another as "Angel of Light," and still another as the "Shadow of the Sepulcher." It was the "Shadow" who first communicated by means of table raps after Léopoldine, Hugo's deceased daughter, came through, informing Hugo and the others sitting in a circle with the medium that "death is the balloon that takes the soul to heaven," and that "infinity is an emptiness packed full," and "use your body to search out your soul." Initially, Hugo was very skeptical, wondering if the table acted through their thoughts. Although he soon came to believe that spirits of the dead were communicating, he then wondered if these were devious spirits posing as wise men, as religious leaders claimed, especially when what they had to say conflicted with established dogma and doctrine. But Hugo apparently had also heard that the "essence" of advanced souls can come down through lower spirits and that "group souls" can take on a fictitious identity for want of a specific identity. Whatever the explanation, Hugo was intrigued, impressed, and inspired by much of what the superior spirits had to say.

Allan Kardec, a pioneering French researcher, purportedly received messages from John the Evangelist, St. Augustine, St. Vincent De Paul, St. Louis, "The Spirit of Truth," Socrates, Plato, Fénélon, Franklin, and Swedenborg. They answered questions on every conceivable subject, including God, pantheism, universal space, biblical accounts of creation, reincarnation, relationships beyond the grave, possession, the fate of children beyond the grave, spirit influence, war, capital punishment, slavery, dreams, free will, suicide, and fear of death, to name just some.

As Kardec came to understand, superior spirits, while preserving their individuality, have no need to be identified with their teachings delivered while on earth, but because humans seem to need an identity in order to fix their ideas, superior spirits who identify with the teachings of the famous personage and belong to the same "family" or "collective whole" may take that famous name to appease us, as it is the teaching, not the signature, that is important.

Kardec asked if taking the name of a famous person would not be fraud. "It would be fraud on the part of a bad spirit who might want to deceive," came the answer, "but when it is for good, God permits it to be so among spirits of the same order, because there is among them a solidarity and similarity of thought."

Kardec had earlier been warned that inferior spirits frequently borrow respectable names in order to give credence to their words. Moreover, some spirits report themselves as fictional characters. "There is always a crowd of spirits ready to speak for anything," Kardec wrote, mentioning that one day a person took a fancy to invoke Tartufe, a fictitious character from a French play. Tartufe came immediately and talked of Orgon, of Elmire, of Damis, and of Valire, other fictitious characters in the play. "As to himself, he counterfeited the hypocrite with as much art as if Tartufe had been a real personage. Afterward, he said he was the spirit of an actor who had played that character."

The superior spirits, Kardec was informed, "have a language always worthy, noble, elevated, with not the least tincture of triviality. They say everything with simplicity and modesty, never boast, never make a parade of their knowledge or their position among others. That of the inferior or ordinary spirit has always some reflex human passion; every expression that savors of vulgarity, self-sufficiency, arrogance, boasting, acrimony, is a characteristic indication of inferiority, or of treachery if the spirit presents himself under a respected and venerated name."

Kardec asked why inferior spirits were permitted to interfere in the first place. Couldn't God or the superior spirits prevent it? "God permits it to be so to make trial of your perseverance and your judgment, and to teach you to distinguish truth from error; if you do not, it is that you are not sufficiently elevated, and still need the lessons of experience," came the reply.

A few years before Hugo and Kardec began their investigations of mediumship, John Edmonds, Chief Justice of the New York State Supreme Court, and George T. Dexter, a New York physician, received numerous profound messages from Swedenborg, the brilliant 18th Century scientist, and Lord Francis Bacon, the 17th Century British philosopher.

"It is not for the purpose of showing to the world that spirits can confer with man, or that God's law obtains in spirit-connection as well as physical, but it is for the purpose of showing you the truths of your spirit-life, after the spirit has left the body, that we leave our high estate and the blissful life of the spheres, and come to teach you," Swedenborg communicated at one sitting.

During the 1870s, William Stainton Moses, an Anglican priest who developed into a medium, was said to be controlled by a band of 49 spirits under the direction of a spirit called Imperator. Some of Imperator's subordinates had names like Rector, Mentor, and Doctor. Apparently,

Imperator was too far advanced and had to relay messages through some of the 49, who were closer in vibration to the earth vibration. When Imperator was asked about his name and the other strange names in his band of 49 spirits, he replied: "These names are but convenient symbols for influences brought to bear upon you. In some cases the influence is not centralized; it is impersonal, as you would say. In many cases the messages given you are not the product of any one mind, but are the collective influence of a number. Many who have been concerned with you are but the vehicles to you of a yet higher influence which is obliged to reach you in that way. We deliberate, we consult, and in many instances you receive the impression of our united thought."

If Jesus was concerned with the welfare of humans when alive, why wouldn't he still be concerned and continue with his teachings? Of course, the religious skeptic would say that if Jesus wanted to communicate he would certainly be able to do a much better job and be more convincing than he has been in those cases in which he has supposedly communicated in recent years. But the student of mediumship comes to understand that inter-dimensional communication has many obstacles and that the obstacles for superior spirits are greater than those facing lower spirits.

If the seemingly credible spirits can be believed, the superior spirits have a much more difficult time communicating than those at lower levels because they exist at such a high rate of vibration relative to the earth's vibration. These superior spirits, we are told, have to use spirits at lower levels of vibration to relay their messages to humans and these messages are sometimes distorted in the process, especially when they are filtered through the medium's mind.

"In proportion as spirits are purified and elevated in the hierarchy, the distinctive characters of their personalities are, in some sort, obliterated in the uniformity of perfection, and yet they do not the less preserve their individuality; this is the case with the superior and pure spirits," Kardec related what he had come to understand. "In this condition, the name they had on earth, in one of their thousand ephemeral corporeal existences, is quite an insignificant thing. Let us remark again that spirits are attracted to each other by the similarity of their qualities, and that they thus form sympathetic groups or families . . . but as names are necessary to us to fix our ideas, they can take that of any known personage whose nature is best identified with their own . . . . It thus follows that if a person's guardian angel gives his name as St. Peter, for instance, there is no actual proof that it is the apostle of that name; it may be he, or it may be an entirely unknown spirit belonging to the family of spirits of which St. Peter makes a part; it also follows that under whatever name the guardian angel is invoked, he comes to the call that is made, because he is attracted by the thought, and the name is indifferent to him."

Why so much research into spiritual communication during the nineteenth century, and less so during the twentieth century? Imperator told Stainton Moses that they (the superior spirits) overestimated their ability to communicate. "It is true that Benjamin Franklin did discover means of communication by raps, and that he was greatly aided by Swedenborg in awakening interest among spirits in the subject," Imperator communicated. "At the time of the discovery it was believed that all denizens of both worlds would be brought into ready communion. But, both on account of the obstinate ignorance of man, and of the extent to which the privilege was abused by spirits who assumed well-known names and personated them and so deceived men, that privilege has been greatly narrowed."

In effect, the superior or elevated spirits seem to have withdrawn because they had given as much as humans could absorb over a period of some 50 years and they weren't getting through. But that does not mean they gave up completely. From time to time over the last century, there have been a number of spirit communicators offering enlightenment for those open to it. Based on the profoundness of the messages recorded by Dr. Marti

Barham, a psychologist, over a 30-year period, Aenka and Mario come across as the real thing. Whether they were individual spirits, a soul group essence speaking as one or two spirits, or some form of spirit beyond human comprehension seems irrelevant. As those pioneers of psychical research were told, it was the message that counted, not the messenger.

Michael Tymn is the author of:
The Articulate Dead
Running on Third Wind
The Afterlife Revealed
Transcending the Titanic
The Afterlife Explorers
Resurrecting Leonora Piper

Editor's Preface

"If at first an idea does not sound absurd, then there is no hope for it" (Albert Einstein).

This is a lengthy Preface because reading this book requires one to maintain a mind as open as Einstein's. For about 150 years, there has been a revolution in the understanding of the nature of the universe in general and the purpose of life in particular. This revolution is taking place with a confluence of strange bedfellows—scientists, psychics, and spiritualists (LeShan, 2003).

47 Billion Years of Evolution: A Case Report indicates that our galaxy is one of seven that were set in motion 47 billion years ago. Three of those galaxies evolved conditions to sustain biological life on one planet and each of the three planets has its own distinct purpose and immutable laws. Our galaxy's planet Earth is one of them. Biological life on Earth, including the human creature, was created 47 million years ago. The majority of this book describes how the human on Earth operated on instincts for 40 million years. Then, seven million years ago, the human creature was selected as the most suitable for endowment of a higher quantity and quality of consciousness (i.e., a soul) than other forms of life on Earth. Some of the evolutionary information presented is supported by mainstream views on both evolution and creationism. Most information is, however, new to world literature.

The content of *Evolution* was dictated by two transiently materialized discarnate entities (i.e. spirits) who called themselves Aenka (pronounce ang-kah) and Mario. They were representing a committee of discarnate entities. The head of the committee went by the name of 'K'. This committee indicated that it is engaged in a worldwide project of expanding the awareness of the modern human being beyond information obtained by the five physical senses and yielded from a reductive materialistic approach to science and life in general. This project is referred to as the

"K Plan". The committee calls this a "revolution against negativity" that was initiated most recently by Buddha and Jesus—but their teachings have become distorted in modern organized religions, whose membership continues to decline (Milliken, 2012).

Information from many entities is being relayed worldwide via intuition, impingements, enhanced psychic abilities, channels, mediums, near-death experiencers, pre-death experiencers, apparitions, after death communications, and materialized entities. Highly respected quantum theorists (e.g., Amit Goswami), astrophysicists (e.g., Bernard Haisch), biologists (e.g., Rupert Sheldrake), physicians (e.g., Larry Dossey), psychologists (e.g., Gary Schwartz), and chemists (e.g., Andrew Collins) have integrated the concept of non-physical energies described by the entities to explain phenomena that a pure reductive materialistic approach to knowledge has failed to elucidate and organized religion has failed to satisfy.

In the common vernacular an entity might be called a soul, spirit, angel, or apparition. Aenka and Mario used the term *a Facet of Divinity*. They indicated that each entity is born from the Source (energy that creates energy). Each human is an entity incarnate. Therefore, each human is a facet of the Source. Terms for an entity proposed by scientists include a high frequency pure energy pattern, living consciousness, living entangled mind, morphogenetic field, living energy, systemic memory, quantum consciousness, quantum monad, and zero-point field, among others. This array of terms indicates that people from many persuasions throughout history and modern times have had a concept of existence beyond the physical.

An entity is defined as an eternal intelligent and creative energy pattern that exists both incarnate and discarnate. While incarnate, the entity exists within and around a human physical body, referred to as endowment. This incarnate condition of the entity is commonly referred to as the inner self, intuition, and also a soul. The physical body and other matter impose an obstructed consciousness

11

upon the entity that is related to the limitations of the physical senses and organ functions.

While discarnate, the entity exists as a pure energy form whose vibration is higher in frequency than matter. Consciousness is therefore unobstructed by physical matter and there is clear perception of both the physical and non-physical universes. While discarnate, an entity is often called a spirit, angel, disembodied soul, etheric body, or an astral body.

The discarnate entities that taught the contents of this book did so as temporarily materialized human beings presenting in the appearance of their last incarnation. A materialized discarnate entity temporarily forms the mass of a physical human body. The process that yields the materialization is described in Martha (Marti) Barham's 1981 book *Bridging Two Worlds*, edited by James Thomas (Tom) Green. Given Barham is the sole copyright holder of *Bridging Two Worlds*, it is reproduced in its entirety in Appendix A.

The materialization involved a complete or partially complete physical body with a working speech apparatus, so the voice was always independent rather than through the vocal cords of a living human as happens with voice channeling or mental mediumship, including automatic writing. The materialized entity will have a pulse but would have no need to create digestive and other unnecessary organs, as they have no need for food or drink. Observers of the materialized entities, with permission, touched them and inspected their body parts. The skin was described to be moist like a newborn baby. The procedure that led up to the materialized entities that taught the contents of *Evolution* is briefly summarized as follows:

The author Marti Barham, her husband Jay, Tom Greene, and up to 25 other interested individuals met in a darkened room. Jay, or at times another person, would lie down and enter a trance state. A trance is an altered state of consciousness similar but not identical to sleep. In a trance state, there is less awareness of the physical environment than during the typical awakened state. For example, meditation or absorption in a movie or book involves a trance state. The channel did not speak, move out of place, or awaken for the duration of a two-hour session (except for brief breaks). The others in the group would say an inviting prayer or some other unifying statement, sing any songs they enjoyed, and explicitly invited the entities to appear.

While a variety of entities materialized in the Darkroom over the years, two of them dictated the lectures for *Evolution*. These two entities, as mentioned, called themselves Aenka and Mario, who generally appeared twice or more a week for two-hour sessions over the course of about 30 years. The lectures were presented using both didactics and the Socratic method and were recorded on audiotape, transcribed, and then checked for accuracy. Aenka and Mario provided lectures on the origin and nature of the Source, the unobstructed and obstructed universes, the structure of the human physical personality, the purpose of life, and universal laws of natural human behavior.

Much of these teachings were relayed in Barham and Green's 1986 book, *The Silver Cord: Lifeline to the Unobstructed*, which is summarized in Appendix B. There were approximately 300 hours of lectures specifically for *Evolution* recorded on audiotape and then transcribed. Additional heretofore unpublished teachings on healing are given in Appendix C.

It was not the intent of the Darkroom sessions to objectively substantiate the existence of materialized entities to the point of satisfying modern scientific methods. However, there are numerous scientifically documented incidences of materialization that used similar Darkroom procedures in addition to numerous verified securities against fraud, group hallucinations, wishful thinking, or other confounds to the findings. One experimental approach to materialization was published in 2011 as *The Scole Report* by Keen, Ellison, and Fontana and also in Foy's 2008 book entitled *Witnessing the Impossible*. These books describe, in detail, a two-year project involving materialized entities appearing several times a week with skeptical scientists from various universities and professional magicians as participants documenting the procedure and phenomena witnessed. Other experimentally controlled examples of materialization yielded by contemporary mediums have been well documented (e.g., Vandersande, 2008, 2012). The only serious critiques from the participating scientists have been unsubstantiated claims of lying and fraud that would have required a multi-million dollar investment and a large conspiracy of reliable liars who received no financial compensation or social status for doing so. The professional magicians concluded they could not replicate the phenomena.

The entities' lectures for *Evolution* were given not only to Marti Barham and Tom Greene; many other professionals were sometimes among those in attendance, including psychiatrists, other physicians, psychologists, social workers, and counselors. One attendant was the physician famous for death studies, Elizabeth Kübler-Ross. She published her subsequent beliefs about the afterlife in numerous books. Perhaps it was her experiences with materialized entities that led Kübler-Ross to declare in *The Wheel of Life* (1997; 188) "Up until then I had absolutely no belief in an afterlife, but the data convinced me that these were not coincidences or hallucinations."

While I myself have not had the privilege of observing the entities Aenka and Mario materialized, I have interviewed numerous credible people who have. I have also listened to hundreds of hours of audiotaped lectures by the entities, including those on *Evolution* that are quoted or summarized in the present book. I am convinced that there is no reason to suspect fraudulent activities or a group psychosis. No money was made by these sittings with the materialized entities and there is every reason to believe the participants were soundly sane. In addition, I have witnessed materialization personally in a different group darkroom with a physical medium. I am convinced that these unique lectures belong in world literature.

As an academic psychologist myself, I know that phenomena with far less scientifically controlled objective evidence of their existence are accepted as face valid. These phenomena are based on anecdotes, case reports, inferences, and self-reports. They include concepts such as thoughts, emotions, consciousness, most personality characteristics, and most so-called mental disorders that are claimed to exist by the American Psychiatric Association and accepted to exist by most other mental health professionals and clinical scientists. Therefore, the concept of communications from discarnate entities is as credible as many psychological constructs. And recognition of the feasibility of spiritual experiences is beginning to be addressed by psychologists and related professionals.

The number of scholarly publications on spirituality in the psychological literature alone has surged in recent years, as evidenced by the database PsycINFO™. In the years 1887 through 1980, there were only 2,799 publications on spirituality. Since 1981 through mid-2012, there were an additional 24,571 publications. Leading-edge psychologists are bringing the soul back to psychology. Indeed, the founders of psychology, such as William James, took it for granted that the soul was part of the human experience.

Spirituality Defined

Spirituality does not refer to organized religion, but does include aspects of it at the basic level of beliefs in a Creator, a meaningful universe, an eternal soul, a purpose in life, free choice, and being responsible for the consequences of those choices. Organized religion is based on social institutions and dogma with teachings that involve threats of fear, guilt, shame, sin, satan, and a hell of some sort, including eternal misery or endless reincarnations. In contrast, spirituality is based on an individual's personal relationship with the universe and it's Source, the importance of mutual respect, forgiveness, unconditional love, and inclusivity rather than exclusivity. In the most general sense, 'spiritual' refers to a non-physical pure energy that has only positive motives, is lawful, intelligent, creative, purposeful, and eternal. Non-physical energy is perceived at times by the five basic physical senses (taste, smell, sight, hearing, and touch). But non-physical energy is often experienced by what some call the 6th sense. This 6th sense involves intuition, hunches, subtle feelings, and experiences of what might be called the inner senses, psychic abilities, having a purpose in life, and being interconnected with the universe.

Specific spiritual beliefs are guided by intuition and personal experiences, and sparked by a burgeoning of worldwide literature that validates those beliefs and experiences. Spiritual philosophies are not only offered by the ancient psychics and mediums whose work led to the development of organized religions, but also, in modern times, spiritual philosophies are offered by contemporary psychics and mediums, athletes (e.g., ocean surfers), meditationists, materialized entities, quantum theorists, astrophysicists, physicians, psychologists, epidemiologists, and other established professionals and scientists. One driving force behind the growth of interest in spirituality is the work of quantum theorists, who are concluding that an eternal, creative, and meaningful consciousness is necessary to understand the universe(s). Where goes physics, eventually, so goes the rest of modern thinkers.

Modern spiritual belief frameworks are generally void of concepts such as a satan, hell, sin, guilt, and shame that are prominent in the world's major religions. As will be seen later in this book, these fear-inducing notions became part of organized religion over a million years ago. For a few million years prior to then, the spiritual beliefs of the early endowed humans were similar to what has been taught by the materialized entities Aenka and Mario.

These ancient and contemporary spiritual belief frameworks tend to focus on maintaining a harmonious relationship with self, others, and the universe as a whole based on the assumption that all forms of consciousness are interconnected and eternal. Rather than involving dictated rituals common in organized religions, spiritual practices and experiences are individualized with the evolving goal of reaching a sense of inner peace and purpose.

People often equate the spiritual with feeling unconditional love, being guided by universal laws, and an inner knowing of an eternal afterlife. People commonly report a variety of spiritual experiences, some of which are also referred to as psychic experiences. Just a sampling includes having a subtle "gut feeling" or premonition that proves true despite no rationale for it, knowing what others are thinking, feeling interconnected with nature, experiencing an altered state of consciousness during meditation, having an after-death communication, remembering vivid informative dreams, and finding that a prayer has been fulfilled.

What these experiences have in common is that they do not conform to accepted laws of Newtonian classical physics. Newtonian assumptions include the following: (1) the physical world is objectively real and a non-physical reality is simply an illusion; (2) locality, meaning objects are fixed in space and can be influenced only by direct physical contact, thereby ruling out the possibility of all psychic and spiritual experiences; (3) causality, meaning the arrow of time is linear and points in only one direction, ruling out interconnectedness, a sense of purpose, and a destiny; (4) continuity, meaning there are no discontinuous 'jumps' in nature, such as a sudden insight; and (5) determinism, meaning things progress in a predictable fashion, ruling out spontaneous experiences such as an after-death communication (Radin, 1997, 2006).

Some aspects of psychic and spiritual experiences, however, do conform to concepts in quantum physics, which complements Newtonian physics (Roberts, 1970, 1972). Quantum concepts include that everything in the universe is an energy field and that this energy field is nonlocal (effects occur at a distance and elements are not fixed in space), independent of linear time (now reflects the past and future), and involves an interconnectedness of the observer and the

17

observed. Like experiences called spiritual, quantum theory posits that there is a non-local subtle energy transmission between minds (or consciousness) and between minds and matter.

Often poorly understood experiences are labeled spiritual to underscore that there are phenomena that do not conform to reductive materialistic science. History is riddled with examples of so-called spiritual phenomena that later were widely accepted by mainstream science. For example, Isaac Newton's (1642-1727) concept of gravity was initially rejected by the scientific community as being too 'mystical' because it is an energy that cannot be directly observed. Even to this day, no one has directly observed gravity. Its existence is inferred from its effects, just as intuitive, psychic, and spiritual phenomena are inferred from their effects. Yet, while the concept of gravity is widely accepted, psychical and spiritual energies continue to be rejected by many mainstream scientists, despite equivalent evidence for them.

Paradigm shifts in science and modern thinking take centuries (Kuhn, 1970). Academia as an institution is as conservative as, for example, the earlier Catholic Church when it vilified Copernicus and Galileo for suggesting the Earth revolves around the sun. Therefore, it is understandable that spiritual and psychic experiences are often viewed with disdain and ridicule by mainstream scientists and the public that adheres to its materialistic values. Yet many events established by the scientific method today arguably can still be seen as spiritual, such as controlling for the placebo effect and using randomized double-blind studies. For example, some of these studies have shown healing by remote prayer without the patients knowing about it and without those praying knowing the person in need of help (Dossey, 1999).

This growing acceptance of the spiritual is in concert with beliefs of the population. Surveys consistently show that over 90% of the American population believes in an afterlife and a creator (e.g.,

). Given most people's behavior includes spiritual beliefs and practices, it is indeed an odd state of affairs that many if not most psychologists and other health professionals neglect this aspect of the human personality.

Even many parapsychologists—those who study psychic abilities (e.g., clairvoyance, clairaudience, precognitions, and psychokinesis)—often eschew spiritual implications of their evidence for the existence of consciousness once the physical body is deceased. It seems as if these scientists on the one hand reject reductive materialism but on the other hand also want to be part of its establishment. So they walk a thin line, claiming psychic energy by inference of its effects exists, but avoiding the big question of whether spiritual energy exists.

I cannot think of another example of a common human characteristic that is so overlooked by psychology and related disciplines, as are psychic and spiritual experiences. But this neglect seems to be coming to an end as work in quantum theory provides an explanatory mechanism for these experiences and their concomitant energies. Also, seemingly independent of quantum theory, the primary psychological literature has grown in the development of spirituality assessment devices and psychotherapies that explicitly address and integrate the use of the clients' spiritual beliefs and experiences in order to promote wellbeing (e.g., Kapuscinski & Masters, 2010; Worthington, Hook, Davis, & McDaniel, 2011).

Overview of Evidence for Psychic and Spiritual Phenomena

Evidence for non-material energies has been documented by research in quantum physics including astrophysics, psychology, medicine and related disciplines. Additionally, there are countless reports of discarnate entities by intuitives, psychics, and mediums. In other words, people who are sensitive to non-physical energy via the 6th sense.

The types of evidence include hundreds of systematic case studies, anecdotes, direct observations, surveys, and laboratory experiments whose methodology meet the standards of mainstream science. This evidence is consistent with the concept that consciousness exists beyond the physical body, and the possibility of both incarnate (soul) and discarnate (spirit) entities. Yet many reasonable scientists and laypersons do reject this notion, often with a disproportionate degree of disdain that suggests the concept threatens some deeply held assumptions related to the material world being the only dimension of existence.

Surveys suggest that more than half of scientists report that they are atheists. Yet these same scientists treat their materialistic beliefs as dogma, a dogma as rigid as in an organized religion, which these same scientists claim to disdain (Collins, 2006). However, as seen in the subsections below, leading edge scientists are beginning to change their stance. The same holds true for some health professionals, including physicians, psychologists, nurses, and social workers. There is an emerging new science that adopts both material and non-material approaches to understanding the universe, sometimes called a spiritual science. Therefore, considering the teachings from discarnate entities and the presentation of ideas in conflict with current science, there is an indication of a shift in how people view the universe.

Below I briefly summarize developments in the last century that reflect this shift. Topics covered include the new physics, evidence of psychic abilities and the new psychology, the new medicine, and various types of evidence of an afterlife, i.e., the existence of discarnate entities.

The New Physics

The field of physics has been undergoing a paradigm shift since Einstein's theory of relativity and the study of sub-atomic particles. It is now widely accepted that the study of matter and physical energy presents an incomplete picture of the universe. It is now known that some elements operate outside of linear time and local space and are entangled with everything else. No event is truly independent and no event has been shown to be random. It has been observed at the subatomic level that the intention of the experimenter, even if blind to the observations obtained in the studies, influences whether a subatomic element behaves as a particle (local matter) or a wave (nonlocal energy). In addition, matter flickers in and out of existence (materializes and de-materializes just as Aenka and Mario have done). Given consciousness affects the observed nature of these subatomic elements, there is every reason to entertain the possibility that consciousness affects everything else. Other sciences have adopted these concepts at the macro level in terms using experimental designs in human research studies that are double-blind and include a placebo control group.

In recent years, numerous physicists and astrophysicists have concluded that evidence from quantum mechanics demands the concept of discarnate consciousness that affects everything in the universe, creating precise order, and yet creativity via free will. Quantum data are inexplicable under a Newtonian, purely materialistic view of the universe. Quantum data also raise the need of the notion of energy that creates energy, meaning a Source (God, Creator).

The quantum physicist Amit Goswami explicated in his 2008 book *God Is Not Dead: What Quantum Physics Tells Us about Our Origins and How We Should Live* that the concept of an interconnected consciousness is necessary to explain quantum observations. What one does to others, one does to oneself. In an earlier 2001 book *Physics of the Soul: The Quantum Book of Living, Dying, Reincarnation, and Immortality*, he applied findings from physics to an incarnate entity (e.g., soul), which he calls a quantum monad. He also argues the necessity of that quantum monad to reincarnate in order to make sense of quantum possibilities becoming actualities and to account for evolutionary change.

The astrophysicist Bernard Haisch in his 2006 book *The God Theory, Universes, Zero-Point Fields and What Is Behind It All* makes similar arguments. He points out that zero-point fields refer to a vacuum that appears to have zero energy but in fact has infinite energy and is lawful. It is this zero-point field that creates energy and the laws of the universe, what the author calls God for lack of another term recognizable to the public. He followed up this work with a 2010 book entitled *The Purpose-Guided Universe: Believing in Einstein, Darwin, and God*. In this sequel, he demonstrates that a science without a concept of purpose (or God) is far more difficult to reconcile than a science with one, due to the underlying organizing nature of the universe.

Psychic Abilities and the New Psychology

Since the 1960's, mainstream psychological science has remained embedded in classical Newtonian physics based on matter, locality, linear time, independence of events, and predictable determinism despite the assumed existence of randomness. Most psychological research is based on this reductive materialistic approach. The result has been dustbowl empiricism with little advancement in the understanding of the human personality. This approach assumes the mind, consciousness, and free will are illusions, and that all human behavior and experiences can be reduced to some neurotransmitters in the brain that have yet to be discovered or understood. This approach is called promissory materialism. Humans are viewed as randomly produced complex machines with no purpose, no meaning. This approach to psychology is well articulated in Cummings, O'Donohue, and Cummings 2009 book entitled *Psychology's War on Religion*. Indeed, mainstream psychology views psychic and spiritual experiences as evidence of some mental disorder, such as schizophrenia or schizotypal personality disorder. However, this attitude is slowly changing. There is a developing literature on integrating spirituality into psychotherapies, such as the empirically supported approach of cognitive behavior therapy that heretofore had been neglectful of a client's spiritual beliefs and practices as a way to deal with the challenges of living (e.g., Koszycki, Raab, Aldosary, & Bradweijn, 2010).

There also have been inroads from quantum physics that may put an end to *Psychology's War on Religion*. As already mentioned, the number of mainstream psychologists investigating spirituality has escalated, demonstrating an implicit acceptance of quantum physics and a non-material reality. But the psychologists who have paid greatest attention to advancements in physics are those who are oddly frowned upon or outright rejected by mainstream psychology to the point they have been relegated as 'parapsychologists', meaning that this field is off to the side of 'real' psychology or what the layperson would call an atheistic psychology. By atheistic, it is meant that mainstream psychology attends to only physical matter, and not non-physical elements such as consciousness or a soul. These same mainstream psychologists will study what are called "covert events" such as thoughts, but these events are then converted to numbers via some measurement device, such as a score on a self-report questionnaire. Once converted to a number, the covert event is now deemed to be material.

For over a century, so-called parapsychologists have systematically studied what is now called quantum human behavior. Indeed, one of the esteemed founder's of psychology, William James, today would be considered a parapsychologist and shunned rather than placed on a pedestal. Parapsychologists are forced to create their own journals and professional associations, such as the Society for Psychical Research, the Institute of Noetic Sciences, the International Society of Scientific Exploration, the World Institute for Scientific Exploration, and the Academy of Spirituality and Consciousness Studies. Research done by these scientists are just as, if not more, rigorous than the research done in mainstream psychology. There is overwhelming evidence from this body of research that consciousness is not limited to the brain and follows the concepts in quantum physics of nonlocality, nontime, and the interconnectedness of all people and all elements of the universe. People are not viewed as randomly produced machines, but instead as having free will and abilities beyond the five physical senses. There is overwhelming evidence of an additional 6th sense, called psychic abilities, intuition, sensitivity to nonmaterial energies, or the soul.

Strong experimental evidence for psychic abilities has been summarized in Dean Radin's 1997 book *The Conscious Universe: The Scientific Truth of Psychic Phenomena*. Findings he reports are derived from over 1000 experiments and pertain to the following abilities neglected by most psychologists: (1) telepathy, or sensing others' thoughts at a distance; (2) clairvoyance, or seeing at a distance (remote viewing); (3) psychokinesis or mind affecting matter; (4) precognition or hunches about the future unexplained by reasoning or temporal conditioning; (5) intuition or being aware of something without rationally knowing how you are aware; (6) distant mental influences of being stared at; (7) distant mental healing; and (8) field consciousness showing group concentration can affect matter, such as a random number generator.

Radin points out that surveys show that over 89% of Americans report having some of the above listed psychic experiences. He synthesizes these findings with quantum theory. For example, intuitive reasoning is deemed equivalent to quantum computing. In a subsequent book, *Entangled Minds: Extrasensory Experiences in a Quantum Reality*, Radin further integrates findings on psychic abilities with quantum physics, noting that these human behaviors cannot be accounted for by Newtonian assumptions.

While Radin steers clear of implications of research on psychic abilities to concepts of spirituality, other so-called parapsychologists do not. In Charles Tart's 2009 book, *The End of Materialism: How Evidence of the Paranormal is Bringing Science and Spirit Together*, he sticks his neck out and declares the obvious. Psychic abilities and evidence of spiritual phenomena create a need for psychology to finally recognize what most people already believe: that there is a non-material reality.

Similarly, the clinical and health psychologist Gary Schwartz has provided extensive experimental evidence that consciousness exists not only outside of the incarnate's physical body, as evidenced by psychic abilities, but also when people are discarnate. Some of his works will be cited below under the subsection *Other Evidence of an Afterlife*. In terms of integrating quantum physics with psychic abilities and spiritual experiences, his 1999 book with Linda Russek, *The Living Energy Universe,* speaks to evidence and logic supporting the notion that quantum fields refer to a universal living memory. The authors indicated how psychic abilities reflect the zero-point field and call for a new science that integrates physical and non-physical energy, and local and nonlocal space, such as particles and waves.

The New Medicine

Recently, the medical sciences have also been highly influenced by quantum theory, evidence of psychic abilities, and the well-established finding that most people report that they believe in spiritual concepts, such as having a purpose in life and being part of a universal consciousness. This openness to non-material causes complements the accomplishments made from a materialistic view of the human physical body that equated consciousness with the brain and attributed all dis-eased symptoms to the physical body.

This openness also is related to a growing interest in the West of psychic and spiritual theory and healing techniques traced to the East as well as to indigenous cultures worldwide. According to the National Center for Complementary and Alternative Medicine (CAM; part of the U.S. National Institutes of Health), about 38% of Americans use CAM. These techniques include prayer, meditation, mind-mediated energy healing, acupuncture, and massage, among numerous others.

One inspiration for the new medicine was the shattering finding that came from the Human Genome Project. The Project involved the tracing of 3.1 billion letters of the DNA code arrayed across 24 chromosomes. Yet the findings failed to produce the detailed insights about life that was anticipated. The Project team expected at least 100,000 human genes but found only 20,000—25,000. This is comparable to the number of genes in an insect such as a fly, failing to explain the seemingly superior intelligence and consciousness of humans. Moreover, it was found that at the DNA level, humans are 99.99% the same. That leaves only 0.01% of DNA to account for all individual differences. The head of the Project, Andrew Collins, has an M.D. and a Ph.D. in chemistry. He provided his reactions to the Project in his 2006 book entitled *The Language of God: A Scientist Presents Evidence for Belief.* He concluded that some non-material explanation for the abilities and experiences of the human being is needed, such as a soul that is endowed with a higher consciousness than other forms of life. He argues that this endowment is what accounts for how the human differs from other living creatures and how humans differ from one another.

Other physicians are making the same claim. In his 1999 book entitled *Reinventing Medicine: Beyond Mind-Body to a New Era of Healing,* Larry Dossey reviews the effectiveness of distant energy healing and intercessory prayer. He argues that medicine is entering a new era based on the use of psychic and spiritual energy as treatment modalities. In a later 2009 book, *The Power of Premonitions: How Knowing the Future Can Shape Our Lives,* Dossey extends this argument to preventive medicine. He cites international surveys indicating 50%—75% of the population report having had psychic-related experiences. Preventive implications are suggested by evidence that 22% of parents whose infant had sudden death syndrome (SIDS) had a premonition or precognition of SIDS happening to their child, whereas only 2.6% of the controls whose infant did not die had a similar premonition.

The neurosurgeon John Turner, in his 2009 book *Medicine, Miracles, and Manifestations: A Doctor's Journey Through the Worlds of Divine Intervention, Near-Death Experiences, and Universal Energy*, has modified his clinical practice to include complementary and alternative medicine based on the health-promoting effects of spiritual beliefs and experiences by his patients. He became convinced of the mind-body connection based on reports of near-death experiences (NDE's) and observing the healing effects of nonlocal energies, such as from prayer and chanting.

NDE's have influenced many physicians to accept the importance of spiritual, non-physical experiences of their patients. While the particulars of an NDE vary somewhat across individuals, they generally include recognizing one's physical body is dead, seeing it from a distance, interacting with discarnate entities, and having an expanded sense of consciousness, including understanding the purpose of life and the nature of the afterlife.

There have been numerous books by physicians who systematically studied NDE's across various patient populations and cultures since the mid 1970's. One of the most recent ones was published in 2010 by the cardiologist Pim van Lommel and is entitled *Consciousness Beyond Life: The Science of the Near Death Experience*. Van Lommel summarizes prior research as well as presents new data on NDE's. He proposes an explanatory framework for NDE's that integrates concepts from quantum physics.

An NDE is a conscious experience while someone has been declared clinically dead. This makes no sense to a material approach to medicine that equates the mind with the brain. Because patients who had an NDE consistently report descriptions of an afterlife that speak to consciousness or the soul existing beyond the physical body, NDE's are convergent with the existence of discarnate entities such as those who dictated the contents of the present book, *Evolution*.

The vast majority of people who had an NDE show the following positive effects: (1) self-acceptance; (2) compassion for others; (3) appreciation of life; (4) loss of any fear of death; (5) belief in the afterlife; (6) increased belief in spirituality but not necessarily the dogma of organized religions; and (7) enhanced psychic abilities (e.g. clairvoyance, precognition, clairaudience, and telepathy). These positive effects are consistent with the developing new revelation of spirituality and a spiritual science that includes not only physical matter/energy, but non-physical energies as well.

Van Lommel reports on retrospective studies that show that 18% of patients declared clinically dead and then somehow revived report NDE's. In general, retrospective studies show 14—80% report NDE's. Even if not officially declared clinically dead, 10% of the U.S. population reports having had an NDE. Some also experience psychological stress due to the rejection and stigmatization of their NDE by friends, relatives, physicians, and mental health professionals. Among physicians in the U.S., only 76% report a belief in God and 59% a belief in the afterlife (vs. 90% of the population). A tolerance of belief in the afterlife is necessary to take NDE's seriously but understandably many keep their NDE's private, making prevalence statistics possibly less than what occurs.

Many non-physician researchers also have investigated NDE's (e.g., Fontana, 2003, 2005; Guggenheim & Guggenheim, 1995; Tart, 2009; Varghese, 2010). One of the most comprehensive surveys was done by P. M. H. Atwater and reported in *The Big Book of Near-Death Experiences: The Ultimate Guide to What Happens When We Die* published in 2007. She interviewed more than 3000 adults and 277 children who were declared clinically dead and revived either on their own or with medical interventions. She found 70% reported an NDE. Like other researchers on this topic, Atwater integrates these findings

28

with quantum physics and spiritual beliefs in an afterlife.

Other Evidence of an Afterlife

In addition to NDE's there is a massive literature on the nature of an eternal soul or consciousness, the afterlife, and the existence of discarnate entities. This additional evidence derives from mediumship/channeling, after-death communications (ADC's), pre-death experiences (PDE's), hypnosis, and reincarnation memories. Evidence is derived from case reports, testimonials, surveys, and scientifically controlled and replicated experiments.

Mediumship

Controlled experiments of the accuracy mediums or channels is critical given they have published hundreds of books on a new revelation of spirituality. Amazon.com™ lists about 22,000 books about mediumship as of mid-2012. Many other books whose copyrights have expired or been released are available for download at this website: http://onlinebooks.library.upenn.edu/webbin/book/browse?type=lcsubc&key=Spirit%20writings. These writings describe the purpose of life and the nature of the afterlife when one is discarnate. There are minor discrepancies among these books, but for the most part they relay the same information given by Aenka and Mario in Appendix B.

The academic psychologist Gary Schwartz has undertaken a series of studies to test what he calls the survival hypothesis and the G.O.D. hypothesis. In his 2002 book with Linda Russek entitled *The Afterlife Experiments: Breakthrough Scientific Evidence of Life After Death,* he studied the accuracy of five well-known mediums. Readings were double blind, meaning the medium did not know or see the sitter and the sitter did not know or see the medium. Both the sitters and control subjects rated accuracy of the readings. Accuracy of the readings were rated 83%-95% across the mediums by the sitters and 36% by controls, which were not involved in the sittings. In his subsequent 2005 book with William Simon entitled *The Truth About Medium,* he reports on replications of these double blind experiments. Accuracy of the medium's readings was found to be about 80% for the sitters and 17% for the controls. Similar accuracy ratings have been reported by researchers at the Windbridge Institute whereby the primary investigator, Julie Beischel, Ph.D., certifies mediums who have undergone highly controlled and replicated experiments (http://www.windbridge.org/). Interestingly, spirit communicators have also said that mediumship or channeling is at best about 85% accurate given distortions made when the medium receives the information. The discarnate entities that dictated this book on *Evolution* and two prior books by Marti Barham and Tom Greene (see Appendix A and Appendix B) indicated that materialized entities bypass this distortion.

After Death Communications

Research on after death communications (ADC's) has also provided evidence of the existence of discarnate entities. Bill Guggenheim and Judy Guggenheim report in their 1995 book, *Hello From Heaven,* the results of structured interviews of 2000 adults. The results yielded 3300 ADC's, some involving two or more people seeing the same discarnate entity at the same time and in the same place. While the authors list 13 types of ADC's and noted some involved full materializations, unfortunately the prevalence of each type of ADC was not reported.

A more systematic study of ADC's is reported in the 2005 book *Afterlife Encounters: Ordinary People, Extraordinary Experiences*, by psychotherapist Dianne Arcangel. She provides the results of a survey of 827 adults who had a deceased loved one. Of those, 59% reported at least one ADC. Materialization of the discarnate loved one occurred in 36% of ADC's. Of those materialization ADC's, 4% saw, heard, smelled, and touched the entity while the other 32% both saw and heard the entity.

These two studies suggest that spontaneous communication including materialization by a discarnate entity is not an unusual experience. Historically, since the 19th century, there are dozens of case examples of invited materialization through the use of a channel or medium, as reviewed in Michael Tymn's two books *The Articulate Dead: They Brought the Spirit World Alive (2008)* and *The Afterlife Revealed: What Happens After We Die (2011)*. Perhaps the most famous materialization is that of Jesus as described in the New Testament.

The positive effects of ADC's found by the Guggenheims, Arcangel, and others, have led some psychologists to utilize ADC's in psychotherapy. Jane Greer, in her 2003 book *The Afterlife Connection: A Therapist Reveals How To Communicate With Departed Loved Ones*, provides a description of her clinical experience with grief-stricken clients. Her approach involves the validation of ADC's and how to notice and accept them as normal and healing. She also encourages clients to use both psychic and spiritual energies via meditation, attention to dreams, and other methods to communicate routinely with deceased loved ones. As an extension of this approach, Alan Botkin and R. Craig Hogan in their 2005 book *Induced After Death Communication: A New Therapy for Healing Grief and Trauma*, have learned the therapeutic value of inducing ADC's. They present 84 case studies involving the use of relaxation, eye movements with the eyes closed, and imagery of past trauma's, including loss of a loved one and related symptoms of post-traumatic stress. Of those 84 cases, 98% experienced an induced ADC and 96% resolved their grief and post-traumatic stress. Prior to treatment, only 8% believed an ADC was possible. Therefore, case studies suggest it is worthwhile to evaluate the effectiveness of ADC's in adjustment to both grief and the effects of other trauma

Pre-Death Experiences

Palliative care physicians and hospice workers have reported pre-death experiences (PDE's). "Deathbed visions" is another term sometimes used for PDE's.

In Arcangel's 2005 book mentioned above, she indicates that while working as a psychotherapist in a hospice, 100% of her patients reported visual and auditory communications with discarnate entities. Case reports of PDE's are described by the palliative care hospice physician John Lerma in his 2007 book *Into the Light: Real Life Stories about Angelic Visits, Visions of the Afterlife, and Other Pre-death Experiences*. The contents of these experiences, like those of NDE's, were remarkably similar and the possible effects of psychosis and medications were ruled out. They contained messages from discarnate entities about the purpose of life being to experience unconditional love for and forgiveness of self and others, with the ultimate goal of merging with God, or the Source. The patients spoke about reincarnation as the way God gives people multiple chances to attain this purpose. They relayed predictions that the human race is entering a new era of enlightenment and that within 500 to 1000 years, the new spirituality will be commonplace on Earth and the present focus on materialism will seem like a Dark Age. The patients noted that currently many humans have chosen to be engrossed with technology and have turned away from spiritual experiences. Concepts of quantum physics are also mentioned; including the interconnectedness of the universe and that it is consciousness that creates matter, not the other way around. They stated that each person has a learning agenda for each incarnation (called the Government of Life by the entities Aenka and Mario), which may or may not be attained due to free will and events that humans are unable to predict (called the Gamble of Life by Aenka and Mario).

The teachings from PDE's reported by Lerma are remarkably similar to the teachings of the materialized discarnate entities Aenka and Mario who dictated this book

32

on *Evolution* and the two earlier books by Marti Barham and Tom Greene (Appendix A and Appendix B). They also are highly similar to the teachings of mediums and writings based on spirit communications and clients who have undergone hypnosis.

Hypnosis

Another form of evidence of the existence of discarnate entities comes from hundreds of case reports by hypnotherapists that, like the reports of mediums, NDE's, and PDE's, converge with the descriptions provided of an afterlife and the existence of both incarnate and discarnate entities via mediums, psychics, and materialization. By the use of regression hypnosis, therapists report that their clients describe past lives, life-between lives (i.e., the afterlife or unobstructed universe), and the purpose of each incarnation.

The psychologist Michael Newton has published two books of case studies of clients who underwent life-between-lives hypnosis where they were regressed to provide memories that usually are subconscious. In his 2001 book *Destiny of Souls: New Case Studies of Life Between Lives*, Newton reports on 67 cases and synthesizes their descriptions of the unobstructed universe (spirit world of discarnates), stages of death while incarnate and discarnate, soul mates, soul groups with common interests of study, reincarnation, and the ultimate goal of soul/spirit evolutionary progression as merging with God or the Source once unconditional love is mastered. These clients describe 7 levels of progression (Appendix B also describes 7 levels), and most of them were at levels 3 or 4, so the information is restricted in that respect. In his sequel, Newton's 2003 book *Case Studies of Life Between Lives* describes another 29 cases out of an unspecified number that provide consistent reporting.

Hypnotherapist (and dentist) Bruce Goldberg replicated Newton's findings. In his 2004 book *Past Lives, Future Lives Revealed,* Goldberg reports on 35,000 past life regressions with more than 14,000 clients. These findings concern the purpose of life, having a specific goal for each incarnation, the nature of life as a discarnate entity, and the existence of reincarnation. It is noteworthy that mediums working with past lives have also reported similar findings.

In the 2009 book by Robert Schwartz, *Your Soul's Plan: Discovering the Real Meaning of the Life You Planned Before You Were Born*, he reports on 10 case studies where two different mediums independently read for the same sitter and provided converging evidence of these notions. He reported that 8 of the 10 subjects had planned life challenges as the primary experience for their present incarnation. One sitter planned challenges as a secondary experience and another changed his pre-birth plan to accommodate an unexpected event at birth that caused blindness. All 10 reported a greater sense of self-understanding, self-responsibility, peace, joy, and unconditional love following the sessions with the mediums.

Similar findings have been reported by the psychiatric physician Brian Weiss in his 2004 book *Same Soul, Many Bodies: Discover the Healing Power of Future Lives Through Progression Therapy*. During his hypnotherapy, he directs clients not only toward memories of past lives but also, in terms of linear time, of future lives. Recall that quantum physics is based on the existence of nontime, where all events occur simultaneously but become an actuality only when consciousness focuses upon them. Weiss reports over 12 cases of hypnosis in which remembering these other lives helped the individuals accept or resolve current problems in living. His findings are similar to those of Newton, Goldberg, and R. Schwartz mentioned above. This approach to hypnosis deserves further study, such as comparing different treatment approaches for the same type of problems in living.

The presumably suppressed memories of these clients who underwent hypnosis or were assisted by mediums demonstrated once again a consistency with messages about a new revelation of spirituality. Whether reported by hypnosis subjects, mediums, NDE's, ADC's, PDE's, and the teachings by the materialized discarnate entities Aenka and Mario, these messages converge.

Reincarnation Memories

Another source of data for the existence of both incarnate and discarnate entities that deserves mentioning pertains to thousands of case studies suggesting spontaneous reincarnation memories reported without mediumship, NDE's, ADC's, PDE's, or hypnosis. Van Lommel (2010) cites surveys indicating that 22% to 27% of Americans and Europeans believe in reincarnation. Atwater (2007) reported that 80% of people with NDE's acquired a belief in reincarnation. Goswami (2001) reported that 50% of people worldwide believe in reincarnation. Reincarnation is assumed to be true in most of Eastern cultures and in Brazil where the work of Allan Kardec (1804 – 1869) on the new spirituality has been highly influential (Playfair, 2011). Kardec worked with highly credible mediums and posed incisive questions to the spirit communicators, so his work has been quite influential worldwide. Many of his books are available for download at http://onlinebooks.library.upenn.edu/webbin/book/browse?type=lcsubc&key=Spirit writings

Reincarnation was an integral part of Christianity until the Council of Nicea in 353 initiated its removal from the Bible (http://reluctant-messenger.com/origen6.html). A controversy raged for 200 years. Then in 553 A.D. the concept was removed by a vote (not evidence) to eliminate it from dogma at the Second Council of Constantinople (http://reluctant-messenger.com/origen1.html). It has been speculated that the church feared loss of control of the masses via threatening eternal hell. If people believed they had countless chances to reincarnate and eventually learn to live a life based on unconditional love and merge with God or the Source, the Church would have fewer means to manipulate society for its own benefit. An analysis of the early Christian church and later distortions in its teachings is described in this book on *Evolution*.

The physician Ian Stevenson in his 1997 book *Where Reincarnation and Biology Intersect* has documented case studies of reincarnation memories based on spontaneous recollection by children worldwide. Stevenson reports on 112 of 225 cases of spontaneous reincarnation memories. These 112 cases are reported because they can be documented by physical evidence, such as birthmarks at the place on the body where the person had been fatally injured in a past life, medical records to corroborate that injury, and by corroboration of the memories of experiences of living people who knew the person in his/her past life. Similarly, phobias that are inexplicable from current life conditioning have been found to converge with past life experiences in many of these cases.

Stevenson's meticulous case studies have inspired other researchers who have replicated his findings. The physician Peter Fenwick and his co-author Elizabeth Fenwick reported in their 1999 book *Past Lives: An Investigation into Reincarnation Memories* report on several case studies of reincarnation that converge with Stevenson's findings. Fenwick and Fenwick also report on reincarnation memories of 8 cases of survivors of the Titanic and numerous individuals who indicate that they were victims of the Nazi Holocaust.

More recently, Jim Tucker reported in his 2005 book, *Life Before Life: A Scientific Investigation of Children's Memories of Previous Lives*, 2500 cases of children with spontaneous past life memories obtained through structured interviews that included open-ended questions to avoid leading the child. Like Stevenson, he too collected birthmark evidence of the source of death of the prior life and that the children had phobias inexplicable from current life conditioning. He also noted these children were fond of food and such that they enjoyed in the prior life but was not modeled or encouraged by their current family or community. Tucker also verified reincarnation memories with medical records, police reports, corroborative reports from the prior life's friends and family, and eye witnesses. Tucker coded 200 variables in determining if recollections met criteria for reincarnation memories. He also noted that almost all past lives were ordinary, suggesting ego enhancement was not a factor in reporting reincarnation memories.

Evidence of reincarnation memories has also been summarized by Goswami (2001), Radin (1997), Fontana (2005), and Tart (2009). These reincarnation researchers tie in the notion of reincarnation with quantum theory, helping to integrate the case reports with an explanatory mechanism. In addition, the number of systematic case studies of reincarnation memories documented thus far is greater than those published for many other personality characteristics that are widely considered to be a mental disorder. For example, dissociative amnesia (an extreme and temporary loss of memory with no known physical cause) is taken for granted in mainstream psychology and psychiatry but is only inferred by theory and rare case studies.

Concluding Remarks

Given the evidence for a new spirituality and the existence of discarnate entities, it would take an assertion of worldwide psychosis, blatant denial, or simple ignorance to refute such converging data from various sources. As I said above, phenomena in both the physical sciences (e.g., gravity) and psychological sciences (e.g., personality) have equal or less empirical support but yet are widely accepted by both scientists and the public.

Science by definition does not prove. To prove involves establishing an irrefutable truth shared by everybody. Only mathematics provides proofs, and such proofs are rendered to work by adding assumptions as well as mysterious constants and weights to formulae. A demand for proof of the new (quantum) physics, psychic abilities and the new psychology, the new medicine (CAM), mediumship,

NDE's, ADC's, PDE's, hypnosis, and reincarnation memories are beyond the abilities of current science. Science provides a relative degree of supporting and refuting evidence for some idea. That is it. Nothing more. Science also by definition is self-correcting given an acceptance that new data can refute old ideas. Therefore, the Editor hopes a case has been made in this Preface to take the information in this *Evolution* book with a mind as open as Einstein's.

INTRODUCTION

"Great spirits have always encountered violent opposition from mediocre minds" (Albert Einstein).

This is a book of channeled information regarding humankind's collective physical and spiritual evolution. The information was presented by two materialized entities that went by the names Aenka (pronounced Ang-kah) and Mario. The process of obtaining materialization is described in Martha Barham's 1981 book *Bridging Two Worlds* (reproduced in Appendix A). Part of the entities' teachings was published in Barham and Greene's 1986 book, *The Silver Cord: Lifeline to the Unobstructed* (summarized in Appendix B). Implications for use of physical, psychic, and spiritual energies for healing briefly mentioned in the prior two books are presented in Appendix C. *Evolution* is the third book of this series.

Overall, *Evolution* presents what would be considered both a creationist and evolutionary view of the history of our galaxy, planet, and its inhabitants. It is the hope of the entities that knowledge of their view of this history will promote humankind to use free will to behave in accordance with the inter-related and collective nature of the universe. They see this work as an effort to direct modern humans toward a life with meaning, purpose, and a compassion for both themselves and others.

Chapter One describes physical evolution of our galaxy commencing 47 billion years ago. It is stated that all life was created by the Source (energy that creates energy; God) 47 million years ago, including the instinctual human, referred to as the human creature.

Chapter Two describes how the human creature existed 40 million years as it physically evolved and until it was chosen by the Source to be endowed with a soul, a consciousness of higher quantity and quality than in other forms of life and a facet of the Source itself. Since endowment 7 million years ago, the human physical personality functions involve 4 quadrants: physical (including instinctual), intellectual, emotional, and spiritual (intuitive). The allegory of the Garden of Eden refers to this endowment, although it took place worldwide. For the first 3 million years of endowment, humans lived rhythmically, adhering to the universal laws of natural human behavior. These laws reflect how each individual is a unique facet of the Source (i.e., has a soul), is equal to all other souls, and is both independent, and interdependent. These laws also state that each human has a destiny (life plan or Government of Life), free will, exposure to events that he/she could not predict (Gamble of Life), accepts responsibility for choices, makes recompense when those choices harm another, and experiences true benefits only when they are earned.

Early endowed humans balanced the physical, intellectual, emotional, and spiritual aspects of their physical personalities. Their 5 basic emotions of anger, instinctual fear of heights and loud noises, unconditional love, grief, and jealousy were expressed in a natural manner, meaning they served to respect both oneself and others and to promote creativity. Unnatural and distorted expressions of these emotions are often seen today in the form of hostility, irrational fears including guilt and shame, conditional love, depression, and envy. See Appendix B for detailed descriptions of the nature of the soul and its progression across 7 levels of evolution, the 4 quadrants of the physical personality, universal laws of natural behavior, the purpose of incarnations, three types of energies in the universe, and psychic abilities.

Chapter Three describes how the endowed human became out of balance and unrhythmic 4 million years ago. The use of free will to not adhere to the universal laws of natural human behavior are described allegorically in terms of Biblical stories, a theme carried out through Chapter Eight. In Chapter Three, the story of expulsion of Adam and Eve from the Garden of Eden depicts the decline of sensitivity to the spiritual quadrant 4 million years ago and thereby a lessening of humans' intuitive use of psychic abilities and connection to the Source. The story of Cain and Abel illustrates the onset of the unnatural emotions of guilt and shame 4 million years ago.

Chapter Four continues the story of Cain and Abel. It describes how the physical and psychological trauma of Cain and his guilt and shame led to the first engagement in war and the creation of slavery. It also notes that neurological damage of Cain's father contributed to this event by his inability to understand that Cain did not kill Abel. His father beat Cain so severely that he too suffered neurological damage. Therefore, brain damage of some influential people has been important in the promotion of unnatural behaviors.

Chapter Five depicts how the control of slaves became problematic. Slaves believed in an afterlife and often chose death by their masters to escape the brutality of their incarnate existence. This noncooperation by the slaves created challenges for the power brokers who depended upon them. This problem for the ruling elite was solved about 1,109,000 years ago by an Egyptian named Ute (rhymes with boot). In collaboration with rulers and priests, he developed the concepts of sin, satan, and hell to encourage the cooperation of slaves. Thus, physical death was no longer an escape from the miseries of slavery. Indeed, noncooperation with the slave owners would lead to an eternal hell. The entities deem this as the onset of organized religions as we know them, which to this day use threats of a miserable afterlife if one does not come under their control.

Chapter Six interprets the allegorical meaning of some of the books of the Old Testament. Addressed briefly are Samson and the jawbone, Noah and the flood, Abraham and the sacrificing of his son, Joseph and his coat of many colors, satan as a fallen angel, the holy of holies, Jonah and the whale, Elijah, and Moses. Each of the Ten Commandments is given a modern interpretation that underscores their distortions over the years, distortions that reflect the teachings of Ute.

Chapter Seven introduces the purpose of the

incarnations of Buddha and Jesus. More detail on Jesus as a revolutionary Jew is provided, perhaps because the recipients of these lectures were more familiar with Judeo-Christian than Buddhist history. The entities did not address Hinduism or Islam, the world's other major religions.

Chapter Eight describes how Jesus planned his crucifixion and the reason he did so. It also explains the meaning of some of Jesus' parables in simple modern English.

Chapter Nine describes how the early Christian church developed. While initially in tune with Jesus' teachings, the church made compromises with Judaism and the Roman emperors for pragmatic reasons. However, eventually the church regressed to the tactics of Ute by emphasizing sin, satan, and hell. While the Protestant movement attempted to reject some of the compromises of the church, it too continued to adopt Ute's teachings.

Chapter 10 points out that organized religions have adopted a condescending attitude toward its followers. Yet, the followers are responsible for their own submission. Followers rejected their own intuitive sense of spirituality and became more and more dependent on outside authorities to direct their behavior.

Chapter Eleven is an Epilogue. It describes how some dissenters in the church who have preached of a loving and forgiving God, the lack of a satan or hell, and a joyful purpose in life have been expelled and vilified. In other words, promoting the ideas of Jesus rather than of church doctrine was deemed unacceptable to the authority figures. The entities, however, indicate that there is a new revelation forthcoming to assist human beings to be more in touch with their individual spirituality. This new revelation is apparent in the surge of interest in the implications of quantum physics and explicit messages that come from modern mediumship, as well as other indicators of the nature of the universe mentioned in the Preface. After all, the founders of the great religions were mediums and those mediums were the scientists of their eras.

Yet the new spirituality has a tough row to hoe. Materialism dominates societies in much of the world. As humans, we pollute our planet, rape its resources, subjugate others, and violence only continues to escalate. Some consider ritual prayer a spiritual life in itself rather than a means whereby we might connect with our inner spirituality. We not only don't practice what we preach, but even what we preach is distorted. More is better, power and status are good, and my belief system and values are better than yours. Greed is not only accepted but also encouraged. More of everything continues to be a predominant attitude. More money, more land, more power, more status, more clothes, more sex, more influence over others. Humankind is indeed out of balance with universal laws, and according to the entities has been for over 4 million years.

So it is no wonder that some people become threatened by the new spirituality. They must face that they have missed the purpose of life and fallen off course of their own spiritual evolution. When they realize it is more important to be kind than it is to be rich, they are bound to become unsettled by if not outright hostile toward the evolving new spirituality.

CHAPTER ONE

PHYSICAL EVOLUTION OF OUR GALAXY AND FORMATION OF THE EARTH 47 BILLION YEARS AGO AND OF LIFE 47 MILLION YEARS AGO

"Evolution is not a force, but a process; not a cause but a law" (The Viscount Morley, John).

"Everyone who is seriously involved in the pursuit of science becomes convinced that a spirit is manifest in the laws of the universe—a spirit vastly superior to that of man, and one in the face of which that we, with our modest powers, must feel humble" (Albert Einstein).

The entities Aenka and Mario said that there is validity in both creationistic and evolutionary viewpoints; that both spiritual and physical evolutionary processes were combined in shaping our planet and its inhabitants. They spoke in terms of the Source (the entities' term for God or energy that creates energy; see Appendix A and Appendix B) designing evolutionary sequences, manipulating physical, psychic, and spiritual energies, and setting into motion processes that evolve over billions of years into a variety of living and non-living forms. Physical energy contains matter and many forms of it have been directly measured by modern science (one exception includes gravity). Psychic energy is a type of physical energy that is of a frequency not yet identifiable by current measurement devices but will be once scientists direct their efforts toward measuring it. Psychic energy serves as a conduit between physical and spiritual energy. Spiritual energy is pure energy, containing no matter and of a frequency and nature that incarnates will never be able to measure it (see Appendix C for how physical, psychic, and spiritual energies can be used in healing a dis-eased body).

Mario says that the current scientific conclusion that humans cannot create or destroy energy is correct, that humans can only help transform it from one form to another.

The entities say that only the Source (God) can create energy and program patterns of complex interactions of energy processes at molecular levels. As Aenka very simply puts it: *all physical energy was designed and created, and the laws that govern it, by the Source.*

Each basic energy form or type created by the Source, evolving through its own processes and affected by interactions with other physical forces over brief or extended periods of linear time, ultimately results in a relatively stable form. Relative here can refer to hundreds of thousands of years, perhaps millions. Another way to put this would be to say that patterns of energy forms are set into motion and, if supported in their development, programmed evolution will evolve in its intended general direction. The entities are clear in their teaching that while the Source sets processes in motion with certain definite aspects of evolution programmed within it, the eventual outcome of evolution is to a significant degree quite undetermined. The Source apparently does not want a simple puppet show where each player is totally manipulated and the outcome specifically pre-determined. Instead, the Source Itself wants to learn from It's own creations.

The following comment from Mario regarding such long range programming about the development of galaxies and solar systems does not sound terribly different from some scientific theories regarding the evolutionary transformation of interstellar gases.

As a galaxy is designed, it is set into motion in gaseous forms, which involve energies and processes having a code of evolutionary development.

A cosmic DNA, so to speak. The physical creation of our particular galaxy is said to have been no different from millions of others in the physical (obstructed) universe. Processes were set into motion, which, through billions of years of evolution, formed our galaxy and it's subsystems. Our solar system was one, which evolved to adequate stability for atmospheres to develop around planets, and our planet developed a suitable environment for physical life, as we know it.

This galaxy you live in has been evolving 47 billion years. Your planet began as nothing more than a cloud of gas or smoke, energy, sufficient to evolve and compress or change to create its own atmospheres until it could sustain life.

Currently, mainstream scientists argue the Earth is only 13 or so billion years old; however, this figure is often modified and may eventually come upon the 47 billion year date of onset relayed by the entities. But before such a modification can take place, a new quantum science based upon the role of consciousness (the Source and the soul) must become more widely accepted. As mentioned in the Preface, this new science is emerging with astrophysicists, physicists, physicians, biologists, and psychologists declaring that a concept of energy that creates energy must be introduced to explain nonlocal causes and effects that are beyond 3-dimensional space and linear time. While some of these leading-edge theorists refer to the construct of God or a Source or a Creator, they also evoke terms that are more acceptable to current materialistic science, such as quantum consciousness (Goswami, 2008), zero-point field (Haisch, 2006), and living energy universe (Schwartz & Russek, 1999).

After the Source has set energy processes in motion and allowed for their evolution, It (i.e., the Source) is described as regularly "scanning" the galaxies created. The Source is, at such points, looking for solar systems or planets suitable for initiation of life forms, which would be mobile and capable of further evolutionary development. We asked why such scanning was necessary. Did not the Source know exactly how things would turn out? The answer was along similar lines regarding our own futures as individuals and as a collective society. The Source is not interested in total predictability for this would be a simple replication of the known. There would then be no creativity, no unexpected events, and no true evolution. The Source sets processes in motion with many probability factors, some interactions of which are unknown even to the Source. Only in this way can true evolution and creative experience occur. Such unknown interactions are now commonly accepted among quantum physicists who acknowledge that quantum mechanics (via a probability calculus) demonstrates that the universe contains "possible probabilities" that become an actuality only when there is an intention from consciousness, in this case the free will of a soul (e.g., Goswami, 2001; Rosenblum & Kuttner, 2006) as well as actions from discarnate entities and the Source.

In reference to current scientific theories regarding the formation of our universe and ongoing changes within it, Mario strongly implies that a contracting-expanding theory is more accurate than the Big Bang idea currently endorsed by many physicists. However, some physical cosmologists are beginning to embrace the Big Crunch theory that includes the notion of the universe expanding after the Big Bang and then contracting (http://en.wikipedia.org/wiki/Ultimate_fate_of_the_univers e). Therefore, some progress is being made in cosmology that one day might reflect the entities' understanding of the origin and nature of our universe.

What you must understand is there is an expansion and contraction, but not to the degree that there is an implosion or explosion, hurling matter into space, to become planets or moons or stars.

Regarding life in other parts of the universe, the answer is a definite yes. However, in our galaxy, our solar system is the only one said to support intelligent (i.e., endowed) life. Mario reports that at the time our galaxy was designed and started on its initial evolution processes 47 billion years ago, there were six other galaxies also set in motion. While he declined to offer any information on location or identification of the other galaxies, he did state *they are not close together at all . . . three out of that seven sustain life.* These life forms are endowed with a *Facet of Divinity* (i.e., a soul).

There are other intelligent species in the universe and they are capable of inter-galactic travel and Earthlings are observed but there is no inter-breeding (maybe in the future but unlikely). If crossbreeding between humans and extra-terrestrial occurred, it would be an experiment and the Source would stop any experiment that goes haywire. Look at the history of attempts to crossbreed. Animals rarely do; they just mutate.

Interestingly, there are numerous authors who also make the case for life on other planets. The Director of the Human Genome Project came to this conclusion (Collins, 2006). Hypnotherapists have reported hundreds of case studies that also reveal claims of intelligent life on other planets (e.g., Goldberg, 2004; Newton, 2001, 2003). Numerous other spirit communicators also make this point via automatic writing or a medium (e.g., Kardec, 1804/2010; Multiple Authors, 1996-2010; Roberts, 1970). Finally, there are countless anecdotes and photographs of "unidentified flying objects" that conform to the assertion by Aenka and Mario that people on earth worldwide are being observed by endowed entities from other planets (e.g., http://www.ufoevidence.org/).

Other planets are evolving in the Universe, of course. There is a planet the entities called Masseca that is almost ready to sustain life but it is still being studied in the unobstructed (i.e. by discarnates in the non-physical universe). This planet gives another opportunity to the Source to begin another research project. The planet Callisio is evolving and developing an atmosphere that is promising to life. In billions of linear years, 8-9 other planets similar to Earth will sustain life.

While discarnate, entities travel to all three galaxies

with endowed life and throughout the universes (obstructed and unobstructed) any one soul primarily incarnates and re-incarnates on only one planet. When humans on Earth sleep, they often have an out of body experience (OBE) during which they engage in astral travel (through space faster than the speed of light) throughout this and other galaxies as well as the unobstructed universe.

During an OBE, the soul is connected to the body by a psychic energy permanence often called the silver cord, which stays in place as long as the body is alive. OBE's are needed to connect with discarnate entities and to escape the prison that is the physical body. Humans would literally go crazy by neurological damage if denied OBE's (e.g., sleep deprivation is used as a form of human torture). Some dreams are memory traces of OBE's but most of OBE's are unconscious while one is in the physical body.

The Evolution Of Life Forms 47 Million Years Ago

When the Source finds appropriate planetary conditions, it 'seeds' the planet with primitive life forms. This seeding involves a quality and quantity of consciousness that corresponds to the level of intelligence of the targeted life form. Modern quantum physicists (e.g., Goswami, 2008) and mediums who voice channel (e.g., Roberts, 1970) refer to this process as the consciousness of the Source creating actualities from probabilities and possibilities so that the Source can experience It's self.

Physical evolution of your planet itself continued until 47 million years ago, by which time the sea was filled with basic elements necessary for biological life. These elements had been specifically designed to evolve through many previous years. Some chemical elements in the saline had the potential capability of creating other chemistries. 47 million years ago, after the physical chemistry of the planet evolved into life-sustaining elements and there was supporting evidence for the feasibility of biological life, the amoeba was. The amoeba did not evolve. The Source of Divinity—how would you say—triggered the elements in the saline, and provided the catalyst for life to emerge. Thus life was planted, created, caused to be. In the Biblical sense, life was cast upon the waters of the sea.

As Mario continued to speak of this event we learned he was using the word 'cast' in the sense of a template or genetic coding as well as a catalyzing agent. It is clear in the following statements:

Out of the casting came the single cell, the amoeba, and in the casting each amoeba was designed. It was not an accident. Each type was designed to evolve into a separate species unto itself. Fish unto fish, fowl unto fowl, beast unto beast, man unto man. The catalysts that triggered the processes had their marking, their identity, and carried with it the design for different creatures. Each species as you know them today, and many that have long been extinct, were designed unto their own kind and their origin was from a single cell, the amoeba.

Each species, if it survived, had its own function and purpose in the continuing evolutionary scheme. The development of specific simple life forms was intended to progressively support more complex biological life forms on this planet, as seeded by the Source.

The first life that evolved were the lower forms of life, the organisms in the sea, plankton, various plant and animal life, all small and simple. This was for the purpose of survival for those yet to come.

The design for the support system of biological life actually began before the emergence of the amoeba.

Prior to the casting of physical life, vegetation was caused to be. What you call physical life began after the vegetation was abundant with water. Most of the globe was covered with water, a greater percentage than now. The seas were harsh and rough, the water around land much warmer.

The entities are adamant that regardless of environmental forces or accidental genetic mutations, no species has ever been able to change its basic predetermined design in any major way and survive for many generations. If the environment did not adequately support a species' evolution there could occur minor mutations or changes, but no really major ones. Extinction of a species is said to result either from (1) the environment not supporting its continuation, or (2) the species having reached and executed its planned evolutionary goal or destiny.

Initial structural changes from amoeba to near final form in some species were planned to be very rapid, and in others more slowly. The picture Mario gave was of an *explosive development of life that occurred within the first three thousand years after the casting.* He described the oceans as literally teeming with life forms, evolving extremely rapidly from their initial amoeba stage. The rate of evolutionary development is said to have dropped sharply after this initial dramatic period. Of course, many animal and plant species did not evolve as quickly but required hundreds of thousands or millions of years longer to reach their final forms and play their role in progressive development and evolution.

The Human Creature (Pre-endowment)

The evolution of the human is described as having occurred within a two-phase framework. First, the human creature was a strictly physical being operating from instinctual responses on a level similar to other animals. Second, as a spiritual being when the human creature was chosen to be a physical vehicle to house souls, endowment occurred (cf. channeled material by Roberts, 1970).

The human creature initially derived from a single

cell organism, each of which would develop into either a male or female form. Only gradually did the human creature evolve into a more complex organism where the female would create its own internal nourishing system for a fetus as occurs today. For the initial 2000 years, there were no births or offspring of the human creature. Instead, the Source directly created the amoeba. For years the human creature was essentially an ocean dweller. While capable of functioning as a land dweller from the beginning, it would be 700,000 years after the human creature appeared in the sea before the land would be capable of supporting larger life forms on a permanent basis.

The time required for a human amoeba/embryo to develop adequately to sustain its own life by integrating use of its basic bodily systems is said to have been *nine months, twenty days or thereabouts.*

The amoeba would develop into the equivalent of an embryo. As the embryo developed it supplied its own saline pouch, its own womb. And as all ova it grew into the fetus and formed into a human form, just as in gestation today. The organism was carried in that saline pouch for the required nine-month period.

The fetus would gain its nourishment from a placenta, much as in present times, except the placenta would at that time gain its nourishment directly from the sea rather than a woman's body as occurs today. *The placenta trailed the pouch, feeding on plankton and nurturing the growth of the fetus.*

The picture of a male or female fetus inside a pouch floating in an ocean filled with basic and simple foodstuff, trailing a placenta to absorb its nourishment as it goes through its gestation period, is to say the least a rather unique and startling image. However, consider the following medical facts regarding contemporary human fetal growth. The female egg, following penetration by a male sperm (both of which consist of one cell) literally moves about in the body until it attaches itself to the lining of the uterus. The lining of the embryo creates its own protective membrane, which is filled with a saltwater solution (amniotic fluid).

All living things were cast into the sea as amoeba. The amoeba that you are most interested in produced the human physical form from a single cell for two thousand years. There was amoeba coded to be human; there were amoeba coded to be other life forms. There were no births and no offspring, in the sense you think of it; in the beginning, one cell grew from its own design into an individual physical adult being. Female amoeba did produce other amoeba, but each being grew from a single cell into a differentiated mass of multiple cells, a physical form determined by the casting.

The embryo and host/mother jointly produce a placenta and umbilical cord, by which the embryo is attached to the uterus. The embryo receives nutrients from the host/mother via absorption through selected membranes. Is this really so different from what we understand happens today?

The human creature was to remain primarily an ocean dweller for about 700,000 years. Although the human creature is described as capable of living on land from the earliest beginnings, it took that period of time for evolutionary processes to provide adequate vegetation on land for protection and food.

Man continued to live in and around the sea for a long period of time until the land could provide. He was capable of being amphibian almost from the beginning, but there was very little land to the surface, so they stayed in and around the sea, living mostly in caverns or pockets near the shore.

However, the 700,000 years was anything but a static period, and the human creature went through a number of evolutionary changes as a sea dweller. The first great physical evolutionary step for the human creature was acquiring a capability for self-reproduction, thus increasing the chances for survival as a species.

There was no reproduction from the female until the species proved viable. Man evolved into beginning life as the egg, or as you would call it, the ovum, after about two thousand years of deriving directly from the amoeba. The adult female of the species then became capable of producing true offspring, either male or female. During this early time period, however, the womb was incapable of impregnation by the male, and the male itself had not yet become potent. Initially, the fertilization of the adult female's ova was a self-fertilization process. For about a seven hundred year period (after two thousand years of the human developing directly from individual amoeba), *there was then self-impregnation. Females fertilized their own eggs or ova for conception. There was a small gland in the female reproductive system, located on the lower center quadrant of the uterus; when stimulated, this gland would secrete a hormone, a chemistry equivalent to that of sperm. It was this secretion that provided for conception or fertilization. In the fertilization process, this secretion determined the sex. The secretion would seek out the tubal canal and the egg.*

Even though male and female were not capable of heterosexual impregnation, the Source's design for interdependency between male and female came into play during this evolutionary period. Mating-type ritualistic behavior by a male was needed to stimulate the female's gland.

There had to be a mating ritual to stimulate or excite the reproductive gland for fertilization. The human species is a very touching species, and it was designed to be. Male and female would court in the water and there would be a ritual of touching and rubbing; a ritual of excitement, which would stimulate the female glands for discharge. The male would caress and explore the female body. They would touch, make sounds, and chase each other. They would wrestle, the male showing his strength or might. During this evolutionary period, the male, not yet having developed reproductive capabilities, could not ejaculate, but did experience a pleasure similar to orgasm. During the 700 year period of this self-impregnation phase, man discovered intimacy in a physical, sensual sense through ritualistic behavior. These processes continued until the male body developed its main reproductive organs, the testes and prostate.

During the first 300 years or so of this 700-year evolutionary period, the fertilized egg was to go through the gestation period in what Mario and Aenka referred to as:

sea incubation . . . external incubation. The fertilized egg was discharged into the water. As it floated in the water, it developed into an embryo and grew a saline pouch.

Since the life expectancy of embryos floating in the ocean was not very long due to predators, the Source's evolutionary design for initial reproduction resulted in many eggs being fertilized rather than one as is more often true today.

During the period when the female was dispensing the egg into the sea for the incubation, there were dozens of eggs. They would float like many other eggs of other species in the saline. Usually, ova would drift, and with a tacky secretion, would attach themselves to objects usually within the area of their group—what do you call it, a school—a school of the human species.

Once the eggs were released into the ocean, they joined the millions of other species' eggs *similar to sperm today. If the female were ovulating, it would enter the egg as it does now* floating in that broth of life; they were unprotected and provided handy foodstuffs for larger creatures. *Adults would offer protection to the young only after the infant was born from their sack or pouch.* Most fetuses of course died before birth from the pouch.

Through most of its growth inside its sack during this 300-year period, the fetus remained submerged in the water. As 'birth' approached it would release the attachment to its object and gradually ascend.

The saline pouch as it grew began to surface. By the time the infant was mature, at about nine months and twenty days, the pouch ruptured. The infant was then freed from the pouch and surfaced, usually surfacing on its back. If it did not surface on its back, the infant merely waited until the water of the sea tossed it so. This was to ensure the first breath would be air and not water. Even after the infant took the first breath and their lungs inflated, it continued to feed on the placenta that trailed from the umbilical cord. As it grew in strength, the creature would increasingly capture or taste surface material. Gradually, the infant would begin to tread very carefully near the shore, always staying in the water so that it could feed from the umbilical if necessary. As it grew, it became more self-sufficient. It learned to consume raw material, break shell, and feed.

The next evolutionary development was "internal incubation". At about 300 years into the 700-year period of self-fertilization, the fertilized egg

began stopping its journey through the reproductive organs and out through the vagina in to the sea. Prior to fertilization, the egg would attach itself in what would later be called the fallopian tube. After opportunity for fertilization, it would them come down into the womb or uterus. If fertilized, there it would attach itself and would stay for nurture until the fetus developed. So its life-

sustaining processes were then within the womb and the
fetus would remain there until the incubation period had
passed. The delivery or expulsion of the infant was into
water. A male would assist the female in holding the
infant, cradling the infant with its face above the water,
and the female would gnash the umbilical. Adults would
offer protection to the newborn, much like marine
mammals today. If a pregnant female today were
submerged in water, she could deliver and the baby would
live in the water as long as it was attached to the umbilical
cord and the water had pressure equal to that of the womb:
the lungs would not inflate.

Breastfeeding is said to have begun *after the first*
uterine delivery in the water.

It is interesting to note that in modern times there is
some new interest in women giving birth in water (e.g.,
http://en.wikipedia.org/wiki/Water_birth). This procedure
was recently demonstrated on a national television show and
is said to be less painful for the mother. As documented in
the films, the infant does not begin to take a breath until it
rises above the water. There are international organizations
promoting water birthing (e.g., http://www.waterbirth.org/).

After the 700-year period of self-fertilization the
male became potent. *Then there was impregnation by*
intercourse. The shift from self-fertilization to fertilization
by another was somewhat of a gradual one, and the Source
had designed a temporary failsafe procedure to assure
survival of the species.

As evolution would have it, if the sperm did not fertilize,
the female would fertilize herself. As many began to
fertilize by intercourse, evolution stopped the self-
fertilization.

Mario emphasized the enormous significance of
heterosexual impregnation in evolutionary terms. He
described the self-fertilization process in a way similar to

cloning, since all chromosomes came from the female. There were few individual differences between offspring. As a result,

all the human creatures, although slightly different, were almost a cloned image of each other. There were self-variations because of certain balances of male hormones that existed in the females. After self-fertilization ceased, the species began to change drastically. What I mean by drastically is that the genetic codes could take a different form, a mixing of chromosomes from male and female. Females and males reached puberty much earlier than now. The rate of maturation had a great deal to do with evolution, the necessity to maintain the balance of life.

The potential life span of the amphibian human creature was approximately the same as now, although most did not live that long.

If they escaped the hazards, it was possible to live quite a few years. It was very difficult to live very long, however, for life was much more hazardous and offered a greater challenge for survival. You see, you live longer now than you did back when life was much more challenging. You were very lucky then if you exceeded thirty years, and you were old if you lived passed thirty-five years. In years to come from your present time, a female will not reach sexual puberty for twenty years and the male probably twenty-two.

Prior to becoming a full time land dweller the human creature had evolved to a physical configuration and physiology generally similar to contemporary humans.

Man, even though he lived in the water for years, did not have gills, nor did he have webbed feet or hands. The overall shape was very much the same. The head changed slightly. You may find it an interesting point to realize that

58

man, when he evolved from the water, was very small. It was very seldom that one exceeded which in your number would be five feet. The hair was much more on the surface of the derma, the skin; very similar to the seal. This hair was for protection of the body. The female had little hair around the face, less than the male. Man was capable of living on land and water but fed in the water. Even though he was upright and had the capability of walking, early man did not stray from the shore much farther than the seal does today because of the element of danger.

The transition from ocean to land dweller was a gradual one, covering many thousands of years.

Man migrated from the sea to land and began to dwell in caves on land, while previously they had sought shelter in caverns in and near the water. During this time of the transition, man's body hair decreased and the skin texture was changing some. The body became not as dependent upon constant moisture.

Females gradually began to birth on land. It was not just one day they all started bearing on land. As they became land dwellers, some of the females would reach out far inland when they were pregnant and they would try to find streams or pools of water in which to deliver. But they gradually began to learn through necessity and accident they could deliver on land. I cannot say at seven hundred thousand years there were no more births in water because long after that, if it was possible and they were near bodies of water, the female would go into the water to bear; it was an instinctual process.

By the time the human creature was firmly established as a land dweller, each one

adapted to optimal survival on land. His basic survival was water. Usually, they would seek out calm places where the water was not so rough. They were capable of sleeping on shore or on rocks, and also on their backs in the water because they could float. As man migrated on land, evolution and the change in diet caused a more strong physical structure. All of the species that were to be amphibian or to survive on land had already achieved that evolutionary growth. Those that were to remain in the sea had established that pattern. Man found his security on the land not too long after other amphibians. Some would live in heavily dense forests where they could protect themselves and construct sleeping habits above ground. Others would continue to seek out caves. Man the animal only dwelled in caves for protection, no other reason. The species spread and covered the four corners of the Earth. All continents were somewhat infested by the human species, and there were tribes all over the planet.

Based on the dates given by Aenka and Mario, the human creature became a land dweller around 46 million years ago. Some archeological finds are consistent with these dates. While archeological dating is not a refined science, some evidence such as footprints and skeletal remains have been dated between 25 and 55 million years ago (Cremo & Thompson, 1996). This stands in stark contrast to mainstream archeologists' assertions that humans are only about 100,000 years old. For millions of years to follow only minor evolutionary changes occurred in the human creature, many of these in reactive adaptation to worldwide climatic changes or local environmental conditions.

The species never changed to the extent they would be classified a different species. Basic skeletal structure has always been the same, as has been the sensory equipment, internal organs and systems of the body. Of course, minor variations in shape, form, and color, were determined by adaptive evolutionary processes according to the environment. As environmental conditions changed on land, the body and skin pigmentation began to change. They gradually lost much of their protective hair protein.

One significant physical change over this long and relatively quiet evolutionary period was in the face, which developed a larger bite and bite surface.

Aenka and Mario spoke of early pre-endowment human creature's keen awareness and sensitivity in using the five senses compared to the present time when we are heavily over-balanced in abstract thinking.

Their five senses were a thousand times more active than humans today. The human species today relies on so many scientific things to offer them protection or help. You take things for granted today because your survival is not dependent on your five senses as it was in primitive periods. What you must understand is that the human species of the animal kingdom was no more or no less primitive than any other species prior to spiritual endowment. It was a constant survival process. Man survived on his instinctual processes for forty million years.

Although not having true intelligence, pre-endowment human creatures were capable of primitive self-protective learning, which helped to ensure survival of the species.

With the dexterity of their body, they learned to manipulate simple mechanical processes for primitive defenses, like throwing rocks and putting up barricades. There was no inventive process. The mind was not yet capable of reasoning, so they could not make any process enlightening. Tumbling stones would strike each other, or lightening would strike and cause forest fires. This was very frightening because it was dangerous. At that time, fire was only something to fear. Man could not reason to the point of harnessing it for protection. There was no creativity. This came only after endowment, which gave man reasoning.

There is archeological skeletal evidence of human forms around 47 million years ago during pre-endowment of humans. For example, evidence of primitive tools, such as the use of round stones and chalk balls, has been documented as being over 25 million years old using current scientific estimates (Cremo & Thompson, 1996). Even though the pre-endowment human creatures were not significantly different from other animals in regard to intelligence, they have always been genetically coded to be a social creature and live in groups. In this way the human was no different from a number of other animal species. Many animals were social creatures then and lived in groups even as many do today. It is important to remember that by "social creatures" Aenka and Mario here are referring to descriptive instinctual behavior, not social groups formed by intelligent and reflective conscious choice.

Historically, humans are said to have always been monogamous, just as some lower animals are today. Monogamy was and still is a result of coded instinct, triggered in adult humans when they began to bear young.

Man was designed as a social creature, evolved as a social creature, and practiced monogamy. Even during the self-conception or self-fertilization period, they would pair off.

The human creature also was and still is genetically coded to be ritualistic. During the approximate 40 million year period as a gradually evolving land animal, the human developed a number of simple ritualistic behaviors. These were of a concrete sort and tied closely to survival value in one way or another.

Each tribe would have their own customs, their own rituals related to survival. All mankind was living and responding and behaving according to universal genetic laws that were designed into the species' behavior pattern: that is, coded or programmed to occur in an instinctual way. One ritual or behavior was that the male would never eat until female was gorged, until her appetite was pleased. Only then would he eat. The ritual was for survival, of course, supporting maternal processes to nurse the young. Males would capture and retrieve and bring the family unit the food: he would be hunter, the gatherer of the food; the female provided the family social structure, and was the disciplinarian. He would bring forth food and none of the family unit was allowed to taste or eat until the mother had gorged or pleased her appetite. Some species were designed to be monogamous; many promiscuous.

Not surprisingly, some of the early rituals in the human creature related to sexual behavior in family life, as those aspects of living pertained very directly to survival.

Many rituals were performed to stimulate certain chemistry. For the monogamous creatures, certain rituals would trigger and release chemistries so that the primitive mind would move towards the acceptance of mating. Like many fowl today, the female or the cock will perform a mating ritual, which releases certain chemistries; these in turn provide or trigger certain behavior in both sexes of the species. Early females of mankind would perform rituals about the male in a flirtatious way to encourage him to choose or favor her as his mating partner. Once this commitment was made and monogamy secured, they continued a relationship. All this, of course, was done in a primitive and instinctual manner.

There were also rituals related to tribal units for protection of the larger group and survival. Keeping out intruders was important in tribal survival, and some tribes would develop simple dances to identify outsiders.

They would usually congregate and dance in circles, making crude rhythms with sticks and stones. For example, females might create one circle and within that circle and linked to it, the males would create a circle. If you viewed it from above it would appear as two rings, as two circles linked together like a chain. Then as they danced, they would weave among each other, never breaking the circle or the link. Each tribe had their own rituals. If a stray tried to mingle, they would be recognized because they would not be able to easily perform the ritual. They would betray themselves in their awkwardness and be expelled.

While survival value was a powerful factor involved in the development of primitive rituals, an equally influential factor was social coding. This coding prepared the human creature's chemistry to respond to simple interpersonal or group experiences with warm and comfortable feelings, a primitive and powerful identification and bonding.

They learned that certain behaviors created greater harmony, a harmonious feeling that occurred within the unit. If they consistently performed some ritual as a body, as a whole, together and habitually, they experienced harmonious feelings. Man, even then, was a creature of habit. Do you see? Designed to be a creature of habit. They performed rituals habitually because, when they did, it seemed to create an instinctual feeling of bond within the social structure of the community.

The pre-endowment human creatures were better off than the endowed humans insofar as they had no responsibility. With endowment came conscience and responsibility to the Source. A discarnate entity chooses to enter into a human physical body (to incarnate) and that involves responsibility to live a rhythmic life.

CHAPTER TWO

ENDOWMENT AND THE GARDEN OF EDEN: THE CHOICE OF THE HUMAN SPECIES AS HOUSING FOR SOULS

"...breathed into his nostrils the breath of life; and man became a living being" (Genesis 2: 7).

The slow and gradual evolution of our planet and all its fauna and flora was the result of a conscious experiment by the Source, not an accident. Modern quantum theorists call this "downward causation" (Goswami, 2008). Some mediums who voice-channel discarnates report evolution as an increased degree of quantity and quality consciousnesses (Roberts, 1970). Earth developed in its evolution to the point where it could support a great variety of life forms, one or more of which would hopefully prove to be suitable physical vehicles for the housing of souls, divine sparks of the Source Itself. It is important to realize that the Source's designs and genetic codes were not mere mechanical exercises but processes that take their own courses once set in motion. Built into the evolutionary design of all life forms are chance (deterministic but unpredictable or chaotic) factors, referred to by Aenka and Mario as the Gamble of Life regarding survival and adaptability over millions of years.

During the long period of evolution of life forms, all animal species on Earth were observed from time to time in their development. The Source would monitor species' developmental processes in a manner similar to monitoring physical evolution of the planet as mentioned previously.

After seeding a planet with the beginnings of various life forms, the Source would send out scouts. A few entities were born into the unobstructed while observation of all the species was being undertaken and the choice was still undetermined.

65

The Source rarely uses scouts now that there are plenty of discarnate souls who add to the Archives of Knowledge (i.e., the fund of all knowledge from the Source, discarnate spirits, and incarnate souls; also called the Akashic Records). The scouts returned to the Source, who then gave birth to them again to be additional souls that incarnate physical human bodies.

The choice they (Aenka and Mario) refer to here is the selection of a species to serve as a physical vehicle for souls or entities to be sent by the Source. At some point the Source is said to have determined that several species would possibly serve as suitable vehicles. Aenka and Mario were quite cautious in responding to questions about what species other than the human were considered. After repeated questions on the subject Mario finally responded.

Some of the upright animals were in mind. For example, the gorilla's and some ape's brains were compatible, but they did not have the most adaptable physical form. Their versatility, coordination, dexterity, and the structure of their body as it evolved made them at home in the more dense vegetation, but their survival in open areas and meadows was very limited, much more limited than man. Just in viewing the skeletal structure of a gorilla or ape, it is really apparent that man's physical dexterity and flexibility is far superior. They were much more adaptable to temperature, water, altitude, diet, and a variety of geographic areas. It is remarkable how many of the species survive, but none was as suitable for endowment as man.

The strict evolutionary theory of humans evolving from a basic ape form is said to be in error, attributable to a flaw in logical thinking, and possibly a distortion in early scientists' intuitive function. For example, during Isaac Newton's (1642—1727) and Charles Darwin's (1809—1882) times, mainstream science was determined to separate itself from anything that smacked of religion or spiritual, non-physical phenomena. Scientists had good reason to separate themselves from the Catholic Church since Galileo Galilei (1564—1642) was declared a heretic and put under house arrest for supporting Nicolaus Copernicus' (1473—1543) assertion that the Sun, rather than Earth, is at the center of our solar system. Thus, a pure materialistic view was adopted that remains dominant today despite evidence to the contrary (e.g., Radin, 1997; Tart, 2009). In addition, there are gaps in the fossil record that render incomplete evolutionary theory based on only survival with no ethics and random selection with no purpose (Cremo & Thompson, 1996; Goswami, 2008).

It was confusing to understand that ape and man were competitive species with the possibility of further development. Many assumptions have been made by brilliant minds and their imaginations as to what the human species evolved from and how it evolved. It is not difficult to look at the face of an ape, gorilla, or chimpanzee, and draw an excellent chart of the possible development of your homosapien. It appears very impressive on the chart to see him walking on all fours, then to be almost upright, with a very hairy body and ugly face, finally being totally erect and becoming the handsome man or woman that walks the earth now.

Before the final choice was made, the Source began to design guidelines for the learning experiences and challenges of physically incarnated entities/souls, which are endowed with the highest quantity and quality of consciousness compared to other elements and species of Earth. As part of this process the Source as the Creator experimented with characteristics and energies of entities in the unobstructed that had been sent out to observe and study evolutionary processes of biological life.

You see, all the universal laws that govern behavior were designed. One of the functions of entities born into the unobstructed while observation of the species was still occurring was to test the universal laws in the unobstructed relative to the energies of the planet, to observe how other energies responded and interacted, to see if it was a positive thing.

The Source gives birth to entities so they can experiment and take something new back to the Source and the Archives of Knowledge. Part of the experiment relates to how physical organisms challenge the soul to evolve. Souls are extensions of the Source and It needs physical bodies to further It's learning. Because the Source was All-That-Is, in order for the Source to know Itself, It had to create parts of It's self that was outside of Itself - a dual version of It's self that is restricted by matter. In agreement with Aenka and Mario, there have been other spirit communicators, mediums, and incarnate scientists, given the discoveries of quantum physics, attempting to address the purpose of life that make this same point regarding why the Source created matter, life, and endowed life (Furst, 1968; Roberts, 1970, 1972; Schwartz, 2009; Von Lommel, 2010; Walsch, 1995).

As time for the choice approached, the Source "gave birth" to many entities with a high degree of quantity and quality of consciousness directly into the unobstructed. The Source seeded the unobstructed directly with tiny parts of It's self. This can be a difficult event to picture. While Aenka and Mario have attempted to describe what a discarnate soul looks like in its pure spiritual energy form, and we are given glimpses of this non-physical form of existence, we cannot pretend to understand. As was told to us in many sessions, while we are in the body we as humans are limited in our ability to perceive and comprehend directly this other life of ours between physical incarnations. The most effective word picture we could get from Aenka and Mario regarding the Source seeding our galaxy with souls was in a simple analogy.

There were many thousands of entities created. To visualize the process, you might compare this event to a fish laying eggs. The unobstructed universe was filled with spirit.

People undergoing past life and life-between-lives hypnotic regression have described this "fish laying eggs" inner vision (Newton, 2001, 2003). The Editor experienced this same inner vision during a life-between-lives hypnotic regression as being countless eggs that were pearly white gathered in a gigantic sack.

The entities born from the Source had begun their individual spiritual journeys and would wait in the unobstructed until time for their first physical incarnation (see Appendix B for more of a description of discarnate souls and how they select and enter physical bodies). Humans were chosen as the vehicle for souls because of the species' functional combination of some central attributes. Aenka and Mario described these characteristics as: (1) a capability of functioning in the three elements of land, water and air; (2) great survival ability across many years of severe environmental changes; (3) adaptability to ensure species survival; (4) potential dexterity in strength for task mastery in the physical environment; and (5) a structural physical brain for adequate capacities for further neurological development.

There were many species considered but none compared to the superiority of the human species. What this species of the animal kingdom demonstrated was that they were far superior in their capabilities of survival. It is amazing how the human species survives. You take some mammals out of water and they cannot survive. Humans can survive in or out of the water and they can tolerate rapid or slow extreme temperature changes. Many species have become extinct, some because they couldn't adapt to environmental changes or the change and process of evolution.

Two other characteristics of the human creature, which were crucial in being selected, were *his ritualistic*

nature and his social or group living traits. These last two
aspects were to figure strongly in individual and collective
spiritual development and continue to do so to this day.

Endowment: 7 Million Years Ago

The choice of the human for spiritual endowment and the
endowment itself is said to have occurred 7 million years
ago. The human creatures were ready for an extraordinary
leap along their evolutionary path. They had previously
learned to use the five basic physical senses with great
discrimination. Evolutionary steps of reproduction by
impregnation and leaving the ocean had given them
individuality and independence. Primitive social rituals had
already begun, emphasizing interdependence. They had
proved they could survive in many environments. Their body
shape and brain capacity were optimal for further survival
and growth in many directions.

Contrary to mainstream anthropological data and
theory that sentient humans first evolved or came to be in
Africa alone about 100,000 years ago, Aenka and Mario
state the infusion of human bodies with a spiritual
entity/soul was a contemporaneous worldwide event 7
million years ago. Yet there is strong evidence that
contradicts mainstream anthropological data that suggest
worldwide use of advanced tool making estimated to be 1.5
to 5 million years old (Cremo and Thompson, 1996). It is
certainly well documented scientifically that early-endowed
humans populated the entire world.

Aenka and Mario did not respond to questions
regarding how much time transpired between endowment
from one continent or region of the earth to another, saying
generally that such questions were irrelevant to the greater
event of endowment itself. They seemed to give the general
impression it happened more or less simultaneously. Mario
refers to the Christian Bible story of God breathing life into
humans as a symbolic explanation of human's spiritual
beginning when souls began to literally enter the body of

newborn babies all around the earth. He put it as follows one night in a rather matter-of-fact way.

The first soul made possession of the first physical body and started spiritual evolution. When this first entity selected and entered a physical body, the first newborn of the human species was endowed with a Facet of Divinity.

This worldwide event is the occurrence, which later gave rise to the legend or symbolic story of Adam and Eve, when higher reasoning became a part of human life.

The Gifts Of Endowment

The infusion of an incarnate entity or soul into the human creature is described as a time of both great celebration and great confusion. The celebration was in the unobstructed in honor of a new chapter of spiritual evolution, a further expansion of the Source now underway. The confusion was on Earth, due in part to spiritually endowed children even three or four years of age knowing more than their parents in the dimension of their ability to think and reason and in the ways in which they looked at the world and each other. There was a quantum leap (discontinuity) in the use of body, mind, and feelings after endowment. As endowed children around the world grew into their own adulthood, human's culture changed, or perhaps more accurately truly began.

With endowment, the human's individual and collective life would gain deep meaning, for the entity/soul within brought with it many gifts. Aenka and Mario described these gifts as new capabilities, which would enhance the human's physical qualities tremendously. The natural hungers of our physical bodies (the physical quadrant) would become integrated and coordinated in increasingly subtle ways with the other three quadrants gifted by spiritual endowment: natural emotions, reasoning by intellectual ability, and our spiritual or intuitive aspect. While these four aspects (or quadrants) are described in

Appendix A and Appendix B, a brief description of them seems appropriate here.

The intellectual quadrant provided the ability to reason, to remember, to reflect and to think. It has within it a curiosity to know, to understand, to learn. It prompts us to examine things and thoughts, to use reason in solving physical, emotional and social issues. It prods us in a positive aggressive (i.e., assertive) way to master or resolve a situation. The intellectual quadrant provides flexibility in applying our learning skills to a wide variety of life situations.

The emotional quadrant provided our five natural emotions of fear, anger, jealousy (desire to emulate), love and grief. These expanded the quality of the endowed human's life. The potential for more elaborate and subtle emotional experiences other than simple pleasure and pain would be stirred and stimulated into developing a tremendous variety of feelings.

Primitive fears related to survival would gradually develop into more sophisticated caution and judgment in protecting oneself from less drastic and subtler threats to our wellbeing. The only natural fears are of falling and loud noises. All other fears are conditioned and many are unnatural forms of anxiety, such as fear of negative evaluation, guilt, and shame.

Anger would become a stimulation to respond to challenges of a variety of sorts, prompting humans to bring about change and resolution to problems. Natural anger is healthy aggression (assertiveness), not hostility. Natural anger prompts us to solve or resolve issues. Hostility is distorted anger wherein the goal is to hurt, not resolve.

The natural emotion of jealousy would motivate individuals to achieve what others had achieved, to incorporate certain desirable aspects of others' behavior into their own development. Jealousy as people commonly use the word refers not to healthy emulation but to envy and hate from an attitude of feeling cheated or victimized. While jealousy is a natural emotion, envy is unnatural.

Caring for others in personal and communal relationships, previously expressed as survival concerns, would develop into nuances of the phenomenon and experience of love. Natural love is unconditional giving and is mutually positive, while unnatural love is not. Unnatural love is conditional upon gaining something in return and used to manipulate others for selfish needs.

Grief, the awareness of loss, would remind us of others' importance to us at many levels, and leads to a greater appreciation of life in general and relationships in particular. Unnatural grief is depression, where sadness serves no purpose regarding interconnectedness but instead becomes self-pity.

The spiritual dimension provided by endowment is the simplest and yet the most difficult to describe. Our spiritual aspect derives from our soul, a very real, tiny piece of the Source that is pure energy, not physical energy as we measure it, but real nonetheless. Our spiritual aspect permits our utilizing the highest level of quantity and quality of consciousness apart from the Source Itself. Here we will say only that our soul infuses and suffuses our entire being in an extremely quiet and subtle way. It is the human's soul, this spiritual aspect, that supports and helps integrate awareness of our physical bodies, emotional development, and intellectual capabilities. It permits the use of psychic abilities (e.g., telepathy, clairvoyance, precognition, psychokinesis, and energy healing). It supplies a feeling of wonderment about life itself, its purpose, and one's fellow human. It compels hunches, gut feelings, dreams, insights, creativity, and intuition. This spiritual quadrant would urge humans on towards an understanding of the meaning of life, the Source, and non-physical reality.

Our soul, the essence of our spiritual aspect, is a very quiet and mysterious thing, although its mystery is becoming elucidated by a fusion of spirit communications and quantum physics (e.g., Fontana, 2005; Goswami, 2008; Haisch, 2006; Schwartz & Simon, 2006; Tart, 2009). We can be aware of our soul and its influences, yet we cannot examine it directly. We can know it only by subjective awareness and experience via intuition. This is true of many psychological constructs that are 'observed' only through questionnaires, and psychologists have been attempting to measure some of the spiritual quadrant in this manner (e.g., Kapuscinski & Masters, 2010).

The incarnate entity or soul is real; it is there, and although in a sense it takes a back seat as we go through life, it is the most important of our four quadrants. Not only is it a silent coordinator of our other three quadrants, it provides the basis for the experience of unconditional love and our connection with the Source, and thereby both the obstructed and unobstructed universes. Our soul, the Facet of Divinity within with its many gifts, truly separates the human from other animals. The human was no longer a simple instinctual being, and could never go back.

Rhythmic Living

Before describing some aspects of human's new individual and collective spiritual life after endowment, it should be said that inventive developments as we know them (language, creativity, technology, formal religions, political systems, etc.) did not suddenly or dramatically occur in one generation, but rather in a progressive fashion through thousands of generations. Endowment provided the equipment for these to be developed, but humans had to learn to use their new equipment just as they still do in contemporary times. Following the initial jump in reasoning/intellectual, emotional, and intuitive/spiritual ability resulting from endowment, there were to be millions of years of gradual development.

Apparently primitive language was important in early development as it related not only to communication but also to community.

Prior to endowment, there was no language: man, the primitive beast or animal had instinctual verbalization, but

there was no reasoning to it. They did not have language in a conceptual sense. They simply made sounds indicating pleasure or displeasure. But soon after endowment, when reasoning came about, man learned to communicate in a more sophisticated manner. There is really no difference in the thinking process of early endowment man and contemporary man.

The thinking process has not changed that much in the way people think; it is just that, through evolution, the mind has become more sophisticated and it has more to work with through past learning and accumulated knowledge.

The way the mind began to assimilate, reason, and judge, was as you do now - primarily through pictures. That was the first step. The mind can see and realize most easily through visual imagery. It is like whatever you are thinking about at the time, you can have a mental image of. Early endowment man did not have an alphabet; they did not have numerals. But if they had three apples, then they could visualize or think of three apples in a picture form. Communication between people at first was difficult since they had not developed a way to communicate these concepts or pictures. They had not yet given names to identify them. They began to learn to motion, to wave, and to point. Body language was learned very quickly. Visual symbols were followed by noises. They found they could make certain sounds to communicate something and then everyone would learn that if they made the same sound it meant a particular thing. Soon, they developed true language, because they began to realize that sounds and tones could be repeated and they could represent many things.

Early endowment humans used a combination of intuition from the spiritual quadrant, jealousy from the emotional quadrant, and reasoning from the intellectual quadrant in making discoveries and decisions. They were close to intuitive abilities and relied upon them for guidance as well as a basis for intellectual experimentation and reasoning.

They could learn how to reason; to use and adapt things of nature to their advantage that they could not before. They discovered how to control fire. Intuitively and with reasoning, they learned to rely on many toxic formulas of plant life for medication. Crude scientific advancement began to grow.

Aenka and Mario rather abruptly declined to spend much time on specific early technology or mechanical aspects of living. As they put it, any good documentary on the subject of early humans will give you a good indication. However, mainstream documentaries of "stone age" technology are based on the assumption that humans first invented them about 70,000 years ago. Other documentations are available from anthropologists and archeologists who work outside of mainstream science, which remains wedded to a materialistic Darwinian approach that omits a purpose to life and the existence of a soul. Much of these other data are described as 'forbidden', or 'hidden', history by Cremo and Thompson (1996) and Kenyon (2005). These authors present convincing evidence convergent with the evolutionary history offered by Aenka and Mario.

As humans slowly developed their thinking and broadened their emotional attachments, they were able for many years to live rhythmically and in harmony with themselves and their fellow humans as well as the environment. The experience and meaning of personal commitment and being part of a community grew and expanded. Humans began to consciously discover the importance of a balance in giving and receiving, sharing oneself and one's skills with others, and passing knowledge along. Personal and social interactions were for a long time said to be very rhythmic, although simple. *They were very keenly aware of the universal laws on an intuitive basis.*

Some of these universal laws are listed in Appendix A and Appendix B.

Humans accepted their spiritual/intuitive aspect as much as their emotions, intellect, and body, and they had a healthy sense of their interdependence. They respected and expressed all of these aspects naturally in themselves and in their dealings with fellow humans. They were continually nudged by a desire to know of the Source, and the part of the Source that dwells within them. At this point in their collective social development humans were described as not only respecting one another but also appreciating individual differences. Variations in biological, emotional, and social processes resulted in personal uniqueness then just as occurs now.

In the human's early spiritual history there was no need to make value judgments about any one person's skills being more or less important than anyone else's. Early spiritual humans were able to see how the combination of differences between people can contribute to a more productive and unified whole. Individual interests were followed to a degree of competence or mastery whether the interest was physical, emotional, intellectual or intuitive/psychic/spiritual.

There are always those who would choose to explore certain feats, tasks, or experiences and become masters at it; others would be content with learning the basics and developing other interests. Each person in their skills was respected and accepted, and all benefitted from combined talent. It mattered little whether the skills were woodcutting, tool making, childbearing, hunting, agriculture, or even psychic abilities.

While these positive and respectful attitudes were shown within each tribe, this did not necessarily translate to inter-tribal relationships. With the basic physical survival drive and human's social nature, one's tribe became the center of life. People from other tribes, individually or collectively, were at times welcomed and at other times shunned. Other tribes were looked at as a possible threat to their hunting and shelter areas (and thus their reproductive areas), and caution in intermingling was very reasonable under those circumstances. But whether any one tribe was friendly with or wary of another, early endowment humans were not willful killers. They killed only when they were threatened. Purposeful killing was simply not a natural part of life, due both to their intuitive respect for others as well as physical survival. Early endowment humans were certainly territorial, but not in a murderous way.

The anthropologist team of Richard Leakey and his wife agree (Leakey, 1994). Both Mario and the Leakey's talk about 'mock' battles oriented toward either territory or dominance, the purpose of which is to accept challenges but not to kill or maim the other. Leakey points out that true violence with intent to kill others of the same species simply doesn't make sense, even on a physical survival level: "The biological advantage in mock battles is clear: a species that insists on settling disputes violently reduces its overall fitness to thrive in a world that offers enough environmental challenges any way...this law is so deeply embedded in the nature of survival and success that for a species to transgress there must be extremely unusual circumstances . . . an animal that develops a proclivity for killing its fellows thrusts itself into an evolutionary disadvantageous position . . . ." (Leakey, 1994).

Aenka, Mario, and the Leakey's also point out either conscious or unconscious respect for the life of others occurs not only on a spiritual basis but on a possible familial basis as well. As Leakey puts it "Because our ancestors probably lived in small bands, in which individuals were closely related to one another...in most acts of murder the victim more than likely would have been kin to the murderer."

The Leakey's talk about instinctual animal behaviors regarding territoriality much as Aenka and Mario do from a spiritual point of view. When 'invaders' approach, there are likely to be "stared downs" with aggressive displays, the intention of which is to keep the intruder or challenger away.

Leakey indicated that these confrontations are ritualized such that only on rare occasion does one win by damaging the other. So this act of aggression is simply an exercise in competition rather than an intention to be physically violent. These practice sessions are designed for preparation for a real threat from a predator. Regardless, the outcome is a resolution with minimal physical damage.

In a manner entirely consistent with how Aenka and Mario talk about healthy aggression and territorial challenges of various sorts, the Leakey's are adamant that the human is not inherently a violent or destructive being. They offer, among other examples, two anecdotal observations of some recent 'primitive' tribes.

Among the Ifaluk, of the West Pacific region Micronesia, violence is completely unacceptable. Instead, rituals used to manage conflicts are taught to children. Leakey described how boys at play who feel offended would chase each other and throw things. Yet they threw in a careful manner so that they missed the human target. Leakey talks about adults from the Kurele tribes in New Guinea who seem to be engaged in potentially lethal behaviors, but notes that weapons were fired outside of the target's range. People may on occasion be injured, but by accident - not intent.

It is important to realize that early in the endowed human's social and spiritual evolution there was no such thing as organized religion as we know it today. Daily living with natural spirituality was their religion. There was no difference between the concepts of spiritual and religious as there is today (e.g., Tart, 2009).

You must understand that with the moment of endowment began the essence of religion. Endowment put spiritual and physical together in a joint effort. Soul now had dependency on the physical body for growth.

From this point on the struggle of humans was to integrate all that they could be into spiritual evolution, compared to previous physical evolution alone prior to endowment. It is reasonable to ask why the discarnate entity must incarnate in a physical human body in order to spiritually evolve. This is a system of duality set up by the Source. Prior to the Source's creation of matter and a facet of It's self in matter, the Source only knew Itself. Everything was the Source. The Source was All That Is. In order to know It's potential, the Source needed to experience Itself outside of It's self. With endowment of the human that includes free will to violate universal laws, the Source could experience all of It's potential, and thereby evolve Itself. The Source learns from endowed human beings, and it relies upon endowed human beings for It's own evolution. The Source grows by the experiences of each endowed human being. As explained in Appendix B, once an entity has fully evolved to follow the universal laws, it merges with the Source. Each entity that merges with the Source renders the Source more knowing than before. Therefore, since endowment, the Source has become wiser. The Source is not all knowing, but instead is on an evolutionary course, a course It set in motion.

Early religions were primitive only in a relative sense. Their commonality was an attempt to integrate universal guidelines for conscious living in positive ways. Primitive religion was not really practiced. It was lived.

While early spiritual humans lived their religion in their daily lives in how they responded to others individually in a sharing and respectful manner, they also developed and practiced community ritual. Consistent with the Source's design, the human has always found ritual to be meaningful and useful in a number of ways.

Rituals are a form of security, a form of grounding. They are a reminder of who you are, what you are, where you come from, and where you are going. Rituals are very good at heightening and stimulating chemistry to trigger insight, to put in touch with their intuitive self. That is why man was designed to be ritualistic. To create a ritual that you can become totally emotionally involved with is very gratifying.

Early human rituals appear to have been not only necessary but also very powerful in many ways. They seem to have served an impressive array of functions in helping to integrate the four quadrants.

One reason man creates rituals is to remember. Before the written word, one of the ways that history could be remembered was through ritual, to pass down facts from one generation to another, and to pass on the ethics and teachings of the tribe and society.

There was then, as now, a need for ritual to serve functions of remembering not only historical facts but of other aspects of life: our need for others individually and collectively; the Source from which we came; the respect of all life; true pride and true humility; healthy interdependence. *Rituals can represent anything, as well as record into the mind of the youth, to remember.*

Early communal rituals did not focus on any particular spiritual teachings or dogma, but on natural phenomena and individual development. They were literally shared celebrations that recognized and showed respect for the Source and the spiritual gift that all had received. There was much focus on respect of the soul of each individual, as well as for the collective group. Early spiritual humans developed many 'appreciation' rituals, being keenly aware of their spiritual essence and all that this implied.

Rituals were created in appreciation of this scheme. There are still such rituals today, although some have become terribly distorted, even destructive. But man has always celebrated through ritual the appreciation of awareness, of being different from other animals. Before organized

81

religion, every tribe, every community, had their rituals.

While each tribe developed their own unique forms of specific rituals it is interesting to note that what the rituals were in celebration of had considerable consistency across tribes. Mario gave some examples.

For those that lived on parts of the globe that had four seasons, they would celebrate each season. These would include the planting or the sowing of the seed and the harvest, and periods in between . . . it would come instinctually or intuitively to create a ritual in celebration of the mutual commitment of matrimony. There were rituals for death, for birth, and there were rituals for puberty.

Regarding the general style or type of ritualistic behavior, *most would be in the context of primitive dances and feasts.* Early rituals of any type, tied to individual personal development and natural processes of the environment as well as to an inner awareness of the Source, had tremendous impact. For example, puberty and the entering of sexual maturity was a very significant event, which involved enormous respect for the soul (a more prominent emergence of the spiritual quadrant) within the adolescent as well as for the uniqueness of their physical, emotional, and intellectual personality. Rituals offered young adolescents emotional support for the added burden of responsibility they would carry and the challenges they would meet as adults.

While some cultures still have very impactful rituals today, many have lost their power to influence and aid in the feeling of connectedness both within the social group and with the Source. Some contemporary rituals can be traced back hundreds of thousands or millions of years to early, generalized forms. In speaking of a few examples of these Mario pointed out what seemed to be some changes in their function and purposes.

Early man would practice things in appreciation like what one religion you have now calls Lent, a minor sacrifice. Catholicism is one of the orthodox religions that have practiced some of the beautiful rituals passed down from very primitive man. Like the natural law of confession, which is a beautiful ritual. The only . . . thing the church did was use it as a punitive process.

Mario was referring to natural confession as acceptance of a mistake, apologizing, and if possible, making amends. This, in turn, naturally would lead to self-forgiveness. He referred also to the Catholic ritual of confirmation.

Before religion became what it is, the seventh year of life marked one's initiation or celebration into reasoning. In primitive man, the boy-child was sent out to slay an animal, and thereby demonstrate the power of reasoning and planning that was considered then. Now, you take vows of confirmation.

The Catholic version of a mass has also apparently changed quite a bit, for originally it is said to have been a celebration of group life.

Every one day out of seven or so, many tribes would hold great feasts and conduct rituals of the entire community coming together. You would today call it a 'potluck'.

The entities used terms like 'potluck' (meaning everyone at a gathering brings food to share) presumably because most of the listeners of their lectures were of Euro-American decent and were familiar with this term. Rather than a celebration of spirituality, via community sharing, mass now offers opportunities for renewal of one's inner spiritual awareness in a quiet setting. While all shared many early rituals, there were also separate male and female rituals expressing appreciation to the Source for each sex's basic social and biological function.

Each sex had their own rituals or customs to show respect to the Source, and they also had shared rituals they would carry out together. In their natural behavior, aware as they were of the unity of life, they would automatically design simple rituals to portray and express appreciation of being a part of it all. One example would be the appreciation of cover, vegetation; protection for their physical body.

In one ritual, not long after endowment, the male would pull from a tree a leaf and hold it over his head; he would dance with excitement around the tree at least three times, making sounds. Translated in overly simple terms, he was saying something like "thank you, thank you, thank you". Many years later, when man began going into caves or other places for tribal rituals, men would cover their heads. Such was the evolvement of this ritual. There has always been that for the male.

However, through the years in many sects, male became superficially dominant and, in a show of authority, reversed the ritual. They made it so that the females must cover their face and head when they enter the holy place. In many of your churches now, females cover their head and males uncover the head if he should have it hooded.

In certain places, some women's ritual for years was to expose their left breast. It was a ritual that was convenient and meaningful, although it may sound silly to you. The left breast was over the area of their heart; it supplied sustenance for offspring. To expose also meant pride in their femaleness. It was like saying "for what you have given me, I thank you." This was similar to the protector male covering his head. As this ritual evolved, female would find great pleasure in shallow water. There, the ritual involved not only exposing but in gently washing and splashing water on their breasts to bring attention by ritual to their respect for the Source.

When such examples of male/female differences in ritual were given, questions arose about evolution of each sex socially in human's early spiritual life. We were particularly interested in issues of relative importance and social equality/inequality then as compared to these issues in contemporary society.

In very primitive life, there was no inequality. The only difference for male is that he has always been physically stronger. He was designed that way. Female is generally far more intelligent than male, other than the intuitive senses for stalking. They think faster. They resolve faster. They are emotionally stronger. They are physically stronger genetically, compared to the male brawn and muscular strength. Civilization has deprived man of his natural instincts, for after natural rhythm was broken man [males] *used his brawn to dominate females. It is very difficult now to explain to the female the superior pride for being female and the natural role or behavior of the female in the Source's design in keeping together a society or a social structure.*

Many females in your time feel inferior to males. They allow physicalness - because their muscles are shorter and less strong—to cause them to feel inferior. However, it is also true that female has psychologically dominated male for centuries and continues to do so. They put males in a role to which they must conform. They educate, treat, and train them to function in a certain role. If the males do not play out the role when they become adults, they are seen as inferior; and if they do, then the female feels dominated. Yours is a female-dominated society and if you do not understand it or believe it, monitor your expectations of behavior towards males in certain roles, and observe your responses. See if it does not conform to this description of expectations.

In several of our meetings we asked when and how it happened that tribes began to recognize or identify one or more of their members as a leader of ritual activities. Did tribal members in some way identify others in the community who seemed particularly attuned to spiritual impingement or intuition? Mario responded to such questions cautiously, answering obliquely in the context of tribes and villages initially selecting people as historians rather than as religious or spiritual leaders. His response is interesting in that it suggests that gradually these historians did begin to be looked at as wise. It also suggests that the aged were well cared for by the younger. The following comments refer to a general sequence of changes over thousands of years, and no specific timeframe was provided.

Of course, some of what primitive man called masters received protection by the tribe and lived to be quite old, relatively speaking. These were the teachers of the people who would pass on the cultural knowledge. These persons would often dwell alone and be celibate. Their sole purpose, at first, was to remember incidents, to record. In their minds was history that would be taught and passed on to other generations. Much later they would begin to create signs to record meaning when written language became a part of society. They would make marks by carving or with berry stains, and place them where they would not erode. Thus, ancestors could show the future generations what happened before them.

It should be noted that Sanskrit writings of India relate to millions of years of human history (Cremo & Thompson, 1996; Kenyon, 2005). While ancient examples of writing carved in stone or with berry stains remain to be discovered, Aenka and Mario indicated that this is because modern humans have not looked in the right places, which could be much deeper in the Earth's surface than has yet been investigated.

Tribal members began to seek and pick out those who could be called priests or wise men also. Such persons were selected on the basis of their spiritual attunement as well as their ability to function as historians. There were many variations in the function and identity of elders or those considered wise, but it was on a less formal basis than we use today.

The celibacy aspect of tribal historians/elders was intriguing in the context of the entities' teachings of sex as healthy and intended to be enjoyed.

It was a chosen social and cultural evolvement that seemed to be practical and appropriate. Before man had symbols for words or slates to mark upon, a disciplined mind was needed that could focus and concentrate on particular issues without being influenced by external stimuli. Also, while it was not always a factor, some of those interested or willing to become such a person of high regard were the physically deformed, whereby there were physical interferences with sexual expression.

Mario went on to describe what is considered positive and negative motivation for celibacy then and now in a person physically capable of sex.

We have always taught sexuality as a natural part of human behavior. Celibacy, if it is by choice, can be practiced and be a holy thing if the motive is positive. By this, I mean when the motive is on the basis of unconditional love, to give and serve your fellow man or your tribe. In this way it is not in violation of any universal laws, and can be a healthy thing. If a choice of celibacy is made through fear and guilt or an attitude of subtle condescension then this is another matter. This is celibacy practiced under the broken rhythm of superiority and is not healthy.

Early Psychic Abilities

Rituals and rhythmic living were two avenues that helped early humans work toward integrating the enormous input of their spiritual aspect. In addition, heightened awareness of their intuitive abilities also offered access to what we would now also call psychic abilities. Early endowment human is said to have had much awareness of unexplainable yet definitely real unseen energies, and to have used information gained via them in a very matter-of-fact way. In modern science, there is a great deal of experimental and replicated evidence for psychic abilities (e.g., Fontana, 2005; Radin, 1997, 2006; Tart, 2009). However, this evidence is often shunned if not outright vilified by mainstream scientists who adhere to a pure reductive materialistic view of the world. In this atheistic mainstream scientific view, causation is a product of random factors that are inherently meaningless. Yet, as mentioned in the Preface, there is a reason to believe a paradigm shift is taking place in science. This shift reflects that a move away from a materialistic Newtonian view of the universe to one that is quantum and non-materialistic, and thus can accommodate the notion of psychic energy and abilities, such as intuition.

They did not question the source of information. It was just an awareness. They felt comfortable to use the faculties available to them for healthy and rhythmic survival.

In addition to using natural intuition in learning medicinal applications of plants and to relate sensitively to one another,

There were many other talents that were available to them. They learned ways of assisting each other in the healing process. They learned to use thought processes to communicate without sound, simple things between people.

If children were out exploring and not in sight, the mother could call them with thoughts, and they would tune into that and come home immediately. They also used their intuitive and psychic processes to warn each other of danger.

The use of energy or mind-body medicine has surged in recent years (e.g., Dossey, 1999; Levin, 2001; Targ & Katra, 1999; Turner, 2009). This interest is based on research demonstrating the effectiveness of the use of psychic and spiritual energy in healing. The details of Aenka and Mario's teachings on healing are presented in Appendix C.

Surveys have shown that over 60% of people believe in psychic abilities such as telepathy, and those with a higher education are more likely to accept these abilities as being genuine (Radin, 2006). Westerners are beginning to be more open to what is called 'alternative' medicine, meaning alternative to allopathic medicine that ignores the intuitive/spiritual quadrant and the use of psychic and spiritual energies to heal.

When we asked Aenka and Mario if early humans participated in channeling phenomena, Mario surprised us when he said:

Every tribe practiced this activity; it was a very natural thing. Before rhythm was broken and man lived in harmony with appreciation of and communication with the unobstructed, they found it was not difficult to have or perform a ritual in a cave where there was the absence of energy or light. In that way, their (discarnate) friends could visit with them.

There is still the practice of performing rituals in the dark in order to communicate with discarnate entities, but its prevalence is unknown. Some call these activities "home circles" and others 'séances'. A Google search of "physical mediumship" got 727,000 hits in early 2013.

Moreover, some mental and voice mediums have been subjected to experimental evaluations, finding that accuracy is about 80% (e.g., Schwartz & Simon, 2005; http://www.google.com/search?client=safari&rls=en&q=win dbridge+institute&ie=UTF-8&oe=UTF-8), which is what Aenka and Mario have indicated (Appendix A and Appendix B).

Mario concluded his comments about such mediumistic activities with a statement that when natural rhythm was broken such darkroom activity began to decrease.

Some of your tribes still practice it, but it is almost a lost art. One example would be some of your American Indians who still use this ritual in the sweat lodge.

With endowment 7 million years ago, the age of human's initial enlightenment had arrived, a true emergence from instinctual animal limitations to reasoning, memory, emotions, and awareness of a divine aspect within via intuition. Early human's spiritual religious orientation was a way of being in the world which pervaded individual perceptions of and interactions with fellow humans and all of life, and with humility they recognized their spiritual aspect that separated them from other animals. They had an attitude of appreciation and celebration in the equality of humans and the awesomeness of the Source.

For religious experience, early humans did not look upward with trembling from the position of sin, fear, shame, and guilt, but outward, supported by their subjective inner connection experiences or intuitions. Thoughts and feelings of equality with respect for one's fellow human were integral fibers in the tapestry of the evolving social human. Although technology was primitive and written language in its infancy, human's constructive use of emotional, physical, intellectual, and spiritual aspects is most impressive. While it is interesting to note that the Hebrew word Eden means 'pleasure' it would be a mistake to picture Eden as an easy life as suggested in Genesis with things provided in abundance and gained with ease. The Garden of Eden story refers to endowment and the introduction of free choice or free will. Humans were no longer just instinctual animals, but faced with balancing the physical, intellectual, emotional, and intuitive/spiritual aspects of their personalities.

CHAPTER THREE

PARADISE LOST: 4 MILLION YEARS AGO

"To err from the right path is common to mankind"
(Sophocles, *Antigone).*

With the endowment of humans with a soul and its gifts of intelligence, emotions, and intuition, the human had been released from the limitations of instinct and primitive conditioned responses. For up to 4 million years, humans lived rhythmically in simple ways as they slowly developed language and technology. Positive and constructive choices were made in pursuit of individual and collective social destiny. It was not necessary for religion to be taught as something separate or apart from daily life for it was integrated in daily behaviors and attitudes.

Humankind held other individuals in high regard and shared freely. People respected the environment and worked with humility towards comprehension and understanding of life. There were never any serious questions or doubts regarding spiritual aspects of life being a reality. However, endowment also brought the ability to question, to challenge, and the opportunity for free choice not available to the instinctual human creature or other animals.

While endowment heightened humans' awareness of their spiritual/intuitive aspect and respect for life, it also put them in charge of their own destiny in a very real sense. No longer would they howl at the moon, or mate on an instinctual basis. They could choose. But with choices comes responsibility for making them, and experiencing their consequences. The potential for greed, egomania, arrogance, status, and a feeling of power has always been present in the spiritually endowed human, early as well as contemporary. Those who use free choice in ways to violate spiritual guidelines run the risk of beginning to attend more to material self-benefit and less to mutual benefit. If continued, such an emphasis, by its very nature, will impair attunement to spiritual impingement and intuition. Thus, the danger in disregarding universal laws (see Appendix A and Appendix B) in making choices was and is primarily that of weakening our spiritual connection and distorting natural healthy behaviors. We can go off course, and off track. This is not a sin in the terms of organized religions; it is simply a misdirected and potentially destructive mistaken choice.

Adam and Eve and The Tree Of Knowledge

The Bible describes the human as being expelled from the Garden of Eden for going against God's directive to not eat the fruit from the Tree Of Knowledge (Genesis 2:15-17). According to Aenka and Mario, the abbreviated symbology in this story refers to humankind losing its spiritually constructive track.

Humankind was not cast out from the Garden of Eden. Humans found their own way out. The Tree Of Knowledge refers not to forbidden information but to free choice and thereby potential for unhealthy choices as well as healthy choices. Guidelines from the Source regarding how to live one's life were and are not commands but reminders to bear in mind universal spiritual principles and laws in making choices. The Source gives suggestions to follow the laws of natural behavior, not orders.

Eating of the fruit of The Tree Of Knowledge refers not to trying to be as wise or powerful as the Source, or disobeying a command from the Source, but to experimenting with free choice into directions that include the possibility of losing a healthy perspective. The persuasive and seductive Biblical snake (Genesis 3:1-7) refers not to a literal devil, but to those thoughts of people that could lead into directions of destructive behaviors toward others or toward self-aggrandizement and ego inflation.

The eating of a fruit based on manipulation by the snake refers to making a poor choice, or perhaps a series of poor choices. In the Biblical allegory, God is warning humans about what can happen, not condemning them for making free choices. Challenging the Source's wisdom and guidelines for living may reflect bad judgment but is not a sin. Free choice is a right and a universal law that applies to all humans, even if the choice is poor (i.e., harming oneself and others).

The above attitude is clearly at odds with orthodox Catholic and Protestant teachings, for most branches of Christianity believe in (or at least support) the concept of Original Sin. Their belief is simple. Adam and Eve disobeyed God, and thus evil was allowed into the world. The basic Christian interpretation of Adam and Eve making the choice to eat this fruit, which would give them knowledge of choice and more awareness of "good and evil", is that it is disrespectful and arrogant. They are then severely punished by the Creator for their disobedience. How dare naive children of God challenge the wisdom, knowledge, authority, and territory of their Creator in Heaven?

Psychologists and people with common sense know that at various times in their development, children and adolescents will challenge the rules and authority of their parents or other authority figures. Psychologically this is at times very healthy and necessary for at least two reasons: (1) to find out if the guidelines and rules set down for them really work from their own experience; and (2) to assert their own autonomy in their evolution towards more self-choice and self-responsibility. They want to gain enough information and knowledge to make more of their own decisions, and to do so they need to find out for themselves. One cannot do this by passive dependence and blind faith.

When a seven- or seventeen-year-old challenges parental authority, is their motive to be like them? Do they want to take the place of their parent? No, of course not. (Perhaps, but only if after their own search for learning they find they respect the parent's values and ways of being in the world.) The motive of children and adolescents challenging parental rules and authority is simple: to come to their own conclusions about what is positive and negative, what feels good and what does not; what is helpful or harmful to them and others. Intuitively, whether consciously or unconsciously, they seek to use their own "God-given" equipment and gifts to develop their own autonomy as much as they can relative to their stage of development. If they are supported in their quest for increasing self-responsibility and experimenting with choices, they can experience not only real-life consequences, but also develop the self-confidence to look within for their own spiritual aspect as a guide in life. We are, of course, speaking here of a healthy challenging of authority, not exaggerated types of rebellion or hostility.

Is the motive to learn by experience evil/sinful, or is it healthy? Do parents have all the answers for their children? Is it healthy for children of the Source to be only obedient? Do we want our children and adolescents to be passive and dependent on us to the point that they are replications or little clones of us with no uniqueness of their own? Or do we want them to find out who they are, believe in themselves, and follow their own destiny in a responsible way? Would not the Source as a healthy Creator want It's children to grow up to be independent, unique, and responsible adults?

But what if human's early poor choices were not the result of sin? As Haag (1969) puts it, "No man enters the world a sinner. As the creature and image of God he is from his first hour surrounded by God's parental love. Consequently he is not at birth, as is often maintained, an enemy of God and a child of God's wrath. A man becomes a sinner only through his own individual and responsive action." (http://www.msgr.ca/msgr-7/hell_jesus_never_intended%2002.htm).

Similarly, Matthew Fox (1983) also seems to support the idea of human's sins as mistakes rather than an inherited guilt burden in his writings on what he calls original "blessings" as compared to the doctrine of original sin. As he puts it pithily "we do not enter (the world) as blotches on existence, as sinful creatures, we burst into the world as original blessings!" (http://www.msgr.ca/msgr-7/hell_jesus_never_intended%2002.htm).

Fox is clearly a theologian who believes in enjoying the beauty of life and creation in all its forms and takes an attitude of enjoying all of God's gifts within us and in our environment. Certainly he believes in the concept of free choice and self-responsibility as central to what he considers a Christian orientation to life. He is taken to task by some as focusing too much on enjoying life, free choice, and pleasure, even though he has lived with the discipline of the Dominican Order of the Catholic Church for many years.

But whether the early endowment humans were born as sinners or as a blessing, the question of course arises that if they were connected with their inner spiritual/intuitive aspect and nourished by their relationships with others, why would they choose to become selfish and seek self-aggrandizement or power? How could such deviation from positive courses occur? And, even if some individuals made poor choices in challenging their inner spiritual guidelines, how could enough people begin to distort their behavior to the extent of gradually shifting human's collective focus from spiritual to material, from broad respectful goals to shortsighted and selfish ones? This is a crucial question and, while we feel we have been given some clues to it from Aenka and Mario, there are aspects that remain obscure.

Humankind's Collective Misdirection

Aenka and Mario talked about three main factors regarding humankind's collective misdirection. They sound simple but on closer inquiry become quite complex.

The first is that spiritually endowed humans, whether in early history or in contemporary times, cannot by their very nature be simply a passive and automatic "yes man". To say only yes to spiritual direction would essentially mean functioning like a puppet or a constantly obedient child. However, the Source does not need or want puppets. The Source endows beings with spiritual essence and free will. Or would God, as some churches and ministers teach, want us to be passive and obedient adult children with little free choice? The author agrees with the entities Aenka and Mario that there is nothing sinful in being self-responsible and seeking one's own truth.

Orthodox Catholic and Protestant churches teach not only that challenging God's rules or guidelines was a sin of Adam and Eve and that they were punished by God as suggested in Genesis (3:16-24), but that all their offspring would be born in sin and carry the burden of guilt placed on the shoulders of their original ancestry. Cavendish's (1980) definition of original sin is generally representative of Christian belief. "Original sin means that all human beings, quite apart from the sins they commit, are infected with an inescapable taint of corruption which cannot be eradicated by human effort alone, that man is a fallen being, evil and guilty from birth."

However, it is interesting to note that the concept of original sin and its consequences being passed on to all of Adam's and Eve's descendants is not in Genesis or indeed anywhere in the Old Testament. This fact is pointed out by Haag (1969), former president of the Catholic Bible Association of Germany and author of *Is Original Sin In Scripture?* Along with other scholars in theology, he says in part, "The idea of Adam's descendants being automatically sinners because of the sin of their ancestors, and that they are already sinners when they enter the world is foreign to Holy Scripture. The Doctrine of Original Sin is not found in any of the writings of the Old Testament. It certainly is not in Chapters 1-3 of Genesis. This ought to be recognized today."

Cavendish (1980) agrees with Haag that the concept of original sin is not in the Old Testament. He attributes the concept of original sin as "a term used by St. Augustine late in the fourth century." Ricouer (1984) refers to distortions in interpretations of Genesis and the concept of original sin as follows: "The harm that has been done to souls during the centuries of Christianity, first by the literal interpretations of the story of Adam and then by the confusion of this myth treated as history . . .[including] later speculations, principally Augustinian, about original sin will never be adequately told."

Additionally, as Matthew Fox (1983) points out "It is well known that the Council Of Trent insisted on the Doctrine of Original Sin" in the 16th century, long after the death of Jesus. The fact that the spiritually endowed human made poor choices in collective evolution is obviously looked at by churches as sinful rather than choice for growth, new learning, and evolution. Challenge is necessary to learn and live fully. In order to fulfill one's destiny, the human must face the challenge of making free choices, which can turn out to be either constructive or destructive.

This is a concept that may be difficult to swallow unless one is willing to accept self-responsibility even though one is a child of the Source. Such an attitude is not paradoxical unless one has been conditioned in their thinking by religious teachings of essential unworthiness and inferiority. For many orthodox Christians it is almost the ultimate challenge to question God's advice and guidance. Yet, to fully understand and appreciate the naturalness and constructive effects of God's guidelines we must try other avenues of experience. How else could we know that spiritual guidelines are solid unless we try others? For some people it may be enough to believe by blind faith or out of fear or guilt that God is good and wise, but many need to learn this by experience.

A second factor in human's collective misdirection relates to seemingly accidental occurrences that were misinterpreted. The misinterpretations, and behaviors that followed from them, had a gradual rippling effect. In the following pages, you are given symbolic examples of such misinterpretations based on the Biblical story of Cain and Abel.

We are very aware that using simple symbolic

examples of a major factor in human's collective spiritual misdirection may be seen as specious or superficial. However, it should be pointed out that all history prior to written language was an oral history (modern recognized language writing dates to about 3200 B.C. but according to the entities is far much earlier but not yet discovered). And of the oral history, like it or not, the Bible is the major source for either fact or myth regarding historical developments in the Near or Middle East, the seat of the development of Christianity and many of the world's major religions. What we will attempt to point out, regardless of the reference, is that endowed humans erred in interpreting some significant life events in their early tribal societies as they struggled with their evolving abilities and civilization.

A third factor is that although early endowment humans were keenly aware of universal guidelines in living, they were, in an evolutionary sense, young as spiritual beings. Their inner spiritual connections were clear and strong, but somewhat tentative. They were still struggling, just as young or older children and adolescents do in their individual development, to find themselves and grow individually and as a social unit. As humans developed simple tools and language, and communal or social life gradually evolved into more complex and subtle relationships, it became more difficult to follow the intuitive.

In a very real sense early civilization with its inherent need for more complex organization challenged the human's integrative abilities. More factors in everyday social life within tribes and in between tribes had to be evaluated. Human's spiritual quadrant began to have to compete with the intellectual and emotional quadrants for attention. Aenka and Mario also said that this struggle has been part of the Source's design for human evolution.

When humans began to use free choice and to challenge their intuition/inner guidance/connection with spiritual guidelines, what happened and why did the Source not actively interfere? Why did It not warn It's chosen people, the endowed human, that there were grave dangers? Aenka and Mario imply that the Source chose not to intervene because humans in this period of their collective development needed more challenge than previously. As Mario put it rather pithily, **up until that time in development, the Source had pretty much spoon fed the species after endowment. Now it was time for man to take more responsibility for choice, and so the Source chose not to intervene or allow souls in the unobstructed to intervene.**

Humans became more material and selfish as they became more intellectual and emotional such that the four quadrants (physical, intellectual, emotional, and spiritual) were out of balance. Humans misinterpreted some events that could not be understood intuitively via the soul. The Source did not interfere with poor choices by more impingement because this aspect of evolution is part of It's design or experiment with the endowed human. The Source wanted to see how humans (being a physical part of Itself) responded to the challenges of a more complex society, what choices they made, and how they handled the Gamble of Life, given they have a Government of Life.

In a sense, the Source saw the necessity and wisdom of letting the 'adolescent' humans struggle to find their own adult identity.

Cain and Abel Part I: Onset of Guilt and Shame 4 Million Years Ago

In describing how humankind gradually shifted from spiritually oriented rhythmic living to superficial ego and materialistically oriented living, Mario used the familiar Bible story of Cain and Abel as a metaphor (Genesis 1-16). This story is said to illustrate how unnatural guilt and shame became a part of the human experience through essentially a combination of apparent accident, natural emotions, and poor choices around 4 million years ago. Cain and Abel were real people. The story symbolizes not only an interruption in rhythmic living and the introduction of guilt and shame, but

100

also, as is evident in Chapter Four, eventually slavery.

When man originally became aware of his existence in the era of endowment, guilt or shame was not a part of his life. People were not judged or punished for mistakes or misdeeds. There was no moral judgment. They simply experienced natural consequences for their mistakes and were counseled or guided by those closest to them. The initial break in rhythmic living is symbolically told in that period or era of the two brothers. Guilt and shame became a part of man after Cain, who was symbolically the first to feel shame and severe punishment.

While the Bible describes Cain and Abel as offspring of an original Adam and Eve, this is said to be clearly symbolic and not literal. *There were many Adams and Eves, more than one Cain and Abel.* As Aenka and Mario told the symbolic story, Cain did not kill his brother but was erroneously accused; it was not God who punished him but his biological incarnate father.

Cain loved his brother Abel very much. They spent much time together as children and as adults and were very close. One day while Abel was in the field he fell and his head struck a rock. It was an accident. Cain found his brother lying dead in the field, and his love for his brother was apparent in his anguish. He picked up the rock; the stone Abel had struck his head upon that took his life. He picked up the stone and lifted it above his head, shaking it and cursing the stone and the heavens for taking his brother's life. He was venting his anger in a very natural way by simply expressing it.

By this time in humankind's evolution self-expression of natural emotions was accepted as a healthy response to a trauma such as the loss of a loved one. Unable to change the situation due to the Gamble of Life, and needing a release for strong feelings, it was acceptable to allow oneself to go through a natural process of frustration, anger, sadness and pain. Otherwise, repression of these natural emotions would lead to physical illness (see Appendix C).

His father caught sight of this scene and thought Cain had slain his brother. He cursed Cain and rejected him. He sent him out into the wilderness and forbid him to return to the tribe.

According to Aenka and Mario, this unnatural response and interpretation by Cain's father (the conclusion that Cain had killed his brother) was in part due to neurological dysfunction. In a very real sense he was brain-damaged and in current terms would be classified as senile. Thus, this metaphor speaks to the challenge of the incarnate to remain rhythmic in the face of life's challenges, including organic ones.

But, symbolically speaking or translated, Cain's father judged him unfairly. As a result of that judgment Cain suffered the consequences. He could not defend himself, even though he was not guilty in a literal sense of slaying his brother. The senility of the father made it impossible for communication to occur.

Cain, reacting emotionally in his anguish, accepted the wrath and accusations of his father.

Cain felt very badly but there was no way he could reason with his father. His guilt was not due to the death of his brother, because he knew he did not slay his brother. Cain's emotional break was related to his devotion or his love for his father. He felt helpless and weak, ashamed that he could not communicate with his father to show him that he did not take his brother's life.

The rejection of Cain by his village and tribe, as

well as by his father, did occur as the Bible relates, but Mario's explanation for the basis of that rejection is a bit different.

In his grief, with limited intellectual functioning, the father openly accused Cain in the village of killing his brother.

Perhaps out of respect for the important position the father once had as the village chief, and still had as a revered elder, he was listened to. Thus, material status and power was deemed more important than intuitive connections to the universal laws (see Appendix A and Appendix B).

In a literal sense Cain had been accused and not cleared. In the eyes of all those present he was guilty. So he was guilty, was he not? Even today a jury finds guilty and your courts place judgment: then society what? Accepts the verdict.

As to the "Mark of Cain" referred to in the Bible (Genesis 4:15) as a visible sign of punishment from God, again that is said to be symbolic and a legend or myth.

Have you ever seen a frustrated individual try to resolve their problem or be caught in the midst of something difficult, banging their hand or head in some way? Cain, in his cursing the rock as he held it above his head, toward the heavens, was literally pounding his forehead against the rock. He was not only cursing God, he was cursing the stone. It was an emotional reaction; he loved his brother very much. The irregular surface of the rock scarred his face. As coincidence would have it, there was an electrical storm after Abel's death and it occurred about the time that his father discovered the incident. The father in his translation had the rumor spread through the village that God put a curse upon Cain. So the story would have it that when Cain slew Abel God became angry and put the mark on his forehead.

The Cain and Abel story is, of course, representative of many events, not simply an interesting tale or isolated event that in itself changed the course of humankind. As such a symbolic pivotal point, it provides an opportunity to explore other aspects of the beginning of human's spiritual decline according to the materialized entities Aenka and Mario. For example, did Cain have any responsibility regarding his part in what happened to him? Was he in some way more than a passive and innocent victim of circumstances? In his response Mario attempted to explain a rather subtle and not very attractive aspect of free choice and responsibility.

Responsibility is sometimes nothing more than a choice to be involved. Cain was involved in that situation. He was involved in the death of his brother simply because he was there. He was present. The consequence of the choice of being there at the moment was his being accused of slaying his brother, and he has never to this day been cleared.

One other aspect of Cain's responsibility epitomizes another factor in spiritual decline. This is the choice to accept or create some type of guilt feelings even though conclusions or accusations levied toward us are erroneous and have no basis in fact. Cain accepting guilt inappropriately thus symbolizes a milestone in humans turning away from their own inner truth and to begin paying attention instead to the judgments of others toward themselves. How many of us have accepted a guilty verdict of one sort or another, even though we know we are innocent, and particularly when we know any defense might be stifled? How many of us avoid self-responsibility for our feelings and still blame Adam, Eve, or Cain for our difficulties in our life or our feelings of separation from God, the Source?

CHAPTER FOUR

EROSION OF SPIRITUAL CONNECTION

"Darkness cannot drive out darkness; only light can do that. Hate cannot drive out hate" (Martin Luther King, Jr.).

The entities Aenka and Mario date endowment as about 7 million years ago and is represented in their revised version of the Garden of Eden story. Life was rhythmic for up to 4 million years. The loss of rhythmic life is represented in the Cain and Abel story. About 4 million years ago is when people developed unnatural guilt and shame resulting from being judged and rejected from one's tribe and accepting that judgment for oneself. Thereafter, humankind's break from rhythmic living was to be a very gradual process that occurred at different rates worldwide. Aenka and Mario linked events after the time of Cain's rejection by the tribe to the creation of slavery, a major marker of unnatural behavior that violates universal laws set into place by the Source.

The species evolved; primitive scientific advances continued. Even after the time of Cain, there were areas in which rhythmic living was not all that distorted. But there was a break in the rhythm for collective man and resulting deterioration. This did not happen in all tribes over the world. Some avoided and continued to live rhythmically even up into recent times. However, the expansion of what you call the Europeans and other 'developed' countries within the last few centuries has resulted in most of them also being thrown off balance.

Cain and Abel Part II: Guilt, Shame, Hate, War, and Slavery

In responding to questions about these developments, Aenka and Mario chose to continue with the thread of Cain and

Abel as an illustrative story. They explained that after the beating from his senile father, the father left Cain in the desert to die. Cain survived but now, like his father, was also neurologically damaged. Specifically, he incurred damage in the medulla oblongata (locus of the soul in the brain, where impingement is received and psychic energy used, and the source of intuition), so he was not capable of being open to spiritual/natural processes and psychologically could not capture natural behavior. Moreover, being rejected by his tribe, which previously would not have been done (as doing so was unnatural), emotionally traumatized him. At most, he would have been forced by the other elders to live on the outskirts of the village, but still fed, sheltered and treated humanely. Instead, these elders imitated Cain's father by failing to forgive and casting out members of the tribe.

Thus, Cain's tribe was out of rhythm and utilized an "eye for an eye". Hate was born. Unnatural fear and its derivatives of guilt and shame were born. As a result, Cain too was out of rhythm.

Cain taught others in an emotionally damaged way. He taught guilt and shame, domination by fear, and physical domination rather than living according to the spiritual laws. Thus it was a combination of the Gamble of Life (Abel's accident and Cain's and his father's brain damage), and power (a thirst for death of another human).

Cain survived in the wilderness and had his own family. After Cain, others were cast into the wilderness and eventually there came to pass a generation of outcasts. They tended to band together to form their own sect, for life was very difficult. In their struggles they survived even though their land has been described symbolically as filled with thorns, meaning that it was very poor land. As rhythm became increasingly distorted over the years, Cain's sect was more and more looked upon as inferior, what you would call today 'second class' or a minority.

Five generations passed and there was a great drought and famine among many having been relegated to an inferior status. Cain's sect was treated by the older, established tribes and villages much like your American Indian. Promises would be made only to be violated. Finally the outcasts had no fertile soil at all on which to dwell. Famine drove them to war against their forbearers who had rejected them, and whom now they declared their enemy. This war lasted on and off for three hundred years after the first drought. Gradually agreements began to be made among tribesmen on both sides. Near the closing of those agreements Cain's sect was what you would call 'sold down the river'.

The sects superior in strength began to sell those captured from Cain's sect using what you would consider a bartering system. That was somewhat the beginning of slavery. Life became cheap. In time it was no longer only the Cain sect that became slaves. Members of many tribes without standing or status were captured and sold at the slave market. This practice was to continue through the years unto times of mighty power and kingdoms that arose as civilization advanced. Much of what occurred from that point on regarding kingdoms and slave markets can be found described in your more distant history accounts.

Humankind progressively divided itself—warring, enslaving, manipulating—for many thousands of years after the time of Cain and Abel. Mario's description of the social decline of the human was chilling in its simplicity.

As man continued to evolve he began to rely on his mind and brawn to subjugate and to conquer rather than to live with one another based on guidelines from their spiritual aspect. They began to kill each other. They no longer practiced the law of natural survival.

The strong began to survive on the weak. Instead of the

species protecting each other, the strong helping the weak, they began to prey on the weaker and dominate as they dominated other species. Wars began among the tribes; rulers and kings became established. Hierarchies of authority were developed.

People ceased thinking of themselves as equals, but as where they fit in ranks established by the authorities. Slavery grew. But, understandably, slaves were not happy with their lot.

Slavery became more of a problem, and for thousands and thousands of years man was to be under slavery. Life became very cheap for the powerful in position. Those in power had no qualms about beating or killing slaves. They would drive men and beat them, and rob them of all dignity. Obedience became the structure and if one did not obey, their life was taken. Many became as animals, and only a few escaped slavery of one sort or another.

The inner light of human's spiritual essence was dwindling to a tiny flame. We were not able to learn a time frame from the entities in regards to this part of human history. Consistently, they would state that the time frame was of little importance; that what was important was how many departed from spiritual track. This resistance of the entities to use of linear time of the obstructed (physical) universe is understandable when one considers that discarnate entities do not operate in this dimension. Time is a human creation, designed to measure a sequence of experiences that are perceived as a sequence only because of neurological limitations of processing information. In other words, there is a brain-induced gap between experiences, as the human knows them. In the unobstructed universe where discarnate entities reside, there is no linear time. Instead, there is only the accumulation of experiences that are noted in the Archives of Knowledge.

Unfortunately, archaeologists and anthropologists

can tell us little of these events due to the lack of discovered written language during this era. Some of the earliest found forms of comprehensible writing discovered to date are traced to the Sumerians in approximately 3,200 B.C. One of the oldest discovered empires to be recorded in writing is that of Sargon who, around 2350 B.C., extended his kingdom through the Middle East. However, some archeologists and historians have found other physical evidence of these ancient civilizations, such as coins, the soles of shoes, figurines, and ruins of massive architecture that support the notion of the lost continents of Atlantis and Lemuria (Cremo & Thompson, 1996; Kenyan, 2005). Aenka and Mario indicated that archeologists have not dug deep enough and in the right places to find evidence of 7 million years of evolution of the endowed human. They also confirmed the existence of Atlantis and Lemuria, which can fill in some of the gaps of their related history of evolution.

It is also noteworthy that some information from psychics, such as
Edgar Cayce (1877—1945), point out that all humans are able to access the Archives of Knowledge (called by Cayce the Akashic Records) and learn about these 7 million years of endowed human history, including highly developed civilizations such as Atlantis and Lemuria (Todeschi, 1998). Also, individuals who have undergone past life regression hypnosis also fill in some of the gaps of Aenka and Mario's description of ancient human history (e.g., Newton, 2003).

We were very curious about why the spiritually connected early humans apparently passively accepted slavery and grossly unfair authority. Had not people prior to this time been guided by their intuitive connection to positive guidelines for living? How could spiritually attuned people comply with tribal leaders or rebels who would be king based on self-aggrandizement or physical authority? Why did villagers not stop such distortions when they saw them develop? Why did collective humans not control the weeds in the Garden of Eden as they used to do, by consensual decisions? These, to us, were very important questions, and still are. While we did receive some meaningful partial answers to these questions, many aspects remain unclear in what the entities teach. Of the factors we were told about, we were at first very sad; our sadness related to what is clearly a statement of vulnerability of early spiritual man that we had no idea existed.

Listening to the 7 million years of history of endowed humankind, it is clear that 4 million years ago people had started to become unnatural. Conditional love is represented in the Cain and Abel story. While unconditional love is described by the entities as a natural emotion, conditional love is deemed unnatural. And the aftermath of conditional love was guilt, shame, hate, war, and slavery. This puts the modern quest for spiritual fulfillment in historical context. Living a rhythmic life has been a challenge for about the past 3 million years. Yet, modern people continue to be riddled with guilt and shame, and still operate in one form or another with the powerful influence of heartless others.

Apparently, it was naïve for artists and anthropologists in the 1800's and 1900's to think of the "noble savage" in a Gauguin painting. Scholars described tribal peoples as 'innocent' and pictured as somehow pure. They were viewed as untainted by the inroads of the industrial revolution and the explosion of commerce and trade. Just as people today have mental images of Krishna, Buddha, Jesus, Albert Schweitzer, Mother Theresa, etc., regarding "what they were like," so some have such a picture of early endowment man: honest, alert, spiritually attuned, community minded, balanced, etc. These mental images appear to have some basis in fact for the first 4 million years after endowment 7 million years ago, but not since then.

Aenka and Mario described some of the unnatural workings of the four quadrants of the physical personality (see Appendix B) that led to a disruption in rhythmic living. After the era of Cain 4 million years ago, some people who were rejected or traumatized in one way or another began to express their sadness, fear, and pain as distorted unnatural anger, i.e. hostility. They began to take revenge on others, to hurt or control them in some vengeful way. They wanted to feel powerful to offset their feelings of frustration and hurt. Some of these people learned that they could use the natural emotion of fear in an unnatural way in order to intimidate others and threaten them. This would work since physical pain and threat to life of a loved one triggered a basically healthy fear related to survival. Thus, some distorted individuals began to learn they could intimidate others by force.

This was not initially a major social problem, as it would occur in personal relationships or between family groups. However, some people with leadership ability who also had unresolved sadness, fear, or pain, began to notice how people could be intimidated and controlled. When they reached positions of some authority, they began to emulate or copy and gradually generalize the personal techniques of intimidation they had observed. The basic natural emotion of jealousy (desire to learn by modeling or emulating others) was distorted as envy of the free choice of others. This was the beginning of social control by force, intimidation or manipulation.

The picture provided by the entities is of an increasing spiral effect. A few distorted people became power hungry and used fear to intimidate, initially in small groups. Family and clan or tribal members began to pay attention to protecting themselves against those who were threatening them. Early human's natural fears related to pain and survival for themselves and their children caused them to avoid doing things to increase the anger of the leaders or to be more physically or politically aggressive. This fear and survival focus of adults was unwittingly passed on to their children.

Children were told to be careful of what they said, even if a child could clearly see that physical punishment and force was not good and the end was unfair.

The parents were concerned that; if the children's natural and healthy observations were overheard by their angry and powerful leaders or opponents, then they would be harmed in some way. Such fearful adults taught their children to keep their personal values and thoughts inside themselves and not share them with others. The adults' fearfulness required more of their attention for protection, which gradually began to affect their inner spiritual connections. Thus, children began to be raised with unconsciously exaggerated fear and their natural inner spiritual aspect gradually began to not be adequately nourished or supported by their parents. By the time they came to be adults, their innate four quadrants or aspects were out of balance. Over many generations an increasing number of children were raised with exaggerated fears rather than psychological balance and a trust in their inner self. Ergo, a higher percentage of them as adults were also enticed into positions of power or authority to "protect themselves" or to seek retribution in their own way.

It is also part of the entities' picture that early local bullying rulers began to interfere with or prohibit certain communal rituals as they knew the villagers gained strength and insight from them. Such strategies by the politically or physically powerful were effective, and the limiting of shared rituals also eroded the strength of individual human's inner connections. Thus, the picture of how early endowment humans strayed off track is a gradual decline in overall balance of the four innate quadrants of the physical personality. In a sense, once rocks are thrown into the peaceful lake, the ripples begin to spread, hit each other, and make waves. The more rocks that are thrown the more turbulent the water becomes.

What became clear from conversations with Aenka and Mario is that early human adults and children had the potential for rhythmic living and inner strength but their spiritual quadrant needed the nourishment of balanced parenting and positive shared community relations to develop this potential. Human's weakening of the spiritual connection was the result of distortions in emotional and thinking functions of two other quadrants. Their spiritual aspect was never lost or distorted; it simply faded more into the background of everyday life rather than being an equal part of it.

While humans allowed themselves to become increasingly passive in the acceptance of slavery, they were not afraid of death itself. This created a problem for those in power.

It was ultimately physical pain and the fear of that pain that caused him to yield to labor. In order to escape pain they would yield to the master's demands: they did not fear death. Natural spirituality was still in existence, although diminishing steadily. Their natural spirituality had left them with the belief that death itself was not painful, but beautiful. The common man's leaders or spiritual advisors taught very heavily trying to strengthen in them an attitude they had nearly lost: that death is not the issue. They emphasized pride and respect for their heritage, meaning the Source of Divinity. They spoke of death as only a small part of growth and as having little to do with their destiny, which they referred to in their primitive way as going home.

The rulers, reacting to people's continual acceptance of death as generations went by, increased their physical brutality and deprivation in an attempt to force them to work harder while they were yet alive. This tactic not only proved futile, but also had the opposite effect.

Slaves were beaten and killed by the thousands. The rulers exhausted various ways to punish the body to force it to yield to labor. The slaves' preference came to be to die rather than to cater or cower.

This long and sorrowful episode in the history of

humans ended not out of compassion or spiritual revelation but of practical necessity. Two factors were ultimately involved in a need for change: the rulers' increasing brutality in forcing slaves to work, and the slaves' acceptance of death.

Eventually the rulers pushed the common man to the wall, and slaves began to talk among themselves of rebelling. After many years of such talk they finally did, but not by forceful overthrow.

Their choice, consistent with their passivity, was more along the lines of what would now be called massive slow down or sit down labor strikes. In many regions over many years, not in an identifiable or formally organized way, those in bondage increasingly rebelled in relatively passive ways.

They knew they might be killed for this but reasoned it was better to die quickly, if one is to live in slavery, than after a lifetime of toil with no compensation of any significant type. They knew their soul would live on, and it was fair not to conform to the demands of the rulers. Death was not a crime or sin under those circumstances. This rebellion caused the masters to have to kill off so many they were running out of labor.

It is clear that by this point in history, humans still had inner knowledge of their soul, and that some were still in contact via meditation, prayer, and ritualistic or mediumistic activities.

Even up to about the 9th century B.C. the Semites still had private rituals. In some of these they would attempt to make contact with their dead loved ones or ancestors, and *venerated their ancestors without the participation or interference of the larger political or ethnic group.* Organized religion was also still practiced with communal rituals. *When the Gods of Heaven rather than the dead were invoked, the whole community became involved.*

However, at a later time in 623 B.C., King Joshua

Got rid of all who called up ghosts and spirits (of the dead)
. . . the traffic between ancestor and offspring, so vital in
polytheistic thought and ritual practice, disappeared. The
living and the dead must be eternally separated.

Unfortunately, some of the priests and other leaders of organized religion had also become power oriented.

Separate classes evolved . . . towards the top were the
priests who . . . tended to become managers on behalf of
the gods; the temples grew into powerful economic centers
which owned much of the land and absorbed a large part of
the product in rents and temple dues . . . the institution of
slavery was but the extreme edge of the fact that the leisure
of the upper classes and the great monuments of early
times rested upon the forced labor of the multitude . . .
more significant socially and politically than the
appearance of slavery was the depression of the tribal
farmers into a position of peasants, from whom the
machinery of state and religion extorted a large part of
their product.

CHAPTER FIVE

UTE AND HUMAN'S INVENTION OF SIN, SATAN, HELL & ORGANIZED RELIGION (1,019,000 B.C.)

"The most frightful idea that has ever corroded human nature - the idea of eternal punishment" (Vauvenargues).

Following the use of judgment, guilt, shame, and conditional love after the time of Cain, rulers were killing slaves by the thousands in response to their resistance to work, and slaves were choosing death over an intolerable life. Then, about 1,000,016 years ago, a genius arose. This is a man Mario refers to as the Egyptian Ute (rhymes with boot), a man who devised a totally new way of coercing slaves to work. His plan would maintain economic/social systems for those in positions of power so that they could continue to dominate others, but with less killing of slaves. Regarding the genius and awareness of this man and the enormous influence he was to have, Aenka said:

This intelligent man, Ute, chose to be negative. He could have at that time been almost as positive as Christ was later. Instead he chose to be selfish and created a monster that would keep the human race oppressed for centuries to come.

Ute was a real person, as Cain and Abel were real people, but also a symbolic story. However, Aenka and Mario spoke about Ute more literally. The entities indicated that Ute survived the flood described in the Old Testament under the story of Noah (further addressed later). Ute's insidious scheme epitomized organized manipulation that used human's weakened spiritual connection to further enslave them. The entities were very clear that while they chose to focus on Ute in our dialogues because of his genius and impact, they were also speaking of others like him.

116

Ute was a very impactful initiator, although he had much support in bringing it to pass. And there were others who adopted his methods or used similar ones. We use names in speaking with you only to identify significant times of changes in man's development.

One session in speaking of Ute as representing another turn in human's evolutionary direction, Mario described what he called a shared responsibility of influential people and gave a few contemporary examples.

Hitler was only a small part of that revolution wherein massacres of Jews occurred. Holocaust was suggested to him by his advisors, he did not initiate it. It was initiated by others in his arm, people of great arrogance and hatred for the Jewish people. Hitler did not even know about it for some time. When he found out he chose not to do anything about it. He eventually supported it and then it carried his name throughout the war. Even in more recent tragedies such as your Watergate (a political scandal in the U.S. under president Richard Nixon in the early 1970's), *your president became involved in somewhat of an innocent way. In trying to justify it, he became involved. During the 'cover up' as they call it, is when he showed his participation and lack of judgment.*

Ute was apparently a very unique man. Born into a family of some wealth and power, he was a person of *unusual curiosity and energy. As a youth and adult he traveled extensively to gather information and experiences, seeking ways to increase his own personal basis of wealth and power.*
To pinpoint his identity by some 'role' or class description was difficult for he appears to be not easily classifiable.

Ute was an Egyptian, a gypsy, and a rebel. But, however you might classify him, he was very clever and very intelligent. He was a traveler and a mastermind of all masterminds. He was a genius intellectually and he would travel and study in gypsy-like style.

In his travels and experiences Ute assumed many roles, functioning in a variety of ways. He is said to have studied warfare and political maneuvering to become what Mario referred to as a *General* at one point in his life.

Fascinated with people's social and emotional behavior, Ute also studied the existing forms of religions and for a short time functioned as a priest. *Over many years, he learned well the behaviors of man.* As he traveled and studied how and to what people responded, Ute became increasingly aware of the subtle rebellion of slaves in many different areas.

He would visit other kingdoms, areas where slavery abounded. He even became a slave himself so he could study the minds and behavior of slaves; what they talked about, how they planned their day, how they planned and plotted to revolt against their slavery. He learned a tremendous amount about their thought processes and what they were most afraid of. Ute saw that the population did not fear death and that killing the slaves or beating them to death simply left the rulers with one less slave.

By the time of what was to be Ute's malicious manipulations and those of others similar to him, humankind's collective spiritual connection had continued to weaken. This occurred despite many spiritual belief systems developing in different places as spiritual leaders tried to invigorate and strengthen individual spiritual connections. These diverse belief systems became somewhat distorted in the sense of developing different concepts of God, or even multiple gods, but the goal was the same: an attempt to re-affirm the essence of humans as more than animals and to teach natural spiritual laws. Generally, these belief systems had no concept of satan or hell, and focused on the positive aspects of human's spiritual connections. They continued the belief in the continuity of life after physical death, but pictured it in different ways.

Ute became concerned about the seemingly pointless process of killing ever-more slaves in response to their increasing passivity. His concern was more practical than humanitarian; he owned slaves and enjoyed power, and he was in danger of losing both. Based on his observations and studies, and prompted by his fascination with power and manipulation, *he devised a very ingenious plan. He thought he had the answer to gain more power over the people.*

Ute knew the crucial element of the slaves' mental frame of reference was their acceptance of dying. Their belief in a positive, non-judgmental afterlife gave them courage to die.

He wanted to stop man's acceptance of death. He knew their preference to die was because they were not afraid of death. It was physical pain they were afraid of, but this was no longer working very well. After an individual has suffered years of physical pain, it can almost become their friend. Ute would design a way to make death so threatening and fearful slaves would not stand and let themselves be beaten to death, they would work. One of the first disguises was to be dignity, distorted to mean man is born to labor.

Ute convinced people that whatever station of life they were born into, or whatever conditions they were exposed to, was the "will of God" and part of God's plan. Thus, if one did not passively accept their lot in life - to not labor to their optimal ability and to not take pride in both of these attitudes - one was then going against God's – or the Source's – plan.

So it was that during the great quiet rebellion of the slaves, Ute began to teach his philosophy that even though they were slaves they had pride and dignity.

While this approach had some influence, it lacked the impact he sought. According to Aenka and Mario, Ute looked for other ways to make people believe his concept that lack of hard work and death were in some ways shameful. He knew he could not directly deny man's inner sense of the continuity of life after physical death. Up until then man was still aware of the origin of his spiritual existence although personal connections were terribly weakened. People were still dimly aware of the failsafe process of returning to their Creator. At some deep level humans continued to know dying was neither an end to life nor a sin. Ute needed a way *to make it an insult to the spirit within to choose death over labor.*

Finally, Ute found a cornerstone for his scheme. *Under the disguise of siding with slavery, he would teach a philosophy in which their attitudes and beliefs toward life and death were sins against God.* Using human's weakened awareness of their spiritual guidelines for living, and their diminishing inner appreciation and respect for their origins, he would convince them they were insulting God. Mario described in simple terms the basic essence of his involved scheme.

He wrote the script of hell. He created a devil that could destroy the soul and prevent it from entering heaven.

Ute consciously and purposefully used the human's weakened intuitive knowledge of unconditional love and acceptance by God in a twisted way. *In his cleverness Ute changed this awareness, and said you do have something to fear because you have sinned against your father.* He thereby made spiritual love and acceptance conditional, and introduced the concept of sinning against God.

Aenka described this stroke of genius another evening from a slightly different point of view.

Ute would introduce an idea with great promise regarding

120

life after death. He emphasized and exaggerated in a distorted sense what the all powerful could do for an individual. He gave a very impressionable description as to what this great power could do in a positive way for their souls. Then, he invented a negative aspect of it. He had to introduce or introject something that would be so frightening and so painful to an individual that he was literally rendered helpless with fear.

Mario described the strategy as follows:

Ute was very aware of man's fears and would use these fears to establish guilt for their fear to feed upon. He would burden them with guilt and fear of everlasting punishment. He painted a picture of knowing that man's greatest fear in the primitive state was fire. He emphasized the torment the soul and possibly the body would endure if they did not yield to the command of the Great Spirit. The only way a person could escape from these imagined punishments was by obeying the rules he would prescribe for them, which were supposedly the rules of the Great Master, or God. So satan was born in legend only, a creation of Ute to persuade people that they would . . . be punished for what he taught them as sin. Guilt and unnatural fear were taught to man.

Next, Ute needed to devise ways to expand and generalize peoples' fear; to bring the slaves' behavior even more under the control and authority of others in position of power. His brilliance showed once again, for he used human's natural and healthy behaviors to weave a matrix of sin and guilt tied to the idea of deceiving God, the Source.

The natural hungers will reach out for gratification and Ute knew this. So he created stories, laws, and rules supposedly coming from God and couched them as 'thou shalt not'. In designing and creating these concepts, and teaching them to the offspring, all of the natural hungers were used and incorporated. In this way, it would be impossible not to violate some rule or commandment. It was an ingenious idea.

What were once positive spiritual guidelines and healthy physical behaviors were thus distorted into rigid rules from which any deviation was a sinful deed. The punishment for violating the behavioral and attitudinal laws Ute created was always the same: endangering of the soul.

Ute cleverly used the hungers of the body and the mind to be in supposed violation, so that many acts or behaviors became sins against God. Of course, the sex drive and the physical hungers are the most powerful. Two hungers of the body that are essential to physical and emotional health are the nutrients of the earth, food (diet), appetite, and procreation. He taught that all the natural hungers were provided as temptation and were satan's attempts to keep you from heaven. So any desire you had was stimulated by the devil; and the will you had to over-rule this desire and not cater to it was the strength of God. Ute knew it was literally impossible, without vegetating, not to indulge the physical body.

Physical intimacy was made a sin. The practices now called lent and fasting were distorted. He made it mandatory to fast up to thirty days or you would not 'go to heaven'. It was a sin to eat any time during that period. Ute knew it was unlikely for the average physical body to be deprived of food for a time approaching that without starvation; but if they did not, then they were guilty. So you see, slavery flourished because he taught that the meek and the dutiful would inherit and receive their rewards in heaven . . . if you can avoid sinful acts.

The design of Ute's philosophical system was brilliant, and his genius was certainly evident in his efficient implementation of it. One means of this was by gaining influence with local priests or their equivalent. Apparently, many of these were quite honest and sincere people, as the following statements suggest:

He was brilliant in his ability to influence and manipulate, he would take a reputable, accepted religious leader and contaminate him. When there is one weak link in your understanding or acceptance of your existence, a very powerful mind can take that link and break it like a weakness in a thread. He would set up doubt. Ute would accuse a leader of being wrong because he could not prove himself on all things, and the leader would become doubtful of himself. Ute would then convince him that if he would fill the gaps with certain concepts he could be a great man. So, many primitive organized religions took his concepts and turned God into a vengeful wrathful being.

Not surprisingly, Ute also in a sense created his own priesthood.

He was very clever at teaching and training disciples to preach and enforce the law. He also began to use false prophets to frighten the people and further support the philosophy.

Ute used his political studies to advantage in achieving the acceptance of local kings and rulers to his system by essentially seducing them. In addition to pointing out the social/economic practicality of his system, he appealed to their vanity. He convinced them that, in the eyes of slaves, they could be seen as God's representatives and suggested they might, indeed, be such representatives.

You see, the slaves had previously accepted the power of rulers as being only in strength and number through the threat of force. Ute used his philosophy to create the idea of kings as being intended to rule. Pharaohs, kings, any people in great power were built up to be chosen by God to create and write laws of God. And as the structure and influences of the religious cults grew, Ute's ideas sounded very attractive to the rulers.

Ute's system came at an opportune time. *Because of the gradual deterioration of natural spirituality, the kind of program he put into effect would work.* He had found a way not only to keep the masses subjugated, but one in which government and religion could complement each other in their attitudes toward - and treatment of - the masses. His system was quite adaptable, a fact which for thousands of years to come would be of tremendous advantage in its application over different geographical areas with various political and economic systems.

It would be difficult to overstate the influence of Ute's philosophy on the course of mankind. Directly or indirectly he influenced all segments of everyday life - work, sex, family life, government, religion.

The impact Ute was to have on later pre-Christian religion was enormous, for his system could be easily altered to apply to any concept of God or gods in many areas. For example, 7000+ year-old Egyptian paintings of The Judgment Scene in the *Book of the Dead* demonstrate an obsession with hell and the end of the soul. Ute and others like him managed to create a deep unnatural fear and cynicism about life after death of the physical body and the nature of God as being vengeful and monstrous that is evident in the minds of many people to this day.

Origin Of Organized Religion

He [Ute] did not start spirituality; he distorted it. He took some of the universal laws and natural behaviors and used them against the people. For example: confession. At one time confession was a cleansing process and he changed that to a punitive and guilt-oriented process. Each generation altered Ute's teachings slightly to make it work better for them. Religion gained the power to dominate. They embellished the picture of a devil and hell and painted them vividly so they could control the masses with fear and guilt. Even today, take satan away from many churches or the clergy and they are powerless. Can you understand that? You would think it would be the other way: take away satan and the church would be more powerful. But what I am telling you, you take away satan and hell and those churches and clergy are powerless to control and manipulate you.

It should be made clear here that Aenka and Mario are not referring to all churches or all religions in the past or present. As for the man Ute who started this insidious and massive movement: ***his stated rationale for his actions was that he wanted to save humanity; that he did not like seeing slaves killed.*** It is ironic that spirituality can be distorted in ways to essentially de-humanize people, yet this has been and still is the case more often than many of us let ourselves see or admit.

Hearing the entities focus so intently on Ute as a significant turning point in the history of the human's spiritual evolution, we hoped for systematic follow-up covering many more thousands of years. We were disappointed in these hopes. Mario and Aenka spoke mostly in general terms of the further spiritual deterioration of collective mankind in a way similar to the decline of humans following the era of Cain and Abel.

Gently but firmly, Aenka and Mario refused to give the specifics of names and dates after about 1,000,016 years ago, such as types of religions developed, and influential events. A typical response to questions about forms of worship or gods that were worshipped before and after Ute would be along the lines of ***there were many kings and tribes that worshipped objects. Your own records provide a good example.*** Then they would stop talking.

We were initially perplexed by such apparent

disinterest and inconsistency following the emphasis on Ute, but as we look back over accumulated transcripts, there is a pattern to what the entities have emphasized and de-emphasized in our discussions. Their focus on people's collective spiritual history is on events seen as turning points in regards to the endowed human following or deviating from natural spiritual principles. Our reading of the transcripts is similar to Mario's statement to the same effect. Between significant change points humankind was spoken of spiritually as undergoing relatively minor modifications until the next directional change point. The stories of the Garden of Eden (endowment 7 million years ago), Cain and Abel (guilt, shame, and slavery 4 million years ago), and Ute (sin, satan, and hell 1,000,016 years ago) symbolize three major change points.

With the lack of response from Aenka and Mario in giving specifics about spiritual processes and religious practices after Ute, we turned questions of relatively modern major religions. The entities were responsive to Christianity and somewhat to Buddhism but minimally or not at all to other major forms of organized religion, such as Hinduism, Judaism, and Islam. We believe there are at least several possible reasons for this: Buddha and Jesus have been among the most influential spiritual teachers in recent history according to the knowledge of the listeners of these lectures; the religions based on their teachings have come to be regarded as the most influential organized religions worldwide, and most people involved in our materialization sessions have been raised in a Christian religious culture.

The entities' lack of response to questions of other religions and/or their founders certainly does not appear based on any prejudice or disapproval. It should be remembered that all religious systems are spoken of by the entities not from the point of view of any one religion at all but from the point of view of what they consider natural spiritual principles or practices from which all organized religions derive. Simply put, all organized religions try to make sense of spiritual truths and present their interpretations as truth.

CHAPTER SIX

THE OLD TESTAMENT

"...not of the letter, but of the Spirit; for the letter of the law punishes with death, but the Spirit gives life" (2 Corinthians 3:6).

It was frustrating to be met with silence or polite disinterest to many of our questions, but as we asked in different ways about issues, people, and time periods, Mario and Aenka seemed responsive to questions regarding early Judeo-Christian Bible stories and scripture. Their initial comments about the Old Testament were at first general, simply describing it as *a collection of writings and teachings accumulated over thousands of years. It was written long after those experiences. You see, the information and events were passed down through history in the memory of those involved.*

Regardless of the source of information that formed the basis for the Old Testament, Mario stressed that many of the teachings and meanings in its stories are distorted. He explained that some distortion in the interpretations of spiritual principles via impingement were due, consciously or unconsciously, to the personality variables and mindset of the recipients. Distortions in historical events were said to be the result of inevitable alterations as history was still predominantly passed down orally through the centuries. Some distortions are said to have been perhaps purposefully formulated to intimidate or control people into further compliance with religious or social authorities. *Much of the material in the Old Testament is symbolic; very little of it is literal truth. Many of Ute's teachings were inadvertently used as material for the Old Testament.*

After initial inquiry regarding the Old Testament, further general questions would elicit little response or a request for the question to be re-phrased. We found by trial and error that Mario and Aenka would respond most to questions regarding specific Old Testament stories. While what they responded to at times seemed inconsistent, they were very consistent in how they responded. Their themes were symbolism, basic spiritual principles involved, distortions of spiritual principles, and/or the historical event upon which the story was based. Their initial comments about the Old Testament were first general, simply describing it as *a collection of writing and teachings accumulated over thousands of years.* Some of its contents were said to be the result of impingement from the unobstructed, some referring to historical events, others being attributed to pure legend.

Samson and the Jawbone

The story of Samson killing an army with the jawbone of an ass is a good example of symbolism, and a legend (Judges 15:15-16). That particular legend symbolizes the honesty of certain tribes or certain societies. The message is simply that truth shall prevail. The strength of Samson is also symbolic. Nobody poked his eyes out, but they did torture him trying to have him betray his people. As legend would have it, Samson in his might destroyed the temple, but he did not (Judges 16:21-31). *Those that were fighting for his goodness overpowered the temple and destroyed it.*

It is also a story about trust and deception and the evilness of broken promises. You see a beautiful woman seduced him. The symbology is of how one can be destroyed through the disguise of conditional love. It reflects the giving away of one's own self-love and pride for a promise of external ecstasy: to be seduced; to be tricked. That story can give you a beautiful symbolic meaning of personal wisdom, personal reliance and strength (Judges 16-4-20*).*

Noah and the Flood

The story of Noah and the flood is said to contain both

distorted history and symbolism (Genesis 6:24 and 8-19). The estimated Biblical date of the flood is about 4300 years ago, but flood legions exist across cultures and dates for each flood are not offered. Aenka and Mario said that there was something like a flood of the Old Testament, but it was not a result of the wrath of God, nor was it precipitous. Over a long period of time there were major changes in Earth's surface due to natural evolutionary processes, and for many years people were aware that major geographic changes were occurring.

Symbolically, yes, there was a great flood. It did not destroy all life on the planet, but there were large areas that were totally destroyed. Earthquakes through the years of evolution caused the earth to separate. Look at the way your continents have separated and created new seas. The story of Noah, naturally, is symbolic of many villages and many races that were debating on how to deal with the impending problems brought on by the evolutionary changes.

Great changes in the Earth's geography over the millennia are widely accepted in mainstream science. Moreover, there is evidence of the possible existence of the lost continents of Atlantis and Lemuria, whose documentation dates back to at least Plato. For example, Plato dated a great flood that destroyed Atlantis to 9500 B.C. Modern scholars debate the location of each of these continents and whether underwater ruins of monumental architecture, roads, etc. support their existence (Kenyon, 2005).

Abraham Sacrificing His Son

In the Old Testament story of Abraham (Genesis 22:1-18) on the verge of sacrificing his only son to God as a test of his faith, who was actually doing the testing, is said to have become distorted in the telling and re-telling of this story.

Mario referred to Abraham as follows:

A very dedicated and sincere man; an acknowledged leader, he wanted to lead his people in a very righteous process, and had, of course, made many errors. There was great famine and his people were having trouble with other tribes. Abraham led his people out into the wilderness. In his desperation, he threatened to sacrifice his son for some insight, to have more knowledge, to be in touch with greater wisdom. It was not a threatening of God, or indeed a threat at all as you think of it. It was a sincere desire to be closer, to be more sure that he was worshipping the right god.

In his desperation he was willing to sacrifice his son for a way to lead his people out of famine. He had convinced himself that if he made such a sacrifice God would pay favor to him and his people. At the last moment he suddenly had the insight that what he was doing was a very foolish process and he knew it would not be necessary for him to sacrifice his son in order to design something to assist his people. But the other way, his being tested by God, makes a good story.

Joseph And His Coat Of Many Colors

Another illustration of spiritual symbolism in the Old Testament is that of Joseph and his coat of many colors (Genesis 37:3-36 and Genesis 41:14-40).

The story of the magician Joseph is another example. His robe symbolically depicts the personality structure. Sometimes, spiritually or psychically sensitive individuals could detect the colors of the aura and they would design a robe to reflect those colors. It was a way to recognize such sensitivity and many thought such a garment improved or increased their magic ability. So, if an individual was seen wearing this particular type of robe, which was very rare, they were seen as carrying some mystical authority. People would almost become mesmerized, and then the magician could create many seeming miracles through the powers of suggestion.

The entities indicated that aura's are physical energy emitted from the physical body forming a field of light or energy around each person. They said that one could learn to see auras. Start by looking at oneself in a mirror with just enough light to see in the mirror. There is no need to see details/features. Just look at oneself past the profile. There will be a little black void or a little grey or misty energy about the body. The energy is sometimes stable and sometimes it moves. It will be a misty circle or halo that will appear a few inches from the head or shoulders. This is the energy that is emitted from the physical body.

Aura's can be used for identifying the physical personality structure. There are 4 colors in the aura that make up the basic personality structure with which one is born and these never change during a particular incarnation. Indeed, when electing to incarnate, a discarnate considers the basic personality structure of the newborn before deciding to endow it. The 4 colors are green, red, yellow, and blue. Green reflects the physical function/quadrant of extraversion. Red reflects the emotional/feeling quadrant. Yellow reflects the intuitive/spiritual quadrant of introversion. Blue reflects the intellectual/thinking quadrant. The two bands of color closest to the body indicate the personality structure. There are 4 basic personality structures of the physical body: (1) thinking extravert (blue first, then green); (2) thinking introvert (blue first, then yellow); (3) feeling extravert (red first, then green); and (4) feeling introvert (red first, then yellow). Perceiving one's personality structure is informative in how to approach an individual and oneself.

Satan As A Fallen Angel

Regarding the story of satan being an angel banished from Heaven, Mario states this is strictly symbolic with no historical antecedent.

Symbolically it is saying that when the rhythm was broken, people suffered the consequences. But, rather than refer to broken rhythm or behavior influenced by guilt and fear, symbolically, it became the devil's work. The devil is only symbolic legend.

Thus the story of satan being a fallen and outcast angel, banished by God, runs parallel to the endowment story of the Garden of Eden. The parallel is of course that God did not cast out Adam, Eve, or a disobedient angel; humans make their own mistakes (Ezekiel 28:12-19).

Holy Of Holies

One night in our sessions we asked about the significance of the innermost chamber of the historical Egyptian temples and Hebrew tabernacles referred to at times as the Holy of Holies and into which only the high priests could go. In this chamber the priests were said to listen to God speaking and giving messages for the people. What did the priests do there and what transpired?

They did like you are doing tonight in your meeting here. It was a chamber where they made contact with spirit. At times they would experience impingement, at other times direct voice, sometimes ether-realization. Materialization is not all that uncommon.

By "like you are doing tonight in your meeting here", the entities were referring to a harmonious group sitting together in the dark and inviting spirits to join them. This process is presented in detail in Appendix A.

Jonah and the Whale

The story of Jonah and the Whale is said to be an example of how an out of body experience (OBE) can be colored by conscious attempts to integrate spiritual or mystical experiences in our daily life. As the Bible story goes, Jonah ignores an impinged message regarding serving God and literally runs away (Jonah 1:1-2:10). In the belly of a whale, he tells God he will serve Him if he can be saved. Mario agreed with the basic interpretation of this symbology as related to consequences of choices, but told a different version of the story with an expanded view of spiritual implications.

It is rather accurate about Jonah. He did have considerable doubts. It is true: there was a shipwreck; and it is true that he was traumatized by this wreck. In an unconscious state, as he was being tossed about on the sea, Jonah had an out of body experience that caused him to be aware of some of his personal thought processes or belief systems. When Jonah regained consciousness, he was being pushed ashore by a school of porpoises. Shortly before the shipwreck, they had experienced a number of large whales. In his dream state and immediately after awakening, there were images of whales, so his interpretation of his experience was he had been swallowed by a whale. Because of his positive out of body experience and his spiritual enlightenment, knowing now what he must do, he interpreted his believed experience as God offering him another chance. It was in this way he told the story that he was swallowed by a whale.

Elijah

The events of one Old Testament story are said to have involved the use of psychic and spiritual energy in a rather dramatic manner (see Appendix C for the differentiation of psychic and spiritual energies). The story of Elijah describes a contest between leaders of two different religions or religious sects (I Kings 18: 23-39). Elijah and another priest essentially took turns at attempting to invoke their respective deities and cause a sacrifice to burn spontaneously. Elijah's sacrifice began to burn; the other priest's did not.

Symbolically it is saying Elijah proved to the people that the spiritual process is evident. With his abilities he performed certain rituals and made it evident that there is only one Source, and that Source governs all matter.

When we asked for a more concrete description of what happened, Mario replied, *he started a fire with psychic energy and a little help.*

Moses and the Parting of the Red Sea

While Mario described Moses as a very spiritually oriented and conscientious man who could be quite open to impingement in his own intuitive processes, at least one incident related to him is also described as primarily a "good story." This is the story of the parting the Red Sea as he was leading the Israelites out of Egypt.

During that period there were very unusual tides. Moses helped his people across during one of the lowest periods. Just as the tribes had left Egypt, the tide began to come in. The army followed some time later, and in their attempts to cross, many of the soldiers drowned. It was a rather wide and desolate area. But it is a good story. (Exodus 14:21-23)

Moses and the Ten Commandments

Many people might agree that the story of Moses and the Ten Commandments (Exodus 20:1-17) epitomizes the thrust of the Old Testament. The tableau is that of a prophet (psychic/medium) in tune with God and acting as his messenger while waiting for a Messiah, a deliverer from bondage of various sorts. Mario spoke at some length about Moses, the Commandments, and how they came to be.

The story seems to contain a slice of many things relevant to a human's spiritual aspect then and now: a sincere person in touch with his/her spiritual essence impinged guidelines for healthy living received from the unobstructed, the intrusion of ego and unintentional personal distortions, compromise within a cultural context, and unfortunate cultural distortions. In this instance, what were intended as positive guidelines to lead humans by free choice back to rhythmic living were to be transformed into ironclad rules related to guilt and sin. As Mario put it:

How easy it is to take the Ten Commandments and use them as weapons against you, rather than guidelines to remind you of your nature. Distortions still cling to the Christian religion.

First, the story of the impingement that resulted in the Commandments; then, a look at them one by one.

Yes, Moses delivered Ten Commandments. And yes, there were certain phenomena both spiritual and physical, which were very convincing. Moses was a very intuitive, trustful, committed man who served his people in the name of God. He worshipped a god, which was not stone, but was the Father. He was aware of the true identity of spirituality. His people believed him, at least when things were going well and when they were not hungry or frightened.

Moses was distressed and disturbed about how to guide his tribes. They were becoming chaotic. He went away into the mountains to let them either destroy themselves with their greed or for him to come up with an answer . . . how to influence them to behave for their betterment.

136

He sought something to offer them hope for the future. He faced starvation by fasting in his attempts to have his mind come up with an answer, a resolve to social problems. While he was in the hills there was a storm, and lightning caused fire to the dry bush. While he was observing this from the cave he was staying in during his tribulation, even though his life was somewhat in danger because the fire was burning out of control, he had a vision. He had great insight. It was probably the clearest impingement he had ever received. And he chiseled with stone into stone the ten guidelines as he received them through impingement.

His people thought he was dead. He had been gone for so long when he returned to the village, emaciated, he dropped the slates and said 'God has given me the answer for that which we are to live by'; then he fainted.

Immediately there were all types of interjections and celebrations. His people put him back upon the pedestal as their leader. Once again they began to listen to him. He never told his people that God carved the laws with 'lightning' but he did not dispute the rumor. He did not because what was important to him was that the people believed God had given guidelines to help them be fair with each other, to stop raping each other's daughters, to end the greed. But it is much more impressive to create the story that God carved the Ten Commandments in stone, and he did not in any way deprive anyone from believing that.

In asking Mario to speak explicitly of the Ten Commandments, the question was phrased as follows: "Would you comment on as many as you could? Would you also speak of the purpose of the Commandments at the time they were used, and also of the distortions that have occurred in their interpretation and use?"

The Ten Commandments as presented here are taken from the King James Bible followed by Mario's responses in their entirety.

1. Thou shalt have no other Gods before me.

Yes, that is not difficult to interpret. There is only one God, one Source, one Supreme Power. What it is saying, is that he is the one you would choose to direct your energy toward.

2. Thou shalt not make any graven image nor any likeness of anything that is in heaven above, or that is in the earth beneath, or that is in the water beneath the earth. Thou shalt not bow down thy self to them, nor serve them; for the Lord Thy God am a jealous God, visiting the iniquity of the Father upon the children unto the third and fourth generations of them that hate me; and showing mercy unto thousands of them that love me and keep my Commandments.

What that is essentially saying is that you are wasting your time when you choose an idol to worship rather than the Source. It is also saying that you should look only in one direction; to accept the universal laws that govern your behavior that will lead you back to the Source. You see it is phrased as if God were talking to people. Well, God never did walk around with his people but they talk as if He is not only there in body, but giving orders. The Source is not jealous or vengeful, nor does It give orders or judge. This individual who is trying to interpret his impingement or his visions was very disturbed at the time. You can hear in his words his anger against the corruption of the society or the people. And so he wrote as if it were God talking, to put fear into man to obey what he is saying.

3. Thou shalt not take the name of the Lord thy God in vain.

You do not speak in anger about Him, you do not curse Him or belittle Him or make fun of Him. Symbolically, it is excellent: to vex or curse the Source is to curse yourself as a Facet of Divinity. So, this commandment speaks about self-love: do not hate yourself; do not take your person in vain; do not speak lightly of your body, mind, and soul; do not take it for granted; do not use your own waste to condemn others, do not condemn the waste of others. Do you understand what I mean by waste? The inadequacies, the weaknesses, the fallacies . . . or that which you have interpreted as fallacies. Also, it is saying to evaluate jealousy of the more powerful. Someone that you view as more powerful with more authority, you have a tendency to condemn. In doing so you are ultimately criticizing your own authority. You are questioning your own authority and your own strength by criticizing the strength of another.

4. Remember the Sabbath Day, to keep it holy. Six days shalt thou labor, and do all thy work.

A universal law is that you must be kind to yourself, and a portion of your time must be set aside for a total narcissistic process. By this I mean self-pleasuring, self-indulgence, in nourishing ways. This refers to healthy self-love. I know of nothing else I could say about that one.

5. Honor thy father and thy mother.

Yes, and what is to honor? To show respect and appreciation. It does not mean you have to agree with them. But you see you can learn humility; you can learn acceptance. I honor you by respecting your opinion if you are an authority. It is not that I have to agree with you, but I respect and I submit and I yield. That is to honor. The interpretation of this law to mean never disagree or become angry is distorted. It is saying to respect your parents' authority as much and as long as possible while you are under their supervision. Who was the greatest teacher (i.e., Jesus*), and what were his words? Give to Caesar what is his. In Caesar's house, do as Caesar does; honor and* *respect the rituals of others. That is what the universal law is saying. As long as a child is dependent upon and under the supervision of their parents they yield to the rules of their home, and the authority that interprets the rules. They do not have to like the rules, and there will come a time when they can change them and no longer have to accept them. This can be applied to all authority. But understand that being subordinate does not mean you cannot express your opinion.*

6. Thou shalt not kill.

It is a universal law not to willfully take human life. There are exceptions to this but they are limited and intended to allow only for necessity. They cannot be rationalized if untrue. Exceptions apply only when one's life is clearly threatened or when one is serving national authority in war. These exceptions are not to be viewed as condoning the taking of life, but as allowing for survival and the Gamble of Life.

7. Thou shalt not commit adultery.

It is to say that the human species is by nature a monogamous creature. It is natural for the male and female after they are in a committed relationship to share their sexual pleasure with each other and not go out and seek to find extra pleasure elsewhere. The commandment says or implies nothing about sex being bad, dirty or nasty. What it means is I will understand and abide by the universal law of monogamy. But it does not say without exception. The exceptions, of course, are rather misunderstood. One could be where two individuals chose to be committed to each other and one refused or was not physically able to indulge in sexual activity so that the physical hunger could be gratified, but all other aspects of the relationship were gratifying and fulfilling the shared experiences needed. The exception would have to be with mutual acceptance and understanding on the part of both for it to be positive. Discretion must be considered. To indulge or consider an exception to monogamy cannot be taken lightly, because every physical body is designed to be self-sufficient. It cannot be a rationalization merely to get pleasure and avoid an unresolved problem. It must be the individuals themselves who would determine exception. No one else can interpret, decide or judge. No minister or priest could interpret because that would be putting the responsibility of possibly violating the universal law on another individual. If you and your mate have made the decision, then that is where the responsibility lies. Then it truly becomes an exception based on a decision, and those two people are the only two that really know.

8. Thou shalt not steal.

Yes, respect the property of your fellow man. That comes under the universal and immutable law that all true benefits must be earned.

This law is related to another one that states that all true benefits must be mutual. See Appendix A and Appendix B.

9. Thou shalt not bear false witness against thy neighbor.

Yes, that means to not tell a lie, to cause harm. The first nine commandments are basically wonderful rules to live by, if not distorted.

10. Thou shalt not covet thy neighbor's house, thou shalt not covet thy neighbor's wife, nor his manservant, nor his maidservant, nor his ox, nor his ass, nor anything that is thy neighbors.

That is probably the only commandment that is in total violation of the universal laws of natural behavior. It is natural to admire. It is natural to fantasize. One would need to be an imbecile or an idiot to abide by that commandment. You could not be a functioning human being emotionally and psychologically and be physically sound, and not at least have a curiosity about what something would be like. The distorted law was that you could not even have a fantasy about a woman, another man's wife, to look at her and admire her. They made it a sin to fantasize. At the time of this commandment the true meaning was do not overpower or seduce. Do not manhandle, maul, rape, or act maliciously against the will of a woman.

The positive effects of the Ten Commandments on humankind have been drastically reduced from what it could have been. Interpreting these impinged guidelines along the dimension of sin and guilt, rather than positive responsible choices, has turned them into limiting laws rather than thought-provoking signposts for one's inner search and self-control of social behavior. Before and after the time of Moses, human's weakened individual spiritual connections continued to leave people open to distorted interpretation and to the influence of those in positions of power.

Unfortunately, a similar fate awaited the teachings and guidelines offered by other spiritual teachers through many years in all parts of the world. The effect of these dedicated and spiritually open persons was simply not enough to stem the tide of greed and power that Ute and others had set into motion. The tapestry of sin, guilt, satan, hell, and manipulation woven by Ute and embellished by hundreds of following generations smothered the individual flames of truth as impinged upon genuine prophets. It is not surprising that many prophets referred to in the Old Testament began speaking of the need for a Messiah, a powerful savior for mankind in bondage.

CHAPTER SEVEN

BUDDHA AND JESUS

"And you will know the truth, and that very truth will make you free" (John 10: 32).

While Aenka and Mario describe much information in the Old Testament as distorted, they are far from critical of the prophets (i.e., mediums, channels) whose teachings are represented there. Given the harsh social structure of the times and historical weakening in spiritual connections for thousands of years, it was unavoidable that a significant amount of impingement and intuition would be distorted. Perhaps also some of the spiritual teachers consciously decided to fight fire with fire; i.e., support the idea of stern rules from God to offset the scare tactics that obviously distorted religions had derived from Ute's philosophy. Strong commandments from a distant and powerful God may have been seen as necessary to try and break up the unhealthy marriage of government and religion established by Ute and others like him.

Observing the failure of individual efforts made via impingement and intuition to remind humans of how off course they were becoming, *the Source realized something must take place to effect more change. Something was needed to encourage a more positive choice for mankind.*

Although humans could not be deprived of free choice or decisions regarding constructive and destructive living, some type of intervention was necessary. The Source formulated a plan that would hopefully gain people's attention but would not violate their free choice. The Source would provide one or more special teachers to demonstrate the powerful essence of spirituality by their own living example.

These teachers would hopefully revive human's memory of their spiritual aspect and its potential. The first part of It's plan was to have impinged upon some religious leaders or prophets the thought that, indeed, a Messiah was coming. The prophets and wise men referred to in the Old and New Testaments were among many worldwide who were given this message. The second part of It's plan was to find one or more teachers. What was to be demonstrated could not be by pure spirit or miraculous occurrence alone, for such could be misused and distorted by those in power to further subjugate humans.

People needed a model to follow, to identify with, to give them courage to accept their own inner challenge and re-connect with their own natural spirituality. It could not be an incarnated soul still working on their individual destiny in the physical, for such individuals had not been influential enough. Perhaps the Source could find a suitable teacher among those who had completed their individual spiritual journeys and merged with It, someone thoroughly familiar with the human body as well as the soul and the Source (see Appendix B regarding merging with the Source after 7 levels of spiritual progression). The teacher/model would need to have great compassion for the plight of humankind, for they would be asked to reincarnate again and face many hardships.

The Source sent a challenge to several who had finished their destiny and merged with Him, and one chose to return to the earth for one more physical life. Without breaking the laws that govern the nature of man, this entity would be endowed with very special qualities.

While the teachers' special qualities would help in their work as once again a physically incarnated being, the curtain would be drawn upon incarnation. There would be amnesia for life in the unobstructed and for prior incarnations in the obstructed. The teachers would need to awaken to their purpose and identity by themselves upon reincarnation. It would be no easy task. In response to the Source's request for volunteers, first Buddha and then Jesus chose the task of yet another incarnation.

Buddha

He who was to become known as Buddha was a soul who had merged with the Source and the first to accept the challenge. During his physical incarnation (born approximately 557 B.C.) he succeeded in awakening to his purpose and destiny and this was reflected in what he referred to as his enlightenment. *Buddha was well aware of the type of structure and philosophy needed to be taught to help man free himself from slavery.*

Regarding his choice of how to influence people:

He chose a rather subtle and thoughtful approach in his attempt to reach the masses. He did not condemn or seek to change. He chose to influence by fitting into the culture in the way he spoke and interacted. His teaching focused on the inner life, not the outer.

Buddha sought to direct humans to their personal salvation via a contemplative life and acquiring patience to endure the physical.

He made no social, cultural, or political waves.

Buddha's thrust was to direct human's attention away from the limitations of the physical body and social bondage by steering them towards their own inner wisdom. Indeed, he is said to have consistently admonished his students/disciples to show no flamboyance of any type in their work. For example, healing was to be done sparingly, and never in public.

The entities speak of Buddha as a great teacher and as having done an effective job during his long teaching span. Unfortunately, in humans' hunger for something or someone to look up to,

145

They made an idol or god out of him. When he died, they erected temples and worshipped him. But it is for the good of the people, and Buddhism is still practiced. It is not a harmful religion although there are many things taught in the name of Buddhism that oppress people, and keep them from being totally with themselves in the sense of their natural physical hunger. It has not damaged man nearly as much as the more orthodox western religions such as Christianity and Judaism.

The entities emphasized that making a god of one who teaches of God is a rather serious misdirection, and point out that this has occurred with Buddha and Jesus as well as Mohammed and others. While Buddha had an influence on many, the changes he helped to bring about were not sufficient. The number of people who responded was not adequate to stem the tide of continued estrangement of individual spiritual connections and collective social distortions.

People's social direction towards self-destruction in a way of life that offered neither harmony within nor rhythmic living with others continued.

Another distortion in the teachings of Buddha concerns the concept of karma as a punishment and reward system. The entities indicate that karma is nothing more than the natural consequences of free choice. There is no consequence that is automatically executed in the next incarnation. There are multiple factors affecting one's Government of Life for each incarnation. These factors pertain to needed positive experiences and challenges. For example, an entity might choose to endow a blind baby in order to learn to rely more on the inner senses. Being born blind is not a punishment for behavior in past incarnations.

Again, the Source offered a challenge to those who had merged with It and another accepted. Like Buddha, this teacher's love for humankind would be so great as to motivate him to return to Earth as a human once again. This second teacher was Jesus.

Jesus

While Jesus and Buddha shared the same goal of directing humans back to their inner spiritual truth, their approaches were different. Buddha worked within existing social/cultural guidelines and rules. Jesus began by attempting to do that through working with church leaders, but became very frustrated with the slow progress. He decided to counter their teachings in a more aggressive manner. While Buddha and Jesus both taught inward directions regarding personal spirituality, Jesus also encouraged people to reject distorted social controls and teachings by unhealthy authorities. In this sense, Jesus can be seen as having become a revolutionary who sought eventual overthrow of cruel social systems (e.g. slavery), harsh governments, and distorted church teachings. Given it's road network, Jesus focused on the Roman Empire; in the long run, he overthrew said Empire. Additionally, monotheism was more accepted in the Middle East than it was in the East where Buddha did his work with the polytheists of Asia, where there was no conditioned need for a Messiah.

Jesus was very much against structured organized religion. He fought it. He went into the synagogues and argued with the priests. He pointed out their fallacies and how they had distorted true spirituality for their own power, to control and manipulate people and keep them oppressed.

Profoundly, he influenced the world in what he taught. Even though much of his teaching has been distorted to be punitive and threatening, nothing of the kind did he teach. He taught equality among all men; that no man, regardless of his wealth or position, is more superior than those who have nothing.

His teachings have affected minds throughout the world.

They have helped re-create the building of morals and principles of faith in oneself. He taught one to be kind to his neighbors so that people could begin to live and build together again.

In the pages to follow, Marti and Tom describe, from the entities' points of view, the development of Jesus' life and his teachings. We are well aware that the information obtained from Aenka and Mario is their picture. The impact of Jesus was great and his teachings are obviously open to interpretation. We have no wish here to criticize or disagree with the many people who devoted years to the study of Jesus' life and the meanings of his teachings. In our readings, we have come upon information or theories that both agree with and disagree with some of the entities' information. We will not in this section do any cross-referencing of other studies, which either agree or disagree with the entities' teachings. That would simply be too enormous a task. We simply present this information for consideration.

Jesus' Life

Prior to his physical incarnation, the entity that was to become Jesus, designed his Government of Life plan as carefully as he could, including the conditions he would need to experience while growing up in preparation for his later work.

Seven of your years prior to his incarnation, guides of some incarnated individuals were given special permission by the Source to make strong and impressive impingements. These would enable the seers of that age to predict the coming of a great change, an event that could alter the political rule of their people. This is where you find the legend of the wise men. They knew far in advance there would be an individual born who would have a very special influence to touch the lives of man. Christ planned

148

it carefully. He planned to be born in an area of the world where the people were oppressed, where they had nothing but fear. The parents that Jesus chose were very poor, deprived; his father to be was a carpenter, a very young man. Joseph is the name familiar to you. His mother to be was named Mary.

The impregnation of Mary has always been a subject of considerable debate and the story as told by the entities will probably in no way clarify the different points of view. However, the entities emphasize that the issue of Jesus' birth was intended to generate interest and controversy as a part of Jesus' plan.

It must be an unusual sort of birth to bring attention to him. It was very important that attention be brought to him from birth to death, because prior to his physical incarnation he knew well he would only have a few years to teach and make his impact. We are not communicating the circumstances of his birth to you to shape or alter any religious or spiritual beliefs in your teachings of the Christ-child. Many of the stories of the Christ-child are very beautiful and, should they be handled with care, could be very meaningful, especially to children.

As much as possible regarding the issue of Jesus' birth we will use quotations of the entities to avoid our own interpretive distortions.

Prior to their marriage, Joseph and Mary were involved with a group of friends in some type of spiritual, religious or psychic meetings.

When they were together they practiced a very similar thing you are practicing here which you call Darkroom communication with entities. There was a very dear friend of Joseph's who so happened to be in the unobstructed, and who communicated with the group very freely. During one particular meeting, Mary and Joseph were impinged upon.

149

Their friend communicated that Mary would become pregnant without any physical person being the father.

Apparently they were not told how this was to take place, but they were asked

to gather together friends of theirs and have a very special meeting for prayers. In this special meeting they were to pray, chant, and create a pleasant and harmonious vibration that would create energy.

And so they did. Far into the meeting Mary found herself betook. She felt herself being pulled in the dark, yet it felt restful and very safe. She later said she had no fear of this because whatever or whoever was tugging at her seemed to be very friendly and loving. She found herself so comfortable with this figure she began to inspect it. She found it to be reasonably like Joseph's body, but she knew that it was not. This body before her in the dark had no beard. Joseph did.

This masculine figure guided Mary into a partition of the meeting place. There he explained many things to her and she accepted the Holy Spirit. He forewarned her that when the child was born they would need to flee for the safety of the child. Then he returned her to the group and wished her well.

When they lighted the room, Mary was somewhat in a daze. Joseph recognized that she had experienced something no other woman had experienced, but it was days before Mary shared with him what had occurred. She encouraged him to believe the experience was very special. She knew she must bear the child regardless of Joseph's decision to believe her or not.

The physical birth and early life of Jesus as presented by the entities seems to be in fairly close correspondence with traditional Bible history.

Joseph decided to marry her, and they became married. They wanted a place to live, and his father owned a goat shed. Being the carpenter he was he took a portion of this barn and made it very comfortable for them. He fixed a very lovely crib. They had no money, no luxuries. They both slept very comfortably on straw and sheepskin. By the time Christ was born, all of the village recognized the coming of this child and the birth was celebrated. That was the beginning of the revolution against negativity.

Because of the impingement that had occurred to some individuals prior to the birth of Jesus, people in many areas were looking for a child they hoped was destined to become a Messiah or savior. Word of this prediction had spread and some of those in power were concerned.

The rumors at this time began to reach the ears of a number of rulers. They began to be very worried about this newborn that was destined to have special abilities, possess great magic, and become powerful. The ruler of the area where Joseph and Mary lived became convinced the child was to be born in his area: with great fear he became determined to destroy this child. The soldiers were ordered to find and kill all newborns over a certain period of time. it was a grievous period for all mothers and fathers.

Mary's special friend had forewarned her that such an event might occur.

She conveyed to Joseph that they must leave immediately for their child to escape the tragedy, and during one night they set out for Egypt. They took with them the burros and oxen and all their personal belongings other than their sheep. They lived in Egypt for 7 years. During that time Joseph and Mary bore two boys, offering Christ two brothers.

Apparently, Jesus was a somewhat difficult child for his parents.

Jesus was a very unruly child. Even at the age of seven he was very rebellious. His two brothers were quite obedient and learned quickly from their father who taught them carpentry and to be good shepherds. But Jesus could not be content with the sound of the saw or the hammer; his mind would not allow him to dwell on those things for very long. He found himself in search of the behavior of people. Even his brothers fascinated him with their behavior. He would watch them for hours, forgetting all about what he was supposed to do, trying to anticipate what they would do next.

By the age of eight he could tell his mother exactly what she could expect from each of his brothers every day and usually it would occur. When he worked with his father he became so fascinated by his father's behavior rather than his assigned work that Joseph would punish him to encourage him to work. But Jesus' attention span was very limited, and he would again find himself observing his father.

When Jesus was around seven years old, *Joseph received word from Jerusalem; it was safe to return, and so they did.*

Jesus continued to be a rather obstreperous child for at least several more years. As psychologists, we would like to point out that today in the U.S., it is likely a child exhibiting Jesus' behavior at this age would be diagnosed with a mental disorder, such as attention deficit and hyperactivity disorder, and placed on amphetamines to diminish non-conforming interests and leave him 'stoned'. It makes us wonder how many children given this diagnosis today are simply psychic and intuitive/spiritual.

As Jesus grew he became more difficult to discipline by his parents. He began to wander into villages and towns where he found minds to observe and behaviors that fascinated him.

In his wanderings he found himself attracted to the temples and the religious leaders' discussions there.

If he should be with his sheep, he would invariably trick his brothers into watching them, and he would be off to the temples. He would ask to enter a temple and listen for hours. He was attracted to one particularly handsome gentleman in a robe, who invited Jesus time and again to talk with him. This man and others realized the unusual quality about the young boy and his great interest in the teachings of the church.

Jesus would listen carefully and ask many probing questions. He would not hesitate to debate with the priests, and made astute comments, which were sometimes embarrassing. Nonetheless, the priests were initially very interested in this precocious boy with such a keen comprehension of religious teachings. He could be stubborn and persistent but provided them a stimulating intellectual challenge.

As these dialogues continued over a period of several years,

Jesus began to understand the practices of the priests as well as their principles. However, his own inner spiritual aspect seemed to him to offer a more accurate picture of basic spiritual truths. He began to see the basic distortions in the priests' teachings and interpretations of the same raw material. He began to understand how the temple leaders had compromised themselves in their attempt to strike a balance between getting along with political authorities and influencing the masses of people for their good.

Jesus experienced many of the temple leaders as quite good-willed in their desire to be of assistance to people:

But he saw that they lacked adequate personal impact or persuasive abilities and instead relied for their influence on concepts of fear and guilt instilled by the church. Most of the religious leaders had learned to educate fears into people, and to control them by this education. They programmed people to reject and fear their natural hungers and responses and to deny these. They labeled these hungers evil. They taught that the Source would punish you for indulging in these activities they categorized as evil and sinful.

For the most part they were unaware of their distorted emphasis. A few were consciously aware of the basic distortions but the rationalization was that if they could control people by teaching, the rulers would not need to control them by physical force.

As his understanding of Jesus' own inner spirituality and spiritual truth continued to unfold, the discrepancies of the priests' teachings became more obvious. He found it more difficult to try to reason with them logically.

He began to increase the tempo of his disagreements. He would say, 'you are wrong, it is not right. It is not that way at all.' They would tell him, 'yes, you make good points, but you may be wrong and we need to join forces with the power structures as a way to survive'.

When Jesus would refute this tactic, even those who recognized his inner wisdom nevertheless *became very belligerent with him. They would not seriously listen to a boy regarding basic teachings of religion about what they considered adult practicality. But by now the curtain had entirely lifted, and his purpose began to be more clearly defined. By the age of twelve he had developed his spirituality to such a degree he began to see and recognize his spiritual destiny.*

While Jesus continued his temple studies and dialogues with the established religious leaders, he became increasingly disenchanted and frustrated. He found his rejected attempts to influence the priests' thinking increasingly frustrating. By the age of 14 he began to realize his efforts in negotiating or reasoning with most of the religious leaders was hopeless. When he realized the limits of what he could accomplish within organized religion, he changed his approach. *He set out to learn more.*

He broadened his observations and studies for the next several years in directions other than religion. He wanted to gain information about the world around him, as well as more about his own inner spiritual workings. *His objective then became to teach his human mind all there was to know in regards to the psychological makeup of man.*

For the next several years

he would study himself and other people even more. He committed himself to a period of personal development, and during this period of physical and psychological growth he would plan what he was to do.

For a while, he became a very good, obedient, and hard-working boy. He began to help his father, and even became a better carpenter than his father. He would tend sheep affectionately and effectively. He would do more work than either of his brothers. His increasing awareness of his destiny helped him become increasingly more gentle and understanding. He became more content with himself and the plan he was just beginning to develop. He began to make friends and everybody began to love him, especially children.

Apparently, Jesus stayed fairly close to his parental home until he was about 17 years old, when he once again began to turn his interest outward as well as inward. Needing to study many more issues and skills, he decided he must travel to gain knowledge.

Jesus talked to his mother and father and told them of his desire. Mary, of course, willingly supported his thinking. She and Joseph agreed that he could go and study as long as he desired to learn whatever he chose to learn. They asked only that he promise to return home.

Much of his life from the ages of 17 to 29 was to be spent away from home. He would study mostly in Egypt but also in other places he could reach, with occasional brief visits home.

After discussing his thoughts with his mother and father he went about planning his first trip to Egypt. He made arrangements with a caravan and off he went. Having no friends there he began to seek out their learned men, studying everything that he possibly could. He did the same in many other areas where his curiosities and studies led him.

This approximate 12 years of study was apparently a great learning experience for this extraordinary being.

He learned much of what there was to know of existing religious cultures and social or political power structures. He studied astrology, mathematics, astronomy, biology, and chemistry. In whatever you might name, he excelled. But I believe the greatest of his studies was that of the magician.

He lived with and learned from what would be considered one of the greatest magicians before him that ever existed, and in these studies he learned to mesmerize (hypnotize).

After these studies he returned to studying behavior patterns in a way similar to the observations of his brothers, and mastered the art of human behavior. He learned about every weakness, guilt and fear man was capable of responding to, and what strengthened their belief in themselves to face these fears. He learned to control his emotions; he learned to control his nervous system. He knew very well that the more he could master himself the more he could influence others. He believed he had developed so highly that he could perform psychic miracles. He discovered he could invoke spiritual energy consistently. He believed anything he wanted to happen would. He would not doubt it. With his many and various skills in manipulating forms of energy he could make things appear and disappear. He learned he had powerful physical and psychological healing abilities. After he learned all that he thought was available to him, he decided to return home.

CHAPTER EIGHT

JESUS' PLAN

"I have come that they might have life, and have it abundantly" (John 10:10).

On returning home Jesus continued his thinking about alternative ways to fulfill his destiny of influence—to create a revolution against the negative beliefs of sin, guilt, and hell as a basis for religion introduced by Ute and his cohorts. Mario described Jesus as agonizing over one of the most basic decisions: whether to develop temporal power, or demonstrate what was possible by teaching and personal example. Regarding temporal power he knew he could use his brilliance and abilities to gain a position of power to the point of becoming a king or ruler himself.

The legend would have it that Christ was tempted by the devil, that satan out in the desert tempted Christ to become a ruler of all Jerusalem. But it was not satan, the imagined devil; it was Jesus on the inner argument. The balance of choice having an opportunity to possibly become the ruler of all kingdoms because of his powers. For forty days he argued the point with himself, 'should I or shouldn't I? I have an opportunity to be king of all kings. I could snap my fingers and they will fall to my feet.'

Jesus knew that he would be a benevolent ruler or king. He knew that he could bring about positive social, cultural, economical and religious changes. However, he also knew that this would not empower people to use their own personal strength and free choice. He knew from his studies in history that while people benefitted from benevolent authoritarian rulers, they would remain passive and dependent on the next outer authority. He knew that after the death of past benevolent rulers people had become dependent on the new ruler, benign or malicious, and that rulers following him would likely return to themes of power, status and greed. He knew he wanted more than temporary influence based on his authority alone.

He wanted to give people their nation to rule for themselves, to take them out of bondage and slavery into freedom. He wanted to show people what they had lost in their spiritual connection and its power so that they could find it again. He wanted to teach people to feel and be equal and self-responsible, not be subservient to and dependent on someone. He wanted to offer them the opportunity to love and respect themselves once again.

He reached his decision and told his family of his destiny and his plan. He was going to start a revolution. He would embarrass and weaken the powers, and cause them to fear greatly. Such impact and upheaval would provide an opportunity for self-rule and his teachings would help show people directions for their self-rule.

Some people may be disturbed to think of Jesus as a plotter or planner. Many prefer to think of him only as a pure and tender son of God, whose mind was not tainted by thoughts of manipulation, rebellion, revolution, etc. But is it likely that someone basing their life on love alone and speaking only of the beautiful nature of humans and God, who could even heal, would be influential enough to offset the powerful and intricate machinery of political and economic power structures? Is it negative for Jesus or any other person to use their entire God given equipment, including intelligence, to bring about positive change? Another potentially disturbing point made by Aenka and Mario is that Jesus was married (as was common in that era). Interestingly, some modern-day archeologists claim that not only was Jesus married to Mary Magdalene, but they also had a son. The documentary "The Lost Tomb of Jesus" (directed by Simcha Jacobovici and produced by Felix Golubev and Ric Esther Bienstock; executive producer

James Cameron, 2007) provides controversial evidence of his marriage and child. While all archeological evidence is open to question (http://www.str.org/site/News2?page=NewsArticle&id=7109), the notion of Jesus as a family man has intrigued many and continues to do so.

In beginning to implement his plan, Jesus' first goal was

to introduce himself to the multitude, to those individuals seeking help. Previously he had not used his powers and abilities in a public way, he had gone about his studies and caring for others in a quiet and very personal way. He was told by spirit through impingement that one had been sent before him to pave the way for the effect of his teaching and that individual would recognize him by his unusual gifts. And so he went to the river and there he met John the Baptist. He admired John because he knew of John's great spirituality. John baptized him and recognized Jesus as his replacement. They met many times in secret, and Christ explained to him much of what he had learned. John witnessed some of Jesus' unusual gifts.

Jesus talked at length with John about his plan, explaining that he would use all of the abilities he possessed to convince people that he was spiritually attuned and to offer them a reason to follow him.

Jesus knew by this time he had to penetrate people's fears to offer them something worth dying for, because that they would do should they speak against the government. He explained to John he had developed his scheme carefully, and there was little time. Jesus understood that political powers would overcome his objective should he not hasten with his plan. John realized that with Jesus' knowledge and unusual gifts he could truly cause the multitude to yield to their requests. He began to inform all of his

160

followers that Jesus was the hoped for holy one. He worked very closely with Jesus to plan a revolution, one that would be achieved without force.

Jesus also told John of his plan to choose his disciples.

He would choose carefully and for specific purposes, because he was aware of individuals' weaknesses and strengths. He could spend only a few moments with someone and know them well.

Even at this early point, Jesus is said to have known his death and resurrection would be a crucial part of his plan to influence.

He knew he would need somebody that would betray him. One of the disciples he chose especially for that, and planned it well. He wanted at least three years to accomplish his effect and set to work in earnest immediately after choosing his disciples. He taught them in an abbreviated form the basic principles of almost everything he knew: spirituality and the continuity of life; the positive functions of natural emotions; the interdependence of man's four quadrants and his social interdependence; healing and psychological persuasiveness; magic and psychic abilities; astral travel.

After he had begun teaching and training with the disciples, those that were destined to help him organize and disseminate his teachings, he began his direct contacts with the masses. *He began to teach, and to impress his followers he started with healing.*

The entities describe Jesus as having had a tremendous ability to invoke spiritual energy from the Source to effect literal miracles. However, as much as possible he is said to have used his own abilities, which he had learned to control. Such an attitude of self-reliance to

161

the limits of his abilities would help him be a more effective model for others in demonstrating the potentials of humans. His physical and psychological healing abilities were impressive, and difficult to dismiss. Jesus' simple, meaningful talks with people not only reflected his inner wisdom but also struck responsive chords deep in the now largely unconscious of those who listened to him. One essential function of his healing activities was to prepare people to listen to his most important teachings: self-love; love for others; rhythmic living; a continuity of life; and that death is nothing to fear.

Jesus emphasized the concept of self-love in much of his psychological and physical healing. He knew that the experience of genuine self-respect and following one's own inner spiritual wisdom was necessary to build up the confidence of people. They needed self-confidence if they were to quietly rebel against the distorted authority both within themselves through personal history and against the current political and religious authorities in their community.

He taught them the first rule in true spiritual acceptance, which is self-love. He said 'before this can occur you must cast out all evil, all the devils.' and he went about the cities and villages casting out devils. And what are devils but a fever or a psychological displacement? His physical healing abilities would help eradicate the former. The psychological devils are those of distorted fear, misdirected natural emotions, and guilt. He would help people eradicate these within themselves by his acceptance, love, belief in them, and guidance.

His impact was tremendously augmented by love and understanding. He would kneel before a wicked man, look right into this vicious man's face, and say 'you are a good man, I love you'. Perhaps this man had just done something quite negative. So Jesus would look at him and cast out the symbolic devil or evil. Jesus did not accept evil

162

because evil does not really exist. It is psychologically caused and can disappear as fast as it happens. It is not a permanent thing within man; therefore, it can be dismissed. He knew how to look into your eyes and tell you what you were doing wrong without criticizing you. That is what people responded to.

In his discourses, sermons and dialogues with people, Jesus continued to emphasize and teach there was no such thing as negative spiritual energy and that satan was a myth created to control people.

Since the time of Ute most people had been trained to believe in a force equal to that of divinity and were told it was a matter of choice which one a person would follow, although this was not true. Jesus spoke against the distorted concept of God being good overpowering the devil. He tried to make people understand that the Source of Divinity would have no need to cause an evil force equal to It's own power; that the force of evil does not exist in the unobstructed.

He emphasized the point of view that the devil represents evil. He taught that evil is a learned and created thing in the physical, not a type of spiritual energy. All that negativity develops in the physical from psychological distortions and poor choices in the physical.

In his teachings and spiritual discussions with people:

He never lied to them. The greatest teacher man has ever experienced is Jesus. One reason he impressed on the minds so strongly was his simplicity. He would not allow his intellect to complicate his perceptions and presentations, and why he would not is he had no need for ego. He was not in a position to tamper with arrogance or superiority. Therefore he could communicate things that were impressionable upon the mind and not difficult to understand when presented simply.

One evening Mario used a well known Bible story to illustrate the marvelous way Jesus had of directing people to their spiritual reflection and inner wisdom. This was the story of Mary, accused of adultery.

What he tried to teach, symbolically, was that she had committed no sin: that what she had experienced was a not uncommon phenomenon as a result of free choice. Jesus knew her accusers and would-be punishers were attempting to hide and minimize their own guilt by directing their self-condemnation to condemnation of her. They were going to demonstrate their innocence and their superiority by stoning her to death, thereby attempting to camouflage their own guilt.

What Jesus did was teach them they did not practice what they preached and that they used a double standard; something I do should be acceptable, but if you do it, then it is wrong. So he merely said to those that had picked up a stone 'those of you that have not sinned let you throw the first stones.' he of course knew there was not one of them that had not satisfied the natural hungers in one way or another.

In dealing with people's fears of punishment by outer authorities he directed each person toward their inner strength and knowledge of the continuity of life.

All of those individuals were condemned to death, in one way or another, and they knew it. They hated themselves and feared their superiors. But Jesus would approach a man and tell him 'fear no more.' he took away the fears, and of course he psychically bestowed upon them courage. This courage was supported by the promise of an everlasting life. He taught people to walk proudly once again and they did. He would say 'now that you believe me, believe in yourself and you can also do it'. And so they did, and they could do it.

He gave them hope. He also gave them back a reason for death as a natural part of life, and when you have a reason for death you are not afraid to die. He said, 'suffer no more, open your eyes and you will see,' and they did.

As Jesus and his disciples continued their work, reaching more and more people as individuals, their impact began to be felt in the social and economic systems.

Some were refusing to pay their taxes, others refused to work. Some who were in slavery would refuse to obey their masters. They knew they might be killed for this, of course, but now it seemed a reasonable choice or even a privilege. They feared not death because Christ taught and helped them remember that death with self-respect may well be better than what you have. Jesus was very effective in his contacts with people in eroding the influence of Ute's teachings. He would say to them, 'rise above your pity, rise above your sorrows, rise above your passive acceptance and challenge your fears. And if it is death, then it is destiny, but let it be your choice, not theirs'.

As Jesus knew would happen, some indeed were killed.

Jesus continued his preachings and healings, directing man to their spiritual aspect within, spreading the truth of everlasting life as compared to their distorted beliefs based on sin and guilt. He continued to teach people to respect themselves, to honor their inner wisdom, to confront distorted authority and deny distorted submission. The results of his work increased steadily. By this time the authorities were very worried about Jesus' influence increasing with the multitudes.

He had begun to undermine and weaken their power structures. Jesus could see the religious and political authorities becoming concerned and feeling threatened. They began to look for ways to discredit and destroy him. He knew there was a chance they could find some legal basis on which to interrupt his work, and this is one factor that prompted him to begin teaching in parables.

It came to pass as he had anticipated. His teachings and impact began to be seen as potentially dangerous in the eyes of the rulers. He knew he could not openly violate the law. So he told his disciples and those in the congregations they were never again to speak openly against the government, it had become too risky. He told them they were making good progress in their revolution and they could not chance failure now. He began to practice what he preached. He found a way to speak and teach without openly defying the authorities.

He began to teach in parables, knowing that anything he said could not be used against him. He would not deliberately tell someone not to pay excessive taxes, but he would tell them in a parable. It was like a coded message or symbolic language. People began to understand and even speak this language. The rulers became very frustrated. Here was a man talking in an unknown tongue, saying things that at times seemed to make no sense, yet everybody was turning to him for advice. But the authorities could not touch him. They could not punish him because he was saying nothing against the law.

Toning down his direct outspokenness against authority gave Jesus more time to continue his influence, and it continued to grow. Unfortunately, one practical aspect of Jesus' approach in working with people provided some priests needed ammunition. *The church first turned against him openly on the basis that he refused to help individuals all the time.*

In his ministry and his healing work, Jesus used his discrimination skills and would at times overlook or not work directly with those who were clearly not ready to make some inner turning point. *He would respond to them, would be with them, but would not use all the powers at his disposal.* Some people might view such practical discrimination as antithetical to the image of an all-loving or sacrificial Jesus, but again when such a practice is examined in context it makes good sense. Jesus was attempting to influence thousands of mostly illiterate people. There were many prophets in his time and quite a few people would initially listen to him out of simple curiosity. Others were interested in his messages but were not willing for one reason or another to take in his influence. Wishing to maximize his influence in his limited time on Earth, he focused most on those who would allow optimal influence.

Jesus could see that the authorities' frustration and anger continued to increase, and knew that his time on Earth was almost done.

He told his disciples he was going to die, and told them what they must do after he died. He told them their life would be threatened. He was knowledgeable of all his disciples and who would deny him. He told them it was all right to deny him because they would anyway. Unconscious fear was still too great for them, and he knew this.

Jesus tried the weakness in all his disciples because of the psychological effect it would have on all of his followers and eventually on all of mankind. His methods of influence, while appearing simple, were in many ways very complex in their implementation. History has shown they have had a profound effect. For generations to come man would be more aware of the heavenly Father and the everlasting life He offered.

167

The Crucifixion and Resurrection

Finally, the government and the church could stand it no longer, and they began to plan the destruction of Christ. They thought the only way to stop the revolution was to kill him. They held their meetings and planned to trick him into doing something that would violate the law. And so they did (not healing everyone; doing healings on the Sabbath). They also contacted Judas and offered him money to tell them where Christ was hiding and so he did, just as Christ had planned. They held their courts and convicted him. Pilot offered Jesus freedom, a way out, but he would not accept it.

The entities describe the crucifixion of Jesus very much as it is depicted in the Bible. He was killed with no more distinction than thousands of others who had been casually put to death over many years. Aenka did offer a point of information on what crucifixion was then, and some comments on why the actual style was not later chosen to represent how Jesus died.

They sentenced him to die on the stake. You have been taught he died on the cross. Well, a cross is more beautiful, but in those days how did they crucify? In those days crucifixion was to attach the body to a post. It was a vertical rail or post, without a cross beam, but that is not the point I am trying to make. It would matter little whether they hung him on a post, a cross, or upside down. The point is they hung him with the thieves, the usual ritual of destroying bodies like cattle.

As he hung there, there was a great darkness over the earth. Sadness, yes, but to those who cared not to believe in him and the passersby, they scorned him and shook their fist at him and yelled at him 'if you are a king then get down from the post, if you are truly the son of man or the son of God then surely this is possible!'

*Yes, Christ could have removed the nails from his hands
and feet, healed the wounds in his body and walked away.
What would he have proved? Nothing. Just another miracle
that would have convinced a few more. But by dying he
convinced the world. He could have escaped his crucifixion
in a number of ways, but he chose it. He could have caused
the stake to disappear, or mesmerized the crowd and made
them like dummies so he could walk away. The crucifixion
was to be a final impression for a lasting effect on mankind
for man to believe what he taught was the truth.*

Aenka and Mario both teach that one of the crucial
cornerstones of Jesus' plan to influence humankind was that
of the resurrection. Knowing that the effects of his healing
abilities and his beautiful messages spoken in love would
weaken and fade shortly after his own death, he hoped that a
vivid demonstration of the reality that the soul lives on
would burn in peoples' minds something that would literally
be unforgettable. He would materialize after physical death,
literally resurrected.

*The effects of his teachings, though impactful, had not
gained the momentum he had hoped for. He knew he must
continue with his plan to die. To cause the multitudes to
believe him, he must become a martyr. His death would be
wicked and cruel, and he would dramatize it to make it so.
By this time he knew he could materialize and thereby
make his teaching more effective.*

The entities also offered their explanation of one of
the last things Jesus said as he was being crucified, one that
has been offered many interpretations: "my God, why have
you forsaken me?" Aenka stated:

*At this moment, near death, Christ was weary. He was
weary and weak as a human being, and he felt for a
moment everything he had taught may have been wrong.*

Aenka went on to explain that such self-doubting by Jesus of the way he had gone about trying to implement his plan was due to simple physical weakness, merely a brief lapse of his spiritual connection.

He thought the heavens had forsaken him. Why did he think this? Because he was in pain. There is no pain to death. He knew this. But he was beginning to feel the pain that many of his followers had been feeling. Also the simple fact that he was in a physical body meant the physical pain and lack of nourishment would cloud his mind.

Immediately upon his death, as Jesus knew there would be, there was a mixed reaction among his followers as well as the population in general.

There were groups of people torn with grief at this taking away of the great teacher. Some were hysterical, screaming and crying, shouting 'you have taken our lord, our savior, our healer. You have taken him and given us nothing.'

Some began to deny the reality of what they had seen and heard, quickly moved away from the teachings, and oriented back to temporal power and values. Others were beginning the process of doubting their own experience of what they had seen Jesus do and would gradually resolve their doubts by proclaiming that while he was a great magician and healer he was not any son of God.

After the immediate tumult following the crucifixion had subsided, Jesus played his trump card. He reappeared in physical form.

He had told his disciples he would materialize and see them again after death, and before he joined his Father in heaven. With the disciples he had the longest period of materialization that has ever been recorded, about three days. It is very plainly stated and written in the Bible to recognize the quality or availability of materialization in reincarnation.

The effect on the disciples was as Jesus had hoped.

They had known him so well in the physical there was simply no way they could be deceived. They literally had no choice but to accept that this figure that appeared, spoke, and touched them was indeed Jesus.

Their lingering doubts were finally dissolved. Others also witnessed materialization by Jesus, including many staunch followers and believers who had already begun to work with the disciples even before Jesus' death. *The disciples had begun to organize and form committees and each chose committee leaders.* Those who were chosen as committee leaders were people believed by the disciples to be most able to maintain their connection with inner spiritual truth. This was important for they would need inner strength to combat previous mental programming which would push them towards collapse of their spiritual connection.

For each such person Jesus would also manage the energies required for materialization. Each leader of a committee would have the opportunity to witness a materialization of Christ. Christ would speak to them and this to many seemed unbelievable. He appeared many times telling them they could love and rid themselves of their guilt and fear. He would teach them and influence them just as he had in the body, attempting to get them to begin to live rhythmically 'let not your fears cause you to be selfish and greedy, let your fears motivate you into kindness and understanding. Work together and love one another as I have loved you. Give to one another as I have given. Die for one another if you need to, as I chose to do, but let your decisions be by your choice.'

171

Satan, Symbolism, and Parables

The resurrection of Jesus, i.e., his materialization after physical death, has indeed proven to be a cornerstone of the Christian religion. His reappearance and continued teaching was so impactful a demonstration of the continuity of life that it could not be rationalized away. But why after his second departure did the disciples continue to speak of evil and satan as real things? Had he not taught and demonstrated there is only positive spiritual energy, that evil comes only from the physical minds of people? Why indeed did even Jesus speak at times of satan and evil as though they were tangible supernatural forces? How is one to view such phrasing? The entities offer the following explanations.

People had been accustomed to thinking of evil and satan as realities from the time of Ute (1,000,016 B.C.) through much or all of the Old Testament times. It is difficult to get people to change life-long or generations-long thinking habits quickly.

Jesus and his disciples tried in the beginning to contradict the distorted Old Testament teachings directly, but achieved that goal only to some degree.

Also, Jesus knew if he disagreed too drastically with some of the ingrained beliefs he would lose his connection with people and thus his influence.

Christ was very careful not to interfere or change drastically some of the concepts because he would not have been heard.

However, Jesus knew people could listen to and hear positive messages about their spiritual essence and other teachings even though they consciously thought of evil as a reality. He simply chose a more easily obtained positive effect by speaking in concrete terms with which they were familiar. Choosing to avoid tackling some of the basic distortions directly, he was content to plant the seeds of truth that evil is human-made. This decision to abide the distorted belief that satan and evil were real supernatural forces as a means to convey his positive messages was similar to an approach he sometimes took with religious leaders.

With those who were significant in positions of authority he would at times exaggerate some of the simple positive principles of the universal laws, holding back from speaking openly about major distortions such as satan. He was trying to minimize the chance of being totally rejected by the synagogue, although it was clear they were in conflict.

Regarding the disciples continuing to use labels such as satan and evil they also decided that it was not only politically safer, but agreed with Jesus that all human evil could be translated and interpreted in terms familiar to them. *At that time some basic spiritual truths needed a carrier by name to be easily grasped.*

Jesus had another reason to avoid directly confronting the artificiality of satan and evil. He knew the importance of people as individuals doing their own part to find spiritual truth and make their inner connections personally. Spoon-feeding or forced feeding had not worked in history and would not work then or now. He knew one must face and accept their own personal challenge to do their part rather than having something given to them with little effort. While Jesus' goal was to re-direct the course of mankind he could not violate free choice or make it too easy.

Seeking meaning and finding truth has always been one of our required learning experiences in the body and a major challenge in developing true autonomy. Jesus knew this and this was one other reason he often taught in parables.

If a person directs himself towards his own spirituality he will find the translation Jesus taught his disciples to use, the symbolic language. as he said many times of his parables, 'those that have ears shall hear'. What will they hear? If the person is guided by his natural spirituality he will find his translation. Jesus and the disciples did not choose to keep the concepts and names of satan, hell, and evil alive for any other than these reasons. They knew evil does not exist.

CHAPTER NINE

THE EARLY CHRISTIAN CHURCH

"For now we see through a mirror darkly" (1 Corinthians, 13:12).

Compromises in the Early Church

It should be remembered that the quotations attributed to Jesus in the New Testament are not his written word, but the words of others written in a time of struggle for the disciples and the leaders of the young church for many years after Jesus' death. Many theologians say that it is important to realize this in reading Matthew, Mark, Luke and John (the four Gospels focusing on Jesus' teachings and alleged quotations) but also the three remainder of the New Testament books as well. There was a tremendous feeling of responsibility by the disciples and their followers to try to keep alive the truth of Jesus' teachings so they reach as many people as possible, and function in such a way that political and social authorities would not squash them. These three motives, compounded by the likelihood that the disciples were not as spiritually aware as Jesus and undoubtedly added their own color into his teachings, provide a context in which it might be easily understood how distortions could have occurred in the early church. Aenka and Mario spoke with great admiration of the disciples and the early church founders, but pointed out that then as now, there are real dangers of unconscious distortions along all the dimensions just mentioned.

We have no doubt that the intent or motive of the disciples and early church leaders were positive and that they worked hard to continue and organize Jesus' teachings. But in attempting to reach their multiple goals, early church leaders seem to have made decisions in four directions that had mixed results. These directions include: (1) compromise in a variety of ways; (2) adding mystery to the life and

175

teachings of Jesus; (3) continuing the Old Testament focus on sin and guilt as well as teaching love and compassion; and (4) investing church authorities with formal power and authority Jesus never sought or adopted.

Certainly the early church leaders needed to continue Jesus' model of compromise in a healthy sense. The church was just beginning and the disciples and committee leaders knew they would have to temper their zeal by compromise with political and social authorities so as not to be squashed. They needed to be accepted enough so they could function openly toward the goal of reaching as many people as possible. Sometimes this meant speaking in parables or symbology, sometimes it meant not pushing someone's thinking or their frame of reference too far or too fast, sometimes it meant subtle subterfuge so that one will not be rejected by authority by divergent ideas, sometimes it meant saying things in ways that would hopefully be palatable and acceptable.

Compromise, like discrimination, is not in and of itself a dirty word or concept. Compromise means to adjust or adapt toward a desired goal, via a balance of positive submission and positive aggression (assertiveness). Discrimination means to notice differences. Whether compromises and discrimination are used in healthy or unhealthy ways depends on several factors: (1) whether moral judgment is involved; (2) whether issues of feeling or acting superior are involved; (3) whether fairness in the sense of respecting the other person is involved despite difference of opinions; (4) whether constructive change occurs in a healthy evolutionary sequence; and (5) whether stagnation results with no new learning.

Mario describes some of the dangers of the coin of compromise for religious leaders present and past, the flip side of a positive bridge function.

With compromise one gets a point across somewhat indirectly. In a sense you are tricking someone into believing the truth. You see, deception in this way - if you care to use that word - has frequently been used by spiritual and religious teachers hopefully the motive is for a positive purpose, but it is very difficult and one must very carefully examine motives. If your motive is not positive and your judgment poor, you are doing nothing more than manipulating, which in such cases is a violation of universal law. Also, with too much practical compromise it is possible to lose touch with some of one's inner truths or values.

History suggests clearly that the disciples and early church leaders used compromise with a healthy attitude and positive motive. These attempts to gain acceptance had mixed results. For example, in Paul's attempts to teach the Gospels to Gentiles as well as Jews he found resistance regarding certain Jewish beliefs and rituals. From various compromises made with the Gentiles *the breach with Judaism became irreparable . . . the Sanhedrin pronounced a curse upon the Nazarenes as the followers of Christ were contemptuously called.*

Paul apparently was in the difficult position of needing to make many compromises in his extensive travels not only because of his missionary zeal but his Roman citizenship. As a Roman citizen *thanks to the tolerance of Roman rule, he was free to debate the cause of Christianity provided he said nothing subversive of Rome's political authority... at various points on his journeys he met quite a variety of peoples representing contemporary paganism, in doing this he found it necessary to temper his comments and compromise his statements.*

Regarding compromising with state authority, *Paul took a median position* (in his epistle to the Romans) *asserting that the government was instituted by God and entrusted with the sword to protect the good and punish the bad.*

At times the early Christian leaders sought to re-align with Judaism for practical reasons, another compromise. The Roman Emperor Augustus was declared a state god after his death and people were required to refer to him and worship him as such. The Jews *were the only people in the empire to enjoy immunity* [from this requirement] ... *one can understand therefore why the Christians were eager to be counted Jews by the Roman government and why the evangelist Luke should insist that Christians were preaching nothing but Moses and the prophets.*

Mystery

From the time of the Garden of Eden or endowment 7 million years ago, the human has been a seeker of knowledge. People have sought to understand the what's, how's, and why's of the physical world, themselves and their fellow humans. Our spiritual aspect, coming from that tiny piece of the Source (God) within, urges us to explore the mystery and meaning of life. Jesus taught of the essence of life, and demonstrated the truth of those essences. However, during his limited time of influence, he did not explain many of the subtleties of the mysteries of life even to his disciples.

Essentially Jesus did what we might now call basic training with them. He met with them regularly in what could be called seminars, but they also had their own work to do directly with people. So the disciples and those who became church leaders after them were all saddled with the responsibility of not only understanding nuances of natural spirituality but explaining them to the thousands of converts seeking answers. This was a heavy task and one not undertaken lightly by early church leaders.

In attempting to rise to this challenge, realizing that each person indeed needed to make his/her own interpretations of basic spiritual teachings, early church leaders found a solution that would not only take some unneeded or unwanted responsibility from their shoulders but would fit the seeking nature of people and the fact that the purpose of life and how to live is an individual search.

Their solution was three-fold: (1) they would acknowledge openly they did not have all the answers; (2) they would emphasize that spiritual connections are a personal search; and (3) they would add mystery to Jesus' teachings and his life, and thereby add mystery regarding spirituality and God.

Mario and Aenka both say the early church leaders were wise to acknowledge their limitations and understanding of the mysteries and nuances of spiritual life and living. By doing so they were acknowledging their own human limitations in understanding God, and provided a positive model for their followers. Teaching people they would need to find their own personal connections and answers in an individual way rather than rely totally in a passive manner on pat answers provided by others was clearly consistent with Jesus' teachings. They knew that the most they could do was teach the basic truths and guidelines, discuss parables and metaphors in stories and teachings of Jesus and others, believe in and encourage spiritual seekers, and provide shared rituals, which would hopefully facilitate insight and inner spiritual experiences.

The entities imply that the third aspect of their solution, i.e., adding mystery to Jesus' teachings and his life, was motivated not so much positively as self-protectively. It was and remains a manipulation that seems to be at best a doubled-edged sword. On the one hand they knew that people found mystery interesting for we are designed to seek answers to mysteries. Thus, focusing on mysteries and even embellishing or creating them would serve to instill a sense of awe of God's plan and lead to further self-exploration. On the other hand, they knew that if they could create enough mystery and imply that the clergy had special insights into them, this would keep the church members dependent on the church leaders for guidance. Thus, the down side motive for creating additional and unnecessary mysteries seems to involve a desire to keep the church growing by increasing its authority.

A major example of the church creating mystery was offered by Mario one evening:

179

The 'Holy Ghost' was an idea, a legend, something that combined with other teachings and some spiritual truths that would be meaningful yet mysterious. Mystery is a healthy function of the mind that is very necessary. When in the body you understand something completely or thoroughly you become bored with it. Great leaders have always been well aware of this. Christianity came to be designed - not by Jesus but by others - to be confusing, just like politics. It was and still is believed there must always be that mystery, the part you do not understand, the part that keeps you coming back, or keeps you hungry. Just like the desire to return to the Source.

Influence And Authority

Through its first hundred years or so the young church did well, in the sense of increasing its members and spreading the gospel, and it did so in a way that sounds consistent with the teachings and attitude of Jesus. "According to the Acts of the Apostles and the Letters of Paul the sensation of divine power still manifested itself in miraculous healings, visions, prophecies, and speaking with tongues. The Christian community still depended on such needed experiences for their worship and devotion. Any believer might see a vision or a prophecy as a part of healing or evangelism. Organized, regular authority had barely developed. Christianity remained sectarian and enthusiastic. First Century Christianity remained loyal to its original inspiration" (McDannell & Lang, 2001).

Different church leaders in different regions functioned independently, made their own interpretations of Jesus' teachings, created their own rituals, and developed their own systems of house rules for how people should behave in and outside of church activities. They created their own church committees and hierarchies. Various sects or branches were in contact with acknowledged leaders of the total church movement, but there was no such thing as a formal pope, cardinal, archbishop, bishop, etc. The leadership of the churches occurred by informal acceptance of those they taught, not by authoritative fiat.

The rationalization was that they were putting themselves in a position of authority only to guide their congregation; anything that would help them keep their authority was believed by them to be in the interest of their followers.

Naturally leaders of various branches or sects would meet together and talk about many issues: scriptural interpretation, guidelines for social behavior, how to respond to members who challenged the local church guidelines, types of rituals in meetings, etc. Gradually, in these aperiodic and scattered meetings some teachers and ministers began to be recognized as having considerable wisdom and perspective.

Often these personages also were looked to by local civil authorities for discussion about the churches' teachings and activities. As they gained influence, these informally chosen leaders began to feel a need for more consistency in church teachings and activities. They realized that consistency in what was taught would be very advantageous in many ways. To achieve such consistency with the goal of reaching more people and increasing their influence, they would need to work together and make agreements or compromises so they could present a united front.

It was not only the need for consistency that prompted church organization. Some sects were felt by others to be in grave error in their interpretations of the teachings of Jesus and his followers. For example, some of the Gnostic sects (who believed in intuitive, experiential knowledge of the Source rather than what is taught to them) were perceived as aberrant in their beliefs and as a threat to the growing church.

The spread of Gnosticism faced the still weakly organized church with a grave crisis. What the church believed to be the real truth had to be formulated and what it did not believe had to be refuted.

In response to such variances, some of the early church leaders, mostly centered round Rome, began to develop ritualistic prayers, which all sects were encouraged to incorporate in their worship services and meetings. One of the earliest of these was the Apostle's Creed.

The Apostle's Creed began as a baptismal ritual wherein new converts *were required to make a confession of their faith. The earliest version of this formal confession, called the Roman symbol, developed later to what we now know as the Apostle's Creed . . . here in direct contradiction to gnostic precepts it is asserted that God did create the physical world, that Christ was actually physically born . . . by such affirmations the church guarded the faith's perversions.*

What is now called the celebration of Mass is another ritual that apparently came under early control. *Presiding at the Lord's supper could be performed by only one person at a time, and perhaps out of this arose the institution of a single bishop in a community.*
It appears that after the first 100 years or so after Jesus' death the young church perhaps unknowingly fell back into the tactics of Ute and older pre-Christian religions: a focus on sin, guilt, and fear rather than love, hope, and compassion. They gradually became more dogmatic, more centralized, more insular, more bureaucratic. They began to feel they had the responsibility to keep people in line as compared to sharing their knowledge with them and accepting diversity and free choice. This gradually increasing focus seems epitomized in the doctrine of original sin, an idea that is nowhere to be found in the Bible, but one produced by Augustine in the fourth century and still accepted by most Christian churches worldwide. The church

grew and growth brought new problems. In the first half of the second century we meet a phenomenon recurrent in the expansion of Christianity. First the church must accommodate itself to the culture in which it takes roots and which it seeks to win converts. The gospel must be couched in images intelligent to the heathen. The next stage is one of assimilation.

This time frame is apparently when problems with the church began to be significant, for their main solutions to the questions of consistency and influence was to develop an authority structure and begin to act from a position of centralized power rather than dialogue and accepting diversity. The church became less inclusive and more exclusive. The centralized church began to make decisions on which religious writings were acceptable or not, and how those that were accepted should be interpreted. They gained more power to appoint or elect leaders in outlying areas rather than allow local congregations to choose their own leaders. Thus, they could choose those who agreed with their doctrines in thinking, increasing consistency and minimizing diversity.

Mario pointed out the irony of the early church leaders themselves falling prey to something that Jesus taught against, i.e., developing external authority to influence and control others whether the motive be benign or malicious. *He taught them the importance of inner authority, not reliance on outer authority.* Yet, is the fact that this happened in the still young church really surprising? People's individual spiritual connections were still mightily weakened.

Jesus could only reach so many people directly in his few years of evangelizing. The disciples, and those who took over their positions, not only were struggling with their interpretations of Jesus' teachings but also felt limited in their own personal contacts in their ministries. There were many seekers and possible converts, and relatively few new leaders and teachers. People were hungry for positive affirmations of man's spiritual life at conscious and unconscious levels. The early church leaders knew they could not spend tens or hundreds of hours personally with each seeker as Jesus had done with the first disciples for their education and training.

Yet, they felt the burden of responsibility to reach as many as possible and teach as best they could. They knew the spiritually hungry seekers would listen to them as an authority for they had placed their authority in others previously.

They also knew if they had the sanction of the state their authority would be further increased. *They knew their motive was to teach, not to use people. So, they accepted the role of authority figure.* It was easy for the early church leaders to fall back in an unconscious manner on attitudes that had been inculcated in them when they were children; so they sought to gain authority by their own positions and by state support.

Regarding the organization and centralization of what was to become the Catholic Church, one of its own historians, Lapple (1986), makes the following comments in *The Catholic Church, A Brief History.* "As early as the end of the first Christian century it proved necessary to point to a 'sound doctrine'. . . as opposed to erroneous interpretations. A fundamental importance became attached to union of those communities and dioceses with the Roman church and to its bishop who was esteemed as Peter's successor." Lapple quotes Iraneaus: "Every other church must concur with the Roman church on account of its special preeminence." According to Cyprian "To be in communion with the Bishop of Rome is to be in communion with the Catholic Church." While the head of the Church of Rome was not officially designated with the title of Pope until the 11th century, "In common parlance today [the title of Pope] is used for the Bishop of Rome since the beginning of the office."

By the third century A.D. other religious sects became threats to the increasing central power of Rome. Some of those considered essentially errant or non-Christian were absorbed by compromise if they were outside direct central authority. By around 258 A.D., Lapple (1986) indicated "The Oriental cults, particularly the Mysteries, flourished as well." But in a manner similar to Ute's system "Certain concepts could easily be fashioned and adapted to Christian beliefs and practice. Blessedness in the fields of Osiris could be transferred to the New Jerusalem; and security under the tutelage of Isis ...could be transmuted into refuge beneath the folds of the robe of The Virgin Mary . . . The Church . . . in the fourth century permitted the transferring of the celebration of Jesus' birth from the 6th of January to the 25th of December, the winter Solstice and birthday of the solar deity of some religions . . . Certain fertility symbols were allowed to become associated with Easter (i.e., eggs and rabbits).

Power And Authority

The actual formal beginning of the Church of Rome and its leader becoming the central authority is dated from somewhere around 378 A.D. with Emperor Gratian establishing Rome to be the legal jurisdiction and by Pope Damsus I (366-384 A.D.) who declared at about the same time that the Holy Roman Church received its preeminence over all other churches by the word of Jesus rather than civil authorities.

The collusion or marriage of the Catholic Church and temporal emperors and kings is well known and documented. The Christian Church based in Rome that was to become the Catholic Church became the state religion of many countries and kingdoms. It began officially with Constantine in about 313 A.D. with the Edict of Milan and continued with the Emperor Theodosius in 380 A.D. The Emperor Justinian supplied the wedding ring and performed the official ceremony in Justinian Code. From then until the Reformation and the time of Luther and Calvin (16th century), church and state enjoyed a lucrative and powerful bedchamber, at times cooperative and at times conflicting, in

185

many Mediterranean and European countries. But regardless of the attitude of the State towards it, the Catholic Church achieved incredible power, autonomy, wealth, land, and influence. The misuse of their awesome and mostly unchecked power during these centuries is a bleak testimony of how well intentioned people can rationalize morally unjustifiable behavior.

Anyone who doubts the travesties that the Catholic Church perpetrated on lay spiritual seekers truly does not want to see that the emperor's body was a bit dirty under his beautiful robes. With the rationale that their behavior was intended for the salvation of an individual human soul, they amassed incredible amounts of money and land, waged wars, fathered innumerable "bastard" children, tortured and killed those believed to be heretics, developed gradations of sins, and allowed people to buy indulgences or literally pay for their sins as various forms of forgiveness. A Bishop Albert in Europe is said to have sold indulgences that would remit not only the penalties for the sins but also the sins themselves, and would give preferential treatment to one who sinned in the future (http://www.aloha.net/~mikesch/tetzel.htm).

The church ex-communicated those who strayed too far from orthodox teachings, supported capital punishment, transformed confession from honest acknowledgement of mistakes to a hierarchy of sins with graduated penances, stole and embezzled money, became involved in international usury, supported ascetic-style punishment of one's body to cleanse sins, imposed unfair taxes, resurrected the Hebrew idea of a middle place for deceased souls with the concept of Purgatory, acted as an intermediary for people who had relatives or friends in Purgatory (often on a financial basis), sold offices in the church, claimed authority or jurisdiction regarding marriage and divorce above that of the state, and had a double standard of how clerical people were dealt with legally compared to the lay people. The Dominican Johann Tetzel proclaimed the power of buying indulgences to ensure immediate release from Purgatory

using the jingle "as soon as the coin in the coffer rings, the soul from Purgatory springs."
(http://en.wikipedia.org/wiki/Indulgence).

It is certainly true that the Catholic Church developed beautiful rituals, and built magnificent cathedrals that helped people get in touch with their spiritual aspect. It is certainly true that many priests, nuns, bishops, etc., have been truly warm and compassionate people who were and are very sincere in their work and their vocation or calling. But on the whole the Catholic Church seems to have gone far astray from the teachings of Jesus on which it is said to be founded.

The Reformation And Guilt

In the 16th century or so the Catholic Church's excesses and distortions finally became too much. What was later to be called the Reformation was symbolized by the courage of the Dominican friar Savonarola who spoke out to "castigate the sins of the church." Unfortunately, but not surprisingly, he was "ultimately tortured, hanged and burned for sedition and heresy by the Spanish Pope Alexander VI. However, enough was enough and others began to speak out. The disenchantment with the Catholic Church crystallized in the development of breakaway churches begun by such theologians as Luther and Calvin. The protestant attempt at 'reforming' the Catholic Church had begun. By rejecting celibacy, papal authority, and scholastic theology the two reformers Luther and Calvin created new churches with different organizations and teachings. From the Catholic point of view, this meant that heresy succeeded in asserting itself, thus destroying the unity of the Christian world. The seamless garment of Christ was rent. For Protestants the true Gospel teaching had now freed itself from distortion of superstition and abuse. Biblical purity was restored. Protestants and Catholics were re-drawing the religious map of the western world" (Bainton, 2000).

Unfortunately the Protestant Reformation did not

throw out all the dirty bath water in its attempt to keep clean the teachings of Jesus. They not only adopted the teachings of original sin and human's essential unworthiness but also continued to focus on fear and guilt as ways to 'reach' people. Similar to the teachings of Ute, one might possibly find grace in the eyes of God by hard work, following rules of authority, and self-denial of pleasure. Regarding the philosophical attitude of a number of early Protestant sects, "the new ascetics did not believe in the natural goodness of human nature: for them the human being was fundamentally sinful . . . from this perspective humankind badly needed salvation. God the Savior rather than God the Creator served as the focus . . . Life therefore must not be celebrated in art or in conspicuous waste and display; hard work became the standard Puritan advice leading to the successful Protestant Ethic" (Bainton, 2000).

It seems clear that Luther and Calvin were point-setters for later Protestant denominations and were deeply committed to the above philosophies. "Calvin had no use for the view . . . that man can be united with God. The chief end of man . . . according to Calvin . . . is not to be united with God, but to bow down before his inscrutable decrees and to fulfill his evident commands . . . . There is absolutely nothing man can do [regarding his personal salvation] because God, out of time, has already decreed who should be saved and who damned. [Luther is said to have been] tormented by terror of the wrath of God, by dread of the judgment of Christ, by panic at the power of Satan . . . [In order to] purge himself from sinful inclination by acts of self-denial . . . Luther chose castigation of the flesh. But the thought constantly obsessed him that he could never be hungry enough, or poor enough, to merit God's favor" (Bainton, 2000).

Whatever the similarities or differences between early Protestant and Catholic doctrines, their emphasis on sin, guilt, and unnatural fear is very clear. Both accepted the concept of original sin, instilled a fear of God, and taught denial of the physical pleasures of the world. And both killed people for being heretics. Catholics had their Inquisition, and Protestants their witch trials. Even in early Reformation times Protestants are said to have joined in killing some who disagreed with their teachings. "Fear leads to repression . . . . The Catholics burned the Anabaptists; the Protestants drowned them. At the Diet of Speyer in 1529 both Catholics and Lutherans agreed to subject them to the death penalty throughout the Holy Roman Empire. Luther was slower than others in giving his consent; but by 1531 his fear of anarchy led him to agree to the death penalty, not for heresy but for blasphemy and sedition. He considered pacifism (one of the Anabaptist attitudes) to be sedition because it would destroy the police power of the state" (Bainton, 2000).

In the many modifications and branches of the Protestant churches that have evolved since the times of Calvin and Luther, some have shifted to a positive focus of compassion, love, and forgiveness rather than one of essential unworthiness. But even in these more positive Protestant denominations and in some of what is now called "new age" churches there is often still an implicit undertone of blame and guilt, however subtle. From a fundamentalist point of view one may get cancer or experience the accidental death of a loved one because of being punished by God. From some "new age" points of view one is 'creating' these events because the person does not really understand God and they must not "being doing it right." Christian churches just seem to have a hard time avoiding the concept of blame.

CHAPTER TEN

SHEPHERDS AND SHEEP

"I will follow thee to the last gasp with truth and loyalty"
(Shakespeare, As You Like It, Act II, Scene III, Line 69).

One unfortunate result of accepting or creating roles of
authority and hierarchy in the Catholic and Protestant
churches has been the gradual development of a
condescending attitude towards everyday people. While
Jesus and his disciples urged people to look within to find
their spiritual connection and their own answers to life's
questions, later church leaders began to wonder if people
were capable of this. They looked at the ever-increasing
numbers of people seeking spiritual truth in the church and
saw naïveté', fear, guilt, and little self-respect. Sadly, they
began to interpret these qualities as suggesting an inability
of people to go within themselves for spiritual truth.
According to Mario:

*They took an easy way out, which was to treat people as
though they had no native intelligence, and no innate
spiritual inner wisdom. They began to treat individuals as
passive sheep who needed shepherds rather than
autonomous people seeking spiritual nourishment. They
saw them as needing guidance and direction, which they as
church leaders should choose. Naturally as time went on
and church members accepted these attitudes, those who
strayed from the flock were treated rather severely in order
to bring them back into the fold.*

However, it is not fair to hold only church leaders
responsible for their attitudes. While it is true a shepherd
needs sheep, it is also true that sheep need a shepherd. That
is to say, everyday people were and are still disconnected
from their inner spiritual guidance. They have become
accustomed to outer authority whether through religious or

political structure. Aspiring church converts thus bring with them an expectation of someone in authority telling them how to think, what to believe, and how to behave. The combination of seekers lacking self-respect and church leaders lacking confidence in the seekers' inner autonomy can only have one result: broken rhythm continued, based on conscious and unconscious compromise.

Compromise has been a bridge between spiritual truth and distorted myths in Christianity for two thousand years. It is true that religious leaders still do not have the courage at this point to make the break, to drop the old distortions. Two thousand years is more than enough time. But what you also have to accept is that you are dealing with unreasonable human beings; the lambs that follow as well as the shepherds that lead. I do not say these things with an interest to criticize or minimize one's intelligence, but to point out how vulnerable the human emotional process is. The responsibility is as much the responsibility of the led as the leaders. Had not people been as dependent on their Christian leaders they could have made greater changes. But man's history of broken rhythm has made it difficult for one to be in better balance, to feel more secure in one's judgment. So there has been a stagnation in Christianity and, at times, regression more than progression.

It is unfortunate that many choose to idolize Jesus. To place him on a pedestal simply serves to separate us from him.

Jesus hated pedestals. He always deferred to God, the Father. It is the Source that grants you the miracles, not the Christ. The Source shall give you miracles only if it is beneficial for your spiritual growth. Jesus performed miracles to teach this, not primarily to heal. Jesus came to show us our essence, to demonstrate our potential and to teach us how to live rhythmically. He did not come to offer us a new god, but to remind us of the Father we already

191

had. His theme again and again was equality and unconditional love, and the attitude 'what I have done, so can you.' That, of course, was the objective; to restore the rhythm, which was broken years past. What did his work prove to people at that time? It proved there was another way, a power greater than obedience for the temple, priest, or king. And should people follow and obey this power they would find everlasting life. Offer Jesus thanks for your opportunity to pray to your Creator, give thanks to Christ for the lesson.

CHAPTER ELEVEN

EPILOGUE

"There is a candle in your heart, ready to be kindled. There is a void in your soul, ready to be filled. You feel it, don't you?" (Jalalud'din Rumi).

It is amazing how Catholic and Protestant churches have turned or returned to an attitude of controlling people "for their own good" rather than supporting humankind's inner guidance system. Rather than teach awareness of life as a joyous creative event and of God as a loving spiritual parent, they continue for the most part to focus on concepts of inherited original sin, a belief in people's innate inferiority, fear of hell and the displeasure of God, and passive obedience to church doctrine. Matthew Fox, a former Catholic priest, underwent expulsion from the Dominican Order in 1993 for teaching and writing of life as a joyous creative event compared to the concepts of original sin and inborn guilt
(http://en.wikipedia.org/wiki/Matthew_Fox(priest))
There was a pamphlet with no discovered author, date, or publisher printed some years ago (prior to 1986), which we found most poignant. It seemed to exemplify the intrinsic condescending attitude of a number of church leaders toward their parishioners. It was written by a devout middle aged Protestant who had been a deacon in his rural church for many years. He saw or had a vision of seeing an angel, and was overpowered by the beauty of the experience and the love he felt. When he told his minister and congregation about it, he was not believed. He was essentially told that he was not spiritually elevated enough to have such an experience and that it was only his imagination. He left the church crushed in the faith he had clung to for years.
Church history shows little true emphasis on Jesus' basic teachings: unconditional love; the ongoing nature of

life; life as a positive challenge rather than a school grade to be flunked, and then to be expelled from school; that life is to live fully with true humility, positive interdependence, integrity, respect for differences, compassion, and forgiveness; that life is to be enjoyed rather than feared; that the natural hungers of the body and mind are healthy and to be used, not rejected. Certainly there are some individual ministers and priests who teach these things in a positive way, but Catholic and Protestant churches as a whole are still mired in negative concepts.

Matthew Fox tells a story of a female social outreach worker, who "had worked for many years with prostitutes from the streets of Chicago. She was asked if she had any support from the churches in caring for these women. 'No, none whatsoever.' 'What do you think of the Church?' she was asked. Her reply: 'I see the Church as a very, very old grandmother who does not see well any more, does not hear well any more, and does not get out much any more. She is clinging too tightly to life. Though we love her dearly, we should let her die'"
(http://en.wikipedia.org/wiki/Matthew_Fox(priest)

The entities Aenka and Mario are very clear from their point of view that most church leaders continue to play safe when it comes to issues of compromise, their desire to continue their feeling of security, their degree of willingness to take risks, and the unconscious lack of faith in individual human's inner spiritual guidance.

Unfortunately time has not seen the eventual elimination of the concepts of hell and satan. The religious leaders have continued to compromise. As intelligent as the scholars of spirituality and religion are, even though they know hell and satan do not exist, they skirt around the issue. It would be a great risk to rise in a pulpit and insist that people give up their thinking about satan and hell. It would be like stripping them nude and asking them to walk down main street. To drop the concepts abruptly would be too threatening to the people as a whole, so religious leaders try to make their points in ways that people will not be too threatened. Until you can convey to a significant degree that it is safe to make a change of concept, people will cling to the past.

In closing his presentations on these issues Mario stated again that his objective was not to criticize either church leaders or followers, but to identify some factors that continue to interfere with spiritual growth within individuals and churches. In a type of summary statement regarding these issues in Christianity or in any other religion, Mario stated:

Time is a factor, but change is the measurable element. We are not concerned so much about time as we are about lack of change. So let us measure by experience and change rather than by how many turns of the clock. Many religions have not dropped the concepts of satan and hell as reality, but a few have moved toward their basic meaning and purpose: to let these concepts be symbolic of destructive processes and chosen negative behavior by man rather than some punitive threatening element that is going to consume you or destroy you.

Jesus, Buddha, and other spiritual leaders were great people with great souls. They succeeded in their goals of reminding people of their spiritual essence and the temporality of physical life. Yet, even with their enormous impact, humankind continues to show severe distortions in many forms of natural rhythmic living. Greed still predominates. "Man's inhumanity to man" continues. Feeling superior in a superficial sense remains a badge of success. Unnatural fear, guilt, and shame continue to be the three main enemies of humans and their spiritual development. We are so accustomed to these basic facts we ignore their presence and indeed may not be aware of them. Yet surveys from the Pew Foundation in 2008 show that nearly 30% of Americans have abandoned their religious affiliations, but less than 2% describe themselves as being atheistic and 74% believe in an afterlife (http://religions.pewforum.org/reports).

Mario and Aenka speak of another great teacher who will appear to show humankind a positive way. Their statement comes at a time when a number of people across the world are speaking of an age of spiritual revolution/evolution that is gaining momentum - sometimes referred to as the New Revelation or the New Spirituality, meaning one with less compromise to Ute's teachings and more clear and straight forward language than what is found in the Bible and preachings of organized religion. Perhaps, once again, some are being impinged upon to announce the coming of another great teacher, another messiah. According to the voice medium Roberts (1970) who channeled the entity Seth, this messiah who will follow Buddha and Jesus is Paul of the New Testament. Seth indicated that Paul has not yet returned to the Source (see the 7 levels of evolution in Appendix B), owing to his dissatisfaction in laying the groundwork for what became distorted organized religions. (Aenka and Mario indicate that Buddha and Jesus returned to the Source as did John the Baptist and two unnamed disciples.) Seth indicated that Paul will appear in modern terms as a great psychic. No timeline was specified but around the year 2070 was suggested. Meanwhile, perhaps the preliminary work is being established with the surge of interest in quantum physics, spirituality, mediums, and psychics - along with a dissatisfaction with organized religion.

On the other hand, perhaps this time the influence will not be by one teacher, but by many people who are personally impinged on and take risks to return to natural spiritual connections and positive attitudes based on universal laws. Perhaps generations yet to come will know more of a taste of the joy and love of creation, and feel less the bonds of artificially induced fear, guilt, and shame of life and terror about physical death.

Modern Developments of a New Revelation

There certainly is evidence of growth in the number of mediums and psychics in the last 150 years or so. A Google search of the word 'medium' yielded 3,380,000,000 hits as of early 2013. The term 'psychic' yielded 62,600,000 hits.

Mediums and psychics are coming out of the closet. While still often vilified and accused of fraud, many have been subjected to enough scrutiny since the mid-19th century to rule out deception (e.g., Foy, 2008; Schwartz & Simon, 2005; Tymn, 2008, 2011; http://www.windbridge.org/).

Other mediums and psychics have published books on what they have learned by serving as a channel (receiver) for discarnate entities, rather than via materialization where the entity speaks independently and is visually apparent in a physical body, as is reported in the Barham and Greene books (*Bridging Two Worlds* in Appendix A, *The Silver Cord: Lifeline to the Unobstructed* summarized in Appendix B, and this volume on *Evolution*).

Channeling can include automatic writing, voice channeling of the discarnate entity who uses the receiver's vocal cords with its own voice, and mental channeling in which the psychic/medium relays in his/her own words and voice the messages received. Many of these books are national (U.S.) or international best sellers and are too numerous to mention in their entirety. While automatic writing, voice channeling, and mental mediumship can involve up to 25% distortion from the physical personality of the receiver (see Appendix A and B and Schwarz and Simon, 2005), the teachings of the materialized entities Aenka and Mario involve little or no distortion. Presumably there is minimal distortion in the teachings of entities that use independent voice, but these teachings are primarily available only on websites that provide audio recordings rather than published books (e.g., http://www.montcabirol.com/)

Just a few of the hundreds of channeled books that underwent editorial review can be mentioned here. The automatic writings of Neale Donald Walsch (1995) in his *Conversations With God* series have been translated into many languages and are international bestsellers (for a list of his books, see http://www.nealdonaldwalsh.com/index.php?p=Store).

Jane Roberts' series on voice channeling of the entity Seth also have become bestsellers (see http://www.sethlearningcenter.org/) These Seth volumes describe spirituality in terms that would be familiar to quantum theorists, such as the nonlocal nature of a discarnate entity that can be in more than one 'place' at the same 'time'.

Perhaps the most widely published mental medium has been Edgar Cayce, whose material has yielded a training institute, numerous books, and other media (http://www.edgarcayce.org/). Cayce is also credited as the founder of holistic medicine. Much of his health advice has been corroborated by allopathic physicians.

Another highly influential writer on teachings obtained via mediums/psychics is Allan Kardec. He used the term spiritualism and many of his works are available as free e-books (http://www.spiritwritings.com/kardec.html). His works have been highly influential in Brazil, where the concepts of the New Revelation of the nature of the universes are widely accepted (Playfair, 2011).

A Google search of "spirit writings" yielded 25,100,000 hits as of mid-2012. Many of these are free e-books (e.g., see http://www.spiritwritings.com).

In addition to the lay literature, academics have shown a rapid increase in publishing scholarly articles on the positive effects of spirituality (vs. organized religion) on psychological and physical wellbeing. As mentioned in the Preface, in the citation database PsycINFO™, which abstracts scholarly works related to psychology, there were only 2,799 articles using the terms "spirit, spiritual, or spirituality" from 1887 through 1980. However, from 1981 through May 18, 2012, there were 24,571 hits for these same terms. Academics are often correctly characterized as materialists (i.e., atheists in lay terms), who assert the only reality is the physical and that physical reality is produced by a purely random process that has no meaning or purpose. One just needs to reduce the physical to its smallest elements to understand the human personality and the universe, an assumption called reductive materialism.

This renewed interest in the intuitive or spiritual quadrant of the human personality shows that even arcane scientists resistant to change are awakening to the importance of non-physical reality, a connection with the Source, and the universal laws of natural behavior. Moreover, many scholars have argued that there is a need for a new science that integrates both the physical and non-physical universes. These include quantum physicists, astrophysicists, psychologists, and physicians, among other professionals (e.g., Arcangel, 2005; Collins, 2006; Dossey, 1999; Goswami 2001, 2008; Greer, 2003; Haisch, 2006; LaShan, 2003; Levin, 2001; Milliken, 2012; Newton 2001, 2003; Radin, 1997, 2006; Rosenblum & Kuttner, 2006; Schroeder, 1997; Schwartz & Russek, 1999; Schwartz, Simon, & Russek, 2002; Schwartz & Simon, 2005, 2006; Targ & Katra, 1999; Tart, 2009; Turner, 2009; Van Lommel, 2010).

The entities Aenka and Mario are encouraging regarding the ultimate destiny of humankind as a whole, but always emphasize choice and challenge for each human being as individuals. Indeed, they say the ultimate destiny of humankind rests on individual recognition of our unique selves as Facets of Divinity (souls), parts of the whole that is humankind.

In spiritual evolution there must be choice and there must be challenge. Without choice there is no challenge.

So it is natural to ask what modern humans can do to improve the condition of humankind and the Earth. The entities Aenka and Mario did give some specific advice. These specifics include, among others, the following:

1. Become more spiritually connected to the Source, which by definition includes yourself, others, and both the obstructed and unobstructed universes
2. Live according to the universal laws of natural behavior (see Appendix A and Appendix B; also listed further below)
3. Understand that what you do to others, you do to yourself and the Source and the universes
4. Love and forgive yourself and you will love and forgive others
5. Loving others is not the same as liking others; it is respecting and accepting them
6. Act as a role model for others by being kind and showing an understanding of interconnectedness
7. Reduce population growth and its impact through birth control, disease, war, and natural disaster
8. Learn from the interdependence of globalization
9. Vote in elections
10. Pressure politicians to work toward population control and reducing environmental impact
11, Change consumer habits to spend money responsibly and punish companies who negatively affect the environment via retail sales
12. Join local efforts and get a rich person to do the same
13. Give money to environmental organizations and those for zero population growth
14. Reduce consumption
15. Alter consumption
16. Recycle
17. Write letters to the editor and on internet blogs (the use of the internet is an editorial extension of the entities' advice)
18. Join demonstrations and initiate them
19. Spread the word of the new revelation of spirituality and the "revolution against negativity" without imposing your beliefs upon others
20. Smile at strangers

The 10 major universal laws of natural behavior listed by the entities are as follow:

1.Every human is endowed with a Facet of Divinity (soul) that ensures dignity and equality.
2.Every human is unique and has an individual destiny to fulfill.
3.Self-acceptance of the physical, emotional, intellectual, and spiritual aspects of the personality structure.
4.Every human has free choice.
5.Recompense: acceptance of responsibility for the effects of one's choices. This acceptance involves owning a mistake, apologizing, making amends if possible, and then self-forgiveness. This is also referred to as the Universal Law of Confession.
6.Independence: each human has the potential for self-fulfillment.
7.Interdependence: each human has limitations and is therefore social.
8.All true benefits are earned.
9.All true benefits are mutual.
10. Every human is equally subjected to the Gamble of Life (events one did not predict) and the Government of Life (one's plan for a particular incarnation).

APPENDIX A

BRIDGING TWO WORLDS

Marti Barham, R.N., Ph.D.

Meetings with Materialized Spirit Guides as described by a former close associate of
Elisabeth Kübler-Ross, M.D.

BRIDGING TWO WORLDS
Marti Barham, R.N., Ph.D.

Editor Tom Greene, Ph.D.
©Copyright 1981 MJB Books, P.O. Box 1085, Valley Center, CA 92082

DEDICATION

In gratitude to all of those individuals who sat in our Darkroom even for one session, for it is through all of the combined energies that these events came to pass.

ACKNOWLEDGMENTS

Combined efforts made this book possible. To my husband, Jay, thank you for walking through life with me and for your contributions in making the Darkroom a reality. I love you and what you stand for.

Elisabeth Kübler-Ross, M.D., just prior to the publication of this book, withdrew her support from the activities of Jay and myself. She stood beside us in a close working relationship and weathered quite a few storms for four years. She is a courageous woman. Thank you, Elisabeth, for all the hours and energy you contributed to the Darkroom. I'll miss them.

If I were to make a list of risk takers I have known, Tom Greene, Ph.D., would be high on it. A clinical psychologist from Honolulu, he has spent many hours editing in what I edited out to keep the words flowing. He dares to stand up for what he believes in. Tom, I am grateful for your help and contribution to this book. Patricia Greene designed the cover and it reflects not only her talent, but also her love. Thank you, Patricia, for your patience and many cups of tea as Tom and I went over pages of manuscript.

To all who have contributed by work or word, I want to say I could not have written this book without you. Just as our meetings were a group effort, so is our sharing now with the world.

INTRODUCTION

This book documents a successful attempt to directly contact and communicate with physically materialized entities. An entity is the essence or spirit of someone who has lived before, and is now in the unobstructed universe. This is a universe not seen with physical eyes, but perceived through other avenues of awareness. Our contacts occur mostly in a group setting. The experiences shared are primarily my own, but those of others are also included. I believe in order for this book to be meaningful, the reader must be willing to at least consider that which I accept now as a fact: life after life is a reality.

The entities, often called 'guides' or "guardian angels," have direct and full communication with us. In our searching and experimenting we were not satisfied with the phenomenon of voice channeling while in trance state as a means of communication. We knew if an entity could communicate with us in a physical form speaking with physical voice that it would be more meaningful to us personally, and we believed the information received would be more accurate than that obtained by voice channeling. These hopes were realized when direct communication and meetings with materialized entities were achieved. The purpose of this book is to openly share what has happened, what it meant to us and what it means now, together with some of the teachings the entities have given us.

Our process took several years. The group began with the idea of making contact per se, with the added hope of increasing spiritual awareness. What happened was far more than we ever expected.

In solidifying our inner beliefs, we moved from believing to knowing. In addition to this affirmation, we developed a unique closeness and solidarity within the group and received information from the entities about the importance of man's stewardship on earth. Our questions came to focus on the purpose of life, self-actualization, and spiritual awareness. We were able to receive information on all these subjects. This, too, will be shared here.

As the group continued to meet, the emphasis was not totally placed on the spiritual aspect of man in the unobstructed. We were told and shown that man's total personality structure—his physical being, his emotional self, his intellectual pursuits, and his spiritual awarenesses—were linked while we live on this earth and therefore no one part could be talked about or dealt with fully without the others. Perhaps the greatest concept we learned is that negativity is the only thing standing between man and an increase in his spiritual awareness. Fear and guilt is man's enemy, and cloud his gifts and abilities.

We met for eight years as a group, investing thousands of hours in our experiments. This book contains a sample of experiences of myself, my husband, and a few of the people in the group. The Darkroom, as we called it, never had the connotation of the occult, and therefore we never called it a séance. We did meet in a darkened room because we were told that light adversely affects the energy involved in the materialization process. Through the years the lighting of the room has increased from time to time, but the name has persisted. We met with a commonality of purpose. An emotional support system developed I find phenomenal even now. Even as a professionally trained counselor I have never seen a group develop a group process in as thorough and ideal a way as ours did.

I believe everyone has a curiosity to know of creation, and to seek knowledge of the meaning of life. Perhaps some of us feel as Plato described: "Every seeker after wisdom knows that . . . his soul is a . . . prisoner chained hand and foot in a body, compelled to view reality not directly but only through its prison bars" (The Phaedo). I believe we really peeked through the prison bars, pushed and stretched out our hands, and bridged two worlds. I know my basic curiosities are not so different from others. What is life after death? What part of us exists then? Is there any connection between here and the hereafter and, if so, how might we bridge the gap? How can we somehow bring that continuity into our awareness?

I hope the reader will find this book a journey, and in doing so have a flavor of my journey. As I gathered the materials for this book, I experienced at time much nostalgia. I shed tears of happiness and of sadness as I recollected. As the past was, I know it will never be again. Many people have come and gone through the last eight years. Some experienced the Darkroom and their experiences as a truth, others doubted, and some left in total disbelief. We never required anyone to participate, nor attempted to change anyone's beliefs or conclusions. The entities gave many proofs of their reality, but never on demand. This also I will discuss. We have met in many locations, with different participants, and have been able to duplicate the experience consistently.

What I share with the reader is what I experienced, and even though some people had negative experiences with the Darkroom, that has not been true for me. I have gained immeasurably. My learnings have not all been pleasant, but they are all worth whatever prices I have paid. I hope what I present here will give the reader something to ponder, consider, and evaluate. Each of us must decide for ourselves what our own truth is, and I believe truth needs no defense.

What I do is share, not try to convince. I do want to say something about the uniqueness of perception. We all perceive situations according to our own physical, emotional, intellectual and spiritual background or balance point. No two people perceive things exactly alike, and the uniqueness of each is something I always bear in mind.

We only have to look back in history to see how man has searched for knowledge as we try to bring focus to life. Mario, an entity who speaks to our group regularly, mentioned in regard to the publication of this book, *the purpose that it would serve is tenfold. Naming only one of them would be that of clearing up some of the myths about negativity in the spiritual world, so that people can more easily move toward the acceptance of the naturalness of their spirituality without fearing, without thinking of those things that lie beyond the physical realm as something to fear.*

I hope the reader will consider what I have

experienced and find the material meaningful and supportive of any unique experiences you may have had. May it be a trigger to your own curiosity to seek that aspect of spirituality, which I know is present in all men, and a support in challenging your fears.

CHAPTER ONE
THE AUTHOR'S VIEW: EXPERIMENTS AND EXPERIENCES

On a December evening in 1975, we sat in a darkened room waiting for our spiritual teacher to materialize from the unobstructed universe and join us in human form. He had in the past materialized many times but we had never been able to see him with the clarity we'd been promised. The fact he had told us we could take photographs this evening added to our eagerness and anticipation. My excitement was overwhelming. My hopes and dreams to clearly see this being were soon to be realized. I put aside the tiny part of me that feared disappointment and, like a child on Christmas Eve, waited.

The words, *"you may turn on the light,"* penetrated the silence. It was a familiar voice with a clipped British accent. Even now as I recall the sight of him standing there with black skin, curly hair, and a somewhat weathered face, I am awed. We saw a male figure who appeared to be in his late 30's, wearing a loose garment covering his chest and lower torso. His angular facial features, long arms, gangly legs, all fully exposed, were black as ebony. He stood silently for a few moments. The group was quiet as he walked about. Then he spoke to each person, calling them by name and addressing each in a very individualistic manner. With his outstretched hand he touched several people. One other person and I were permitted to give him a hug. Some of his remarks were serious, almost a religious greeting, and some were humorous.

The room was illuminated to the point that features

and forms of everyone present were clearly visible and identifiable. I gazed at Aenka and remembered we had first heard him speak to us in September of 1972. We had accepted him as the leader of our Darkroom activity, and we had heard many, many words from him. Some people in the room were crying, while others sat and stared in silence, as did I, apparently overwhelmed. Words cannot adequately describe my response—awe, humility, childlike wonder; all would be close. My thought at that moment was that surely this must be the high point of my life regarding a sheer feeling of spiritual awareness.

I looked around at some of the newer members of the group and their response appeared to differ from that of the older members. They appeared more complacent. I wondered if they could fully comprehend the time, emotional pain, and energy that had been invested from 1972 to 1975 in working toward this happening. For me, even 1972 was not truly the beginning of my search. I have long been interested in psychic experiences, ESP, and other metaphysical matters, although I did not use those labels. My interests were coupled with an awareness of an existence outside of myself and beyond the physical level. However, since I had been raised in a strong religious background, which emphasized that only the 'good' go to a pleasant hereafter, many of my religious teachings had been associated with fear rather than positive attitudes. As a result, I had built a barrier between myself and my spirituality without knowing it. I had been more afraid than I realized. Because of my own personal therapy, my background in professional counseling, and counselor education, I intellectually believed these fears had been resolved.

I smiled to myself as I recalled my early meetings in the Darkroom and how frightened I felt when I realized the experience was genuine. This was not a hoax or a trick—contact had been made with our guides. The residue of unresolved fears of punishment and associated guilt for imagined sins had come quickly to the surface. Fortunately, even with the negative conditioning I had experienced in organized religion, I had a deep personal belief in mankind, in God, and in myself as a Facet of God having a soul, which is part of Him. It was in fact this very personal spiritual belief that brought me to a group of people seventeen years ago and led me through personal growth and further development of my spirituality. The remainder of this chapter will document the history of the Darkroom as it unfolded, and will include a few of the teachings as well as personal experiences.

I first became involved in spiritual exploration as a consequence of personal counseling. I was 24 or 25, had finished nursing school, and married. One day I happened to meet an old friend from high school days, and when I saw her I knew there was something different about her, an inner peace not there before. She told me about some personal counseling and a group she had been involved in, and mentioned a foundation which offered a combination of personal counseling and educational classes that had helped her with some of her personal issues and problems. Since I liked the changes I saw in her I decided to see for myself. Even though I was a psychiatric nurse, I was still very naive and fearful regarding my own personal involvement in therapy or counseling. After attending one of the classes at this foundation, I knew for the first time in my life I could do something about some of the unpleasant ways I felt. Up until then, I really was afraid that if anybody knew how I felt they would think I was crazy. I thought I was dumb and stupid which obviously wasn't so because I had been through nursing school and had a good job. I felt nobody liked me. Intellectually I knew I did have friends, and that other professional people I worked with also cared, and yet deep down I felt as if no one liked me. Up to that time, even though I had psychiatric training as a nurse, I feared that if I had gone to see a therapist or a counselor that even they would think I was crazy. I had such anguish inside me about many things. For example: my thoughts and feelings about my mother. I believed people would think I had made up some of the things I remembered. No one would believe anybody treated a child as terrible as I remembered being treated. So with new hope in my heart, and a bit of trepidation, I became involved in some personal counseling and a self-study group at this foundation. And I benefited.

From time to time while I was there I would hear people mention, usually in whispers, about contacts and entities. I didn't know what they were talking about, but that was all right. Finally somebody said to me, "Well, you know Wes is the channel." That still didn't make any sense to me. I had no idea what a channel was. Even as I became closer personally to Nan, the director and principal teacher of the foundation, and to Elaine and Wes who were usually her right-hand people, they never mentioned any type of psychic or spiritual contact. After I had been at the foundation about a year during 1954-55, I finally asked a fellow student when I heard him mention a channel what he was talking about. He replied, "Well, you know, Wes goes to sleep and entities talk to him." That did not clarify the issue; I still didn't know what channeling meant.

I was curious and, after doing some research, learned a voice channel is a person who has developed an ability to enter an altered state of consciousness in which he serves as a receiver of information from the unobstructed universe and as an instrument for the expression of that information. This type of channeling might be simplistically compared to a radio system containing a receiver and, in the case of a voice channel, a speaker.

As I began to put the pieces together I concluded Wes was a voice channel, and assumed he, Elaine, and Nan would meet together. I further assumed Nan was the one who presented the teachings based on what had been gained through channeling. As I reflected on this detective work somehow it felt right. Regardless of whether I was right or not, or where the information was coming from, I knew the lectures and my personal counseling were answering many of my long standing questions about my feelings and attitudes. At this point I was interested in nothing but personal growth. For me at the time there was nothing spiritual about my experiences and learning, at least not to my awareness. I couldn't care less where the information came from. All I knew or really cared about was at last I was having some experience in a subjective way that I had previously learned about only objectively in nursing school. I was learning how to deal with myself. I should point out here that when I had my psychiatric training it was actually a good thing I couldn't touch my feelings. At that time in my life when my memories boiled up I would just hook right into them and feel really miserable. I didn't know what to do with them. I felt like I was holding a hot pan without a potholder.

Prior to these early exposures at the foundation, my only direct encounter with anything having to do with spirituality occurred when I was going to high school. I had a job in a beauty shop; helping to clean up, wash the towels, etc. One day a customer said to me, "Who do you know by the name of George?" She then described a man and his physical handicap. I looked at her and backed away, very frightened. I remember asking the shop owner, "Who is this woman and what is she saying?" She told me the customer was a spiritualist, like a fortune-teller, and she knows things about you. She said to just listen to what she has to say and if it makes sense believe it, and if it doesn't then don't pay any attention to it. You must understand at this time I was 16 years old, and was a "good Catholic girl!" All I could do at that time was to file this experience in my memory. To my way of thinking at the time, this woman had no way of knowing she was describing my Uncle George who had been almost totally deaf since age 10. This shows how naive I was regarding psychic or spiritual experiences prior to my days at the foundation.

Liking what was happening to me, I continued my involvement. I became emotionally close to Wes and Elaine. I finally asked Nan about Wes and channeling and what that meant to her. She talked freely about it, and my curiosity escalated. During this conversation she asked me if I knew what a Ouija board was. I had heard of it, though I had never seen one or seen anybody work with one. After that initial conversation, which included information about contacting guides, or entities, I experienced such a strong inner push or impingement that it could only be equated to somebody's foot on my behind. I felt I simply must find a Ouija board.

Later I was to learn that entities guide and direct by what is called impingement, an influence on our awareness, which can be either strong or subtle. Hopefully the influence, coupled with our own free choice, prods us or motivates us in a direction that will be of positive help in the successful completion of our personal learnings, destiny, or goals in this life. Another way of describing impingement is as a transmitting of information to a human by a spirit guide, a soul mate, or one in the unobstructed to support or perhaps add to a person's wisdom or learning. This may be recognized as a hunch, or it may be experienced as coming from a feeling.

In the late 1950's, Ouija boards were not easy to find. After looking all over San Diego, I finally did locate one. When I shared my thoughts and feelings about the Ouija board with Jay, my husband, he agreed to participate. He is the type of man who, as long as my requests were within reason, would usually support and go along with me. We practiced with the board and the marker or plachette moved around a little. After sharing our experimental attempts with Wes and Elaine, they wanted to observe us working the board. Soon Wes and Jay would be comparing information received, Wes from his voice channeling, Jay from the Ouija board.

Instructions we received on how to use the Ouija board, and information regarding the actual mechanics of using it, are as follows. We were told two individuals are required to use the board. It is necessary to sit close together. The letters on the board should face the 'balancer.' A balancer is defined as a clarifier in some respects of information. The channel can close his eyes. The channel can be the only one with hands on the marker, or the plachette. The two working the board need only to touch each other with their knees or feet. This leaves the balancer's hands free to record. For example, when the marker paused in its movements under Jay's hands, I would write the letter, and the letters would eventually spell out a message. While I am aware for many people the Ouija board is used solely for entertainment purposes, in our experience we found it to be a useful and helpful way to initiate contact with the unobstructed.

Many times the information Jay and Wes would receive from their different processes was identical word for word. Other times the words would be different but the information would be the same. This was all very startling for Jay. We continued to experiment and practice with the Ouija board on our own. Eventually, I began to feel as though we were receiving information from friends I knew, but had never really met. Kind of like a pen-pal who was a friend and teacher.

Organizational problems began to develop within the foundation, some of these involving Wes and Elaine. In our attempts to assist with these problems Jay and I continued to work the board on our own for information. Jay's hands were moving very fast now. I would write down the words and the letters that came through. His speed finally increased to the point that I just couldn't keep up. I began to notice he seemed to be going into some type of altered state of consciousness. Now when we worked the Ouija board he would have his eyes closed, and begin to say words prior to and in conjunction with words and letters spelled out on the board. Finally he would just close his eyes, go into a trance, and talk. I continued to touch him during these sessions. As the entities contacted us, we identified two of them as 'L' and 'M'. These became their call letters, so to speak. Our contact had definitely begun with these two entities.

Soon after this development, Wes and Elaine left the foundation. The organizational problems had not been resolved. Jay and I began meeting with Nan at least once a week. Utilizing the contact we had made, she would ask questions regarding teaching and counseling. Jay and I would combine the Ouija board with his voice channeling for responses. Within a year the board was discarded altogether.

This arrangement with Nan lasted for several years. Continuing difficulties among the members of the foundation and differences of opinion regarding directions of the group precipitated our resignations in 1967 after 13 years of various involvements there. Jay was very disappointed he had not been forewarned by the entities of these happenings. It was not the difficulties themselves and the accompanying unpleasantness that he could not handle; his disappointment was he could have been warned. He was quite dejected about the lack of warning, and was ready to give up channeling. I asked him to at least one more time talk to L and M for my sake. He did and I asked about the situation. The response we received was along the lines of, *we are sorry. Yes, we did know there was a possibility. No, we didn't tell you because minds have many ways to go. What you are left with now is having to go your own way.* They didn't really say anything specifically or lay out any authoritative statements. The general theme appeared to be that we had learned many things. *Now put yourselves in a position where you can help others and put into practice some of the teachings you have learned.* To do this Jay and I would have to return to school for formal credentials. We talked about this, not knowing what the suggestions fully meant. We had not made any plans. Jay had little academic background, but we accepted the message at face value.

I returned to nursing as a night supervisor in a convalescent hospital. Within a few months I went back to psychiatric nursing, working on a unit with children. Again I began to feel the now familiar 'push' of impingement, this time as an urge to return to school. The feeling was the same as I recalled having experienced in regard to finding a Ouija board. Jay and I talked about it and at Christmas in 1967 we decided I would return to school. I began to take classes at a local university. He had an interest in hypnosis and half-heartedly considered a class in the subject. At this time there were no clear-cut goals for us; my objective was an academic career and professional training in order to move legally and independently into a counseling situation.

By this time I felt confidence in my skills clinically but I wanted further training and needed formal certification. Over a 13-year period at the foundation, I had studied, counseled, and taught. I actually had to persuade Jay to attend the hypnosis class. He began gradually to be re-involved with experimental trance states. We both began attending classes in hypnosis conducted by a retired career military man named Major Roberts. He was a wonderful man who truly liked Jay and me. We became two of his demonstration subjects in many classes. One evening at a parapsychology institute Major Roberts was to talk about his experiences in Haiti with hypnosis. During a break in the presentation, a woman in the class removed her beads from around her neck and handed them to Jay saying, "Tell me something." She said she had a feeling Jay was very psychic. "Tell me what you think." Reluctantly Jay told her several things. She became very excited and commented on the accuracy of his statements.

The term 'psychometry' is applied to the phenomenon of receiving information by handling objects. Psychometry might be defined further as the ability to touch an object and experience an awareness of its history, ownership, etc., including some past or future experiences of its owner. Many people who have this gift describe their experiences as a 'feeling' about something. I would explain the phenomenon as an awareness from the intuitive aspect of their personality. Like most psychic or intuitive abilities, this skill can be developed considerably, or be allowed to lie dormant.

One thing led to another after this experience with the beads, and Jay was invited to meet with a group of people who were experimenting with telepathy and other psychic phenomena, including the Ouija board. For several years now Jay had avoided voice channeling and other experiments in contacting the unobstructed. During those years he chose to allow his gifts to lie dormant. Jay began meeting with this group fairly regularly, and his interest in contact with the unobstructed was rekindled. It was at this time he met Sally, who proved to be the only person other than myself who could balance him on the Ouija board. The board just wouldn't move for Jay when he was alone or in physical contact with other people, but with either Sally or me the marker would jump all over the place and the messages were many.

There were a number of months during this period when I wasn't very involved with Jay and his experimenting. I had decided to go for a Master's degree and was in Arizona from September 1971 until September 1972. Jay was staying in San Diego and working to maintain our home. As his meetings with the group continued, he began to tell me about experimenting with a trumpet, receiving touches, and small objects moving spontaneously about the meeting room. Again I found myself feeling naive, for I didn't understand what he was telling me. Something about sitting in the dark. I had no idea what he meant when he was talking about a trumpet; the only kind I knew was one you blew in a band. I thought maybe he blew through it. He talked about being touched by entities, and the realness of the touch. I would say, "I want to understand it," and would try, but I had a hard time grasping the nature of the experiences. The purpose of this particular group had begun as an exploration of psychic phenomena such as telepathy, precognition, clairvoyance, psychometry, etc. It had expanded to include establishing contact with the spiritual world through voice channeling and later to physical contact through materialization. Even though at the time I really didn't understand what Jay was describing, this group was actually beginning to make some contact and have materialization phenomena.

Then accusations began in the group, people began to mistrust each other. One woman began to accuse Jay of standing up in the dark, going around and touching people, and making objects move around. Once again Jay was very disillusioned and said, "To hell with it." He called me in Arizona and told me about the accusations, his feeling bad, and his decision to drop out of the group. I told him I didn't know what was going on, but to just forget that group and find another one. I tried to encourage him to continue his searching. His response was that he just would forget the whole thing. At that point in a practical sense I couldn't spend too much time thinking about him. My work was to return to my statistics courses, etc., and finish my academic work. I decided reluctantly I would talk to him more when I returned. Then he called a few days later and told me about Daniel.

Daniel was a spontaneous materialization Jay encountered in our little house in San Diego. We had a small two-bedroom cottage about 50 years old. A small hallway connected the bedrooms and the bathroom. Jay described his experience to me as follows: as he stepped out from the bathroom at one end of the hallway, he could see something that appeared to be an outline of a person standing at the opposite end of the hall. He could see through the image, even to the extent of seeing his own reflection in the mirror that was on the wall behind the figure. He described this person/entity as very tall, standing almost to the ceiling, dressed in a white gown, but ethereal in substance. The figure introduced himself and said he was there to say that Jay knew his physical destiny and he was not to abandon activities necessary in his pursuit of it. At this point the figure disappeared. Jay called me on the phone and rather excitedly said, "I don't know whether you'll think I'm crazy or not," and proceeded to describe the above. I told him if he said he saw an entity in the hallway, then he saw one. I trusted his reality testing. My only other feeling at the time was, "God, I wish I could see one myself."

I completed my schooling and returned to San Diego not many weeks after that in the fall of 1972. We talked at length about his experiences. I tried to envision a clear picture in my head about what had actually happened in his group. They sat around being touched. I tried to understand, but could not really comprehend it. I did understand the group had disbanded, that lack of trust and accusations bouncing around within the group had destroyed it.

One member of that original group stood steadfast in her support of Jay and his integrity. Even after I returned home, she would call Jay many times sharing her belief in him and asking if he would be part of a new group she wanted to form. This was Lily, who became in the years to come a very important part of our experiments and our experiences. Repeatedly she would call up and want to know how Jay was, asking when we would visit, etc. Jay had much appreciation of Lily. He experienced her as a person who had never been negative in the group, and one who was always very supportive and positive toward people. Lily persisted in asking us to come over, but Jay stated he didn't want to be involved any more in those types of experiments. He had been disillusioned by his experiences with the people in his channeling and psychic experimentations several times by now. Yet, one night he finally asked me if I'd mind if we went over to Lily's. She had said she had some interesting tapes she wanted us to hear. We went and Lily, being a lady who is full of energy and excitement, began to talk about what had happened in the group that broke up. I still could not comprehend what was going on. Lily talked about materialization, and I didn't even recognize the word or really know what the phenomenon was all about. I was familiar with channeling and entities, and concepts of spirits and souls, but was ignorant of any materialization phenomenon. Lily described how they make bodies, etc. A good part of our conversation was directed toward the subject of fraud and fakery, and Lily had her own ways of discriminating phony from genuine. For example, she would ask about non-existent relatives and pay attention to what answer she received. She spoke of things such as voice quality and body textures of materialized entities, and how they would respond to different types of questions. It seems her mother had been a channel so her personal experiences with the unobstructed had begun at an early age. From my point of view her discriminative ability seemed quite keen and acute. She had good eyes and ears and was neither gullible nor naïve.

Lily had managed to invite some other people for this evening and, sure enough, we found ourselves sitting in a dark room and experimenting. I remember this night clearly, as it was my first time to sit in the dark with a hope for physical phenomenon. I wasn't in there two seconds until I realized I had not finished with my fear of the dark. In addition to having a very Catholic background that in my case focused mainly on fear rather than positive aspects of spirituality, I had a number of very traumatic experiences in the dark as a child. I was punished by being locked in a dark closet. My aunt thought it funny to send me to the basement after wine, knowing I was always afraid somebody or something was going to come from behind the big furnace down there and grab me. As much as I thought I had resolved my fears, this particular fear of the dark came right up on the surface again. This same night Lily showed me the trumpet I'd been hearing so much about. It turned out to be nothing more than an elongated telescope-type tin object that was larger at one end than the other. And that's all the trumpet was. I thought it was funny.

Lily later became our group's informal historian. She kept a journal and would make entries after most of our meetings. While none of us at that time had any thought of writing about our experiences, I am very grateful for Lily's efforts. She gladly supplied a copy of all her journals for this book. Portions of her dated entries, as she wrote them, will be preceded by a date and are direct quotations from her personal accounts. I urge the reader not to expect Lily's entries to be an explicit elaboration on the text material. They are included only to give a sample of generally related phenomena at different stages of our process, from a very conscientious and enthusiastic participant. Her account of my first evening in the dark on the night just described goes as follows:

9/9/72 . . . Marti got scared—and asked to sit near her husband.

A few nights later we met again, and had quite an experience with the table tipping which was also new to me. We had a dim light on in the room and while the room was not fully illuminated it was certainly bright enough to see clearly. We brought in a table, perhaps a foot and a half in diameter and two feet in height. We stood around it and the next thing I knew the table was so high up in the air that I had to stand on my tiptoes to hold it! I think there were about four or five of us in the room at the time. Nobody's fingers were under the table; all of our palms were on top of the table, all bodies were away from the table, nobody was touching it in any other way. That table just went straight up, all the way up until I was on my tiptoes holding on (I am rather short). My reaction, surprisingly, was one of curiosity rather than fear. How could that happen? We were the only ones in the room and we all had our hands on top and nobody was touching the table with their knees. With my fingers I pressed downward and the table felt as though it were suspended on a huge air bag. But of course nothing was visible.

Never had I experienced such unusual phenomena, and I was uncertain what was expected of me. Although I knew everyone in the room, I could feel my residual fear stirring— "something will grab me in the dark." These mystifying activities offered an excellent opportunity for me to work with my fear, which other types of growth counseling had not helped me completely resolve. I was eager to come back for more meetings, but Jay didn't really want to be involved again. I was so motivated to try to satisfy my curiosity and interest, and to resolve my fear, that I pleaded with him. He didn't have the heart to say no. We came back and at the next meeting the table went up again, although not as high as before. We would hear knocks on the table, but I really wasn't interested in that very much.

221

As a result of these sessions Jay and I began to be involved once again. At first everything was quite informal and our meetings were sporadic. One member of our group introduced us to a psychic named Shirley. Jay and Sally began to work the Ouija board for spiritual teachings with Shirley, and they talked about materialization of an entity she had encountered in some of her meditations. As a result of this interest we also had some meetings at Shirley's. There we sat in a darkened room with very lightweight luminous scarves on the floor. We also put luminous paint on little peanut shaped pieces of styrofoam, which I later fondly referred to as our 'peanuts.' We would place these luminous peanuts on a little chalkboard with X's marking their positions. In this way we could easily see if these light objects had been moved even a fraction of an inch when our meeting was over and the lights were turned on. We made sure there were no drafts of any kind in the room, and that no person moved the objects.

Our meetings with Shirley involved praying and saying the alphabet over and over to establish energy. This is what Shirley thought was necessary. We had met two or three times in the dark, saying the Lord's Prayer and the alphabet repeatedly, and one evening in October one of these little peanuts actually moved. We knew it wasn't the wind because all the windows and doors were closed. But we thought maybe one of Shirley's dogs had come in and bumped the table, even though we hadn't heard anything.

By this time, after a meeting we would frequently go back to the Ouija board and ask, "What can we do to make it better?" Always the answers were things like, "Just continue to try . . . be patient . . . try to get together as a group," etc. Several times, Lily had a couple come who did what they called "table tipping". After watching them I had to admit I didn't think it was all spiritual energy raising the table. Their knees were very close, and I think they were giving it a bit of assistance. I just didn't feel right about what I saw happening.

Then, one night at Shirley's, one of the peanuts

jumped off the table onto the floor. Jumped! Everybody hollered and became very excited. I said out loud something like, "Boy if you can do that, make it go back on the table and we'll quit for the night!" And that peanut just came right back up on the table, just jumped right back up. I couldn't believe it! I was just so excited I could hardly stand it. Truly, I couldn't understand this. Even skepticism isn't the word for it. My scientific mind continued to repeat . . . what goes up is lifted up, but if you can't see it, it isn't there. The day after this I of course regretted saying that we would quit for the night if we saw a second jump. Something else might have happened.

You must realize I really did feel the people in the group were trustworthy. I felt no one had anything to gain by faking or rigging the activity. At this time in our meetings, Jay was sitting with us as part of the group. We were all in this together.

People in the group, both men and women, had mixed backgrounds and interests. Some were interested in psychic phenomena, others came out of curiosity, and there were varied responses to the phenomena and activity. Some accepted it as natural and were comfortable, some felt afraid and revealed this in their actions and body language but not in words; others felt mostly delight and excitement! I was verbal and expressed, among other reactions, my feeling of fear. This resulted in generating doubts in some of the members about my continued participation, but I was finally accepted along with my fear. Looking back, I suspect many of the group members at this early time were not accustomed to hearing people express and externalize feelings openly. Perhaps they did not have my viewpoint, which was that the emotions I was expressing at the time were feelings I had at that point in my development, not a fixed reality that would remain with me forever.

By this time in our meetings, we were experiencing phenomena such as breezes and little flashes of light; light touches on our arms, and a variety of noises. As these things happened I had to deal with my doubts and my disbeliefs even though I experienced them and couldn't explain it. I would ask Jay if he were making these things happen, and he'd always say no. To give the reader some idea of my sensitivity to being fooled, I need to interject here another aspect of my history. My aunt thought the naïveté of children was very funny. For example, I always loved animals, and was particularly fond of baby animals. To her it was humorous to tell me there was a baby lamb in the garage and of course I'd run quickly to see. Later she would laugh at me for being so stupid as to believe her. Yet there was always a part of me that would have to go look, every time she would say that, just to make sure it wasn't true. With experiences like this in my background, I know I could not have tolerated any tricks from Jay or anyone else. I just could not have put up with that. Fortunately there was a part of me that simply knew absolutely Jay was not doing those things. But I still had to ask him. I just had to ask him. He was always very beautiful about it and would say to me, "No, not to my knowledge."

Although our meetings at this point were short (30 to 60 minutes) a strong bond developed among us as we continued to meet. On some level of awareness, I think we knew it would be a positive experience. We all became increasingly committed to continuing our experiments to develop further contact with the spirit world—the unobstructed universe, the reality that exists for us all when we are no longer in a physical body. We began to meet sometimes three evenings a week.

I see emotional growth and self-discovery as an endless process. Since I believe a person must confront their fears and guilts in order to realize their own potentials, I continued to see this environment in our meetings as helpful in resolving some of my uncomfortable feelings. Intuitively I recognized others would soon follow and choose to challenge their own fears and prejudices of the unknown. And that did indeed happen.

One night I became very courageous and decided what I'm going to do is put that peanut in my hand and hold it out. I was shaking so much I held my wrist with my other hand. As I held it out, I asked aloud for the peanut to be taken. Immediately, I felt the most delicate female hand I had ever experienced. I have seen few women with hands of this type, very tiny hands with slender fingers. Excitedly I told Sally, "Hey, there's nothing to it, stick your hand out." I should point out that Sally and I still both became very scared at times. We would laugh and make jokes trying to reduce our nervousness, sometimes screeching out loud when something unexpected happened. Following my lead Sally stuck out her hand, and from underneath she felt a large masculine hand touch her. Needless to say, she expressed her considerable surprise quite feelingly before she could describe what she had experienced.

We added what has already been described as a 'trumpet'. Ours was made of aluminum, shaped generally like an elongated megaphone. One night the trumpet began to move of its own accord and finally lifted slowly in the air. By November of 1972 the trumpet, now painted with bands of luminous paint so it could be easily seen in the dark, would float freely within the room. We would often feel hands touching us about the face and on top of our heads. Little bells we had placed on the floor would ring when we would sing, particularly when we sang "Jingle Bells." As Lily describes in her log:

11/18/72 ... It took a little longer than ordinary to start the trumpet moving. The trumpet did not move violently and would not answer a single time by tapping yes or no. Once it spoke between Jay and myself. Couldn't understand the word but it was independent voice. Later it clearly said **Goodnight.** Then the trumpet was near the ceiling and fell to the floor and there was a great rush of wind—cold—then some more cold right after that. The bell jingled many times while singing "Jingle Bells" and Alice felt large hands touching her.

In early December of 1972 the trumpet's movements became more brisk and animated, occasionally keeping time

225

with our songs. We would hear noises coming from the trumpet, which sounded like kissing sounds and what we identified as little **hellos.** We placed a small slate and chalk on the floor, hoping that an entity would write on it. Often after a meeting, when we would turn on the lights, we would find words like 'love' written in mirror writing. We learned we could ask yes and no questions of the trumpet. It would move up and down for yes, side to side for no. This allowed us to ask questions regarding understanding the activity and expanding on it.

12/1/72 ... So we were only four and it was fantastic! Trumpet moved all over. It did not touch any of us. It kept time with the songs. The bells rang and rang. Also both went up in the air and many kisses were heard. Spirits didn't say anything this time. The slate moved along the floor and wrote Love backwards which could be read looking at a mirror.

We found that we were making progress while moving against some of what other people considered 'taboos'. We were told by the entities via the Ouija board, and our experience later confirmed, that an atmosphere of lightness, laughter, singing and generally having fun, as well as being sincere, was the most positive way to create and focus the energy. L and M had advised that we did not need to be super serious, chant for hours, wear certain kinds of clothes, have shoes off, or face in certain directions. We could touch the trumpet; in no way did this interfere with the entities or their activities. It was suggested that it might be better if we sat in a circle rather than a square. We were told to touch the entities only with their permission, and they would touch us only if we agreed to it. Anything that would alter the chemical balance of an individual was of importance. For example, alcohol was not good to drink because it is disturbing to the energy. Certainly if somebody has had enough to drink to where it would be noticeable, their mind would not be in a place that would be very receptive to a spiritual experience. Regarding our physical procedures we frequently asked for guidance from the Ouija board. We felt we could trust this information and we would use this method for questions and to confirm our experiences. We didn't know then, as we do now, that the maximum accuracy of voice channeling and the Ouija board can only be 80% correct. There are always distortions with these methods, as the information must pass through the 'filter' of the channel's psyche. Although we consulted the Ouija board for information, the Darkroom was our focal point.

I remember one night a woman was there who was confined to a wheelchair. She and the chair just came up off the floor about six inches and glided right out to the middle of the room as we were all sitting there watching in the dim light. One man in the group had been talking about fraud, and to this date I don't know how he figured we did something like that. Nobody was touching that chair. Perhaps somebody knows how to do that, but I certainly don't. I have never seen anything like that happen again. Sometimes I would tease Jay and say things like, "If that's you why don't we just go to Las Vegas and make a bundle, and then we can have money to build the best clinic in the world?" Of course he would just laugh and say, "I don't know how to do that, I can't even move a toothpick."

At this time in our development we were hearing some noises through the trumpet. We would ask the entities to throw us a kiss, and then we would hear little kissing noises come out of the trumpet. Looking back on it, I now know the entities were using the trumpet to amplify the weak energy just as we use megaphones or power horns. One night we were talking about hearing the kisses and Sally asked for a kiss. Suddenly, she saw a black ball like a shadow move around near her face. Then she felt two lips on her cheek, and received her kiss from lips with no body connected. Did she let out a yell!

Sally was truly startled by this experience and became afraid. She knew she did not want to leave the group but she felt she wanted or needed some extra support. She

227

asked her husband, Don, to come to the group just to give her such support. Don did come and the first night he was there it was as if all creation broke loose. The peanuts flew all over the room. The chiffon scarf went all over, making many different shapes. I saw that scarf make shapes and do things that were just unbelievable. For example, it would suddenly wad itself up and then begin to assume the form of a bouquet of roses. At another time it formed an arrow of itself in midair, then shot about ten feet clear across the room. This marvelous show went on for quite awhile. As the scarf would be gradually making a shape, we would guess out loud at what it was or was becoming. As soon as we guessed correctly and all could see and agree, the scarf would wad itself up again and begin to make another shape. One other shape I especially recall was a parrot on a swing. Now I just don't know how you could do that with a piece of rag! I do know that after the meeting we sat around trying to duplicate the shapes and it was simply impossible for us to do it ourselves. Many other things happened that evening. Later we were to learn that Don's energy and excitement were very special, and with his addition to the group the total energy was strengthened very much.

Don had never experienced anything like this before, and the whole evening had a tremendous impact on him. But as excited and startled as he was, he said he had no doubts about the authenticity. Some people are ready for such experiences and he was. He knew there was no way the things he saw could have been done by a human being. We never had another night with that much sheer phenomena happening.

Many times at our meetings people would personally experience an awareness, a sensation of a change in the feeling or atmosphere of the room prior to visual evidence of materialization. Someone might say, "I have the feeling somebody's very close to me." We would always check when this occurred and ask outwardly something like, "If somebody is close, would you knock on the wall." This was our method of seeking some confirmation of personal experiences. "Would you do something to give us a sign if you are here?" We would often see pale light patches in the Darkroom, similar to smoke. If you can picture cigarette smoke in a cluster or a lump, it would be something like that. We later were told this was ectoplasm trying to form in a more solid way. Ectoplasm is nothing mystical, as some would have you believe, but simply a type of transformed physical energy that is used in the materialization process. From time to time we continued to feel touches even when we couldn't see anything. There were also weeks of only seeing little white or colored flashes of light in the room during the meeting. These were the months of non-verbal communication.

We asked the entities via the Ouija board if any one of us in the group had the ability to be a channel or catalyst for the energy, which enables the materialization process to occur. We were told several of our members present had such ability. In fact, we were told all people have such abilities and can learn to develop them. But it was made clear that in our group Jay was especially gifted in this regard.

We were a very close-knit group by this time. Since this factor clearly facilitated our experiments I would like to offer some comments about group aspects. One of the essentials was the establishment in our group of a dedication to purpose. Not personal purpose, but a dedication and awareness that this is a group experience and is to be shared as such. The purpose as stated is one of working toward the goal of establishing contact, and doing whatever we could as a group in that effort. We pooled our energies, allowing the entities to eventually solidify and materialize. For this to occur the energy must be stabilized. The channel somehow acts as a catalyst or stabilizer, a function that might be likened to making bread. The channel is a starter, but the starter without the group is of no value. The yeast without the flour is of no value. The group without the starter isn't going any place regarding materialization and vice versa. It cannot be emphasized enough that the motivation and

229

attitude can't be only "I wonder what I am going to get out of this"; the desires and energies must be shared and pooled. The direction of energy and focus of attention from each person must be outward. Meditation is beautiful and can offer much learning or awareness, but that process is not useful in our type of activity. Meditating is a productive and useful way to tune into one's own spirituality, but does not enhance a group effort for materialization. The energy must be directed outward, not inward.

A bit here about Jay, since he proved to be a very powerful channel for our group. He is a gentle and quiet man of 52 years. His childhood was one of poverty; he was a sharecropper's son. He has had many psychic experiences, dating back to his boyhood years. The channel tells of this and some other personal experiences in the chapter devoted to him.

Via the Ouija board, it was suggested any channel be physically separated from the group to better facilitate the materialization process. Jay would sit in a chair in the corner and we would make a curtain by putting a sheet in front of him and tacking it to two walls. Since the house where we were meeting at this time was old, some moonlight or streetlight would filter in around the doors and windows. So even though the room was darkened, there was sufficient light to identify moving forms and shapes. Once Jay was separated the forms and shapes became even more identifiable.

In that particular room it was very easy to tell if it was one of us standing up and moving around. At times we could see some form of energy (which we later came to call ectoplasm) outlining a freshly formed body against the curtain. At other times we watched the entities form themselves. First a shadow would appear, and then the shadowy form would begin to move. Sometimes the shadow would appear about seven feet tall. Arms would unfold. We could see what looked like stovepipes for legs, and watch the outline of hands moving down the contour of the legs. As the hands lowered we could see them fashioning the stovepipe shapes into leg muscles. The entity would form a thigh, then a calf, where before there had been nothing but a straight pipe-looking shadow. Even though all we could see were outlines of body parts, it was wonderful! No voice or other phenomena or any sounds, just the shapes forming themselves.

12/8/72 ... It gets better all the time. Trumpet went all over. Bells jingled on the floor, in space and up high. There were winds, trembling of leaves in my ear. Kisses were heard. Many times it looked as if there were two trumpets instead of one. The slate had Christ written on backwards. Mary felt fingers press on her forehead. Finally Jay went behind curtain and ectoplasm was seen against the black curtain— top part of curtain on the right. We sang and there was the shape of half a person in the middle of the curtain, then some more forms here and there.

The next evolutionary step was the recognition of an audible voice speaking in more than one or two word phrases. We became aware of this communication in an unusual way. During our meetings we had tape recorders running and sometimes people would play them back later to listen to the group activity. One day Sally called, very excited, and said she had played back our evening session just to hear the group singing and she heard this voice whispering on the tape. We both knew there was no way that the voice could have been superimposed on the tape loud enough to be heard. Our equipment certainly wasn't fancy and, as I've said, we had trust in one another. This first voice said in a whisper, *this is all for Don.* It wasn't too long after this that we began to hear a weak, tinny voice coming through the trumpet. We would also continue to see shapes form. At this time usually the shapes forming and the voice would not occur simultaneously.

1/7/73 . . . Tonight there was more talking, voices coming from all corners of the room. Talking in and out of the trumpet. Independent voices. Shirley brought foam peanuts, which moved all over and so did her bells sound. Others were touched; a peanut was grabbed from my hand. They were large, thick fingers.

We began to see what I might call the "real thing". I remember vividly the night when out of the silence came a rustling sound. We were speechless and spellbound as we watched an entity walking amid the group. The whole body was illuminated like the scarf. You could see wrinkles in the face, like those of someone maybe 80 or 90 years old. He had a couple of days' stubble of beard. All the male group members were clean-shaven, and since I knew it would have been literally impossible with the amount of light coming into the room to play any tricks, I had no doubt this was the real thing. This entity walked around, came very close to me, and brushed his cheek across mine. As his face touched me, I could feel the stiffness of his whiskers. I remember thinking to myself, "Oh, my God, how could I ever have doubted that this is anything but real!" I remember feeling guilty about my doubts, but it wasn't long after this that I was taught honest doubt is healthy.

The particular night just mentioned ended up being quite an evening. Before the meeting ended, we had four entities who walked around and faced everyone in the room. They leaned close to us so they could be clearly seen. All four bodies were self-illuminated, the effect being a bright glow. I thought I had been hooked before on these activities, but this evening really did it! I was astounded and filled with questions about what is all of this going on? I remember, even from the beginning, feeling such love and tenderness from the entities. In a way it was like meeting someone you had known forever, yet had never seen. It's difficult to describe my experience. In my memory I can still see them walking around the room. We were all very excited that night, of course, and Sally and I were just kicking each other and poking each other, hugging each other and looking at them. It was just great. Lily, of course, was beside herself with glee. She was the only one who really knew what was happening, since she had previously had similar experiences.

232

By this time in our meetings we had, of course, long ago stopped saying the alphabet and were now singing most of the time. Don sang and played the guitar and was faithful in his contribution. Of course, we continued to go to the Ouija board after our meetings and ask the same questions, what can we do to make it better, etc. The Ouija board, until now, had been the only contact with words from the spiritual world until we began to hear the few very weak words through the trumpet. Initially, we couldn't really make out the words too well, and certainly there was no talking back and forth. Regarding the weak trumpet voice, frequently we would ask for repetition of what had been said, or would feed back what we thought had been said. When we finally had the words right, the voice would say very weakly, *that's a fact.* We had been able to make that particular phrase out with some clarity. Naturally, we developed our own parlance and began to call that particular entity, "That's A Fact". The voice sounded male, and the shape of the physique proved to be male. We would see his shadowy form appear. He would stand and try to talk through the trumpet. That's A Fact was for a long time the only entity to try to speak with us.

We had no names for any other entities, but many of them did things we found humorous. For example, one entity would come and lights would flash from his body. They appeared to be like small, weak camera flashes, a flash of light that would occur for a split second and then be gone. It was as if lights were contained under the surface of the skin. First you might see a hand outlined when this light flashed, then the light might flash in the middle of the chest, down on the thigh or up on the shoulders. You never knew where the next flashes would be.

I should mention how the group would attempt to validate genuine phenomena to rule out individual perceptual distortions or unique personal experiences. Our procedure has remained constant through all our meetings. If one person saw or heard something they would describe it out loud. Others would say whether they saw it or heard it, or would reply that they had not. Our rationale and feeling was sometimes we might have been thinking we were seeing things, and we wanted to check that out. We wanted to find out if other people were seeing the same thing. If we verbalized our perception and described the location as best we could, others could also make their observations. We had enough mutual trust; we knew people would be honest in their self-reports. We would also ask possible entities present, "If you did that, would you do it again?" If it happened again, then we would conclude it wasn't just our eyesight, for everybody could then see it. Usually what one person saw, at least two people would see, but whenever there was any doubt, and many times when there was no doubt, we would ask, "Do it again" anyway so that everybody could respond.

Our group grew to nine people. During our meetings, we would begin to hear voices saying, *"Hello; glad you came tonight"*, or *"We love you."* One evening we found written on the slate, *"I love you, Mother; be happy."* Under that was what appeared to be a straight line. It was this evening that the voice suggested we take an intermission and return for a second session. We were very excited! This was the first time that our meeting continued beyond the usual period. When we went back for our second session there were more comments from the entities and we heard the chalk move on the slate. When the light went on at the end of our meeting, we saw that the straight line on the slate now formed the base of a Christmas tree. The group members felt that the picture of the Christmas tree, and the statement "I love you, Mother, be happy," were intended for one of the women in the group. Her son had recently died. This particular woman took this as evidence of life after death.

One night the trumpet moved over to a scarf and sucked it up inside itself as though the trumpet were a vacuum cleaner. We were quite startled and amused when the tip of the scarf came out the small end! Later that evening we were electrified when we observed an entity standing in the middle of the room. We could see his entire body and he appeared to be at least seven feet tall. The entity stepped forth and asked one of the women if she would stand up and give him her hand. She stood and extended her hand as far above her head as possible. In the dim light we could see the entity bend over and kiss her hand. His enormous height was experienced as most impactful and inspiring, but in no way as frightening. He began to answer our questions, and we knew That's A Fact was with us once again.

2/3/73 . . . This tall That's A Fact one seems to be taking over. He showed us all kinds of demonstrations. Held the trumpet above the scarf and the scarf crawled slowly in the trumpet. Another time it went again from a couple of feet into the trumpet and out at the small end. He also stuck his finger from small end and kept touching my out-held hand. Then stuck his hand up the large end. Scarf made all kinds of movements. He was standing in the middle of the room and touched everyone and took Jean's hand and kissed it and held it and swayed Jean's hand from side to side, then felt her fingers and lifted her hand way up and kissed it and moved it some more and kissed it again. Scarf was open flat in the air and his arm could be seen against it. He put scarf against his long legs so we could see his height and over his hips, then over his head. He then asked me, *"Lily, please stand up,"* which I did. *"Stick out your hand."* He took my hand lifted it way straight up and he stooped over more, and pulled me more towards the middle of the floor then with his covered scarfed head he bent and kissed my hand and then he led me back to my seat with my hands still way up and said, *"You're a short one."* Oh yes, he showed his hand when he put it over the scarf making the scarf into a ball. There was much talking. There were less hellos. The tall one likes to kid along. To our questions he would answer, *"Is that a fact?"* or *"That's a fact"* or *"Heaven's yes"* or *"Heaven's no."* After a continued performance he said that we could have a break and come back and he would talk some more. We asked him if he would write and show his hands so he put the scarf around his hands somewhere on the slate and we could see his hand holding the chalk and writing. Well, we had tea and came back and there was more talking, and more movements of scarf and peanuts and we could see his whole figure in the middle of the floor, then he said, *"That's all for tonight."*

By February of 1973 our group had increased to 12. One night we heard several voices simultaneously from all corners of the room as well as from the trumpet. The entities were now regularly speaking in short sentences such as, *"Please come again,"* and *"You're nice."* When we would ask their name they would answer, *"It's a secret,"* and we would laugh. The laughter seemed to make the energy intensify.

2/9/73 . . . For the first time we had two trumpets up while voices came out of both. The tall one was talking through the larger trumpet, while a new voice was trying to say, *"Hello, I cannot stay."* The tall one jokingly said, *"Poor little fellow, he's having a hard time, I'd better go help him."*

One evening, one of the men in the group asked if he should see a doctor because of a physical problem and medical condition, explaining it had been some time since he had seen one. That's A Fact laughed and said he thought it was a good idea. He explained he himself had not seen a doctor for a long time either—remarking it had been over 3,000 years!

Gradually, That's A Fact began materializing a stronger voice. His voice sounded very English, clipped, almost like an African black that has been sent to an English school. He finally gave us his name, and we had quite a time learning how to spell it. We finally got it—Aenka. One night in response to questions about his own past lives or identity, he told us that in his last life his mother had been very beautiful and his father had been a wise man, that he had lived on a mountaintop by a stream and fished every day as a boy. He said that in this life he was black, fuzzy-haired, and stood seven feet eight inches tall. His father taught him to love all living things. Most exciting of all on that particular evening was his telling us he was to be the coordinator of our group and that he had chosen this job for himself in the unobstructed. He was to coordinate all activities of other entities who would come to visit, guide, and assist us in our development and growth!

New people joined our group and since the meeting room was small it would be filled to capacity. Someone suggested Jay sit in the hallway adjacent to the room. After a session, as we were dragging a chair in and out between the room and the hall, Jay said, "Why don't I just lay down on the floor?" So began our technique of the channel lying down within or adjacent to the meeting room.

Aenka began speaking to us with increasing frequency, and most of us acknowledged him as our leader for the Darkroom activities. We detected a continual ribbon of humor within his teaching, which caused a few group members to be unsure about his leadership. It was difficult for them to let go of some of their beliefs and some of the attitudes and teachings frequently associated with spiritual experimentation. They seemed to believe it should all be much more serious. Some group members claimed a 'gatekeeper' was needed to ensure that only 'higher' entities could enter a room and materialize. When we asked Aenka to comment, he responded with a chuckle and the statement, *"There is no fence."* In this humorous way, and later in a more serious vein, he assured us no gatekeeper was necessary. There is no class or caste system in the unobstructed as there is in our physical, obstructed world.

I would like to say a few more things about the dynamics of our group. There was something happening in the group that was very impressive. Many of us still only knew each other through our meetings, not on a social or personally intimate basis, but somehow we began to form increasing support and caring for each other. If someone missed a meeting and we had a particular phenomenon, we would share the experience before the next meeting started.

During the meeting, as phenomena began, we would ask if entities would repeat something from the last meeting (like the light flashes) for so-and-so. Often, the phenomenon would be repeated for the person who had missed it. We became more attentive and responsive to each other's moods, fears, feelings, etc.

Now we were still meeting regularly three times a week, and in addition would meet spontaneously in different homes. The activity was intensified in some places more than others. The voices were becoming clearer. We could ask questions now and receive verbal answers. Only rarely would an entity stand in front of a group member answering questions with the tapping method. Every activity we experienced stimulated us and there would be never ending requests for more!

I would like to share one of the more fascinating ones that happened. Lily was the source of the idea. Lily was and is a very open and expressive person. Some people in our group would object to her directness and lightheartedness, but in my opinion she added much positive energy to our group. For example, one of Lily's greatest desires was for an entity to come in, scoop her up in his arms and hold her like a bride. She would freely express fantasies and desires of this type in the group. Since she was 65 at the time, the reader may have some idea of her energy and spontaneity. Sure enough, pretty soon in walks an entity and lifts Lily right up to the ceiling! As she is up in the air, she is describing this big broad-shouldered guy. We are all sitting there yelling like kids, saying, "We want it too," etc. Over the next few weeks everybody had that experience. This entity we began to refer to as Hercules. His shoulders were broad, his biceps massive, and he picked up people from 105 to 150 pounds with the same apparent ease. We were, of course, delighted with these experiences. When it became my turn with Hercules, he stood in front of me and asked me to stand. I stood beside him and I could feel the width of his body. He took my arm and set it on his shoulder. My hand could in no way cover his deltoid muscle.

Then he guided my hand across his back, which felt very wide. There was no one in the group that had a physique anything like his. As I stood there, he reached down and picked me up with one arm under my shoulder, and the other under the bend of my knees. He lifted me to the ceiling straight up like he might a baby, rocked me, and set me down. Then he gave me a little pat on the head and guided me back to my chair. How can I say I felt? Very excited. I think if I had any thoughts it would have been something like, "It's over too soon." You know, like it is there and it happens, and it is gone. I remember one night Hercules knelt down by the luminous scarf and flexed his arm so you could see the muscles. We couldn't see him but we could see the shape of his arm and the muscles. Lily describes another night:

3/3/73 ... I asked the tall one to ask the lifter to come and lift June and Peg like he did me last Friday. So he went to June and stood her up—then sideways and swung her way up in the air with her arm around his neck and then he did the same to Peg but ran around the room so fast like she was paper. She went right up to the ceiling. He went around after and let us feel his muscles. He went to the curtain and I thought he was gone—so I got on my hands and knees in the middle of the room to straighten the scarves and he came to me so quick he put his arm under my belly and carried me all around the room with my arms and legs dangling in the air! What a thrill!

By this time in our group evolution, our many experiences had helped me decrease considerably my fear of the dark. I had asked the entities specifically to help me resolve this fear any way they felt would be positive. As I said previously, I had not totally resolved it even though I'd done a tremendous amount of work on it. When I would mention my fear to Aenka, he would respond very reassuringly with statements like, *"We will never harm you."* I would say, "I know that, but my reaction is more than being startled." With my permission a number of

239

entities began to touch me unexpectedly over a period of several months. A touch on a shoulder or a touch on an arm, and I would let out a yelp. They were using, if you will, a behavior modification approach. I would share with the group fears I had learned and soon began to connect with grief I had inside me. The entities began to talk about the reaction of being startled as a natural and healthy protection, but that panic was unnatural. Ironically, the feeling that "someone or something would come out of the woodwork and grab me" was coming true; however, I was now delighted with the idea.

Our group now began to have what we referred to as private visits, a time spent with an entity apart from the group discussing private issues. These sessions might last a few moments or two hours. A room adjacent to our meeting room was always available once these visits began. The first private visit was a bit shaky for some group members but not for the person who received it. It happened to a young woman who was using drugs and exhibiting paranoid behavior. She was sitting with the group for the first time and the entity approached her, tapping her on the head indicating that he was there to visit her. She stood up and he led her out of the meeting room into an adjoining room. Since this was the first time this had occurred, we were all a bit worried. This particular lady in her very first meeting was to have this powerful experience? I was especially concerned because I thought something might happen to make her feel more afraid. To my great surprise, she came back emotionally in a very positive place, much more peaceful. Her comment in part when she came back to us was, "Yes, I distrust people, but I trust the entities completely." She said as soon as the entity walked up to her, she knew he was someone she could trust. The entity gave her his name during the private visit, talked with her about her fears, and emphasized the need to take better care of herself physically. I can remember her saying at least she didn't feel like she was being given another "goddamn sermon." After this incident, we began to expect these brief private visits, and they indeed began to occur with increasing regularity.

In our meetings now the voices of the entities, though not crystal clear, were understandable. We discontinued using the Ouija board for clarification. If we were unsure of what was said, we would repeat it until we were assured of accuracy by the entity. Often when we touched the entities they felt moist or damp. Not wanting to shock or frighten us, they had gradually introduced us to this feeling.

5/21/73 ... A large spirit came out and let a couple of women touch him. He was very tall and big. Some of the other spirits touched some of the women's toes. One entity ruffled some of our hair.

Each meeting we would naturally strain to see with as much clarity as we could. Often, the heads of the entities appeared to be wrapped in something. We asked about this and they said they often wear turbans out of respect for the Source of All Divinity. They would not comment further. This apparel continues to be frequently present to this day, although some male entities have appeared with shoulder length hair and some females with hair to their waist.

By May or June of 1973 our meetings were beginning to develop a general pattern. Aenka would come, greet everyone, say some funny things to a few people and begin answering questions. The questions were usually of a personal nature. Frequently they were psychically or spiritually oriented, touching on such subjects as reincarnation, past lives, etc. We would ask him many times about himself, but he said very little. After the greeting and some questions, another or several other entities would come and sometimes one person would go out for a personal visit. Some entities, male and female, allowed all the group members to touch them. We would recognize differences in their body structure and say, "Oh, this is somebody different." The shadows of their feet, legs, and other parts of their form were readily seen. One entity was recognizable by the leanness of his stature and skinny legs, easily identified even at a distance. Eventually, we came not only to recognize a number of them but gradually to associate who they were there to visit. It was joyful to watch the entity walk over, tap the person on the head, and then take them out for their private visit. We experienced a great variety in the shapes and sizes of the entities: tall, short, fat, and skinny. One we referred to as the 'doctor' since he would manipulate or massage our backs. His hands were very stubby, his fingers short.

5/25/73 . . . The doctor came and treated Xavier. He let us have the scarves out and we saw his robe. He treated my throat. I asked him to. I had a bone stuck in my throat when I ate today.

The doctor appeared at several meetings and then did not return. We concluded his absence meant that such activity was not one of the main purposes of our group. Looking back, it seems as if the message was it's time to move on in our group process experiences and evolution. One other entity I'd like to describe we called Harry. This particular entity was perceived as small boned but he had hair on his chest that seemed about five inches long. Each time we were allowed to touch him he would jump about in rapid, jerky movements. Then he would stand, let us touch him, and again act as if he were skittish or supersensitive to being touched. One evening when Aenka appeared he was wearing a long robe and allowed us to touch it. The texture was a rough home woven feeling material.

6/10/73 . . . The tall robed man came out and walked around the room, pushing the scarves while he walked so we could see his feet, which were bare. He threw part of his robe (which was partly dragging on the floor) on our laps so we could feel the texture—which was wooly and heavy. He went around putting his hands on our eyes and our hands.

Even though our meetings were now taking on a more serious flavor, there continued to be times when some lighter experiences would come along. By now we had become accustomed to the unpredictable and the unusual. If the entities didn't do something unpredictable, Lily would. For example, Lily was a cat lover. She began to talk in the Darkroom about a sick cat and asked the entities for help. One night she brought the cat with her to the meeting. Sure enough, one of the entities worked on the cat. We observed the outline of the entity silhouetted against the light, reaching down brushing his hands over it. The cat, which was wiggling around a moment before, began to stretch and lazily lay down. After the entity worked with it, he gave Lily specific advice about caring for the animal. After this Lily began bringing a number of her cats to different sessions. Some people in the group began to be a bit irritated about this, but Lily went ahead and did it anyway.

Consistent with their own unpredictability, one night the entities told us we might be able to use a dim red light in order to see them more clearly. We had previously talked about wanting to view them in a clearer light. A group member had heard using a red light did not affect energy in the same manner as white light. This was confirmed by Aenka, although we were never told in depth why. He simply said red light does not interfere with the energy as much as white. We wanted to see the entities more clearly and we experimented. We began by putting a 25-watt red light on a dimmer switch and asking at each meeting if we could turn it on. Many times before we had asked and received a 'no' in response. We never hesitated to ask anything; questions were our specialty. The reader is reminded that by this point in our meetings, all of us were more comfortable in the presence of the entities. Some of us were of course more verbal than others. And one night an entity said, *"All right, turn it on very, very low."*

6/20/73 . . . First time we are permitted to use red light! Put scarves on floor and they didn't take them away. So an entity came (male) in white. Very fine gauze hanging and also tied on his body, like cheesecloth. Walked all around.

That's A Fact came and told us to take all scarves away and an entity would come—for us to count to 15 when the trumpet fell and then to put the red light on as strong as we wanted to, then turn it off at 15 (i.e., we could view an entity in the light for 15 seconds).

After this we repeatedly asked to use the light again. One night we were once again given permission. When the light went on, I clearly saw a figure kneeling in the middle of the room about two feet from me. The group was sitting around in a circle and I could see the entity and all the group members very distinctly. The light from a 25-watt red bulb, when your eyes are dark-adapted, is actually a good bit of light, and visibility is extensive. Those familiar with a photographic darkroom will certainly be able to understand this. The entity I saw had shoulder length blondish hair, a classical Roman nose, and little eyes that were looking at everyone in the room. His face looked as though he'd had a bad burn, which had left scarring. The skin was pulled very taut. He asked if we were frightened, and we all said no. He spoke and said that we could look but to please not touch. We were told to stay in our seats but we could lean and look from different angles from our seated position. Believe me, I really learned how to lean! I wanted to see as much as possible. I didn't want to miss anything. I figured I may never see this again and it would have to last me a long time. He stayed quite a few minutes, talked a bit, and apologized about the quality of his face. Lily described another evening with the light.

8/18/73 . . . Aenka came and said we should have tea and the vibration was very good. I asked for red light and he said he would consider it. After tea we came back in. Nina went out for a visit for 30 minutes with Patrick. Aenka then said to put the light on. So the entity appeared all in white with medium blond hair. He turned his face to Don and said his face looked like a bad plastic surgery job. He talked before we put the light on saying, *"I don't want to frighten anyone."* He just turned slowly —a short turn—then

244

another came in and said to put the light low, and then a little stronger, and stronger yet—he came to the middle of the floor saying he didn't want to frighten us and we said of course not, we were not scared. He stayed at least fifteen minutes turning around and peering into our eyes. Then he went in front of the curtain and made himself into a little white shape then opened the curtain from the floor, went under the curtain.

It would be some weeks before we were to use the red light again and see the face of an entity with such clarity. After some months we were able to see Aenka and see his skin coloring—black. Aenka's facial features were different from other entities we had seen. In the months that followed an entity might walk in at unexpected times and turn the red light on using the dimmer switch we had attached, and put their face near the light. The turban could be clearly seen, as could their garment. Sometimes they wore like a lava-lava, or little loincloth. Our private visits continued and, in fact, were increasing in frequency and duration.

8/22/73 Esther's friend Johnathan came and took her out. They touched the channel (Jay).

More and more people were requesting permission to attend the group. I myself was so fascinated I would have been willing to meet every night if I could have. However, since it was necessary for Jay to continue his gardening work so that we could live, that was not possible. The excitement of the Darkroom has never worn off for me.

Don continued to bring his guitar each session he attended. We all sang loudly though not always well. One night, as we were singing, the group became aware of an additional male voice. The group was quiet but Don continued to sing and play the guitar. An entity who was also singing stepped forward and moved to Don's side. They sang many duets, and soon the voice of the entity was so loud both Don and the guitar were background. We would in time learn the singer's name was Willie. He was to become a beloved entity, one we would look forward to hearing and would hear many times in the years to come.

9/9/73 . . . The singer came . . .

Another subject of interest to the group was apports. Since our group was feeling more and more comfortable together, many times we would laugh and joke about apports and about wanting a four or five carat diamond ring, etc. Apports are gifts the entities are able to materialize and give to someone. We were told apports are usually objects that had been lost. An apport was not created from energy, but was something someone had lost, misplaced, discarded or was as free as flowers. The entities repeatedly stated they could not or would not steal. One apport they brought was a small Indian ring with three small stones. Aenka asked Esther one night to step forward in the group and said to her, *this ring will not fit you, but I shall give it to you in the hope that with it, your mind may offer you success. It is only a small token; it is inexpensive. It is turquoise melted in silver, made by an Indian. It is in the shape of a heart for your own warm understanding for your fellowman. It has three small turquoise stones planted in the heart for the three steps you must take until you merge with the Source of Divinity.* This is an example of the gentleness, love, and support the entities offer. This ring continued to serve as a symbol of loving support in this woman's painful pursuit of growth. She moved away from a life of drugs and welfare toward a more positive interaction with society. One session, a female entity who would come and dance tossed us her yellow dress. When we initially touched it, it was damp. We were advised to pass it around to the members of the group, and were told by the time we had all touched it, it would be fully materialized and we would be able to keep it.

9/19/73 . . . The dancer came and danced and she left her dress. It was cotton, very hot on Marti's lap. We were just thrilled. He said it belonged to a material being who had discarded it and it was dematerialized and materialized and then she put it on. That we should bring it every time and leave it in the middle of the room—it then will be easier for the dancer to put it on and leave it when she left. It was cotton, mustardy yellow with little flowers and a white cotton border with a little black cotton belt.

One person playfully asked for a copy of a certain magazine. This magazine had just appeared on the market. Sure enough, one evening Aenka presented her with a copy of that magazine. It was as if it had just come hot off the press, with not even a creased corner. Often flowers were materialized.

When I made my choice of an apport, I shared with Aenka my desire for a gold ankh to wear on a chain. Several years would go by before this request was granted. In May of 1976, Aenka asked me unexpectedly, *"What is it you've been wanting?"* The question was vague and at the moment had no meaning for me. Then he asked me to put my hand at the bottom of the trumpet. There was no sound, nothing occurred. I spoke up, saying, "Nothing's happening!" My mind was stirring with curiosity. Again Aenka spoke, *"Put your hand at the bottom of this contraption."* Then I heard the tinkle of metal against metal and felt something drop into my hand. I quickly identified a chain and the unusual shape of an ankh. I was told this particular ankh had been located on a San Onofre beach. The clasp was broken. I still wear this ankh daily, a gift from my beloved Aenka.

On many occasions, we were able to witness the materialization process. When energy begins to congeal it appears to me as dense cigarette smoke, white, a bit like a little cloud. At times, the energy would form like a small cloud, then glide across the floor. The shape was not perfectly round like a ball but more elongated or irregular. One evening, I was especially awed as I witnessed a materialization process. Cloud-like material glided to the luminous scarf on the floor and there it remained stationary and unchanged as I looked, not blinking an eye. A thick and dense inner core formed as I watched spellbound. I saw a turbaned head and shoulders appear gradually. As I watched, the entity gradually formed the rest of his body. When completed he could be seen kneeling on the floor before me. To say the least, this is a humbling experience and you can believe when it happened one could have literally heard a pin drop. It absolutely took my breath away. Not many things leave me speechless but that experience did.

Now, there were many entities that would come, talk to the entire group or let everyone in the group touch them. Others who came singled out one individual for a touch or talk. In the private visits the entities were very selective and individualistic.

9/29/73 . . . Everyone went out except me, my friend Joseph came to see me last. He danced and answered a few questions. We held the shawls up a little and I asked if he could help me with money and he said he couldn't violate the government of life. I asked about someone to take Jay's place so he could enjoy the entities with us, and he said there was one.

There were only two entities who would address openly at length everyone in the large group. One was Aenka, our leader and co-coordinator. He is involved with our group alone. Later, an entity who would introduce himself as Mario began working with our group. He has been involved to a great degree in teachings related to the importance of our physical body and its role in our physical, emotional, intellectual, and spiritual development. K has spoken at rare intervals with messages to all participating in the group. He usually spoke of an overall plan. He is said to direct a movement against negativity and is responsible for all groups on the planet Earth involved in this particular plan. K refers to this concerted effort as a revolution on negativity. Rarely did a main guide of a group member materialize. We were advised that entities who did come for personal visits were usually a representative chosen by one's main guide. We were also told this was a method of preserving objectivity between a person and their main guide. If for any reason visits were discontinued, it would somehow be easier for the relationship between the entity and the person to remain a positive memory. The loss would not be so profound. This procedure enhances the awareness of our guides without an intense personal involvement.

The theme of growth work was occasionally interrupted by unusual phenomena, perhaps to remind us of the need also for joy and lightheartedness. I remember one night we looked at the ceiling and saw what appeared to be illuminated x-rays of two hands, the bony structure and the soft tissue clearly outlined. Another night we were at Lily's and an entity entered the room by walking through the wall. I was sitting by a built-in dresser leaning my head against the wall, an empty chair beside me. I heard a noise on the dresser and I wondered if Lily was over there doing something. Looking around I saw an entity coming through the wall from the direction of the kitchen, walking through a picture on the wall, and stepping down onto the chair. Nothing was disturbed on the dresser. I stared amazed! Since I was sitting in front of the dresser, there was no way anyone could have moved from the doorway, climbed up on that dresser, turned around and walked down. There was no window in that part of the room, only a wall. There is no doubt he came through the wall. The entities have responded to questions regarding this and explained the phenomenon as a rearrangement of molecular structure.

Repeatedly the entities commented about the group purpose and process. Aenka talked at length about how our meetings were very unusual. He would say if we continued there would be great risk involved. As I look back, he was even then preparing us to expect repercussions, but at the time we were hearing on a different level. I remember clearly thinking, "Oh well, my father will think I'm nuts or turn against me." Or, "Well, there are several people I work with who already think I'm kooky anyway, so that won't make any difference." That was the extent of my thoughts regarding people turning against us. We were not told explicitly or specifically by Aenka or any other entity exactly what to expect, or when. They would not elaborate about the risks, and we didn't pursue it. We simply did not comprehend what they were talking about. Now I know that I would not have stopped coming to the meetings even if I'd known what was to come. I speak only for myself here when I say I was hooked, not only because of the way I'd watched the entities talk to the other people and to me, but because of the beauty of what they said and did.

I was fascinated with watching the entities' counseling techniques with people in deep feelings and pain. There were many times when this would occur in the large group, and much personal therapy was done by participants in the group setting in addition to private visits. I would sit, watch, listen, and think to myself, "If I could do half that well I'd be a terrific counselor." I considered myself good but their work was superb. Their techniques were so simple and basic, yet so profound. They would always give free choice to people allowing us to use our own discrimination and self-permission as to what to share or not. As we were being clearly offered a counseling opportunity in both the group meeting and in private visits, the focus and interest of most of us shifted primarily toward personal growth. The changes I observed in self-image and behavior of group members was at times very impressive. For example, shy people who in the beginning were unable to even ask questions of any sort were now beginning to take charge of their lives. One young man no longer needed to rely on drugs to support his identity and attitudes of maleness. His interest in academic pursuits surfaced and he returned to school. Presently he is completing his doctoral studies. One woman, a single parent, began to truly enjoy her children. As she learned of unconditional love and firm, fair discipline and incorporated these, relationships within her family blossomed. As she challenged her own fears, her love of self also deepened.

As this growth work process escalated, entities would at times suggest a person talk with me about selected subjects during intermission or break. I would present some basic information and later the entities would elaborate. This also stimulated questions to be asked within the group setting by the participants. Initially, when the entities suggested my presenting basic information, I felt I couldn't do it. I felt I didn't even know what I was doing. Just like everybody else, I was there as a member of the group. But the entities continued to direct me into teaching by saying things like, *Marti will talk to you about anger.* I finally figured if I were willing to present some basic information, then the entities might have more time and some energy might be saved. So I accepted this challenge, and my teaching and sharing began. What I shared was a combination of what I had learned from my professional studies, my personal therapy, plus what the entities had taught us. Occasionally someone in the group would express intense feelings such as grief or anger, and the entity would talk with them for a while. As I became more comfortable with presenting basic information, the entities would at times suggest to someone, *talk with Marti at the break.* As time passed I gradually became more accustomed to this new role of assistant. If someone in the group began to share strong feelings, we would wait for an entity to come work with the person. Counseling in that setting was not my purpose, it was not my group, I was still there as a participant like everyone else. If an entity didn't appear in a reasonable time I might say to the individual, "Is there something I might talk with you about or do for you until an entity arrives?" Initially, I felt I was interfering and did not respond to anyone in the group on my own initiative. I always limited my participation to talking and sharing, and did not perform any personal counseling per se.

9/19/74 . . . Aenka came and told us there was so much inner feelings that we would be better off if we exposed them and had Marti talk, so the meeting was terminated.

We continued to meet and to tell others outside the group about our happenings. It was now well into 1974, almost two years since we started. More people wanted to come, and the meetings were getting crowded. Regular members were beginning to feel a little resentful when our intimate meetings with familiar people began to include strangers. We always asked the entities for permission for individuals wanting to attend. As the numbers grew we developed one other solution to dealing with new people and that was to begin a visitors' night. The regular meetings were then reserved for our core group of established members. Visitors' night would start late on Saturday afternoon and might last until 5:00 or 6:00 Sunday morning. Regular members of course could attend the visitors' group and the channel and I would always be there. We would begin with prayer and singing, entities would visit one by one (sometimes two by two), after awhile we would take a break and start all over again. Each session might be from two to three hours long. Many would have an individual visit lasting a half hour or an hour. We never knew what criteria would be used by the entities in selecting the amount of time. When people during these long meetings would tire, they could simply leave and go home. The entities would always say to those who remained to support the long group process that if we really got tired, to lie down and take a little nap. However, it was necessary there be a number of people to remain awake to sustain the energy for materialization. By this period in the evolution of our group, the materialization phenomenon was not only consistent but also strong and clear both in regular meetings and visitors' night. The contact we had in both could be maintained for lengthy periods of time.

Mario began to appear frequently. He would come, sit, and talk with the group. We would be expecting Aenka, and Mario would appear making jokes like, ***"The energy is lousy tonight and I can work with lousy energy."*** It was in this way he eased us into working with him for extended periods. Up to this time Aenka had presented all the teachings. It was not long before we recognized the direction of Mario's words and the recognition of the subject of body acceptance. In the lectures by entities given to the entire group there had been questions by participants regarding sexuality and body acceptance. In general the entities' response and approach to these subjects was to emphasize the importance of our physical being in general as it relates to our overall personal, spiritual, and intellectual development. Sexuality was looked at from this perspective, i.e., how does it relate to our emotional and spiritual development. Since there were many questions and personal issues regarding this area, Mario even proposed scheduling workshops specifically focusing on these subjects, to be attended by Darkroom members only. Naturally neither he nor any other entity could promise to appear, since the materialization would depend on so many factors regarding balancing of the energy. However, schedule them he did.

The objective of these workshops focusing on body acceptance and function was to work on issues and attitudes associated with sex, body acceptance, and sexuality. Emphasis was placed on the effect of childhood conditioning on interpersonal relationships and body functioning in mature behavior. Mario and other entities in their teachings would discuss how sexual urges can be triggered, and they would consistently guide and direct people toward integrating those responses with their spouses or mates rather than acting it out with others. The entities in their talks about sexuality stressed that promiscuity was not a natural activity. They stressed that insights be evaluated to see what one might learn about themselves.

One evening when asked directly to comment on the sex drive and sexuality, Mario stated, *"It is one of the most frustrating subjects for any human being until they resolve their attitudes about it."* He went on to say, *"The recognition of the hunger of the physical body for physical gratification is terribly necessary for physical growth, physical health. It must be separated from the emotional quadrant and be recognized as a totally physical phenomenon and nothing more . . . Now it is wonderful to become emotionally involved with it but it is not love nor can it be used as a substitute."*

At times I assisted Mario as he conducted these

workshops. However, the majority of my energy at about this time (by now 1975) was directed towards the establishment of my own private practice and conducting my own psycho- drama workshops. Psychodrama and my private practice have always been activities separate from the Darkroom, and different from it. Counseling was and is my profession, and my involvement in the Darkroom was and is strictly personal. It is true I have adapted some of the techniques and teachings of the entities to my psychodrama workshops. These adaptations will be elaborated on in a subsequent book.

New people continued to be admitted to the Darkroom, and permission to do so was still up to Aenka. Occasionally, someone was given permission to attend and I would question within myself whether it would be or had been a positive experience for them. In other words, there were a few people Aenka permitted to attend that I might have said no to had it been up to me. Discussing this with the entities they would always reply, ***"We must take the risk. If three are helped and two misinterpret it, it is still worth it."*** It took me some time to think about that.

An example of their risk taking might be what we refer to as "Black Monday." A troubled young man came to the group after receiving permission from the entities to attend. He went out for a private visit when all of a sudden I could hear noises sounding like a scuffle and a fight. Somebody was hollering, "Tell them you're a man!" And you could hear another softer voice replying, ***"I am a man."*** There were sounds of blows, and the striking of a wall. After a few moments the young man returned to the room where the group was seated and yelled, "Turn on the light!" I was sitting there saying, "Please don't turn on the light for the channel's sake, I beg you, don't turn on the light." The young man finally sat down. I could feel my heart pounding. I continued to plead with him, "Please don't turn on the light until the channel awakens." To this day I'm not sure why he didn't turn the lights on. Perhaps it was because I tried to say what I did in a voice that was nonthreatening and nonconfrontative. Perhaps he figured, "Oh, this stupid idiot." For whatever reason, he did sit down. Jay awakened, I turned the light on, and I looked at the group who sat stunned. I did not know what to say to this man. A million thoughts were going through my mind such as please leave, why did you do it, etc. One group member put it into words as he turned and said to the young man, "You know, we didn't ask you to believe it. If you didn't believe it why didn't you just go and leave it to the rest of us who do?" At this time Jay came into the room and paused in the doorway, appearing a bit groggy from coming out of his altered state. This transition might be equated to waking up from a sound sleep in an abrupt manner. Jay seemed to sense something had happened. I must have been as white as a sheet. As he stood there trying to figure out what happened, Jay said, "What's the matter, what happened?" The young man began to talk about the entity and his conversation with the entity, describing how he had grabbed the entity and threw him up against the wall. This explained the sounds of punches we heard from the other room and sounds like someone being thrown up against a wall. Jay listened to the young man and said, "Well, gee, you know, I'm sorry." The young man just stared at Jay. I believe he was very surprised to see Jay just standing there, obviously not even disheveled. Jay was not the man who had received the beating a few moments before. I believe the young man expected Jay to be bruised, bleeding, and sore. The young man looked at Jay and continued to insist there had not been any spirit. He emphatically insisted the entity was a man and by God he was going to prove it was a man. There was no question in my mind he was very afraid and covered this up with anger. He left the room and the group at this time. Some of the group members began to cry. My big concern was now the Darkroom was spoiled. In a few moments several of us walked into the room where the private visits were held. There were big black scuffmarks visible on the floor. The young man had been wearing logging boots, and the marks of his boots were apparent. The metal doorknob was completely twisted askew. It looked as though someone had been shoved up against it. It was quite all right before this encounter.

We talked for a while, tried to settle down, and then met back in the dark. We were singing and hoping for materialization and there was nothing. We kept on singing, and still nothing. Sally and I were hanging onto each other almost crying, when finally the trumpet went up and Aenka spoke. I asked him, "My God, why did you do that . . . why did you let that man in?" And Aenka replied, *"High risk, high gain,"* adding that the man needed to come. A choice could have been made that would have changed his whole life. Aenka said the entities would not only take risks now but that they would do it again if they felt it was necessary or positive. I just didn't want to hear that and asked quickly if this experience disturbed the energy for the Darkroom. Aenka said, *"No."* He added, *"You must remember the group will be shaken. This experience may alter things for a while, not because of what this man did but because of the effect on the group members."*

Another shaky experience occurred when a woman turned the light on while the channel was still trancing. This woman had also been given permission by the entities to attend the meeting. We had 10 or 15 people in our meeting that night.

An entity appeared and offered her the opportunity for a private visit. I knew the woman had been told and introduced to what was happening in our meetings by the friend who had brought her to the group. The friend was a regular group member. When the visitor returned to the group from her private visit, she was very quiet. After a time she shared what the entity had said. What she reported sounded to me very distorted, and did not agree with what I, and others, had been taught regarding the same subject. One thing she said I knew flat out was incorrect, but I didn't say anything. I figured she would have her own experience. She came back for a second evening and went out again for a private visit. As she returned to the group I heard her say something like, "I have to show you the truth," or, "I have to prove the truth to you." She was talking directly to her friend who had introduced her to the group. With that, the overhead light went on. Everyone began shouting, "Turn out the lights." The entity who was in the room immediately bent over as if hit in the solar plexus and folded forward. We could see the entity crouched but still in a standing position in the middle of the room. Later, the woman claimed she had seen Jay in the nude. What I saw was an entity of an entirely different stature from Jay. Each person later shared what she or he saw to compare perceptions. None supported or affirmed her description. Naturally, people were very upset. We had never had anything like that happen before; the breaking of one of the basic guidelines. It was a very painful experience for all of us. When Jay came out of his trance, he was very weak. For the next few days Jay experienced a physical condition similar to having the flu. This experience with Jay's weakness supported what the entities had told us regarding possible danger to a channel should the energy be abruptly interrupted. That is, the effect on a channel is a weakening but not necessarily as life-threatening as some people believe.

As a result of these occurrences and subsequent threats of forced entry into our meetings, we simply stopped having visitors' nights' altogether. Our regular meetings were held less frequently. While up to this point our attitude had been to allow people to have their own experiences, we now began to recognize a need to be more cautious.

Critical and accusatory newspaper and magazine articles began to appear about our activities. We did not respond. The entities had told us truth needs no defense. I think if I didn't understand what I do about people's fears and reactions, I would have found it difficult to understand the accusations of fraud. But the articles nonetheless were very painful for all of us to read. Some who made accusations had been active in the Darkroom for months. Jay experienced much grief. People with whom he had spent hours and hours of free time turned on him. There were times all I wanted to say, was, "Leave us alone!" I never really let myself say that; I tried to understand what was happening. When anyone is personally involved in something it is difficult to be objective.

Combining personal reflections, talks with Jay, plus the input by the entities, I would like to share a few thoughts about what may have happened to change some of the group members' attitudes and beliefs. It may be that whatever some people experienced in their personal visits became so threatening to them the only way they could deal with it was to blame someone. People kept private much of what occurred in the personal visits. Entities in early meetings and throughout our activities stressed one only had to ask and they would immediately be returned to the group. There was never any forcing. Everything was by permission and with respect. I feel the entities would try to help people in whatever area was most valuable to them. Free choice was always emphasized. If someone did not want to even talk about a subject, all that was necessary was to say, "I don't want to talk about that," and that was the end of the subject.

I have no reason to doubt that what people said is real to them. Whether or not it is reality, I really do not know. To me, real is how we perceive something. Reality is how it truly is. And these are not always the same. I have never seen the entities do anything that was destructive or deceptive.

What is real or true for someone could be their honest experience and yet not be what other people consider reality. When the Darkroom was still large and open, sometimes people would come up outside the meetings and say Mario or Aenka told me I was to join your group, or Aenka told me this is what your group needed to do, etc. My response usually was, "Thank you, we'll check it out." In a later meeting we would mention to an entity that someone had told us such and such, and that an entity had said it. If what we reported was not accurate the entity would usually reply, *"I am not familiar with that individual's energy pattern."* Entities never put anyone down. This would be their way of saying to us there's nothing to discuss, the information did not come from them. This doesn't mean the people were making up what they said. It could well be they were tuning into their own spirituality, received some information, and distorted it in interpretation. If I asked Aenka about a particular statement supposedly said by him he often would state he was not familiar with the statement. I would then know it was not our Aenka, maybe an Aenka. It is not up to me to judge, it would not be fair to judge another's spiritual truth. What I can do, if I'm asked to be involved, is to check on what might be a common reference point and see what my truth is. Perhaps this is what was going on with some of the people who made the accusations. They were convinced what they were saying was real; it just wasn't everyone's reality.

Positive experiences have been numerous and the teachings of the entities have been very valuable to a number of people. In general the entities taught that an important focus for man is to tune into the general spiritual experience, making contact with the unobstructed in whatever way suits them and thereby getting in touch with the spiritual part of yourself. They shared also that while being in touch with spirituality was very important, it was not the first issue for us to deal with on earth. Regarding our development the important issue is to understand what destiny is. Human life is the first step in that destiny. We asked frequently what happens in the unobstructed between reincarnations. They would acknowledge the question saying, *"Yes, we'll talk about it in the future."* Emphasis was consistently placed on discussing physical life. However, they did tell us of experiences and occurrences on different steps or levels of development in the unobstructed and told us of other spiritual matters. These will be presented in part in another chapter and elaborated upon in a later volume. From time to time they'd talk about the over-all plan of human destiny. They spoke many times of the importance of the four basic aspects of our personality, what they called quadrants, and of the importance of intuition. They would talk at length about Christ and complete the teaching by reinforcing the focus of man's need to learn how to be at peace with himself and with others.

Many who came to the meetings didn't want to hear things about physical life and emotional growth. However, it made more and more sense to me personally that a person could not build a superstructure until they have laid their groundwork. One cannot use spirituality as an escape and have it to be true spirituality. While it is true the more sensitive a person is, the more they can feel the presence of entities around them, we all must integrate our lives physically, emotionally, intellectually, and spiritually.

There's a part of me that knows it is important to learn why we are here and to experience what is necessary. That is, to learn of man's evolution and purpose. I do believe one purpose of our particular group was learning to help ourselves and others touch and resolve unfinished emotional business. This enhances the awareness of our spirituality. Whether you see entities materialize or not, they are there and can impinge on you through your awareness in a meditative state or in other ways. Why many have not had the kinds of experiences we have had, I do not know. I don't think I will know exactly why until after I make the transition. Entities allow us to learn primarily on our own, and will not give information that interferes with personal destiny or needed experiences. Sometimes the generalities of many of their teachings can be quite frustrating. They often will feed back the issue in a guiding way to stimulate the person's own development. Perhaps our group happened because we were dumb or stubborn enough to sit for hours. In a way we were foolish enough not to be afraid to try. Perhaps a factor was that Jay and I had experienced considerable growth work and personal counseling so we were more open.

People have different expectations regarding spiritual experiences, and some latecomers to our group were disappointed. Sometimes an entity would appear that did not fit a particular image. At times there were appearances or presentations that brought awe to many in the group on those particular occasions. For some people that met their spiritual expectation. In my experience that is not what spirituality is. It certainly can be that, but it can be much more.

The entities would, I think intentionally, tell jokes and take a very light mood, doing silly things to shake us up a bit. Letting us know spirituality is not always super heavy, serious business with a somber mood. Yet if we would ask for prayers they would readily share one. This is one Aenka offered in December 1973. *"Forgive me, Father, I have been unfair to myself. I pray that I shall overcome this weakness and to love those facets within me that You so lovingly placed in my being."* The remainder of this book will give you some flavor of our experience and some of the teachings.

CHAPTER TWO
PHENOMENOLOGY AND PROOF

This chapter addresses issues regarding the reality of the materialization phenomenon. It includes comments from the entities in response to requests for proof.

While there were many occasions when the entities provided us the opportunity to reinforce our belief in their existence, in general those people demanding even more proof did not find it forthcoming. When we as a group were not seeking proof but were demonstrating positive curiosity, we were provided countless varieties of phenomena, which staggered our traditional belief systems and scientific minds. Those participants not willing to look at their doubts within themselves but who insisted on repetitive external proofs went unsatisfied.

A portion of a quotation from Aenka regarding repeated requests for more and more proof of the reality of materialized entities will be given here. The complete quotation can be found in the chapter entitled "Frequently Asked Questions." Aenka stated, *"If you rely upon an empirical method for belief in our existence you will never attain it because it falls out of the scope of the dimensions in which your five senses operate. To seek knowledge of the truth through the witnessing of phenomena, or even through what I might hope to teach you, is not possible. It must come from a personal experience gained through an inward searching and a trusting of one's self to recognize the truth when it is presented. Many minds say, 'But Christ offered proof through the performing of miracle" Indeed He did. And most continued to be skeptical and suspicious. He performed demonstrations in front of thousands. Yet at the time He was crucified there were only a handful of supporters who had glimpsed the truth within, and had gained the inner strength necessary to carry on under adversity."*

Some group members continued to request or suggest scientific instruments be brought in to attempt to measure changes in the channel's body or readings from the entities themselves. One night in responding yet again to this idea, an entity in a personal visit permitted his response to be taped and the group member shared the tape with us. The entity said with our current measuring devices it was pointless and he went on to say, *"If you are going to believe it, you are going to believe it. If it is positive for you, you will take advantage of it and apply it to your personal growth. If you doubt it you will continue to try to prove that it does not exist. You could bring in all of the CIA and FBI and continue to research, and every positive factor that you prove about its existence, its positive existence, there would still always be that scientific unknown that you would need to do more research on before you could really believe it. So would you prefer that we turn ourselves into a laboratory for examination or would you prefer that we continue with our intent—and that is to try to contact individuals that are truly interested in their personal development, and help them gain that without putting them in a goldfish bowl?"*

While the entities thus set a limit on their attempts to "objectively prove" their reality, they are not critical of those who want proof after proof after proof. They not only respect, but also encourage what they consider positive or healthy doubt. As an entity said one night, *"It is trickery that one fears so deeply, and that is why they have a deep emotional and psychological need to know what they are dealing with at all times. It is because of this trickery they cannot truly believe that the Darkroom is authentic . . . the mind is so accustomed to being tricked and fooled, and lied to."*

Some examples will now be given of the humorous, loving, or unique events, which occurred regularly. They are essentially anecdotal, as were examples in Chapter One. If the reader finds his belief stretched it is hoped he will nonetheless read on.

At one time a registered nurse in the group, fascinated by the cloning process involved in materialization, and in particular the reproduction of the speech mechanism, asked an entity if she could examine his mouth. She was curious about the peculiar sound of their voices. The entity allowed her to place her fingers in his mouth. She discovered he had a full set of teeth but that his tongue was very thin, pliable, and paper-like. She described the texture as similar to cellophane or thin plastic sheeting. She asked whether he could materialize a more human tongue. He left her for a moment and returned, then allowed her to touch his tongue again which she now found to be as her own.

One woman in the group for some reason was singled out for a special favor. On one particular evening a male entity approached her and placed a yellow rosebud in her outstretched hand. To those of us who had been in the Darkroom from the beginning, this bringing of a flower was a new experience. The rosebud proved to be damp and freshly picked. Each time this woman attended a subsequent meeting the entity brought her a yellow rose. At times it was a bud, at other times a full blossom. No yellow roses grew in the neighborhood.

One evening in June of 1973, Aenka appeared and

asked for a period of silence. A female entity had been appearing, but not with the frequency of Aenka or other male entities. She had danced about the room, never talking; her feminine outline very visible. Naturally, we had asked if it would ever be possible to touch her. This evening, following Aenka's request for silence, an unknown entity then brought us forward one by one and we had the opportunity to touch seven female entities who were now in the middle of the room. Some were tall, some were short; some young, some old. One female entity had the physical structure of a child about ten years old. It was a very awe-inspiring experience and allowed the group members during these still early days to further diminish their doubts.

A group member asking how he might respond to some still-doubtful people participating in the Darkroom received this answer from an entity. *"What they need to understand is if they feel that it is not true then they must accept this and work with it and choose not to come—and continue to believe what they feel to be true—rather than trying to prove that it is wrong . . . If it* [the Darkroom] *offers them something positive, work with that rather than the negative side of it, because it does not validate truth when you try to seek proof that it is wrong."*

The group curiosity about the process of materialization was increasing at a particular point in our group evolution. We wondered how this phenomenon compared to the scientific experiments with cloning. How do the entities accomplish it? We were most anxious to witness this miracle and asked Aenka for permission. He did not promise we would ever witness this, but witness it we did, and many times. The experience was so meaningful to me, and although I shared it in Chapter One, I would like to share it again. We sat in stunned silence one night as we observed a white mist about 18 inches in diameter appear on the floor at the doorway. This mist or cloud of ectoplasm drifted to the center of the room where we could all see it very clearly. As we stared, not daring to blink, the ectoplasm began to solidify. Slowly, a portion of the mist became denser and formed a small sphere at its center. As this process continued we would perceive the outline of shoulders and of a turban-wrapped head. First the head, then the shoulders took on a physical appearance. The entity, in a kneeling position, began to develop a fully formed, beautiful body. Arms still folded on his chest, he rose to one knee and then to a full standing position. We gasped as he unfolded his arms, palms up, and slowly moved his extended arms to the side, as if to demonstrate his love of God and of the group. Several members of our group were most fortunate in that they subsequently observed this incredible event as many as 14 times. No one has felt able to adequately describe their feelings regarding this experience. This phenomenon seems to me in some way to represent symbolically an essence of a perceptual spiritual experience.

There were only a few instances wherein the process of dematerialization was observed. One such instance occurred while an entity was dancing with a female member. In our eagerness to see him we brought the dim red light closer and he disappeared in her arms before our eyes. There was no puff of smoke; he was just gone.

After witnessing these processes we would ask they be repeated when new people joined the Darkroom. To our persistent requests for a promise about this impressive phenomenon, Mario stated, *"We will promise nothing other than the opportunity for you to share what you believe; that there is everlasting life. The concept, the idea of being born from the Source of Divinity; and, through the steps of destiny you take, you will again merge with the Source."*

Some of our group members, because of their fears and doubts, or lack of faith, were eager to observe the entities in brighter light. We were thrilled when first granted the opportunity to see an entity in light brighter than our darkened room offered. As mentioned in Chapter One, they allowed us to turn on a low red light for short periods. Although most male entities appeared with turbans, one particular entity had blond hair to his shoulders. Slowly entering the room, he seemed to have a little heavier than average build. His face was round, with what appeared to be scarring about the eyes. We were very excited and curious. The great love which came from the entity touched us all. Had we been allowed to reach out and hug him at that time, we certainly would have. He asked we all remain in our seats. He moved closer, enabling us to see his features distinctly. We were able to see him clearly for about ten minutes. We could see great love and acceptance in his eyes as he looked at each of us. This was the first of many encounters in the red light that we would enjoy with the entities. The entities continued to have fun with us from time to time and played jokes on us. During an intermission at one meeting the channel noticed his wedding ring had been removed. When the meeting resumed we questioned Aenka about it. He said it was in one of the women's pockets. She looked and said she did not have a pocket in the outfit she was wearing. Aenka said, ***"Oh no, in your big pocket."*** Later, we decided he was referring to her purse. Her purse was on the porch, 40 feet from the room where we met. Sure enough, we found the channel's ring on a key ring in her purse.

One night, we heard a noise in a very small closet in our meeting room. Don was near it playing his guitar. After he finished a song he pushed aside the sliding door and reached in and was startled when a hand reached out and shook his. Another evening an entity came and allowed us to feel his chest. The sternum, or breastbone, was extremely prominent. He had materialized a body having what is known as pigeon breast.

I believe I have previously stated that once we achieved full and strong materialization with clear voice, the phenomena per se decreased markedly. In response to a request for dramatic phenomena which some members thought might offer additional proof for those who doubted, Aenka said, ***"We continually put the emphasis on personal growth rather than the supernatural or the mind expanding phenomena that gives you a sense of awe and wonder that those things are possible. You can lose yourself in a world*** *of non-reality or fantasy that things could exist or possibly exist, and the knowledge would mean nothing to you without some application of the knowledge. So you can learn one simple fact about yourself and if by application it could give you a sense of fulfillment that would cause you to be a more dynamic individual."*

Many times when we were allowed to use our tape recorders we would be uncertain if they were working or of the status of our tapes. Since we were meeting in a darkened room, we could not visually inspect them. We were concerned about this because we didn't want to miss anything or record over anything previously recorded. Routinely, the entities would help us out. At first they offered to assist us at their initiative when they would discover us fumbling with our recorders; they would tell us if our machines were recording, how much time we had left on a side of a tape, etc. After this initial assistance, if we had any doubts or difficulties with our equipment, we would just ask and they would advise. They were never wrong.

Some who wanted to join the group were allowed to participate on visitors' night and were not encouraged or invited by the entities to continue. They were always given a personal explanation of why. An example of the gentle way the entities would present this issue is reflected in Aenka's statement one night to a visitor. *"I believe that your visit* [on visitor's night] *will cause you to check your destiny. You have a wisdom that will extend and become very meaningful to many lives. For you to become involved with this would cause conflict of your understanding, particularly for now. I believe that you are in the process of serious evaluation of yourself, and if you become involved with this it would cause this evaluation to be less meaningful to you."* This person then asked if that was why an entity had not come for him personally that evening. Aenka's response was, *"It would not be fair for you to become addicted to his presence. It would be easier for you not to return again for some time. Once you have visited with an entity personally it is very difficult not to return."*

Among those who asked to join our group were representatives of organizations, which at that time were conducting scientific studies of such phenomena. Like most others who asked to join the group, we chose to trust the entities' judgment for evaluation as to whether aspiring members or observers would be allowed to join us. Some observers or experimenters were allowed to join. Of those who came, some were disappointed when they found the entities to be so human-like physically. Others were upset because the entities would not allow the Darkroom to become a laboratory. They would not accept the entities' explanation that belief is not based upon outer proof.

Many people were surprised to find they were never asked to pay any money or to give some form of donation in order to participate. This was true for visitors' night as well as regular members. Some of those who remained after an experimental visit or two joined us in our struggle for personal growth and began to find rewards in helping others. They have many times over received the proof they originally sought. To those who did not remain, Aenka encouraged them, saying, "Believe that with which you are most comfortable."

Usually, we were granted permission to tape Aenka's and Mario's talks and retain these for future reference and enjoyment. Aenka was asked if there were other Darkroom groups such as ours and whether he ever materialized before another group. He answered, *"Heaven's no! All entities in every segment of human interest and endeavor form in groups to support those interests, which are constructive and positive for the betterment of your growth. All groups that organize for the purpose of generating positive energy sufficient that they may contact us directly gain our support for that which the majority of the group desires. This particular group was from the beginning a manifestation of self-support with the hope that information could be gained to understand one's relationship with himself, his fellowman, and his Creator."* He went on to say, *"I have accepted this group only because I have been associated with the energy patterns that study man's psychological development, and of course being particularly interested in its relationship to the Source and the importance of this balance, I took it upon myself to introduce you to my energy pattern. You shall find that all who have attended your group have specifically grown or gained with themselves psychological meanings and self-understanding. Other groups you may attend only learn about past lives, or of great masters who have taught, or become somewhat introduced to loved ones . . . All of you have been carefully selected to support what you have gained and learned, to pass on your knowledge to others, the better you may help them understand themselves, to bring harmony to their souls . . . it is not a coincidence that 1 chose this group or that I have chosen this channel. Your group will continue to be therapeutic in nature, physically and psychologically. You cannot possibly find your Facet of Divinity unless you are emotionally balanced. The search becomes too frustrating. So I say to you, find your self-love and you shall find your Creator."*

I will conclude this chapter with a comment made by an entity during a personal visit to an individual questioning the authenticity of the Darkroom. *"There is nothing more that we would like to do than to clearly and distinctly make it possible for you to really believe I am an entity here with a materialized body. The only part of this body that belongs to any one individual is a combination of energy and fragments of the molecular structure of the various individuals in the group . . . there is no convenient or permanent way that I can convince you that I am an entity and not the channel or anyone within the group . . . nor am I somebody who has come through the window or who has been paid or hired to talk to you here . . . I could possibly take you in there to the channel and let you drag the channel in here by the foot and let him sleep here before the two of us . . . I really do not believe that would prove anything to you . . . it might possibly prove one thing, that there is a possibility I am not the channel . . . and if I*

269

am not the channel, who am I?"

CHAPTER THREE
PERSONAL GROWTH—A FOUNDATION FOR SPIRITUAL DEVELOPMENT

As stated, once personal visits became a regular occurrence, we began to clearly experience a more serious direction in our meetings. It became even more evident the entities had a particular focus in mind, and they began to emphasize psychological and philosophical topics. This trend first began to be apparent in the extent to which entities would respond to certain types of questions. For example, as people persevered in asking questions about subjects such as past lives, the entities would give more limited and briefer answers. To questions regarding such issues as astral travel or life on other planets, the entities would also answer briefly, adding a comment to the effect that responding to such questions was not the purpose of this group. Aenka at one point stated that if individuals were interested primarily in these subjects perhaps they should seek another group. With the decrease in time spent on subjects such as past lives, out-of-body experiences, etc., some members did indeed leave the group. Questions from individual members regarding psychological issues and personal growth began to increase. The entities would respond to these issues, speak at length, and offer the opportunity for more frequent private visits. The private visits allowed us to ask very personal questions and the entities to elaborate in their responses. While some people would work on personal issues in the group with an entity, often members would do their personal work in private sessions. The entities always accepted their choice and respected confidentiality.

With the increase in personal visits and emphasis on personal issues, we became even more curious about who the entities were. Aenka explained that entities who came for personal visits might be a person's soulmate or one of their guides, but not necessarily. Soulmates were described as entities created together from the Source. By the Source, the entities were referring to God, the Creator, or Source of All Divinity. A guide was described as an entity who chose the assignment of helping an incarnated individual fulfill his physical destiny. This is done via impingement or the sending of thoughts or awarenesses through the individual's intuitive processes, for the purpose of assisting people in making more positive choices. The entities who materialized only for personal visits never gave presentations to the group as a whole. The entity would materialize, go out with the person they were there to visit, return with them, and dematerialize. Usually, several entities would visit during any one meeting, but the number varied quite. While Aenka and Mario worked in a counseling format with people in the group room and at times would go out for personal visits, they were also teachers who would talk to the group as a whole. With regularity Aenka would give talks to the group on subjects relating psychological and philosophical issues. Many times a philosophy of living, the purpose of life, and psychological processes were interwoven. Some attempts will be made to separate them here, but the reader should be aware they are closely interwoven. A few quotations from the entities will be given here, and other teachings are elaborated on in a subsequent chapter. Aenka began to talk to us of the levels, or steps, of spiritual evolution. He spoke about the earth and taught that in spiritual evolution, our physical life is the first step and the most important. He emphasized the benefits of loving our physical body, the physical vehicle which houses a Facet of Divinity, or our soul, and spoke briefly of the seven steps or levels we must complete in pursuit of our chosen destiny. There are certain tasks and learnings to be experienced in each level. The experiences necessary for completion of step one can only be achieved while in the physical body, and involve the integration of personal development with all aspects of our physical being. The first step must be completed in the body. While it is possible that someone could complete step one during a single lifetime, reincarnation provides as many

271

opportunities as needed.

The other steps are completed in the unobstructed or spiritual universe. We may work on steps two, three, four, and begin the fifth in the unobstructed universe, but we cannot complete the fifth until we have completed the first or the physical step. In the unobstructed between physical lives, in addition to working on steps two through five, we personally evaluate our own progression and contemplate our self-chosen requirements for completion of the first step. Each time we reincarnate it is our choice in furtherance of step one or physical destiny. Someone asked if we progress spiritually when we are in a physical life. Aenka replied, *"You are progressing spiritually because you are working on the first step of spiritual evolution. Do not separate the spiritual from the physical; they are inseparable. You cannot live in prayers, you cannot lose yourself in spirituality or religion; you cannot escape reality. You cannot escape physical responsibility. Your responsibility on step one is your physical being, your physical and psychological development. While doing so you will recognize this lesson and improve your knowledge of spirituality, and the spiritual facet within you."* Someone asked when you finish step one, what would you have accomplished. Aenka said, *"You will have accomplished the most important step of the seven, for it is the most difficult."* We asked when you leave the physical step do you have to come back again. Aenka answered, *"When you have completed all the experiences physically and psychologically and handled them well, then it is not necessary to return."*

This prompted someone to ask about the relationship between spiritual evolution and ego. Aenka replied, *"Well, of course, ego is the feeling of pride in your individuality. Should it be rhythmic and naturally felt, it is wonderful to feel pride. But it is negative to feel arrogant. False pride has always been supported by arrogance. It must be supported by arrogance, because it has no value. It is fear that causes the self-doubt. You must realize this*

272

subject is so difficult to speak of because it is so simple. There is little to know really about yourself. Without fear and guilt it is so simple. Life is so simple. It is beautiful. When you see an individual who truly enjoys life, observe their movements, watch their faces and you shall know. You shall feel the radiation of the beauty from them. If you are in the presence of an individual who is frustrated with life, you shall feel this frustration, and you shall feel uncomfortable in their presence. Their arrogance is supported by the superiority of false aggression, and of false extroversion. They tend to build what they consider to be an ego more powerful and more destructive than one can imagine. In so doing, they approach all those in life with an arrogant manner, with a taste of arrogance that is quite bitter. A true phony is an arrogant person."

Aenka continued to be our main teacher, and his lectures helped us understand the importance of dealing with our emotions and our personal growth as a foundation for spiritual evolution. When asked about natural and unnatural emotions Aenka replied, *"Hate is an unnatural emotion. All of you have felt hate, unless your aggression has been positive and balanced with submission. Hate is a product of congealed and unexpressed anger. It is literally impossible to hate should one express their natural emotions. Anger as a natural emotion is always in proportion to the situation. If anger is not expressed, it is suppressed, becomes congealed, then it erupts into seething hate. Tolerance is not an emotion; it is the product of emotions. It is the product of understanding and the basic emotion love."*

Over a period of meetings, the entities taught us that the basis for all negativity, or unnatural behavior, is programmed into our minds from infancy until approximately six years of age. There is no inborn evil or negativity. Negativity stems from traumatic conditioning that comes to us in varying degrees. It can come from our parents, family, friends, or other people with whom we have relationships during those formative years. This is not to say that our friends and loved ones failed us or did something wrong. Their own emotional responses, after all, came from their parents and outer authorities and the way they were programmed. Thus it has been passed on through generation after generation. In this manner " . . . the sins of the father are visited upon the sons."

A tragic mistake many of us make is to accept that not very much can be done about this cyclic process of passing on negativity. We then become victims of our own limitations and of others who continue to say we cannot cause significant changes in our personality structure. I believe, and I have seen evidence to support my belief, that not only are such personal changes possible, but they are available to all who have the courage to follow the guidelines the entities teach us.

Aenka explained the meaning of positive and negative behavior as follows: *"Positive is natural behavior and negative is unnatural. To merely disagree is not necessarily negative. An unnatural behavior creates a negative environment or an unnatural environment that usually causes disharmony or discomfort to the individual. You may call it an unnatural behavior or act, or a negative behavior or act. The reason it is better understood in these terms, rather than right or wrong, is that there is something so cruel and definite about it. It* [right or wrong] *has an air of superiority about it, and is usually associated with an unrhythmic nature."*

A follow-up question was asked, "What is it that makes a behavior unnatural?" His answer, *"What makes an act unnatural is that it is unnatural to deliberately, or with intent, commit an act that would harm another individual— such as revenge. Revenge is an unnatural behavior. It is not a natural emotion. Therefore, it creates an unnatural environment that causes negativity. Any behavior detrimental to your growth or the growth of your fellowman is unnatural—and produces or creates a negative energy that will leave both persons uncomfortable. Neither person will gain any positive experience through unnatural behavior. At the time it may feel or be very gratifying, or seem to be gratifying to you. However, if your behavior is causing pain to another individual, then it can only be unnatural. An exception would be those instances where the individual is responding to his own fears and guilt. In response, he may project upon you his negativity or unnatural behavior.*

Accordingly, in these situations your own behavior is not necessarily unnatural. It is for you to evaluate and allow your own wisdom to determine whether your own behavior is natural or unnatural. You will always base this upon the laws, the universal laws that govern the social creature. You would have the tendency to be governed by fears and guilts rather than choices and judgments. A feeling of spiritual togetherness offers a blending of personality that is harmonious . . . negative thoughts are usually responsible for fear. Without negative thoughts there would be no fear. To be truly free you must accept all feelings. And of course when you identify, accept, and externalize a feeling it becomes harmless and releases part of you."

One night, in response to Aenka's talking about man's need to resolve his own fears in order to live a more positive life, I asked him to talk about positive qualities such as patience. He stated, *"A wonderful quality; should you permit me the evening, I would be most happy to discuss patience with you. There are several ramifications of emotional traits that will induce malfunction of the individual's psychological balance. This causes the inability to be patient. The more kindness you feel toward yourself, the more patient you are with others and the less critical. If you are critical of others, you are impatient with yourself and with others."*

Someone asked if one could be too submissive. Aenka answered, *"You certainly can be too submissive. It is most likely that the individual with this behavior would endure hardships rather than speak out against them. That is not patience. That is the negative part of endurance. It is that you suffer to save yourself the embarrassment of aggressive acts.*"

Another evening Aenka elaborated on submission and patience. "*Submission is to submit to those things you cannot change. Patience is deciding the necessity. Patience is the quality of accepting natural finality and natural procedure. The individual knows exactly how long it takes the clock to go around—it takes exactly 60 seconds, or 60 minutes. But an impatient individual does not accept this. They would be too impatient to accept the natural phenomena of time to come. Submission is the quality of not caring whether it passes by or not. You submit to it whether it is right or wrong. But of course, there are many factors involved in this procedure. You must realize patience is a quality of waiting for certain natural laws to take their course. Submission is the ability to submit and accept the conditions or the result of certain laws, facts, or actions. There is a time to submit and accept that which you cannot change. There are also times when you must use positive aggression and attack those obstacles in your path. Yet you should not be continually submissive to the dominance of others, or you would continually endure, and never progressively move forward. Being aggressive does not mean you abuse your rights, but you must stand up for your rights and use your aggression with wisdom. Submit to those things you cannot change, and have the patience to understand them correctly. Patience involves your mind, decision and indecision, and the opportunity to function between decision and indecision.*"

He went on to speak of love. "*My friends, you are not born into this world to experience love. Of course, you do experience it; you must experience it. Love is not a privilege; it is a right. It is a God-given right to experience love. You cannot experience understanding until you experience love, and this love shall be experienced from birth to adolescence. If it is not, the mind is often crippled. It is then difficult for the adolescent to change into adulthood and live successfully because positive, rhythmic or balanced patterns which should have developed, begin to*

276

take on a negative aspect supporting negative action."

At this point someone asked, "Then, love is really the answer to everything?" Aenka replied, *"That's a fact. Was it not Christ who said love is everything; love thy neighbor? All His teachings were based on love, and as they began to accept His teachings, they began to mellow and feel tolerance toward each other, forgiving each other and not being so critical. You are only so critical with others as you are with yourself. Try it some time. For every fault you find in your fellowman, you will find a magnified fear of this fault in yourself."* As Aenka concluded this particular passage I remember the group being quite silent, each of us contemplating the wisdom and beauty of his words.

Aenka talked frequently about the facets of personality, personality structure, and man's destiny. Though many people in the group did not have training in psychology, I was impressed that the group members could absorb and apply the group methods Aenka presented. Aenka talked about the quality of interdependence. *"A wonderful quality, because you can truly feel interdependence but you cannot use this quality until you balance positive dependence with positive independence. Without this balance, you can only respond with fear or anxiety. Why should an adult feel fearful? It is because psychologically there are so many facets of the personality structure still arrested on the autoerotic level of development. It is difficult to believe you are walking around in an adult body fully developed, functioning on the level of a three year old. I have not accused one of you. Yet does it not stand reasonable to believe that a child who is continually pulling away from authority to venture into the wilderness, only to be scolded, will be instilled with fear? Even as early as two years old he will be filled with fear and anxiety toward authority. This type of fear is learned. It is not a natural development. It is forced upon a child to be fearful of independence. You have been made to feel insecure within your own environment, and this fear becomes so intensified you do not allow the young adult to cast it off. Protective devices give coverings for the development of your personal qualities. It is as a snake's delicate skin. At the age of the young adult, you should shed it like a snake would shed its skin and forever be free of the controlling, frightening attitudes which forever interferes with your adult behavior."*

Also that same evening Aenka talked about adolescence and the great stirring of the spiritual interest. *"Without the fears of childhood, feelings would have developed and blossomed into the proper recognition of the Facet of Divinity within. Without the development of the spiritual quadrant and recognition of the other three quadrants, you would be hampered in your functioning as an independent individual."*

On another evening, Aenka was asked to discuss a blessing. He said, *"It is to be blessed with, or by, something; it is not an event. It is something no individual can bestow on another by force. Blessing is an act of love. I cannot bless you unless you are responsive. Blessed, indeed, are those who believe in themselves first and then in their fellowman. Without believing in yourself, you cannot possibly believe in your fellowman. If you possess these qualities, indeed you are blessed. No force, no energy can bless you without your will to be blessed. If you are open and receptive to accept, you will be blessed abundantly and so shall you bless others. Evaluate your sincere desire, commonly referred to as prayer; evaluate your prayers and make them sound and sensible. There is a quality of science that must be obeyed. The universal and immutable laws govern the heavens and all matters in it. All that has a molecular structure is governed by universal immutable law and it shall not be disobeyed. Because of your neighbor's needs for a spiritual journey, he may require more varied things than you. Cannot he be blessed with this without your being jealous or feeling slighted? Recognize your own blessings not by comparing, but by your needs. Your desire is not a quality to evaluate your needs. You evaluate your needs by your total psychological structure. Yes, indeed you are blessed; I too, am blessed by your existence. Without you I would not have the opportunity to speak with you this evening. Each of you is so dear to me. If I could I would bless each of you, and if I do, it is because you have accepted whatever truth you have gained with my existence. If you have gained with what I have offered you, indeed I am blessed."*

This was the first time we heard the phrase, "I have been blessed by your existence." We would begin to recognize this as Aenka's way of saying goodnight. He told us the entities greeted each other in the unobstructed by saying, *"I am blessed by your existence."* We now looked forward to hearing his voice and having the opportunity to receive this greeting.

CHAPTER FOUR
TEACHINGS REGARDING PERSONALITY STRUCTURE AND DEVELOPMENT

It has been described how our group began to realize our main goal was to be that of personal growth. The entities provided didactic information at their initiative, responded to our questions regarding psychological functioning, and actually conducted personal counseling sessions. Not surprisingly, these activities resulted in our receiving much information from the entities about their beliefs and attitudes regarding psychological functioning and the development of healthy and unhealthy personality function. The entities seemed to emphasize generally the more a person has their psychological house in order, the more able they are to become aware of the spiritual dimension of their life and to develop their spirituality.

This chapter presents a condensed summary of the entities' teachings regarding healthy and unhealthy emotional functioning, descriptions of the basic structure of the personality and personality development from their point of view, together with some comments on their counseling techniques. A book presenting their teachings in a more elaborated and complete form is presently in process and will soon be published.

In our early days during one meeting when there was much laughter and joyful feeling a member was prompted to ask if laughter could interfere with the activities or harmony of the group. Aenka's response was, *"Laughter is one of the highest forms of spirituality." This* response encouraged us to begin to ask more questions regarding other emotions, feelings and attitudes, etc. At times, Aenka's response was limited to the specific question, at other times he would use a question as a springboard and launch into a lecture. Aenka described the basic natural emotions as fear of falling and loud noises, anger, grief, love, and jealousy. Other feelings and emotional responses are derivatives of those. He would contrast these natural emotions with their distortions, such as hate being congealed anger and pity being a distortion of genuine compassion, an aspect of love. Compassion offers true emotional support rather than "feeling sorry" for another.

According to Aenka, *"All your natural emotions, should they be in harmony with their opposites, would allow all negativity to be washed away and then you would live in harmony. There would be no hate or laziness. Laziness is a negative expression of distorted submission. Overbearing behavior is a negative expression of aggression. Anxiety is a direct derivative of guilt and fear . . . you should not confuse joy and grief as one being negative and one positive, for they are both positive. This is an example of qualities that are rhythmic, as the ebb and flow of the tide. You cannot have one without the other." We* were taught man's true nature is one of self-worth and self-confidence with pride and respect for others. Such a person would be involved with the positive attributes of life, and love for his neighbor as himself.

In the sections that follow, the reader will find considerable similarity between the teachings of the entities and some systems of thought developed by various psychiatrists, psychologists, philosophers, etc. Some of the material shared by the entities was similar to that received by Jay and Wes when they voice channeled. Other material was very different. When we asked about the difference in accuracy between voice channeling and materialization, we were again advised voice channeling is at best 80% accurate. Regarding the similarities of information from different channels or sources the entities responded with a familiar quotation. Truth, the entities said, is as . . . *"A rose is a rose is a rose . . ."*

It is suggested similarities found herein be viewed as a function of truth emerging from different orientations. Certainly in the material presented here there is no intention to be totally unique, nor is plagiarism intended or involved. A number of readers will no doubt see similarities to some of the teachings and thinking of people such as Freud, Carl Jung, Karen Horney, Fritz Kunkel, Fritz Perls, to name a few. This brief list is not meant to be exhaustive regarding similarities to the teachings of the entities, but offers a small sample. The entities also explained some concepts are mutually 'discovered' due to the presence of the Universal Center of Knowledge and the functions of intuition and impingement.

One night, Aenka drew a cross in the air with his trumpet symbolizing four quadrants. He identified them as physical, emotional, intellectual, and spiritual. Each quadrant has a specific purpose or function. In general, Aenka taught that basic attitudes about life and living are programmed into the child before the age of six. It is on this foundation man builds his behavior and continues that behavior until he makes a change. We have a magnificence in a potential form. As we acquaint ourselves with an overall picture, we see the self within us in a state ever changing. This is truly what growth is about. Certain qualities manifest from each of the four quadrants. Some of them will be discussed in the following paragraphs. I have synthesized and condensed much material into the following formal presentation.

The Physical Quadrant

The purpose of the physical quadrant is acceptance of physical realities. This is reinforced by input of the five senses. The action of the physical quadrant is acceptance of the realities of daily life. The physical quadrant is first rooted as an instinctual drive for survival and physical growth in the child. What the child sees, hears, touches, tastes; how his or her body responds, becomes the child's primary source of information. Thus, the five senses pave the way to relate to the physical reality of environment. The child will relate from these attitudes as an adult or until they have been changed. The sex drive emanates from the physical quadrant. The objective of survival in the adult encompasses survival of the species.

The physical quadrant links the five senses to the body, encompasses the ability to accept our physical nature, and allows us humility with personal uniqueness. Each person is different physically, emotionally, mentally and spiritually. Each one of us has the uniqueness of a personality different from all other human beings, much as oak leaves from the same tree are similar, yet each is unique. There is humility in this awareness, rather than the arrogance of superiority, which stimulates competing and comparing. Patience from the physical quadrant would allow one time to wait for change and the courage to be imperfect. Man's awareness of growth is a never-ending process that comes from the physical quadrant with the awareness of change.

The qualities found in the physical quadrant are submission and extroversion. Extroversion is the quality of warm outgoingness and moving toward the acceptance of others. This outgoingness provides us with an ability to communicate, to speak, and to interact on a physical level. Extroversion orients one toward the environment as opposed to one's inner world. One must have both an orientation in the direction of the outer world plus the movement toward it to be able to interact successfully and satisfy physical needs. Extroversion can become negative when one involves themselves in the outer world to run away from their inner self. Aloneness then becomes equated with loneliness.

Submission is that quality in the physical quadrant recognized as acceptance or patience. This quality is expressed in the attitude "this is how things are for now." Man must accept certain limitations in his environment. The healthy developing child learns limitations and begins to learn submission and patience. Submission in a positive sense refers to an acceptance of conditions that, at a given time, one cannot change. The quality of patience goes hand in hand with positive submission. Patience is required when one must stay in a situation that cannot be changed. Thus, patience facilitates the ability to be submissive in a positive sense. This concept of submission is different from the more accepted one in which submission is thought of in a negative sense; a person unwillingly "giving in" to another person and/or situation or "gritting their teeth" and enduring a situation or relationship they do not want to be in but feel they cannot escape from.

The Emotional Quadrant

Relationships are the purpose of the emotional quadrant, and the action has the objective of integrating feelings in focusing on interactions or relationships with self and others. The sex drive from the physical quadrant is added to and enhanced by the aspects of love and concern, which stem from the emotional quadrant. The emotional quadrant endows the individual with the need to belong so that he is strongly influenced by family standards and thus becomes socialized. In later years, the individual who has achieved a positive sense of belonging also has the desire to make a commitment to another human being or cause. The great need from the emotional quadrant is to belong. The child recognizes this at an unconscious level as the need to be part of the family. Later this is recognized as one's need to be part of a group, still later a part of the universe.

The small child wants to please their father or mother, yet does not have the awareness of good or bad because he has not learned to be 'bad.' His feelings of bad have only to do with the disapproval of the adults around him. His great desire is to belong, to be loved and to be a part of. He will respond to unconditional love and firm, fair, consistent discipline. Dependence on outer authority exists in the small child who is aware intuitively he cannot function without the care and protection of the adults. Children who are given no care, love or protection will die either figuratively or literally. The quality of conformance on the adult level manifests in the ability to accept, for example, that laws are made for the good of all and must be respected as the rights of others. It would be balanced with nonconformance in the ability of realizing that certain actions might be appropriate for one person and not for another. Each of us has many choices, particularly if they do not infringe on the rights of others. The quality of dependence in the adult becomes interdependence and allows relationships to grow and mature. Dependence refers to the capacity to rely on an outside source for satisfaction of various physical and psychological needs. Dependence is a personality quality that is appropriate at earlier stages of development before the individual has the capacity to become independent and also ultimately interdependent. Dependence becomes a negative quality if one stays fixated at that stage throughout one's life and never develops the capacity to rely on themselves for need of satisfaction.

An example of negative dependence would be a woman who has been raised by a very controlling and domineering father who never allowed her to make independent decisions or perform independent actions. These women fairly consistently marry husbands who basically keep them in the same emotional position as did their father. They know nothing of the family finances and how to handle them. All the major decisions are made by the husband. Should he die prematurely, these women suffer a catastrophic loss and are unable to handle any financial transactions because they never were encouraged to learn. This type of situation is commonly seen in grief counseling with widows who feel totally lost and devastated as a result of the combination of the loss and lack of emotional independence. They are incapable of making even the smallest decision and are often unaware of the tremendous anger, which their "dependent state" prevented them from expressing. They have spent their lives fixated at a child-like level of dependence. This is different from one who decides to go along with a group, set of standards, etc., because this is what they want to do. Negative emotions do not play a role in motivating positive conformance.

An illustration of positive conformance would be an individual who smokes cigarettes having to curtail his habit in portions of public buildings where smoking was not allowed. The individual would conform to the laws without anger or resentment. He would wait to smoke until he was in an area where there were no laws banning it and other individuals did not indicate his smoking was objectionable (e.g., in a restaurant).

Negative conformance is associated with a sense of resentment and feelings of fear and anger. An example would be an individual who acts like the rest of the group when he really does not want to because he is afraid of being rejected if he does not conform to its standards.

We often call it love when we overprotect our children and disguise it as loving concern. But, in fact, we are projecting our own anxieties, guilts, and insecurities onto the children. Love from the emotional quadrant has the flavor of nurturance and caring, a giving freely to another of one's warmth and physicalness. Yet it takes possibly the greatest amount of true genuine love to see someone dissolve in tears at a time of severe distress without having the need to put your arms around them and say, "Everything is going to be fine." Such comfort can be a projection of our own inability to tolerate tears and pain in a fellow human being. By putting our soothing arm around them indiscriminately we often prevent them from externalizing their pain so they take it home with them. This type of band-aid treatment may leave the individual in a position where they have to seek counseling at a later date due to their un-externalized emotions. A good example of another type of band-aid treatment is when parents are informed in the emergency room of a general hospital that their child has died. Instead of allowing them to externalize their feelings in a safe, secure, protected and caring environment, all too often we fill them with sedatives and call it 'love.'

To illustrate a state of healthy interdependence, consider a woman who has been raised to develop the ability to think and act independently, her source of authority coming from within herself. Upon marriage, she and her husband could decide who would perform which tasks. If they decided it was to be the husband who handled the family finances, she still would be knowledgeable of their status. In the event of his death she would have the skills necessary to deal with financial reality and thus be able to function independently. However, while they were together they would perform a division of labor between them based on their mutual assessment of who could best function in a given capacity.

The Intellectual Quadrant

Thinking is the function of the intellectual quadrant. The action is directed against ignorance, outdated attitudes, or outmoded behaviors, in order to bring about change. The intellectual quadrant has the basic drive of supporting survival by reasoning and is its purpose. We recognize this drive for knowledge as need and desire to know.

The intellectual quadrant contains the qualities of aggression and nonconformance. Aggression provides the energy to attack obstacles in one's path for survival and development. Positive aggression would not be directed toward an individual, but against problems preventing the fulfillment of destiny and the expression of one's unique abilities. Nonconformance is a quality manifesting in the child even at the age of two. The child is beginning to recognize his own feelings of independence, and uses the quality of nonconformance to find a new way to express himself. This phenomenon has nothing to do with negative rebellion so common in our society today, where it is too often "hurrah for me, and to hell with you!" In this latter defiance and negative rebellion, all attitudes of society and basic norms are tossed out the window. Such attitudes and actions are not based on good judgment but on the idea one can do as he jolly well pleases. The quality of nonconformance, used constructively, is based on good judgment and development of one's uniqueness and making one's own choices rather than simply swallowing whole something that is provided outwardly by an authority. A new life style is adapted appropriate for each individual and his environment.

When aggression is distorted, people attack each other and act in a violent fashion which is out of proportion to the actual situation. Aggression properly channeled can also be called assertiveness. The line between distorted (negative) and natural or healthy (positive) aggression can be drawn when one differentiates between actions which protect and assert one's rights, ideas, and actions and those that infringe on another's rights, physical self, property, etc. A simple illustration of positive aggression is to be able to say 'No' firmly when someone makes demands on you that are unacceptable. Nonconformance means to find a new way.

An example of negative nonconformance would be a group of teenagers who raid father's bar and decide to get blasted while the parents are gone for the weekend. Their behavior is a result of the parents' constant nagging and preaching about teenagers' vices and the parents setting a poor example by having a few martinis after they come home from work. Youngsters who watch examples like this will often rebel against the discrepancy between parents' preaching and their poor behavioral example by getting stoned on weekends and encouraging visiting friends to do the same. A participant at a teenage party who can understand their peers' behavior but has no need to act out in a resentful way will simply not join them in excessive drinking. They have enough good judgment and courage not to participate or conform.

From the intellectual quadrant can come courage to combat obstacles in the path of our individual destinies and to take step-by-step actions to achieve our goals. This would be true whether the person were in academic pursuits, business, sports, etc. Man would have the courage to combat the obstacles, the disappointments and the many problems that life presents. Persons choosing effective forms of psychotherapy, those involved in our Darkroom experiments, and others in their own ways find the courage for self-change and begin to more healthily use the quality of nonconformance. They allow themselves to move against old ways of behavior that are no longer appropriate. It generates the courage to change when distorted behavior patterns bring pain, frustration, feelings of inadequacy and nonfulfillment.

The Spiritual Quadrant

Intuition is the function of the spiritual quadrant, with the action of inner direction, inner awareness, or finding out "Who am I?" This includes creative processes and the recognition of intuitive hunches or flashes. The deeper hunger from the spiritual quadrant, to know one's Creator, manifests early in adolescence with stirrings of such questions as, "Why am I here, what is my destiny, what is my purpose?" By the time of puberty and adolescence, the young adult has hopefully moved from self-centeredness and early autoerotic orientations to the recognition he or she is one among many similar creatures, yet retaining uniqueness and awareness of a specific purpose. The great hunger to know one's creator includes a sense of 'knowing' that something more exists beyond one's self. Early man, with no organized religious beliefs, across many cultures, shared the experience of awareness of existence outside his physical being. They shared the hunger to discover what this was. I believe this was the basis for the world's religions.

The spiritual quadrant has within it the qualities of independence and introversion. Independence manifests itself in the child when he or she begins to be aware they are not part of the parent figures, but rather a unique and independent individual on their own. Early awareness of this quality occurs as the child takes his first steps. Taking these steps, he becomes more independent and the quality is one of moving away from and beginning to feel his own self-worth and his own ability. As a person matures they develop more of the quality of introspection. This introspection helps us to balance outgoing interactions or extroversion. We begin to listen to ourselves, and to listen to what may be impinged upon us. The qualities of introversion and independence become stronger as the child develops and moves into adolescence.

Of the four parts of the personality structure, the spiritual quadrant is the last to fully unfold. The developing awareness of our spiritual essence and its manifestations occurs during adolescence. This is the time when an individual is working on crystallizing their identity—they are striving to establish their independence as an individual. The only exception to the awakening of the spiritual essence in adolescence is in the event of a child approaching death. If a life-threatening illness occurs prior to adolescence there will be premature awakening of spiritual awareness. This occurrence is apparent in spontaneous drawings of children.

Independence in the spiritual quadrant is the quality of depending on one's self rather than others for need of satisfaction. Independence becomes a negative quality when one goes to the extreme position of "I don't need anybody, I can do it all by myself." In the developmental sequence of dependence, independence, and interdependence, one must master the first two in order to successfully interact with the environment.

In reality, man is interdependent with his fellowman and his environment. Therefore it is important an individual recognize there are appropriate times to be dependent or independent, then he can be comfortable with both of these qualities and arrive at interdependence.

A person who has successfully mastered the stages of dependence and independence and has truly become interdependent would be comfortable being taken care of when they were ill and unable to care for themselves. While they were temporarily dependent they would not feel anxious or guilty about their situation. However, as they became healthier, they would use positive assertiveness to express and act on their ability to do more things on their own. This would be communicated to those about them without resentment or anger.

The quality of love stemming from the spiritual quadrant is associated with faith and trust in another human being's ability to master their own obstacles. It is a good example to say that genuine, true unconditional love from a mother would be that of a mother willing to put training wheels on her child's bicycle. However, she would be just as willing to remove them, and have a sense of pride and joy when she felt the child was ready to master the skill of riding without their aid. The quality of humility from the spiritual quadrant allows man to know he is one with the human race, and yet one with the Creator. Man recognizes his uniqueness and also his sameness. Within man is a Facet of Divinity, a soul that binds all humans together.

Counseling Techniques

The entities presented several general techniques to achieve positive emotional health. These techniques were evident in the processes used to help the Darkroom participants identify basic personality attitudes associated with a variety of problems. Aenka encouraged working with feelings. He stressed the need to express feelings of fear, anger, guilt and grief, etc. Their teachings supported verbalizing and externalizing emotions associated with earlier life experiences responsible for the distortions of our positive qualities. The entities not only helped participants with personal growth, but also from the beginning were willing to teach therapists to utilize these techniques. Some therapists and counselors applied these methods. They would continue to ask about specific methods, techniques or approaches that might be even more advantageous in helping specific clients after they discovered that the teachings were indeed effective. In the Darkroom, the entities have helped people reach a depth of feeling that is very impressive, helping them drain what the entities have referred to as a "pool of repressed emotion."

One therapist commented on applications of her Darkroom experiences as follows, "In general I learned to treat my clients as important, unique human beings with something very special to offer. Sometimes we needed to look for what that might be . . . I learned to care in a genuine, real way for the people that I work with . . . something I learned the importance of in the Darkroom that I now use in my therapy with others is to create a safe place so that I really am worthy of their trust. They can risk expressing feelings that perhaps have never been expressed before—guilts and fears of many years. Another important aspect was to learn that a therapist best serves as a resource person but not as a replacement for the client's capability, ability and potential." Aenka was asked to comment on growth work in a group setting. He suggested each individual be allowed to express emotions without comment by others in the group and without confrontation, each person having a turn to verbalize and/or physically express to the extent he or she felt capable. He did suggest a knowledgeable moderator be present to passively monitor the activity, present basic guidelines, and ensure no one is allowed to act destructively towards another. The group was to be supporting and accepting.

The entities also offered guidance in the development of a unique form of group therapy dramatizing the traumatic situations that are responsible for repressed feelings. In this specialized form of psychodrama they suggested a realistic approach, recreating the original situation and allowing the individual to express his or her feelings as they felt them. The individual should be permitted to move from emotion to emotion without interference or comments from the director or therapist. This technique has been developed into a system known as the Barham Method of Psychodrama, and I have systematized and officially named it such. It differs from traditional methods of psychodrama in several ways. One of the most interesting differences is the use of meditation or visualization to facilitate correlation and evaluation of experiences after externalization of the feelings. The participant correlates his or her responses and behavior at the time of the original traumatic situation to their adult behavior, seeking insight and active relationships between the traumatic experience and current difficulties. A logbook or personal journal is often used to assist in processing this information bridging the past and the present. This Barham Method of Psychodrama is elaborated on in a forthcoming book.

The entities stressed that by resolving fears and guilts associated with damage to the basic personality structure, man can indeed be reborn. He then can utilize his qualities in a positive way. Man can live a life that will bring pleasure, not pain, and meet the conflicts of life with a feeling of strength and determination as he proceeds and searches for the completion of his or her destiny. Life can become a challenge, as it was intended to be, rather than a threat. Above all, the new awarenesses we learned in the Darkroom awakened in many of us a new pathway to expanded communication with a higher self. The path was and is not an easy one. It is covered with the underbrush of fears and guilts, and is at times a painful path to follow.

CHAPTER FIVE
HEALING

As briefly mentioned in the chapter on our early experiments and experiences in the Darkroom, there were several entities who administered healing processes to group members. One of these entities, Mario, came to be a frequent and welcomed visitor. He demonstrated considerable healing skill in addition to functioning as a personal counselor and teacher regarding philosophy and spiritual development. Since the channel had voiced an interest in healing, and particularly since he could not participate while channeling, the group was prompted to ask in-depth questions. This chapter will be an introduction to healing processes as taught and demonstrated by the entities. It includes quotations from Mario, and leans heavily on teachings and practices of Jay in his healing work.

This chapter is only an introduction to healing. The reader is urged not to consider it as a manual presenting basic techniques. In a later publication different aspects of healing processes, energies involved, various body systems, relationships to psychological distortions, etc., will be discussed in more detail.

There are three dimensions or types of healing processes: physical, psychic, and spiritual. Man can learn to influence and channel healing energies in the physical and psychic dimensions, but not in the spiritual dimension. Spiritual healing is a miracle. As Mario stated, *"A miracle can only come from the Source. We in the unobstructed can only deal with the reality that exists in the physical."* Spiritual energy cannot be manipulated, harnessed, handled, or managed by man. Man does have the God-given ability to invoke it. He does this through prayer, through desire; but man is not a channel for spiritual energy. This energy is transmitted directly from the Source to the recipient. It is an energy that always remains outside the healer. Spiritual energy has the power and the right to disregard genetic and universal laws in order to bring about a complete change.

Healing with physical energy involves an actual physical energy produced within the body of every human being. In this process, the healer applies his own energy to help balance and unblock the recipient's energy. In psychic healing, the healer channels psychic energy and applies it through the processes of visualization and imagination. This also influences the physical energy of the recipient.

Mario has taught of the interrelatedness of the four quadrants of the personality and their effect on our physical wellbeing. He states, *"It is very difficult to communicate the truth of the simplicity of physical life, about the true beauty. Life is so simple and so beautiful but within it has been designed some of the most magnificent and fantastic challenges the human specie of the animal kingdom has ever witnessed. There are only two enemies the human being has: fear and guilt. Fears and guilts feed only on negativity. Try to understand the nervous system, understand the energy, the spiritual and psychic energy that flows through your beautiful bodies. All quadrants are involved in physical healing. Primarily, it is a physical/psychic phenomenon; it is with the mind that one directs the healing forces, the healing energy. The social creature was designed to be interdependent, and each one designed to have the inherent ability to help their fellowman in need. That does not mean every living being in the village will take an interest in, or be specifically interested in, healing. It is like every child in a household will not be a carpenter or a plumber. But it does not mean that they could not."*

The entities state that physical symptoms can be the result of several basic factors acting independently or in combination. These are given as disorders in genetic inheritance, physical trauma, and emotional displacements. These factors can weaken the body's self-regulating and protective systems. Thus the body is more susceptible to the "enemy" outside whether it be virus, fungus, stress, etc. The healing processes are a way to relieve symptoms, but if the basic factor involved in the symptom is a psychological displacement, then this must be worked with psychotherapeutically in order for the symptoms not to reoccur.

Physical energy is the energy emitted by the physical anatomy, by the structure of the body. Physical energy flows through every fiber, every tissue of the body, and as long as this energy is flowing the body is going to stay healthy. Any time the energy is blocked the tissue starves, and the body becomes weakened and susceptible. If any part of our body becomes weak, we become vulnerable. The enemy is going to attack the weakest part. The energy in the body can be blocked by muscular armor, which is nothing more than the muscles in our body becoming tense, tight, and shutting off energy. When this occurs the blocked part of the body begins to suffer. What else can cause this blockage? Physical trauma can cause it. For example, if you cut your finger and your resistance is weakened, then energy flow is decreased and infection could result. The less energy that flows through the tissue, the more difficult it is for the body to heal itself. Blockage of energy also occurs with distorted or unnatural emotions and sets the stage for muscular armoring to begin. People are emotional creatures and as long as we accept our emotions we feel good, comfortable and relaxed, and our energy flows. Most people do not accept emotions; that is, they don't escape their childhood training. There are so many no-no's, and we deny our emotions. These repressed emotions affect us physically.

Physical or body energy that flows through tissue behaves in a manner similar to a magnetic field. It has negative and positive polarities. In a physical healing process the healer's physical energy is used to influence the blocked energy of the recipient. Mario states, *"Energy in a body is polarized and associated with natural emotions that have been repressed and which affect the correlated organs. The body's energy flows from negative to positive and when you are applying this energy with the hands, do not think of it as a circle. Think of it as elongated, vertical, or horizontal. It will flow up the body or down the body."*

Basically, the body heals itself. No physician or scientist would argue that point. Medication primarily kills the enemy and sets up a condition where the body can heal

295

itself. There is nothing yet medically discovered that actually does the healing. What one does in healing work is to send energy to the dis-eased and damaged organ; then, the body begins to strengthen itself and starts its own healing process. The healing process is accelerated in this way. Psychic energy is available to each and every one of us. There is no trick; it is not a mystical thing. One need not be a Zen master, a Buddha, or have many years in meditation or training. Any human being, no matter how illiterate or how well educated, can use psychic energy. Man can harness and house psychic energy in a way similar to a condenser or capacitor. It can also be released at will. For example, with psychic energy you can drill through tissue or even work your way through brain matter. This is the energy at work when we hear of people who bend spoons, or perform other unusual acts. This ability depends on a person's capacity to build up and harness this energy and to project it. The only thing that will inhibit the use of psychic energy is self-doubt. If you do not believe you can do it then you may as well not try. You have to believe it works; you have to know it works, and only experience will give you that.

How does one collect psychic energy? Where does it come from? It is everywhere. It is independent energy and man can be the receiver. Man takes it into his body, draws it through his mind, and projects it using the technique of visualization. Psychic energy enters the healer's body through a specific area of the brain called the medulla oblongata.

The entities emphasized never to use psychic or physical energy to remove pain. Pain is a protection for man. It is a warning system and that is its only purpose. Pain provides knowledge of the condition of the body. It provides a symptom or a feeling to bring attention to that part of the body malfunctioning. Only when the cause of the pain is identified is it safe to work on or remove the pain itself. Pay attention to the body, nurture it, protect it and, if possible, it will heal itself. The purpose of pain is to put us in touch, to remind us that something is wrong with our body. Physical symptoms are frequently related to distorted or unnatural emotions. If this is the case and a person does not choose to become involved in psychotherapy or otherwise allow catharsis to occur, the healer might find himself treating the same symptom over and over. Physical or psychic energy can release the blocked energy, initiate a person's energy flow, and the body will begin to heal itself. The recipient may feel better for a while, but if they return to the stressful environment or allow the same personal dynamics to come into play, they will probably block again. Such a person would find himself returning to the healer so their energy can flow once more. Once a person makes natural emotions their friends, they are less apt to have many of the psychosomatically related illnesses.

In Mario's words, *"Emphasis* [in healing] *must be on the individual themselves. The person that is being worked with must be co-operative mentally for any effectiveness on a permanent basis. If they are not accepting, they can consciously or unconsciously reject healing."* Some additional comments by Mario obtained in a question and answer format follow.

Q: Are there any avenues that could be followed that would enhance the acceptance of the energy by the physical body. That is, is there something that the healer could do?
A: *"Then one would need to become involved in the psychological process why the individual is determined to be ill and why they have made the choice to suffer. Naturally, all of this is on the unconscious level. No one can very easily admit that their physical difficulties or pain is of a chosen nature, you understand."*

Q: If someone thought they had a healing gift, what might be suggested to them as preliminary work or training?
A: *"Any person that feels they have a healing gift, all they need to do is understand the nature with which energy works. Then, experience the results. Everybody has the ability. But everybody cannot easily open the line to*

harness the energy and work with it. After they have demonstrated the ability to heal, then the efficiency with which they work becomes more obvious."

Q: Is there anything you might suggest to someone doing healing to prepare themselves before a session? Is there anything that would enhance what they do?

A: *"The only ritual necessary is to clear their mind of doubt. Doubt is the only enemy."*

Q: What about some beliefs or theories of people such as shaking your hands so you don't take on the disease or disorder, making sure the recipient's feet are to the east, etc. Would you comment on that?

A: *"Yes. Those are all myths, of course. It is ritual. They are being ritualistic creatures. Some of those rituals are practiced and the necessity of them is to offer the individual, the practitioner, confidence in what they are about to achieve. Their ritual then minimizes their doubt. It is clearly a ritual to free oneself of doubt. Once doubt is gone, then the energy, the healing process, begins."*

Mario offered the following statement regarding his assessment of the relationship between physical symptoms and our current society. *"Your culture, your society, has programmed you to suffer because it offers you ultimate rewards—the more you suffer and the more you endure, that someday you will be rewarded for it. But until that someday comes, you play games with yourself and your fellow man to get this intimate reward in little bits and little pieces, like pats on the head, sympathy and self-pity, and you live in this masochistic superiority of reaching out for these bits and pieces."*

The reader may find himself thinking that healing is easy. This is not true. Healing processes are simple, but the subtleties and complexities of either person involved can interfere in many ways. Simple does not necessarily mean easy, and in healing, our individual psyches are intricately involved. Faith, belief, and goodwill cannot be faked. Blockages in psychological processes can be denied consciously, but still operate in an interfering manner.

CHAPTER SIX
THE CHANNEL'S VIEW: EXPERIMENTS AND EXPERIENCES

Jay Barham evolved into a very reliable and powerful channel for the Darkroom group. This chapter contains some personal history regarding the evolution of his interests and abilities, and some of his comments on channeling and the unobstructed. All information is directly quoted from interviews. From time to time questions of the interviewer will be included to provide a context.

Question: Jay, would you talk about your own personal history, in particular focusing on experiences you may have had that influenced the development of your interest in things psychic and spiritual?

The first thing that I ever experienced that I would associate to the awakening of any hungers for knowledge regarding the purpose of life or where I came from happened when I was about six or seven years old. My dad and I were on the farm where we sharecropped in Arkansas, and we got caught in a big rainstorm. We were heading for the barn, and just about a hundred yards from the barnyard fence the sky opened up and rain really began to come down and it was really lightning and thundering. The rain was just coming down in sheets and lightning seemed to be striking everywhere. I remember that Dad had me by the hand and we were walking up some steps that were over the barnyard fence. The fence was about five or six foot tall and we had built steps over it on the path. So we were over the steps and in the barnyard and this big bolt of lightning struck in the barnyard. It was so close and so bright and brilliant, and the noise from it shook the earth. The next thing I remember, we were walking over the steps again. That was very vivid in my mind, that we had to climb over that fence, that is walk over those steps again, and down into the barnyard twice. I never forgot that. We didn't talk about it very much; I think my dad mentioned something about it to my mom in an offhand fashion. But then, my dad was not very talkative or expressive. It was an authoritarian type of household where you didn't get too enthusiastic about things like that. If you did you were kidded out of them or it was just minimized. So I never did really make any mention of it, even though it really stood out for me.

Nothing else unusual happened in my growing up after that until I was about twelve years old. By this time most of my brothers were off in the service, this was World War II or just before that, and my dad had died when I was eight. I was helping out a lot on the farm and I was the only male at home by this time. I was there with my oldest sister, my youngest sister, and my mother. I took care of the cows, hogs, chickens, and did the plowing for the crops. In the morning I would work until it was time to go to school and then after school I'd come back and work some more. I tried to get to school as much as I could, but I guess I missed a lot. One Saturday I was clearing off some new ground. New ground is ground that has saplings or like small trees and shrubs on it that has never been farmed before. So you cut all those down and you clear it. I was plowing the new ground and I had a big horse pulling a plow. He was the only horse we had and he was a really big one, around two thousand pounds. He could pull a plow very easily even though the plow would knock me around when it hit a rock, the horse would keep going. Quite often the plow would get stuck under a stump or a root and then you would have to wiggle it, and fight it to pull it out. I guess at that time I weighed less than a hundred pounds, so it was kind of hard for me. I remember the plow getting stuck under this root and I couldn't get it out. I kept tugging and pulling; I must have spent an hour and a half trying to get that thing out. As

I often did then when I was very frustrated, I lied down and started to cry. I remember struggling with that root and I was really scared that if I didn't get that strip of ground plowed, mama was going to come down and beat the hell out of me. I just lied down in the plowed dirt and I was crying for a long time and then something happened. For a long time I just struck what happened off as a dream, knowing it wasn't a dream, but it was the only way I could deal with it at the time. I was lying down there in the dirt and I heard this voice, which said, 'Son.' I looked up and it was my dad. I could see him just like he was standing there. He said, "It looks like you have a problem." I was just dumbfounded. Then he said, "Well, why don't you let me give you a hand?" I watched him and he wiggled the plow and he pulled it out, then he took the horse and he hooked it back up to the plow. Then he placed the plow in the ground and had the horse pull it a few feet to get it started. I had unhooked the horse from the plow in trying to get it out. I don't recall speaking to him. I was just dumbfounded, I just watched him. I think he had a very pleasant look on his face, just like I remembered before he died when he was up and well. The look on his face reminded me of the very few times that I ever sensed his protective love and concern about me. He was a very matter-of-fact person, and seemed to be very frightened of my mother because she manipulated him. He wasn't verbally expressive; he was more introverted. I never saw that particular expression very much, but I remembered it being loving, sincere, and concerned. Very gentle. That was the closest I could relate to my image of him. Anyway, after the plow was out, it was just like he disappeared all of a sudden. It would be like he took two or three steps away from me and then he was just no longer there. To me it seemed like hours that he was involved in this but I'm sure it was only minutes. I couldn't move; I was immobile. It was like I was mesmerized or in shock. So I just sat there and watched all this. It seemed like it was going on for hours. I remember getting up off the ground and it was almost like my mind then let fear come in again about my mom's reaction. So I continued plowing and I finished up the piece of plowing.

All the rest of that day I was there in the field, but I wasn't there. It was as if I was in a daydream and I remember being very quiet. I never did mention it to my mother. I tried once, by asking her if she ever thinks of dad and she said something to the effect of, "Son, I never have time to think about anything, there's so much work around here to do, who has time to think about it. Your dad is dead and that's all there is to it."

I guess the next experience would be somewhere around a few months or a year after that, when something happened with a friend of mine. This was a kid who had tuberculosis and spent a lot of time at an institution because of it. His uncle lived about a mile from us and occasionally he would come to visit his uncle. He was visiting me one time and was spending the night. I remember the incident very clearly. We were out in the front yard. We used to play tag, do a lot of wrestling and stuff like that, and play with the dogs. We were sitting on the porch trying to grab lightning bugs. We had a fence around our house about 80 or 100 feet from the porch with a gate at the road. And all of a sudden he pointed and said, "Jay, look," and I looked over at the corner of the fence to our left and there was an orange ball of light. Oh, it must have been six or seven inches across and it was just dancing on the fence. We were real scared; we thought maybe somebody was playing a trick on us or something. It rolled on the fence, stopped at the gatepost, and just sat there. It was kind of orange, a bright-ish orange light. Maybe a little dimmer than a sixty watt bulb. It was around dusk and we were kind of scared. Then a voice came from this light, and said, "Arthur, come here." Well. Arthur was always much braver than I was, so he walked out there. I was too scared. He walked out to the gate toward that light and he stopped about five or six feet from it. I could hear murmuring sounds like a voice, but I couldn't hear what the words were. Then it was just like the light went poof and went away over the road, just whooshed away very quickly and disappeared. Arthur turned and ran back toward the house and me. He stumbled and fell and got up and he stumbled and fell again and then he came and sat down on the porch and grabbed me. He said, "Jay, that was my father." Now his father had died some time before. I said, "What do you mean your father?" He said, "That was my father talking to me." I tried to brush it off and said something like, "Oh, come on, that was just somebody playing a trick on us." He said, "No, couldn't you hear what he was saying?" I said that I couldn't, and he said, "My father told me that I was going to live and not to worry any more about it." Arthur had been in the TB sanitarium off and on for years and they hadn't expected him to live. The following week he went back to the sanitarium and in less than a year they had released him and he was totally cured.

Question: Did you two ever talk about that again?

Well, it wasn't too long after that he went back to the sanitarium, and my family moved away. We did move back, and I saw him about four years later. His uncle had a big truck and Arthur and I decided we would saw wood and sell it. We would go out in the woods and find hickory trees and saw them for ax handles and stuff. I remember Arthur asking me, "Do you remember that experience I had over in your front yard that day?" I said that I did and told him how that was really scary for me. But that was the end of it; we never did really talk about it. I think we were both so conditioned about devils, ghosts, spooks and goblins and the fear of the devil, hellfire and brimstone that something like that was just too scary for us to talk about.

I guess the next thing happened [was] after I left the Air Force. The service had been scary for me. At that time in my life I still had a lot of inferiority feelings in almost every area you could think of. In a sense, I grew up in the three years I was in the army. The way I survived the service was by drinking, and by the time I got out of the service I was very heavy into alcohol. I was a weekend drunk; I was too scared to drink on duty. After I was discharged, I wasn't quite so afraid of life but I was still feeling very inferior and made very few friends. When 1 was drunk I was kind of like a clown and people thought I was funny. If I wasn't drinking I was like a recluse, very introverted. Then I had an experience that I wrestled with a long time and really didn't understand until maybe ten years later. I was still drinking very heavy, living in southern California, and we were out drinking on a Friday. We were getting pretty tanked up and we decided we wanted some tacos. Well, in southern California if you are drunk and young, where do you go to get tacos? You go to Mexico. Well, we took out for Mexico and on the road we decided that my friend was too drunk to drive but that I could still drive. I talked him into letting me drive, and I got behind the wheel. As soon as I started driving he just passed out. I was driving what I thought was very sensibly. We were in Mexico on a very foggy and winding road going up a mountain. I remember we were coming up out of the fog and the weather cleared up a little. Even though it was nighttime, I could see the road better so I speeded up and I was probably doing maybe 60 or 65 mph. when I came up on this corner. I managed to get the tires off the side of the pavement and the right front wheel spun on a pile of gravel and the car jackknifed right up on the mountain. I could feel myself bouncing around inside the car. As the car rolled down the mountain it landed upside down and one of the doors opened. The car was upside down, the door was open and the car was jammed on the road. There was something interesting about all this. One is that if the door hadn't opened and stopped the car from rolling it would have gone down about a thousand-foot cliff. Another is that if we had gone off the road thirty or forty feet further around the curve there would have been nothing to stop us going down that ravine. Something else that was interesting was some of the funny things that I experienced. Again, it was like when things happen and you can't understand them so you brush it off as a dream. Which is what I did for a long time. I remember very clearly what I felt in that situation, and that is when the car landed I was up above the car and there were three wheels spinning around on the car and one of the wheels was jerked off. I could see two bodies in the car. The headlights were on and the motor was still running. I remember seeing that. I thought I was dead. Then next thing I knew I was in the car and I couldn't move. The reason I couldn't move was that my buddy was lying on top of me. I could hear the engine running and I thought we'd better get the hell out of there, that the car was going to explode. Finally I wiggled out and dragged him out onto the road. I looked in the car and there was a light on in the glove compartment. I opened the glove compartment and there was a flashlight. I got the flashlight out, turned the ignition off, and turned the headlights off. Then I brought the light out and shone it in my friend's face. He was all bloody. After a long time a car finally came by and picked us up and we got back across the border. The next day we went back down to where the accident was to check on the car and get it. The car had been towed away but we finally found it. The right front wheel had been pulled off and the steering wheel was bent over. The glove compartment had been caved in. The windshield was broken where my friend's head went through. My chest must have hit the steering wheel and bent it. There was an imprint of my chest also on the dashboard. An interesting thing was that the roof of the car was literally six inches from the seat. Anyway, years later when I really got into spiritual and psychic phenomena I began to think more and more about that accident and my experience. I think that was probably the first out-of-body experience I ever had. That is I was out of the car, over it, and seeing what was happening.

Question: Would you say a little bit more about that accident experience in regard to your own growth and interest in things psychic and spiritual?

That accident did a lot for my awareness that physical life is not all there is to it. I don't really know how I correlated that at the time. I know that after the accident I quit drinking for a while, but then I got back on it even

305

heavier than I had before. Even though I did start drinking again, I had begun to change. When I was drunk I began to be almost arrogant and I began to even pick fights with people. Up until that accident I was afraid of my shadow. I was afraid of physical pain, I was afraid of being hurt, I was afraid of hurting other people. It was almost like death was the ultimate fear. After the accident, physical harm didn't seem to be all that tormenting to me. That experience didn't seem to do anything about my inferiority complex, but it did somehow change the way I felt about dying.

It wasn't too long after the accident until I started giving my life some serious evaluation and wanted out of drinking and inferiority feelings. I wanted out of always feeling less than, even feeling less than nothing. At that time I still felt everything and everybody was more important than I was. I literally felt like a nothing. I began to take an interest in some of the things my brother was doing. He was my idea of being intelligent and articulate. I would try to read some of his books and found out I couldn't read or enjoy reading because I couldn't understand the words. I began a self-study method to learn words and how to read, and learned a little bit about grammar. You see, I had missed a lot of school, and really could hardly read at all. I had trouble even reading a newspaper. So you can see where I was regarding school, talking, and reading.

My brother and I got very interested in Religious Science. I began to consider in a very direct way questions like what is God? Who am I? What is life and living? Evolution? Spirituality? My brother and I would study. We would go to meetings. There was a friend that we had and we three would study together. It was about this time that people began to say to me that my comprehension and ability to understand some of the things that were being talked about in the books was very vivid, in some ways more vivid than other people's. I found it interesting that people would give me that kind of feedback. I met someone who told me about an elderly woman who was holding some classes and had weekend workshops. My brother went a couple of times and liked it, and he asked me if I would be interested. I finally did go.

Question: Could you say some more about where your driving force came from at this time in your life, what do you remember about these issues regarding living and spirituality being important for you at the time?

I don't know where it came from; it was almost like you wake up one morning and suddenly the world is staring you in the face. It is just like the world is out there but there is a fog between you and the world. You sense there is something over there but you are not a part of it. That's the way I felt about my whole environment. I am here and there is a gate but I don't have the key to it. I must say that after the accident my life didn't make much sense to me. The way I felt about myself, the way I behaved; it was as if something was wrong with my life. I began to have the idea that whoever designed this life, God or whatever, didn't intend for human beings to be in the position I was in emotionally or psychologically. Up until that point I thought I was just stuck with being miserable and feeling inferior and unimportant. I had just accepted that I would never be anything other than one of the lowliest creatures you could ever think of. I thought other people were either born different or were just lucky or somehow had intelligence and wisdom that I didn't have.

The elderly woman who did the classes and the weekend workshops was called Nan. I took a couple of evenings off work and started going to classes she held. Things that were said in the classes began to turn little lights on psychologically and spiritually. What people were saying there was somehow what I knew inside, and I felt I was getting a key to open a door. I ended up staying involved with this woman and the foundation for thirteen years or so. She was doing work that was really an early form of the psychodrama that Marti and I later developed. I remember working a lot on my early life experiences and being surprised at the changes I felt in myself. I really got hooked by the personal benefits of my experiences, and stayed with the classes and workshops.

It wasn't until after I had been there quite awhile that I learned some of the advanced students were in some type of special meetings. I began to learn they were talking about spiritual subjects. During this time I met Marti, and about three years after we met, we married. She was very involved at the foundation and was on staff. I was also helping out in some of the psychodrama sessions. Gradually I began to get a feeling that Nan was into something important. I didn't know in what way, but I knew that I wanted to get involved in it. About that time Marti bought the Ouija board and we started playing with it. We found out through experimenting that if Marti were touching me, the thing would move. It worked out to where we would sit down and she would have her knee touching mine under the table. The plachette would just go wild and start spelling out all kinds of words. She'd ask the questions. One day she shared with Nan some of what we were getting. Nan told Wes, another staff person, and that's when I found out that Wes was a channel of the information she'd been giving on philosophy, spirituality and even psychological material. Wes and his wife, Elaine, had started out on the Ouija board. They had graduated to the point where they would simply sit and Wes would go into a trance, or semi-trance, and start talking. His wife was his balancer, as Marti was for me on the Ouija board. At that time Marti and I were still with the Ouija board and I really didn't know that Elaine and Wes were channeling. Finally, Nan invited Marti and me over and had Wes and his wife there. Nan checked us out and found we were getting the same information, Wes through his voice channeling and me using the Ouija board. Apparently, she was impressed with the similarities of responses.

Within a few months after this there was a big shake-up in the organization. The foundation was reorganized and Marti and I became part of the board of directors. We were to stay with the organization for a number of years after that. After the reorganization Wes and Elaine left, and I began to move into voice channeling. We became the contact person for Nan with the unobstructed universe through voice channeling. We would meet with her regularly once a week. I would go into trance and she would ask questions. This had nothing to do with any kind of materialization. I really didn't know what that was at the time. I was just going on faith that what I was doing had some value.

Question: Would you describe a bit some of your feelings and personal experiences with the Ouija board and auditory channeling, particularly experiences that you found convincing or validating.

What fascinated me was that when I would go into semi- or trance state, I could hear my voice even though I was detached from it. I was amazed at the words that would come out of my mouth. Remember that at the time I started with Nan's foundation I really couldn't even write. I had to learn how to write and spell words. I was just fascinated by the things I was saying. It was as if somebody else was talking and I was kind of asleep. Later I would hear it on a tape or read a transcript. I just wasn't that knowledgeable! All these sentences and communications coming out, very articulate; there was just no way that could be me, even though it was my voice! At first, that really scared me. I wanted to quit, but Marti and Nan convinced me to continue. I used to get real panicky feelings when I would suddenly become aware, my God! This is me? It was as if I just couldn't tolerate this coming out of me. Who am I to do this and do these things? I was still hanging onto that inferiority and in a way it was almost like a false humility. Looking back on it, it was like I was almost too humble to be important enough to be a person that such incredible insight was coming from. In a way I was almost afraid that if I did get to be important or smart then nobody would like me. I felt nobody likes a smart ass, nobody likes an intellect. It was almost like I felt I was damned if I did and damned if I didn't. Also at that time I guess I still hadn't completely given up the concept of satan as much as I hoped I had.

Question: At this point you were thinking that maybe there was something evil about what you were doing?

I had been taught, or heard, and kind of believed things like satan will take many faces to trick you or deceive you, those kinds of things. Also, you see, at this time I hadn't had any other personal experiences to validate the material I was coming up with while in trance. I really didn't have any personal validation for my intellectual belief that there wasn't any devil or there wasn't any evil there. I was using words and sentence structure and saying things I simply just didn't do.

Question: Would you talk about how you dealt with your fears and doubts regarding your experiences with auditory channeling?

Nan helped me a lot with that because I counseled with her. I was also assigned to another counselor and I found that helpful. I remember going up and saying to my counselor, "Am I crazy, what's going on, is this real, is this me, etc.?" I was wondering if I really had a need to make all this up. Or if it was real, was it something that was coming from a part of me, or an unknown factor that was impinging or influencing my mind to say all these things? I would challenge my counselors, I would ask things like, "What is it about my personality that I'm going on a superiority kick . . . am I making this up?" Pretty much the response I got was that I was not on an ego trip or a superiority trip; it was real. I remember one thing that stood out was Nan saying something to the effect of, "Why can't you be important? Why can't you be a human being with a gift or a talent like this? Why does it have to be someone else?" She would talk about people that were in the beginning of their life somewhat insignificant and grew up to be talented or gifted. She would ask why couldn't I deal with that with a sense of honest humility and just accept it was happening to me? She was quite convinced what I was doing was very real, and she made that very clear. At that time I trusted her wisdom and judgment because she was to me like a guru might be to some people now. I trusted her honesty, sincerity and wisdom. For a while I really had nothing to base my experiences on other than that trust. The fact that nobody saw me as having a need to manipulate people or going on an ego trip helped me accept it and go ahead with it.

A couple of years later I began to have out-of-body experiences and that helped me feel much more comfortable with my channeling activities. The first time I had a really powerful experience with what I now call the unobstructed was when I was voice channeling for Nan one particular night. I was in a kind of semi-trance and I slipped off into a deeper state. When I came to, it was almost as if I had [had] a dream. While I was in that deep trance state, Nan and Marti had been asking me questions about my experiences and things about entities and the unobstructed. I had verbalized in the trance what I was experiencing. When I woke up they played the tape back to me and I had no memory or knowledge of what I heard myself saying. As they replayed the tape I could get a little of the feeling back. If we had not captured that experience on tape I wouldn't have been able to bring the knowledge back to me. Even hearing it, I couldn't correlate the experience. Hearing it still didn't awaken a full memory of what I had experienced. What I did remember was probably the most fearless and pleasant experience that I had ever had. I experienced the tunnel, the light, and then moved through that transition phase into the unobstructed universe. After that, I had more out-of-body experiences into the unobstructed and I began to have more memory and retention of my experiences. There were times when I almost had full conscious awareness of my experiences out there. There were a dozen or more such experiences. After that I began not to do it so much.

Question: Could you say more about that?

It is very difficult to deal with this reality after you have experienced that one. It is difficult to keep your feet on the ground and to continue to appreciate the limitations of the physical world. It is very important to keep your senses on the importance of the physical life and the growth process. There is a continuity of life. Living in the physical fully is essential to your spiritual growth. We really have to keep a handle on the significance and importance of our emotional makeup and living day to day, to not let living be a small insignificant process. Even the highest sensation that we can experience in the physical, which I would think of as sexual orgasm, is really insignificant compared to the ecstasies you sense and are aware of in the unobstructed. I can clearly understand why some people, who either spontaneously or by some mechanical or chemical process, experience these kinds of things lose contact with everyday reality and become disoriented.

Question: Would you say a bit about what it is like in the unobstructed?

I don't think there is any way at this point that my physical mind could articulate or translate the things that I have experienced. It would be impossible for me to find words in my limited vocabulary. I can say a few things. You can experience in three to five minutes out there the equivalent to five lifetimes of learning. You can get into profound knowledge, wisdom, and a sense of what the totality of the entire universe is. What it is made of and what makes it tick. But it's also like our physical body can't tolerate that energy. You have to be in a spiritual form to experience it because of the brilliance of it, and if you weren't it would be like looking into a welding arc. If you looked at a welding arc from six to eight inches without a welder's mask, you would be blinded. Yet, if you could measure that arc light it would be only one tenth of one percent of the intensity of spiritual energy! Then you would get an idea of what a physical being would experience if catapulted into the unobstructed unprepared. That is why stages of transition are needed in order to enter it and be able to experience it. The words we have are just not adequate. For example, if somebody asked what are the divisions between the universes, what does it look like? I'd say, well you can't go from the unobstructed into the Universal Source of Divinity. They would ask, well what keeps you from it? I would say, an energy pattern or a division. And they'd say, what is that division or energy pattern? And I'd try to describe it and say it's like glass or cellophane, it's as if you came to an obstruction and that's as far as you can go. Can you see through it? Yes. Can you penetrate it? No. Well, what is it? It's as if something is there but it's not there. It begins to sound like double-talk when you try to put words to these experiences.

Question: Would you say some more about how you handled your doubts and in particular your fears of evil energy and of the devil when you began to do auditory channeling?

Before I began to have out-of-body experiences but after I started auditory channeling, I had consciously and intellectually accepted there was no devil and no hell. This was based on the material and the experience with the Ouija board, and trancing. But the thing that really took care of my fears was the out-of-body experiences, in which you can get in touch with the Archives of Knowledge directly. Then you know. It is like looking at your watch and knowing what time it is. When you are out there you know.

I could bring back some of the awarenesses as I began to have more out-of-body experiences. I could come back and say to myself, "Oh, that's the way it is, now I understand." It was a memory of the knowing and not just an intellectual or belief process. When I experienced that, my fear of the devil, hell and negativity was erased permanently.

I knew because it was right there, I could see it. You see, until you can remember experiencing something like that, you have only a belief and all you can rely on is based on faith, belief and hope. Hope and belief that what you've been taught is real. But when you have experienced it, all doubt is erased.

Question: To get back to the chronology of your personal experiences, what happened with your channeling and your work in the foundation at this point?

I continued to channel and I was more comfortable with it. There was again a big shake-up in the foundation's organization. I ended up feeling as though I had been misled or deceived by some people in positions of power in the organization. I became very disillusioned and felt overwhelmed by these experiences. So what I did was to reject the unobstructed.

Question: How do you mean?

Well, I didn't reject the reality of the unobstructed or of the entities. I simply felt betrayed. I felt I could have been warned about what was happening in the organization. I felt the entities let me walk right into a big personal problem for myself, and big disillusionments, and gave me no warning.

Question: You use the word entities; were you using this term at that point?

At that time we called them invisibles. I had never seen one except in the unobstructed, in my out-of-body experiences. I had never experienced materialization. I was convinced the entities existed in the unobstructed and I knew they were the ones impinging on me and helping me channel. I was disillusioned, I rejected them, and I was angry with them. I refused to channel any more. Marti and I resigned from the organization, and I decided to hell with the entities and didn't make any more contact with the organization or the people in it.

For a long time Marti couldn't even get me to talk about entities. I was really disillusioned. I rejected it all. I guess that lasted about two years. But I just couldn't leave it alone, even though I tried. During those two years or so, my attitude was I knew pretty much what I wanted to do with my life, so why bother with them anymore? All they were going to do is give you a lot of headaches, a lot of responsibility, get you in jams, and then you have to get yourself out. When you are really in a jam and you need them the most, they are there the least. Then they call that a growth experience. By this point I knew what I wanted to do with my life was help other people and work with them in their growth, so I figured why bother with going out on limbs?

Question: How did you get re-involved with the entities and the unobstructed?

Marti went back to school working on some credentials so we could start our own work. We never gave up the commitment to work with people. I had decided I wasn't going to use any more outside influence. I figured with our experience, our knowledge, and our own intelligence, we would just do it on our own.

During the next couple of years I took a greater interest in hypnosis and Marti wanted to learn it also. We began studying that with a Major Roberts. We became good subjects of his and finally became very good friends with him. He would invite us to class and use us as demonstration subjects. One night he did a lecture and a presentation at a parapsychology foundation and Marti and I were invited to come over and demonstrate hypnosis. At one of the breaks I overheard a small group of people talking about psychic and spiritual phenomena. They were talking about learning how to be psychic and use ESP. I found myself moving a little closer so I could hear them. As much as I didn't want to be interested, I still was. Just before the break ended I went up to this woman and told her I had heard her mention some classes and asked how would one get involved in that. She said she had them in her home and we were welcome to come. She said the fee was $2.00 a night. I began to find myself there, one night a week. Marti was working full time and going to school in the evenings and I didn't have anything to do with my time so I went to the classes.

It was also at one of Major Roberts' demonstration sessions that a woman came up to me and handed me a big strand of beads from around her neck and said, "Tell me something about myself." I stumbled with the idea and had the thought, "Well, okay, I'm here to learn and if I'm going to learn then I am going to have to get egg on my face, I'm going to have to give it a try." I just thought I'd say whatever comes to my mind. If a first hunch is supposed to be correct, I'd just throw it from the top of my head and let the cards fall where they may. I just started rattling off about her, and her eyes kept getting bigger and bigger. After I got through, she says, "Well, everything you said is true." After that incident people would want me to do a psychometry reading, tell their future, tell them things, etc.

The woman with the beads invited me over to her house. She called up and said she had some really fantastic psychics coming over. I was still wanting to learn and I figured if I would go and hang around these people I might learn something. I ended up going to her place regularly. We got involved with trying to develop ESP and psychic abilities. It turned out to where people would stand in line behind me and put their ring in my hand so I could tell them something. I got pretty good at psychometry and word got around. The maximum accuracy in something like that is supposed to be around $80°/_c$ but I started batting around 90-95%. I began to develop my own kind of measuring devices for when I thought I was being accurate or not. For example, if I could get three specific factual things about a person correct, then I found I could go into their future with some

316

assurance I was on their lifeline and not on somebody else's. That held pretty steady. If I didn't get three clear specific hits, where there was no doubt, then I would tell them that it just wasn't working.

Question: What kind of specific things?

Things like specific accidents that had happened to them, how many times they had been married; how many children they had, personal traumas they had in their life. If I couldn't pick up anything specific and all I could get was a generality that could apply to anybody, then I would say I'm sorry, I'm not picking up on you, and wouldn't go into anything. One example of a specific hit would be a man who put his watch in my hand and I fumbled with it and suddenly I got this image of a young kid falling out of a wagon and getting run over by the wheel. Or another time I heard sirens, saw an ambulance coming, and a young boy taken to the hospital. Or I would get an image of a funeral, and see a little girl or boy standing there, pulling at the coffin and crying. I would put these things out and people would say, yes that happened to me, or no, that didn't happen to me.

Using psychometry or anything psychic is an interesting thing and hard to predict. The mind works in very organized patterns for behavior but it is predictably unpredictable. When you try to sift out your thought patterns you will probably find you have a number of thought patterns going at the same time. It is kind of like watching four TV channels, four different stations, or listening to four different radios all tuned to different stations and you have to tune in to the right station. You just have to pick one. With me, I would just get visions, picture images, and sometimes they would come in still pictures and sometimes moving pictures. Mental pictures. It would be as if you had seen a movie and you shut your eyes and could see the action of one particular scene again.

Question: So what happened then?

I began to be invited by a number of people to do these things for money. In other words, I got offers to be exploited. I didn't like that idea. I began to recognize what could develop. As your credibility is building up you begin to say things that are generalities. There is pressure to say things that will not be boring, flat, or un-entertaining. There is a subtle push to get into future predictions. By the time you are far into the process with someone, you know quite a bit about them. There would be situations where I could be very accurate on past events and then I would be asked to get into future events. People have a hunger or curiosity to know what is going to happen to them. Now the only way you can really be sure that these things are going to happen is that the prediction has to fulfill itself. My concern was that while it may be true that these things are going to happen to this person, what if I'm influencing them to make it happen? Knowing as much about hypnosis and suggestibility as I did, I could say to somebody, "Within three months you are going to get a new automobile." I have planted an idea and their mind is going to work toward that. So in three months they sell their old car or it breaks down on them and they say, "Well, he said I was going to get a new one, so I might as well go ahead and get it." So they wind up buying a new car and they come back to me and they say, "You're right." It was as if the more you told people, the more they wanted to know. Especially if you are accurate, people begin to come back. It is easy to manipulate people's lives in that situation. It was usually the future they were wanting to know about. I didn't like that responsibility and that influence. I didn't like the idea that I could manipulate people and influence them in that way. I knew that I could either be right intuitively or psychically, that these things may happen to them, but I also had a keen sense of knowing that if I said it, it would also influence them and I would be planting a seed. I began to see a negative potential in such a process and that I could be a part of it. Say you are a person interested in this and you come and want to know what your future is. So I 'see' in your future you are going to be divorced or married three times and I tell you this. Now you go home and you have a very loving relationship with your wife and your kids but for some reason you have a little spat with your wife. You are mad at her and you might say, "To hell with you, baby, I just found out that you are not the only one in my life. I'm going to be married three times, so I might as well get it over with." Literally, I have interfered with their life by creating a negative suggestion. There was no way I could deal with that issue without getting out of doing psychometry. I just couldn't deal with it. I really had to accept I didn't want to be a part of that kind of process. I wouldn't influence people's lives like that. I wouldn't do it for a million dollars. I wouldn't exploit people and take on a possibility of being wrong in any of the aspects of people's future. So I got out of that. I just quit.

During this time of my life in addition to doing psychometry I was meeting with a group of people and we became interested in what we considered the "real thing." We wanted to move into and experience phenomena more than telepathy or psychic ability. We wanted to get more into the mystical, spiritual, the ethereal aspects. We even talked about materialization. Someone mentioned meetings where they had experienced some materialization. I was invited to one of these meetings. My hunger, my curiosity, pulled me. I had never been to such a thing. I had seen them on television and heard about them, but I had never been to what was called a séance. It cost $10.00 a session per person and if you could get ten people together then the channel would have a meeting. It was an interesting experience. I couldn't honestly say that what I experienced there was real or fake. All I know is that, before the session was over, there were some very interesting phenomena that occurred that even scared the medium. I got a feeling that something happened in that group that scared him. The meeting was interrupted very abruptly by some very unusual phenomena. Lights appeared in the room under a person's face illuminating their features, and evidently they weren't the channel's lights.

As our group experimented I found myself involved again with the unobstructed and psychic experiments. For example, we would write a message on a piece of paper, loosely wad it up, put it in a metal pan in the middle of our circle and burn it. When it was your turn you would go up, take a match or a candle, light your piece of paper that you had written on and put it in the pan. While it was burning, everyone would concentrate or meditate to see if they could pick up the message written on the paper. It was at one of these meetings that I met Sally, who became a good friend. Sally and I connected in those evening groups. We found that Sally could also balance me on the Ouija board. I started working it again for fun. Other people in the group took it seriously, but I was doing it this time for the fun of it, the amusement of it. I took the same attitude with psychometry, even though I had stopped doing any real future readings. I was enjoying meeting people, learning from them, and I was willing to play around with the Ouija board.

After the first séance experience there was considerable discussion in our group about our personal experiences and what it had meant to us. I guess that was the jumping off point to become more seriously involved with the invoking of contact with spirit. I had been introduced to some people in other groups who were meeting and holding sessions. They would chant to raise the energy. I became a regular member of a group over at Lily's house, and that's when it got serious.

Before I go on I want to say a bit about impingement and voice channeling. I think I've already said if you are using a Ouija board or doing voice channeling and getting impingement, the best most people can do is to be about 80% accurate. I saw people do a lot of funny things when they channeled that I don't think was really necessary. It's an interesting experience when you are with a group of sensitive people, impingement is going on, but somehow people believe they need to add something to it. I'll give you an example. Sometimes a person's voice will relax because of the relaxed posture of the physical vehicle. A woman's voice may lower some and a man's voice may lower or raise some, depending on what's coming through. But there is no real drastic change. I remember one woman who seemed very psychic was trying to trance. She would start using this hoarse voice as she felt it was a male entity coming through. I told her it was totally unnecessary to change her voice and after that she would go into a kind of semi-trance and let herself just talk naturally. People can make themselves believe they need to do these drastic things. Most of the things people do are rituals or beliefs, but I can also see the seriousness of it. I certainly don't want to laugh at the people or their sincerity.

When I was invited to join the group at Lily's house, that's when I consider my serious involvement began again. In the first two or three meetings we had a power struggle develop, as in most organizations or groups that form. The issues were things like who is the most intelligent and who is the most knowledgeable of the subject. After a few meetings there was a split in the group. I had pretty well committed myself to my own teacher or guru, the person I thought I was learning from in that group. When the group split, I went with the group she was in and we had our own sessions. During those sessions we began to get phenomena such as noises and touches. All of us in the group thought one particular person was the potential channel. We were nurturing and zeroing in on this person because we thought she was the person who was stabilizing and focusing the energy. We were starting to meet in the dark by this time. Several people had said that's what was necessary to help the energy focus and to get the phenomena we were interested in. We continued to meet, and the phenomena were getting more frequent and more vigorous. We were getting more touches and feeling more energy in the room. I was getting touches along with other people, and we worked out a little rule that if you got touched you would say something. In that way other people in the room would know there was some activity. I was enjoying these meetings but one night I got a call from a woman in the group and she sounded very nervous. It was as if she wanted to say something but didn't know how to put it. Finally she came out with it. What she came out with was accusing me of getting up, walking around the group, and touching people. She even made a couple of threatening statements. My saying I wasn't doing that didn't seem to help her cool down any. I never made contact nor heard from her again. Others in the group called me and I saw them, but I withdrew as a part of the group. I was disappointed and disillusioned again, and I decided again that's enough of this stuff. By now I had almost concluded that everybody involved in the spiritual process was neurotic as hell. I had [had] enough of fears, [of] talk about evil entities, higher and lower spirits, suspicions, I had just had enough of all that.

After I dropped out, Lily called many times. She had stayed with the other group after the split. I never would respond to Lily's request to come over to her place and meet. Marti returned from school in Arizona. She was very curious about all the activity. Lily continued to call, and one time we did go over. I thought it would just be Marti and me. When we got there and walked in, Lily had "just happened" to have invited seven or eight other people. She lived up to her promise to play some tapes of a séance she had attended, and which she had mentioned over the phone. We listened to some of it. It was interesting but the tape recorder broke and we couldn't play any more tapes. I was ready to go home then, but Lily said, "Well, since everybody is here, let's just have a little session." Lily is quite a character. We did just that, and got some phenomena. We went again and this time there was some table tipping and wiggling, and at one point the table just floated right up off the floor. A couple of times it went so high some of us had to stand on tiptoe and hold our hands up. You could look under the table and see nobody was doing it. We were all looking under there to see who it was or what it was holding it up. It was very exciting. I got hooked again.

I started meeting regularly with this group. We thought another person in the group was a channel, but Lily got me off to the side and showed me her journal. She had been keeping notes over a long period of time about who was at different meetings and what phenomena occurred. She told me the reason she was trying to get me back in was because she knew I was a channel. She had figured this out by using her logbook and correlating. Looking in her logbook and at her data it seemed pretty clear, at least on paper, but I was reluctant to assume responsibility for channeling again. Because of my experiences at the foundation I wanted to learn and be a part of, but I didn't want to be one of the initiators or a channel.

Question: What was your reluctance?

Based on my experience, I just didn't want the responsibility. Part of it was because of my disillusionment with the entities in the past and how I felt betrayed. Yes, I wanted to experience the real thing. I wanted to be able to experience materialization and be able to talk to the horse's mouth because I had learned through my own experiences and voice channeling that there was a possibility of a 20% distortion. My theory was if you could talk to an entity directly it would be more likely to be accurate. I was searching for truth and I really wanted to experience materialization. That was my reason for getting involved, but I didn't want any active part. I didn't like the idea of being a channel, I would much rather it have been somebody else. I didn't want the responsibility or to set myself up as a target again for another disappointment. I had to decide whether I wanted to get involved. At the group meetings, if I weren't there, phenomena and independent voice wouldn't happen. We constantly tried to have other people channel.

We continued to try different processes like isolating the channel behind curtains, because we were still searching. Different people would have different ideas and would say let's try this and see what happens. Somebody

323

would read a book and say well this book says such-and-such and we would try that. We wanted to be able to get materialization. Through trial and error it finally happened. The trumpet began to float and move around and objects began to fly through the air. That was really exciting. And it began to get scary. At that time I was still sitting out in the circle with the group. I was not going into trance and I was able to experience and witness all of the phenomena. This included touches, hearing a voice from the trumpet, and seeing it move. As we began to get voice, we would ask questions and get directions on how we could stabilize the energy. We would follow these guiding factors and then one night it happened. I remember the first night when someone put their hand out and touched a solid form. That was an exciting night. It just progressed from there. The entities began to materialize and one night someone had a very private, personal issue they wanted to discuss. They didn't feel comfortable discussing it in the group so the entity took them out in the hall. It got to be a humorous thing, everybody hoping that their night would come when they would be taken out there for a private visit. Lily fixed up one of her bedrooms down the hall for a second meeting room. Then we began to get two entities materializing, and at times two private visits occurring simultaneously.

From that point on lots of things began to happen, and you can look at Marti's account for what happened chronologically (Chapter 1). By this time I was separated from the rest of the group, and I was trancing. By the way, that was discovered almost accidentally. One night we were having a session and there were phenomena going on and I went to sleep. The group members found out I was going into a trance, and when that happened more phenomena would occur and there would be more materialization. They would call my name and I wouldn't answer. If somebody would reach over and touch me I'd wake up.

Question: How were you feeling at this point in the development of that group?

I had disappointment more than anything because my channeling excluded me from the phenomena. If I went into an altered state more phenomena and materialization occurred, but I wasn't aware of what happened. I was kind of left out, the only satisfaction I would get out of the group would be their sharing with me after the session what had happened.

Question: What was it like for you to deprive yourself of the direct experience in the group?

It almost felt inevitable. Meaning it put me right back where I had always been. People began to share with me things that were happening with them and how positive it was for them. Up until then it was more of a curiosity, but I was beginning to be aware of the seriousness of it. Our meetings became an important and positive experience for people. I began to notice psychological changes in people and the productivity of the entities' visits. It became more difficult for me to say no.

I agreed to continue, and told the group a promise I had made to myself. The promise was, "I will be a part of this as long as it is positive, but if anything negative ever happens to anybody, that's it. I don't want that type of responsibility." Finally, something happened that shook up one or two people, and I made a decision that I wouldn't have any part of it anymore. I told everyone I couldn't support things happening that were negative for people. But everyone reassured me, even the ones that had the negative experiences. So I continued.

Question: So you let yourself be influenced by the group and be reassured; were there other things that happened where again you wanted to say no, or that you didn't like?

Many times I'd question it, but after that I concluded within myself I was just not going to take any responsibility for it. That's when I told people that I'm not going to take any responsibility for what happens during the meetings. I will channel, but it is your experience. I am not responsible for what happens in there. I was freeing myself of that responsibility. My attitude was you are all grownups, you are adults; you will have to evaluate your own negative and positive aspects of your experience in the Darkroom. I really began to wash my hands of that responsibility, which helped me quite a bit.

We continued meeting, and word got around of what was happening. Many people wanted to have that kind of experience. Some people were being invited and they'd come in and almost freak out because they couldn't deal with the experience. We began to turn the responsibility for permission to attend over to the entities. The entities would say that yes, it would be positive for that person to come or no, it would not be a good time for this person to come. By this time we were having about three meetings a week, and anywhere from 15 to 20 people in each session. Within a year and a half or two years, almost two hundred people had experienced the Darkroom. For the most part it was a positive experience for them. For some it was just too frightening and they would never come back again.

Question: What was it like for you when you began to get materialization that steadily and strongly? You were not actually in the room.

All I can say is it was interesting. Naturally I kept my ears open to people's experiences when they wanted to share it at their initiative. I was still interested in whether or not it was a positive experience. Many people would try to praise me, cater to me, and put me on some kind of pedestal and I was constantly fighting that. I didn't like being sought out as some special person. I think much of my energy went into not allowing myself to become a special person or some kind of guru. I always fought that. People would ask me how I feel about it and I'd say, well I do it because it is positive

326

for people, but I really don't take any credit for it. I can lie down and go to sleep and these things happen. That's very nice. I could understand what was going on at the time; that evidently I was the only link they had at the time. It was like they wanted to keep me fat and healthy so they could keep having experiences. They didn't want something to happen to me, so they tried to make me very comfortable. And all the time I just wanted to be one of the group. I kept going back to the responsibility aspect. The way I continued to deal with it was: just take no responsibility for what happens, let their experiences be their own.

Question: Would you say something about negative experiences people had, or your thoughts about negative experiences and spirituality in general?

I knew by this point there was no such thing as negative spiritual energy. Any experiences people had would have to be at their own choice. I was thoroughly convinced the entities have no aggressive process themselves. I was aware of the possibility of psychic phenomena, that it was possible to create materialized forms in a psychic sense. There might be something destructive in that. But I was also thoroughly convinced that psychic energy could be manipulated and spiritual energy could not. There was much discussion and debate on various phenomena and how it was occurring and why. There were questions on what part I had in the phenomena. My position was if I were producing the phenomena I would have control over it. In other words I could manipulate the energy; to have it do what I wanted it to do. I knew I wasn't doing that, so I was very comfortable with the fact that I wasn't involved with my own psychic energy.

Question: How do you know that since you were in an altered state when you channel that you were not producing something psychically in a materialized form and somehow programming it?

If I was then or am now I have no conscious knowledge of that. Somewhere along the line I know I would be aware of that motivation. There would have to be some intent, some purpose, some motive to my doing that. That just doesn't fit for me, because I take no responsibility for what people experience. A person who would program or pre-design some psychic production would have to have some need to create something and give it direction. The only thing I am aware of is making my energy available. That's the only investment that I have in it. The only reason I continue doing it is because people have positive experiences. I supply the energy I can for that.

Question: At some point after the Darkroom group got larger, something disturbing and negative happened. Would you talk about that?

One of the primary reasons we turned the responsibility of who to invite over to the entities was that as the group got larger more people were being invited at random. Friends bringing friends and things like that. I think some people were having frightful or negative experiences and this was becoming obvious. Some people would get scared; it was too much of a challenge to them personally. We felt if the entities did the evaluation regarding any one person's attendance, there would be fewer people being scared and having negative experiences. We asked the entities about that and they accepted the responsibility. Things began to go much better after that. When people got scared after that I had to rely on the entities' judgment and the participant's judgment that they knew what they were doing. There were times when I really wondered, like when someone attacked the entity.

That's a scary thing, because there was a potential danger or harm to people; not necessarily to the entity, but they could have harmed me or the participants could have harmed each other. It could have caused a panic and in the dark people could have hurt each other. This was what we called Black Monday. That night I wasn't angry with the guy because my mind went to the purpose for which he was there. He had been given permission by the entities, and the entities explained it to us later. They said that yes, they had given him permission. People were even angry with the entities for letting this happen. The entities said in their evaluation there was a risk, but there was also a chance that it would be a very positive experience for him. The entities were willing to take that chance. It could have been a very positive process and changed his whole life.

Question: What made you go underground?

There were threats and negative reactions that happened when there was a division in the group and some chose to pull away. Some people in the group began to be suspicious and they got into the never-ending desire to 'prove' what was happening. Things were very positive on the surface. People were learning things, changing, and the experiences were growth producing. There were some who continued to doubt. They made a compromise to themselves, something like, "Well, it could be Jay, but it couldn't be. But as long as it is positive, what the hell is the difference." For a long while, even for the people who were doubting it didn't make much difference to them whether it was me or entities because the experience was positive. As far as I know there could be some people who still meet with us that question whether it is me or an entity. I don't care as long as they don't try to do anything that will disturb me or harm others. I don't care about people's doubts; what I care about is that they take care of their own business and learn whatever they can.

Those people that stayed with their doubts and their wanting to prove absolutely one way or another couldn't resolve that question. They just couldn't get enough proof to validate the fact that it was not deception or fraud, or me up walking around. As the Darkroom group grew larger and curiosity was still very strong, the entities would really do nothing to prove or validate their existence. They would say that if they did one thing, or create some phenomena to give proof, you would want another phenomenon to prove that proof. It would become an insatiable thing, an impossible process to please. If an entity walked out, materialized, tolerated a lot of light, and let everybody kiss him right in the face, and the people could see it wasn't me, it still would not be enough. If someone had a need and they doubted strongly enough, they could conclude, "Well, Jay paid somebody to come in the back door or crawl in the window." Curiosity is insatiable. There is just no way to satisfy that, if somebody doesn't use their experience as their proof. If you have doubt, and that doubt is creating a fear, it is hard not to conclude it is some kind of trick. Most of us have been tricked so much in our life, in our growing up, it is very difficult to outlive that and let go of it.

Question: You talk like you have a lot of compassion or understanding for those who accused you.

I do. I have no animosity against anyone who has accused me. I believe I understand their process. I've been there. By that I mean I have been there with my own doubts and the way I tussled with them and how insatiable they are. It's up to each person to deal with their doubts in their own way, to question their experience. That is a process they have to live with. There is no one that can deal with it for them. Getting back to the idea of being tricked, if you see something floating in the air, what is your first reaction? There is a string tied to it, it's a trick, or it is a hallucination. So you can imagine how easy it is for people to reach that conclusion rather than accept that there is an energy of some as yet un-measurable type or an entity doing that. And when you can't see that entity then it becomes even more difficult.

We began to get threats by people, and we began to get concerned about people disrupting the meetings by actually breaking in. It never happened, but there were threats of it being done. We would hear a rumor like, "Don't have a meeting tonight, because you are going to be exposed. Somebody is going to turn the lights on or something else nasty is going to happen." But we continued to have the meetings, we just ignored these rumors and threats and challenged them and nothing ever happened.

This was a rough period for people in the group. Some were pulling away. Some were trying to understand the conflicts, turmoil, and pain that many were having. People who had been friends for years had suddenly changed their mind and were against you. People put pressures on one another to choose sides. It was very painful for a lot of people. People would ask me about it and I would try to stay out of it.

Question: Somehow you were the focus for a large amount of this conflict; people were saying either that you were real or that you were a fraud?

That went on all the time, but at the break off or explosion point things got really tight, that was a big crisis. I had to question myself also. Are they telling the truth? I mean are they right or is my experience right? There were people who never doubted and who never had any reason to doubt and yet they had to go through anguish and the loss of friends. People close to them that they had been associated with every week left; people who had been very involved with the process. To suddenly have that kind of division . . . is like a death. You love somebody very much and suddenly they are no longer a part of your life. I suffered a tremendous loss in this but I no longer feel the pain because I grieved about it.

Question: Could you say something about your own feeling of loss regarding that time?

Well, that's the way it was. I had dozens of friends,

and suddenly I was their enemy. It was very painful. I worked through the process of accepting and understanding their need to do what they were doing, and my need to do what I was doing made it all right. I go on. Part of my personal process is not dwelling on my own selfishness and my own need. I have a commitment and a responsibility to continue to share and to help people deal with negativity so they can become more comfortable with themselves. Whatever I can do to help people be free of aches, pains, hurts and destructive processes that go on inside of them every day, I will do. I would like for people to be able to experience some of the quietness, the assuredness of a feeling of knowing about the purpose of life. I would like for people to have that positive feeling, a nonthreatening feeling of their destiny. I let my natural emotions deal with those processes. Then it is easier to let go and I go on. I don't love those people any less now than I did then. I just don't have a need to try to destroy them because they tried to hurt me, or because they didn't believe in me. That is their prerogative, their right and their free choice. It is a part of their process. My lovability and my self-worth are not dependent upon external approval. You see; you will not be devastated from losses like that unless your own love-ability is totally dependent on the outer. That is why it is so important for people to understand and move toward self-love, self-acceptance, a sense of self-worth. Self-love is a natural process that helps keep you together. It sustains you through some hard times in life. I need experiences with other people, I couldn't survive without them; but I also know that too much dependency on external resources or love is not constructive. That's why so many people are devastated when they lose someone in a relationship, or when they lose something and can't let go of it.

Question: Getting back to the crisis in the Darkroom, what happened next?

We decided to go underground. I began to discover I

really didn't know whom I could trust anymore. There were all kinds of rumors going around that somebody had been paid money to be a 'plant' of some kind, etc. I haven't heard anything like that for a long time now, but for a while there were all kinds of rumors. In a sense, I don't know whom to trust anymore, and I'm comfortable with that. I put no energy into it. In a way I have a definite conviction about that, and I stand very firm on it. As far as putting any emotional energy into evaluating whether people in the Darkroom now are trustworthy or not, I just don't get into that.

For a while now, since we have been quiet about our meetings, there are no rumors I'm aware of. There haven't been any threats, there haven't been any attempts or efforts to prove or disprove in an outrageous way. No lights being turned on or people getting up and walking around to see what's going on, etc.

Question: Did your meetings go underground before or after the Time magazine article that was so accusatory of you and Marti and Elisabeth Kübler-Ross, M.D.?

I don't remember whether it was before or after. I know that the information that the journalist got was directed at the Darkroom and at me. The people that gave him the information were not necessarily trying to strike at Elisabeth, they were striking out at me. Evidently they were willing to bring her down in order to bring me down. Other journalists picked up on it as a juicy story because, with Elisabeth's name, there was money in it. They could make a big story of it. If she hadn't been involved in it, the magazines wouldn't have bothered printing the story because who in the hell am I?

Question: So how did you react to the Time article and others?

As far as being personally threatened by it, I wasn't.

Naturally I had a lot of concern as to what effect it would have on Elisabeth's credibility. She had been involved since 1976. We talked about her involvement and the decision was made we wouldn't yield or do anything to defend our activity; it wasn't worth the energy. We just went ahead and did our thing and let the brushfire burn. It evidently burned itself out. It took a few trees with it, as all brushfires do. But symbolically speaking, any forest fire always leaves areas of new growth and stronger timber anyway.

Question: Could you talk about your own personal experiences with an entity, when someone else was channeling?

Yes, I've had personal visits with materialized entities. I've sat down and discussed many things with them, particularly later on in our process. There was at least one other person who could help channel. As long as I was within at least ten feet of that person, the combination of both our energies would provide for materialization. Once materialization occurred, the other person's energy could sustain the materialization until I got my visit. I would go out with the entity and would talk to them. The first time I had a visit with a fully materialized entity it was scary - exciting - apprehensive - spooky. And I still had to battle my programmed messages. You still have some apprehension about the unknown until you directly experience it again and again. Anything you haven't directly experienced, there's a possibility for fear or apprehension. My experience was, and I think this would be true for most people, that the more time I spent with the entities the more comfortable I was. The entities would explain to me very clearly the naturalness of what was happening. I had a chance to have positive experiences going on inside of me, and I began to accept it more and more. The anxiety or energy becomes positive instead of negative. You may get goose bumps or be a little anticipatory, but it is not a negative process. I began to understand and experience those types of excitements, and to enjoy it. It may be like your first dive off the high board; after you have done it fifteen or twenty times, it is not as tantalizing. It may still be fun, but your adrenalin is less after you have experienced it. For me the most obvious thing in my personal visits was constantly an experience of unconditional love. The sense of that unconditional love exudes from their presence, their being. You feel totally safe and even though they can be very tough disciplinarians when it comes to factual things, you know the love is there. If you have ever been criticized or disciplined with love, you clearly understand the difference between that and a rejecting type of criticism or the aggravating effect of judgments placed on you. It is in a sense addicting in developing a hunger for their presence once you have experienced it. It is just nice to be around them. You touch them and it is flesh and bone but it is different than touching a real human being, the energy is different.

There was one entity with whom I had many visits. He and I spent a lot of time talking about the issues for me in my life of commitment, responsibility, moral and legal liability. We also spent a lot of time talking about spiritual evolution, destiny, healing. Much of my knowledge of healing came from those sessions, discussing methods, ways, techniques and processes. I would talk to him regarding my issues on channeling. Regarding my questions to this entity of "why me" as a channel, I would get pretty much the same response every time. Something like why not you? In general his simple approach to me was if I didn't have any need to argue about or defend it, and I wasn't getting any real prestige out of it, there was no way that 1 would be on a power trip or a prestige trip. I talked about my concern that I might become arrogant, demanding, or selfish and manipulate people because of the fact that I was one of the apparently few people that was able to solidify the energy. The entity said it simply was that I didn't block the energy and made it possible. He said there wasn't anything special about me; everybody has this type of ability or energy. It is a matter of freeing yourself of fear, shame, guilt and the need to manipulate. Then the energy is available. Anybody can do it. I'm not really somebody that special. So as long as I am not on some type of ego trip or have any secret motives to manipulate others then all is positive. I was told that was one of the pluses. I wasn't doing anything for my own ego that would interfere with the energy. We didn't spend a lot of time on that subject, my greater interest was in spiritual evolution, the why's and the why not's and talking for hours and hours on universal laws.

Question: Would you talk some about what is the make up or composition or processes of a group providing energy for materialization?

The channel is the focuser or stabilizer of the energy; the group participants provide the bulk energy. Regarding the materialization itself, the entities describe the process in a way similar to when they launch a space rocket they need a 'window.' Conditions and vectors have to be just right. We've been told that if the energy is slightly off in any of a number of ways, materialization may not occur. It could be the weather, the mood of someone in the group, something in the channel's chemistry; it could be almost anything. Sometimes the conditions are right for the entity to materialize and sometimes they are not. We never know when we have a meeting whether something is going to happen or not. We've asked again and again when we didn't get anything what went wrong, we were negative? They might well say that no, conditions just weren't right. It seems to be something no one individual or the collective group has any control over. If one main ingredient is not fitting, it just won't happen. That's a frustrating thing to try to teach someone who is trying to have a Darkroom group. The entities say just try and if it happens it happens. If it doesn't, you're not doing anything wrong, just keep trying if you want to. They won't spell it out for you, if there is any such thing as spelling it out for you. The channel's energy is a catalyst or a stabilizer and the group provides the bulk energy. One needs the other.

We found through our experience, and it seemed to be validated by the entities, that singing created a positive mood and boosted the energy. That's why we sang. Lively music seemed to help even more. That's why we used a lot of country western music at times, something cheerful or something that had an upbeat to it.

Question: How about people being afraid, does that seem to affect the energy?

We have had materialization where people have been scared out of their wits. If it were a very small group and a large percentage were very scared there probably wouldn't be any materialization. If you had a group of fifteen or twenty and one person is really very scared the entities would probably go ahead with the phenomena if in their evaluation that one person would be protected enough and feel secure enough with the other people around. Naturally the entities wouldn't do anything in a deliberate way to add to one's fear. What they would do is deal with it in a manner designed to help the person to become unafraid. But it can happen that if a very few people are really scared, that fear could very possibly interfere with materialization. One of the main things to remember is that the entities will not do anything that will be deliberately painful to you, like deliberately scare you or frighten you. That is a basic rule. That doesn't mean that if they materialize you might not think, "I'm scared to death." Someone might become angry because they are frightened. That is the person's own internal process and if the entities appear they have already evaluated that person's level of fear and whether or not they could deal with it if they wanted to. And they would be working with that person on any of several levels.

I don't know if I've said this before, but one of the most deteriorating processes to the energy is if people in the group are hostile toward one another. Now if you had a large group and two of them were at each other's throats there may be enough energy to override that. But if you have a small group and there're a lot of negative projections toward one another, more than likely there wouldn't be any materialization because that interferes with the energy. That doesn't mean you have to like everybody there, but it seems that there's a not liking somebody in a positive way and this is different from not liking somebody in a negative way. It is a person's own emotional response that interferes with the energy. They told us you don't have to like everybody, you don't have to be chummy and hugging and kissing everybody. You can be together and not really approve of someone's behavior or you could even dislike them, but there's a lot of difference in not liking somebody and having a strong negative reaction to them.

Question: Would you say something about the sex of the entities as that relates to the channel?

More than likely there will be a male entity with a male channel, and female with female, because of the cloning process. There have been females to materialize with just me channeling. Very little is known about the cloning process. About as much as I know is that from the group, either one person or a number of persons, they take very small fragments of tissue. To give you an example, when Lanika would come and materialize, some of the women in the room would begin to get a little itch or like a little pin prick feeling somewhere on their bodies. The entities explained they were taking fragments of the physical body. They would say that all they need would be a few cells and they could clone from that. Sometimes, the number of people they would take tissue from would determine what the entity is going to look like. They can clone an entity to look like any one person in the group, a combination of people, or different altogether. That's really all I know. Once they go through this process of getting the tissue, they use the energy available and once it is stabilized it can begin to manifest itself in what is called ectoplasm. Along with this ectoplasm and the fragments of tissue they clone the body. Sometimes in the very beginning of our group, you could see the ectoplasm form and collect. Then you could see an ethereal form and soon it would solidify.

We started referring to our meetings as Darkroom because when we began to get independent voice they said that natural light or artificial light of most kinds was detrimental to the cloning process. It is like using sensitive film, and like developing film in the dark. That is how we came up with the idea of using a red light. They said that if any entity came out in the light it would preferably be a red light because that was less disturbing to the entity.

We were finally given permission to photograph and were told to use a strobe rather than a flashbulb, I guess because it was faster. People that experienced that photography session said that every time the strobe light would go off the entity would be practically knocked to his knees. He would recoil from the light flash. They took seventeen or eighteen pictures that evening. Needless to say, I was wiped out. I woke up vomiting and very weakened. This happens if an entity is exposed to light. When the channel goes into a deep trance, the entities have control of the channel's nervous system and body. They can take you down into a very deep state and can alter your respiration and pulse rate. Supposedly when Aenka came out in the light my heart rate was practically nothing and so was my pulse. If they get the channel that low and take that much energy they go through a careful process of dematerializing and putting energy back into the channel so that by the time I woke up I would have enough energy. The only other times I remember feeling nauseated (other than when Aenka was photographed) was when Mario would come and would be in much light for an hour or two. Sometimes I would also be a bit confused and disoriented. For our regular session when I awaken and come out of it I feel I've taken a nap and don't have any measurement of time. It might have been only 20 minutes, but it seemed as if I have been sleeping all night.

Question: Would you talk some about what you do when you channel, in a sense how do you do it?

I can describe it in the physical sense. First I empty my pockets so I won't be laying on my wallet or keys or whatever. I take my shoes off, my glasses and my watch. Then I lay down. I take a couple of deep breaths and I hear the people singing. Then it is just like I begin to feel myself floating away, and that is the last I remember.

Question: Could you say more about that?

It's like going to sleep. Physiologically and psychologically for me I don't feel a lot of difference. When I lay down I don't know whether I am in a regular sleep or a trance sleep. The only way I know which one I have been in is through the experience of the people in the Darkroom. When I am in regular sleep, nothing happens. When I am in trance sleep, phenomena occur.

Question: Do you have any awareness during your trance sleep?

No.

Question: Afterwards do you have any memory?

Probably about five times in my ten years or so of experiencing trance. It was explained to us that it is similar to flashback. Sometimes after I wake up, it would be like I had had a dream. I would be aware of someone's experience.

Question: How would you know that?

When they would share some of the things with me, some of their experiences, I already knew it. I'm glad I haven't had any more flashbacks or memories than I just mentioned, and I try not to have. It wouldn't be right to try to have them. If I did that I would be violating the confidence of the other people. That has been one of my vows or promises to myself, that if I ever have any psychic recall of any of their experiences I will never reveal it. I've held to that. It was a concern of people in the group. On some level they didn't want anybody to know what they experienced because their visits were very personal. Naturally they were concerned about me being aware of it. That's a very firm commitment and not one I really have to bother about often because it has only happened those few times I mentioned.

Question: Marti talked about other people who wanted to channel, and who got some instruction from the entities and would practice. Would you comment on that, and also say whatever you could about how you might teach other people to channel?

I don't think anybody, not even myself, can teach anybody how to channel. It is something that just happens. There's no way I can teach someone what happens with my energy so far as preparing myself. I can go through the simple mechanics of saying that I go in and I lay down and I clear my mind. I don't become personally involved with any expectations with what is going to happen; I just relax. In the beginning I used self-hypnosis to relax and put myself in a trance.

I would give myself suggestions for physiological relaxation and then it was automatic. I would lie down in a certain place and would hear the music and I was out. You see, whatever they do with my energy, how they use it, or what happens I don't have any control over, I just trust. It's more like not interfering, just giving permission to the entities, than my actually doing something. It just happens, I have no control over it. My energy is available to be used in whatever manner that is positive.

Question: What have you found that interferes with

channeling?

We've been told that if the channel has alcohol during a number of hours beforehand, that affects the chemistry and alters the energy and does interfere. Other than that, I don't know. We've tried to figure it out on nights that nothing happened, we would ask the entities, but I think I've already talked about that.

Question: Let me put a hypothetical issue to you. Say a group of six people came to you, all of whom had some psychic or auditory channeling type experience. They seemed okay to you, and asked you to teach them or to guide them. What guidelines would you use, what would you try to steer them toward and away from?

I would only tell them the same thing I tell everybody else. Don't be a damn fool. I wouldn't wish it on anybody. Or the responsibility.

Question: Would you say more?

If you get involved with channeling and you start having materialization, I feel you would have a sense of responsibility to share that in some way. Then you are stuck with it. Now you can say, well, I can change and get out of it anytime I want to, I can make that choice. But your choice was made in the first place, you see. When you make a choice you make a choice.

Question: You mean a person could not choose to get out?

Sure somebody could choose to get out, but then you would be shirking some responsibility. I could very easily stop or quit. I wouldn't feel good about myself. I would feel it was a cop-out.

Question: And if this hypothetical group of people were still determined to do it and thought they were willing to accept that responsibility?

Then I would say get involved, be my guest, if that's what you want to do, do it.

Question: What else might you say to such people?

Well, I would tell them to get ready to experience things that would be soul shaking, things that they may never understand, things they may or may not have a need to understand. Things they would have no way to explain. You would probably experience things about people and the environment, which would require you to commit yourself to a lifetime of confidentiality. I would ask them to do a little soul searching. How honest can you be with yourself? How honest can you be with other people? What is your motive for getting involved? Are you willing to put in hours of sacrifice and dedication? Do you have the willingness to develop the patience to stay with it? What is your level of tolerance for disappointment? For loneliness? For isolation?

Question: So again, if these people were willing to look at those issues in themselves and still they wanted to go ahead, what else might you say to them?

I would tell them to avoid a need to be important or to feel responsible for what happens. When you get into these things and you begin to experience things, your intuition develops at a higher capacity. You are able to know more things sooner, and to me that can be very dangerous. If you can become an observer and not a responsibility taker, and be involved with other people but stick to your own business, then you can deal with it. But if you are on an ego trip where you have to prove something, brag, or point out things about people that would break confidence, that's very dangerous business. If you are on an ego trip you get into the attitude of "setting people straight" on where you think they are wrong in their beliefs. I would say to avoid any kind of ego trip, and to take this very seriously. If you are not on an ego trip, you have a better chance with getting involved and letting other people go through their struggles. Let them learn their way without trying to rescue, reform them, or be judgmental in some way. The danger of an ego trip is that you are going to ultimately violate a confidence or mess people over. If you can respect other people, stick to your own business, keep confidentiality, etc., then the entities are going to trust you in being a channel to deal with information.

I believe that a person really has to evaluate their motives for wanting to get involved and wanting to be a channel. You really have to ask yourself, "Why do I want to be a channel?" And each person is the only one that knows their motives. You can make a lot of assumptions or you might even create a test that would predict reasons for motivation for different people, but when you get right down to it only the person themselves really knows. It is quite possible that in a conscious process they would say such and such is the reason that I want to get involved, but on some other level they are being motivated for some other reasons that are not very healthy.

Question: Like . . .?

Status, money, power, things like that. Since I have no vested interest in those then I am an open target. That makes me like an instrument to the cause of serving mankind and helping people get on with their lives. I can deal with unpleasant situations and I can have fortitude in circumstances that otherwise might not be tolerated by someone else. My commitment always makes that very clear to me when I am challenged. My position is unshakeable.

Question: You have mentioned a commitment or commitments you have made. Would you say more about that, have you made other commitments or promises to yourself regarding channeling?

One other commitment is that I would never stop doing it as long as there was somebody that was interested and sincere enough to participate. I will provide my energy for them. This relates to my commitment to Divine Guidance and the need to learn more and this contact offers this opportunity.

Question: In spite of your disappointments or disillusionments in the past?

Yes, because I am older and wiser. I am even more convinced that there is nothing negative out there, and anything a person experiences of a negative nature, comes from themselves. It is some problem of theirs and not the energy out there, not the entities being negative toward them. I am not bothered by that anymore.

Question: Do you feel this commitment to continue is a totally willful choice of your own or do you believe that you have been asked to do this?

I have definitely been asked to do it. I've even been asked to promise that I would never give it up. This happened well into my personal visits with materialized entities. I've sat down and discussed with them for hours all kinds of things, this included. Of course I could have said no, I had free choice as we all do.

Question: Jay, would you talk some about how you know the experiences of materialized entities are not hallucinations, or some product of an altered state of consciousness, rather than being 'real'?

I guess I've had both kinds of experiences, and for me I know the difference. For me, a hallucination is a very personal experience. I can't hallucinate your hallucinations. When you are out of your body or you are with an entity, it is a very real thing. When you come back in your body you can remember that experience. You can repeat it and repeat it in ways that have continuity and further exploration. I don't believe that people hallucinate in sequences of events that hang together and build one on another. You know, I just don't believe that people can hallucinate at will or on command, at a chosen time. So there are similarities in the consistency of experience with materialized entities and out-of-body experiences. I can say some things about out-of-body experiences that I might apply here. So far as I know, total out-of-body experiences are always positive. There are some people who have had very frightening out-of-body experiences, but the fright is not in the experience itself, the fright is in the translation or interpretation after they have experienced it. The frightening aspects have more to do with a person's own psychological process. I don't think hallucinations have any control or command. It is something that you are not in charge of. In an out-of-body experience of a total type you are definitely in command and in charge of it.

Question: How do you mean?

By the processes and the things you experience when you are in the unobstructed. You can go anywhere and experience anything you want when you want to. So far as I am concerned, a hallucination is a spontaneous random thing that you have no control of, and that is not true for out-of-body experiences. One other thing is that when people who have had total out-of-body experiences have experienced the Archives of Knowledge, when you hear them talk you know they have experienced the same things. The experiences are basically identical, even though we have the experience totally independent of one another. Now the way each person would individually translate it, or try to describe it would be slightly different. But when two people who have really had such an experience talk about it their experiences consistently agree. Out-of-body experiences and visits with

346

the entities have some real similarities. I don't think people who hallucinate have those kinds of experiences. One factor, which makes communications about these kinds of experiences difficult for people, is that many times we simply don't have words. So when we try to put words to it, we do it each in our own way. But there is enough consistency and enough contact and identification so that there is no doubt that it was the same experience.

Question: So when you hear people talking about their experiences you can get a sense of whether from your perspective it was an imagined experience—a hallucination—or a genuine one?

Yes. By the way they describe their experience - that is the only thing I have to go on. One difficulty here is not becoming judgmental. You see, if I have any vested interest in their experience or in my proving something then I will become judgmental and not be able to really listen.

Question: To compare a bit between voice channeling and materialization channeling, you said there was always the chance for distortion in voice channeling but not in materialization. Would you elaborate some on that?

I consider that what I am told when I am talking with a materialized entity is 100% accurate with no distortion of my own. I trust them 100%. I've been challenged on this many times, with questions like do you believe word for word? Do you follow their instructions? I say yes. I know they have more information than I have. I trust that. They have availability to the Archives of Knowledge. This is different for me from voice channeling, where I believe I have already said that it is 80% correct maximum and distortions occur through filtering through the channel's mind and personality.

Question: Would you talk about the effect on your life of

your experiences with the entities, whatever comes up for you?

I am committed to the K plan. In a simple or general sense the K plan is a process of teaching people who are willing to learn and receive information and techniques that have a therapeutic quality. It is helping people get in touch and free themselves of their negativity. It is an attempt to get the human race back on the track of unconditional love. I am committed along with some other people to teach and disseminate what we have been taught through the various contacts we have had and not to deviate from those teachings any more than is necessary.

Question: Deviating?

Meaning not to deviate by personal distortion the teaching of what the entities consider the truth about the naturalness of man. What they teach is based on unconditional love and the universal laws that govern natural behavior. Psychodrama as we developed it and Marti elaborated on it is one effective tool in that direction. As I've said before the entities do not put things in terms of orders or "thou shalt not" or "thou shall." We are given suggestions, and have been told that if we would follow certain laws and processes what could eventually happen regarding influencing a lot of people.

Some people ask me why I've made the commitments I have, what do I get out of it. I answer the same way. When you see someone experiencing growth there is no question. You don't even have to argue about why you do it. That's why I do it, that's my gratification, to participate in people having those experiences and those feelings. That is my way of giving. I get pleasure out of this, watching other people grow, watching other people find themselves. I get the chance to watch other people figure out something or experience an awakening they have been looking for all their life and it is simply thrilling to observe this. I don't know if I can give you any idea of the pleasure and gratification I get from observing this. It is soul food to me. It is a privilege for me to be involved in this.

The entities exist, they are just as real as we are and they are always awaiting their opportunity to communicate with us in whatever way they can.

CHAPTER SEVEN
GUIDELINES AND PROCESSES OF THE ORIGINAL GROUP AS THEY EVOLVED

This chapter will be a summary and overview of our Darkroom group procedures as they progressed over the years. It includes a compilation of comments regarding what I feel and believe to be basic purposes of such activities in general. The primary purpose of our group came to be promotion of personal growth and self-awareness. In order to move in these directions, it was necessary for participants to have a very high degree of commitment over a period of many months to several years, coupled with courage to face their fears and to experiment with changing attitudes and behaviors.

Other people who choose to experiment with activities such as ours will need to bear in mind that our objective was and is to explore and discover man's magnificence, and not limit ourselves to the excitement of phenomena alone or attempt to attract any followers or converts. Naturally any persuasion, coercion, or misrepresentation is out of the question. Unfortunately many if not all good things people are capable of doing have at one time or another in history been manipulated and distorted by people with selfish interests and this no doubt will continue. Feeding off of people's fear, guilt and anxiety, some individuals have distorted psychic and spiritual phenomena for personal profit. As with any other human ability or endeavor, Darkroom-type experiences can become a vehicle for destructive forms of self-gratification.

The reader is cautioned to use their own judgment in selecting a process and/or people presenting a spiritual path.

From our early beginnings in the dark, literally and figuratively, it was months before we began to get voices and about two years until we had full physical materialization. While some people who came to the group dropped out in a number of weeks, those who remained had a typical commitment of two nights a week. In other groups similar to ours, one group met regularly for a year and a half, another for two and a half years before they could rejoice in the experience of materialization. In these groups, as in our original group, once the materialization was initiated it continued to be experienced by the group as long as the members had a positive commitment to personal growth. Considerable effort, practice, and experimentation with group interaction and group energy were essential in our being successful. Each member was willing to devote a portion of time and energy to our common cause and interest. It was trying and emotionally painful because it necessitated a high degree of mutual openness and honesty within the group. In the difficult quest for a balance of energy, feelings in the group during our meetings would shift from ecstasy and joy to frustration and back again. In a very real sense uncommon patience and dedication are called for. Homogeneity of purpose was a key factor. One of the purposes and functions of the group came to be to support the physical, emotional, intellectual and spiritual development of each member. The emergence of a positive group focus helped generate and sustain the energy needed for materialization. A primary focus was on the group process and involvement, even after personal visits began. I believe all groups, which meet for purposes similar to ours and achieve full materialization, will receive identical information.

We found a group of seven people was probably optimal to produce adequate energy and yet allow for much personal contact among ourselves. As the group progressed and materialization became more consistent and stronger, we found that we could achieve materialization with as few as one or two people in addition to the channel. We met in a darkened room. This was to eliminate most types of white light, which the entities later told us interfered with the type of energy involved in materialization. Very low levels of moonlight and red light interfere the least, and both could be allowed at times. Luminous or phosphorescent that paint that glows in the dark also interferes minimally; both were also quite useful and used intermittently, as has been described. In our early days, we would have enough moonlight to see outlines of the group members, which was helpful in discriminating movement. We found one hour was adequate for each session during our experimental stages. If phenomena were forthcoming, activity would be observed within this time. In longer sessions we would sometimes use short breaks to stretch, move about, revitalize ourselves. We found if we met too long without a break, the available energy would decrease due to fatigue of group members. The group meetings were begun with the Lord's Prayer and several other prayers having particular personal meanings. The prayers might be Christian, Buddhist, Sufi, or of other orientations. In my point of view, the important factor was not the religious orientation so much as sincerity and a feeling of harmony and humility. While initially we met two to three times a week, once we began to have clear phenomena and materialization, I must admit that our group met as often as possible.

Singing came to be our primary vehicle for sustaining a single group focus and unifying our positive energy to help promote entity materialization. One of the members took a popular song, "Welcome to My World," and wrote a version appropriate for our group which we called "Welcome to Our World." It was one of our favorites. We would sing anything; contemporary pop music, religious hymns, folk songs such as "She'll Be Comin' Round the Mountain," even childhood rounds and Christmas carols, any music that would help create a joyous outgoing mood was preferable.

After we began to get phenomena, we began to use some props for further experimentation and verification. Such simple props might be a light piece of styrofoam chip or a scarf painted with luminous paint or a simple medium's trumpet as described in Chapter One. In the early days of our development we would tape record each session and listen back. Often, comments and greetings, which had been missed by our human ears during the meeting, were heard at playback. Later, when voice developed sufficiently to allow conversation, we began to ask permission to tape. This was often granted, but not always. Occasionally, permission would be given for an individual to tape a personal counseling session with an entity. Professional therapists hearing such tapes have consistently been very impressed at the effectiveness of the counseling techniques used by the entities.

Touch was an early form of contact. Therefore, it became a rule or custom in our group that if one member moved or touched another he or she would acknowledge this action. This, of course, helped in discriminating our behavior from that of the entities. Regarding sounds, if we made any ourselves, we had a rule of verbally acknowledging it immediately.

We continued to find that sharing of our thoughts and feelings, whatever they might be, resulted in a positive form of focused group energy. This was in fact encouraged later by the entities. We tried to give full attention and nonjudgmental support to any verbalization or expression of feelings. Sharing of fear, guilt or anxiety might seem to be potentially explosive and fragmenting, but the honesty of expression and acceptance by others reduced such negativity to a minimum. The entities stressed that critical feelings toward others should not be acted out in a confrontational manner but rather be examined in oneself. We found feelings could be expressed and accepted more readily in the dark than we had expected. Doubts were expressed and understood as a natural activity of the conscious mind. We found many hours in the dark in a group setting consistently tended to strip away the mask we all wear to hide our inner fears. In a very real sense, one may see more clearly in the dark.

We found the most destructive or negative type of forces, which could interfere with our group processes, were generated not by fear, guilt, or anxiety, but from negative, envious, or competitive feelings associated with anger. We found anger was destructive only when envious or resentful feelings were directed from one group member to another without looking inward for the original sources of these feelings. We found that lack of trust is perhaps the most difficult fear confronted within the Darkroom. Even after we had known each other for some time, some people's old fears and lack of trust in humanity could still be re-stimulated and they found the fears needed to be challenged again and again.

When the entities began to make their presence known it was of course startling, although they do not intend to frighten. Indeed, the very gradual process with which they present themselves and make themselves known serves a purpose of reducing fear of the unknown and thus facilitate more full contact. They assured us there was a basic qualitative difference between a negative or neurotic type of fear and natural or healthy fear-like shock or response of the human nervous system when exposed to something new. This latter response is seen as positive rather than negative. However, as careful as the entities were, we found group members would suddenly sometimes become very aware of unresolved fears after materialization had occurred; fears of dying, ghosts, evil, etc. These feelings were also expressed openly within the group.

All the teachings were ultimately directed toward emotional growth, even though humor might at times be the vehicle. On a particular evening or over a series of evenings our meetings might develop a somewhat different focus, but the topic would always swing back to personal growth. Among the emphasized topics were death and the stages of transition, the obstructed, the unobstructed, relationships, healing, therapy, stages of development in the unobstructed, etc. The entities seemed to evaluate the areas of need in the participants and would respond in a wide variety of ways, in my opinion always toward a positive facilitation of growth. In an over-all sense, one of their goals with us was working toward the full development of all four quadrants of the personality structure. A rhythmic balance of the four quadrants would enable us to experience self-acceptance, self-worth and self-love. They provided information and guidance to those willing to understand themselves in order to better understand others. As our group began to experience more phenomena and materialization and increased in size, it became apparent it would be advantageous to form smaller groups rather than to have one large one. For each group a channel was needed. Many people in our group were eager to meet the challenge of attempting to channel and asked Aenka if they could become channels. Aenka replied that everyone has psychic abilities from the intuitive quadrant of the personality structure, but fear and guilt interfere with the natural development of these gifts and they go largely untapped. He stated repeatedly, a person must be willing to challenge their fears and rid themselves of guilt to become a channel. Aenka acknowledged that this was no small task. In order to channel, it appears a person must dedicate much of their life work to what is referred to as a revolution against negativity. For now suffice it to say that this requires not only an attitude and desire to overcome one's own negativity, fears, and guilts, but a willingness to do whatever is required to achieve this. It also involves a free giving of one's energy, love and time to others and assisting in their efforts to overcome their personal or unique fears and negativity. To be an optimally effective channel one must be able to achieve an altered state of consciousness, which appears by observation to be a deep trance. Different channels known to this author have different favorite positions while channeling. One may be relaxed comfortably in a chair, another on a bed, another on cushions on the floor. They might lie on their side or on their back. While most channels are in such a deep trance they are not aware of activity around them. I know at least one who remains aware of singing or other group activities. Two important elements needed for channeling are a feeling of physical security, and relative comfort.

By the time we closed our original Darkroom group to visitors in the late 1970's due to very accusatory publicity, several other groups had started with new channels. While channeling does drain some energy, it does not appear to have any long-term negative effect. While we were still meeting openly Jay could, after a period of five years, channel five or six times a week for periods of up to eight hours. Occasionally, group-teaching sessions conducted by the entities lasted up to sixteen hours. The average meeting once we got full materialization lasted about four hours.

CHAPTER EIGHT
SOME PARTICIPANTS' VIEWS

In this chapter, Darkroom members share some of their experiences, reactions and responses. Little if any editing has been done on their contributions. This will hopefully allow some personal aspect of each to be apparent. I have chosen to change the names of the individuals in order to protect their privacy.

Lon

I became involved with the Darkroom in 1973 when I went to one of the meetings my brother and his wife had been attending. I had talked to them about what went on, and had become more and more interested in going myself. One night I got a chance.

As we first started the meeting everybody was sitting in the dark and singing. Soon there was some noise, like somebody walking across the floor. Everyone had been instructed not to move or to get out of their chair. There were two trumpets in the room, one large and one small. During the meeting one of them rose up. Out of it came a squeaky voice that was very faint. This voice talked and would answer some questions, mostly yes and no. During this time you couldn't really see anyone. The voice didn't sound like anyone in the room, and I don't think anyone there was able to imitate a voice like that.

The first meeting was really interesting. I didn't get many questions answered because to be truthful, I was pretty scared. I didn't even know what I was getting into, but I figured at least I would go and see. After the meeting, I asked if I could come back. Even though I was afraid, it seemed like a nice place to be and all the people seemed rather nice. My sister-in-law told me the entities said no, not at this time. So I put it aside and figured that for whatever reasons the entities had, it wasn't the right time for me to be there. So I accepted that.

The first time I was in the Darkroom, I wasn't sure if I should believe it or not. The people there seemed to accept strange things with such certainty. The first feeling I had when the lights were turned out was anxiety over what was really going to happen. Yet there was excitement over the possibility of truly meeting an entity that was not part of this world. There were strong fears of facing the unknown, the dark, and not knowing what was going to meet me. The not knowing of what kind of creatures existed had always been a curiosity and a fear. I had always wanted to find out, but was afraid. The only thing that kept my fear from increasing and taking over was the calmness and pleasure of the other people. After the singing went on for a few minutes, I started to enjoy the music. There was an interesting change in the tone or mood of the room when the entities came out. This continues to happen to greater or lesser degrees in all of our meetings. The change isn't in the people; it's in the air. It is a new energy entering the room. The quality of the energy is different from any other that I've felt. Even at my first meeting I recognized the energy as strong, constant, balanced and positive. It made me feel energetic and peaceful. At the time my fears of what was to come blocked most of those feelings, but they were there. There wasn't any way for me to know if the entities were partially or fully materialized. Much later I learned that at times when entities tried to materialize there was only a slight change in the energy. Sometimes I could see a whitish light move into the room and take a more solid form. This depended on how close I was to the entity when they materialized. Many times I could see flashes of lights or flowing waves of faint light.

About a year after my initial meeting I met a woman who is now my wife. She told me again about the meetings. She was going to them and she asked for me if I could come. This time I got permission. Again, the meetings were in the dark. The members always said a prayer before they started. So on this, my second time in the group (the first of what began to be regular attendance) there was an entity that came and his voice was completely different from the initial meeting. It was much stronger. It was interesting how much better he could speak, during a year a lot had improved. The entity would go around the room using the trumpet and ask people questions or ask if they had any questions for him.

The biggest thing that stood out for me at that time was the feeling of being accepted; not only by the group members, but by the entity. I had a strong feeling this just wasn't a regular person. It wasn't so much what he was saying at the time, but it was more the feeling that was there. It was as if there were no feelings of negativity, no feeling of pushing people, wanting more from them, or being aggressive. Yet he also wasn't submissive. The entity was just himself. It seemed like he was very much at peace with himself. I think that's the thing that impressed me the most. There was no pretense or arrogance. I forget what I talked about that night or the questions, but people did get visits out of the room. Whatever they discussed with the entity, I am not sure about. Aenka would talk, then leave; then another entity would enter. They would walk over, touch someone, and the person would ask if they were there for them. I guess they either got a tap on the head or something to indicate they were going out. It would vary how long people were out; for private visits there was no set time. I became a regular member of the group about June 1974.

Most of the time people in the group were happy at the meetings. Often, people worked on their feelings, and that is an important thing in itself. In the first few meetings I went to, most of the questions and issues were on very light things—entities, soulmates, and energies; things that are in this world that we cannot see. Looking back, these seem like very superficial questions about what people were doing or what they should do. There was never really much work with feelings. That went on for a while, but not for very long after I joined.

One night Aenka came out and talked about the importance of making a change in the purpose of the meetings. I remember feeling threatened at the time, because it was a change from just playing around and having a good time to really investigating seriously why we were there and what we were to gain. It was like somebody said kindergarten is ending. All the little games that people had played with the entities were really not the primary reason they were there. They were there to work with all the unfinished feelings they had. Now we call it "unfinished business," the holdover of our fears and guilts. At the time I wasn't really sure what it was. The entity was very serious about the importance of dealing with feelings. Up to this point, some people would deal with some things, but not really their major issues.

I noticed as the group went along that certain people didn't come back because they didn't like the change in the structure. They didn't want to be delving into their feelings. At this time the entities would start working with people in the room, trying to guide them to talk about their real problems in their life. They began to be much more confrontational, but not in a derogatory or an abusive way. Sometimes they were very blunt in what they said. The intention was always to teach, to have the person learn, to give them something to grow with. Many times people left the meetings with the awareness of feelings they could work with.

Growth work continued to be the emphasis in our meetings. The psychodrama workshops (conducted by Marti) didn't exist yet. The entities always said our experiences were preparing us. But for what, they were pretty vague. Sometimes I wish I had the knowledge then that I do now as a counselor, to observe the entities work as counselors. I think I would have appreciated a lot more of what they were doing. What they did was amazing at the time but I didn't really understand a lot of what they were saying. I think now I could learn more about working with people if I could see that more. That's one thing I miss.

The first time I ever worked with any feelings was interesting. I hadn't had a visit for a long time. Certain people got a chance to go out with entities and talk with them. At the time, without admitting it, I had a lot of fear about what to do, what to say, or of what they would bring up. Being assertive has always been a major issue for me. It has come up on different levels and in different forms. Just saying something and standing up for myself is always a major issue. I think it was Aenka who said to me one time, *"You don't have to justify your existence to anyone."* That's really what I was doing. I learned very young I didn't have a right to say or do anything without permission. At a time when I apparently needed to work on this, I had a personal visit with the entity called Carlisle.

We'd had two visits before, just getting to know each other. Our talk got onto the subject of past relationships I'd had. I was looking for an understanding of why I still hurt and was still reluctant to trust. There was a tremendous amount of shame for having feelings of grief. When I went out with Carlisle at that time, I had never talked about my thoughts, feelings, or my wanting to let go of my feelings. All I did was mention I wanted to talk about the relationship. It was as if he was following my thoughts and not my words. At that time I was very careful about what I said. He would talk more to what I was thinking than what I said. What I really wanted was to let go of the things inside of me but had not really felt comfortable with doing that. I was hoping being out of the room, away from the other people, I could work with it. So what did he do? He took me back into the group meeting room and sat me down and had me work there. It was very interesting, because that was the one thing that I was so afraid of. I felt secure enough and I trusted enough to let my feelings come up. Even though they were painful, it was good to let them out.

The issue of loving yourself came up many times. Different entities talked about enjoying your life and not letting negativity run your life. I felt very justified in my resentment of others because of how they had hurt me. The entities kept pushing the issue of free choice and how I was responsible in the interactions with others. On many occasions Carlisle would discuss how I was responsible for things that had happened. He would let me complain about someone and then he would explain, step by step, how I ignored my responsibilities and tried to blame others.

That was the beginning of the work that I am doing now, as a dramatist and staff person in psychodrama. Ever since that time I've had good feelings for the entities. There is nothing that has ever been negative to me. There have been a lot of painful things, a lot of things I haven't understood; but if I took the time to explore them, I would get some answers. It is only when I would close myself off and fight that I didn't understand, that things didn't seem to make sense. Anytime I could get clarification on issues, there was a tremendous amount of logic and insight into myself and how other people are—the very existence of people. One of the basic things I've learned from the entities is that some peoples own negativity is the cause of many of their problems. Such negativity manifests itself in numerous ways, often resulting in a person's distrust or unwillingness to look for an explanation that they may not be comfortable with (at any particular time in their lives). Additionally, some people may not want to address their negativity because such an action requires extensive thought and deep soul-searching. The entities always said no one would take such avoidances away from you—and they don't. They haven't at any time tried to coerce, push, or in any way make someone change their opinion. They would rather let that person keep their opinion and their free will and have them leave the group than to jeopardize or take away that person's free will.

One thing I've found that was amazing to me was that Carlisle, the entity I went out with, could talk to me the way that I talk to myself. I've never found that in another person. He used my language to explain, so I didn't find it hard to understand what he was meaning or saying. I remember, too, that the entities would not always go into as much detail as I wanted. At times they would leave things very open, or even ambiguous, to have me use my logic and figure out what they meant. The entities talked a lot about my family when I was a child, and how I fit into it. They would show me how other people in my family saw things differently from me, and that it was important I see this. Other people don't see things exactly the way I do.

There was a tremendous amount of balance in the visits. At times the entities were very serious when things needed to be worked on and people's feelings needed to be worked out. They were very understanding and warm and comforting, when the time was right. And sometimes the entities were very silly, and used humor as a great way to help us look at things. It seemed no matter what was said, there was always a lesson in it; there was always something to be learned from it.

When I think of all the things the entities did with the people, in a way all people really needed to do was listen. In a lot of ways they would push people's fear to the limit until they would face them. That is, when they had been given permission to do so. They said, "You are here to finish unfinished business, and that is the purpose for the group." People seemed to forget that, and would get caught in their fears and away they'd go—losing their perspective of why they were there.

There were many meetings when there would be only one entity; other times there were two simultaneously, both male. Some of the females in the group wanted to channel and see if they could get something to happen. The first meeting that I had a visit with a female entity, she had a very weak voice. It was high-pitched, but it had the same quality of softness that the male entities had. We talked a lot about the relationship that I had with my wife. She tried to explain sexuality to me to help with that. Relationships were an issue I had never really faced. It was important to me at that time to have a female I could talk to. I think I could have talked to Carlisle, but it helped to have a female there to talk to.

I never really learned who my soulmates were. All I really learned was there are two of them. The entities never told me if my soulmates were in this life or in the unobstructed. They focused on the point that there were definite things to learn. One thing that always stuck in my head was why I was here on earth at this time. I would ask this often and it always came back, "To succeed," whatever that means. Sometimes they would answer people's questions in a more definite way, like they were there to experience authority or submission or to learn to cooperate. I never got an answer like that and I always wondered. That is still an open question, whatever succeeding is. I have always felt that was what I wanted to do anyway, to learn to be comfortable with that. They left it as an open question.

I remember the time the subject of marrying my wife came up. That was something very important. I have mentioned here about never giving myself permission. I had talked to Carlisle about that, and he would go through asking me questions and having me answer. How do I feel about her? Do I feel that I want to have a commitment with her? Do I love her? You know, all the questions. Then in the end he said, "Then why don't you marry her?" It kind of clicked in my head again; I just had never given myself permission to do it on my own. He helped me with that. That was one of the nice lessons that I learned from him. One of the things that I wish I could have shared with my father was the experience of coming to the Darkroom. He just never really felt he wanted to. When my wife and I got married my family didn't come to the celebration afterwards, which saddened me. I wish they could have.

The groups kept getting larger and larger, and I wondered about where was this going to go? How many people can they let come in? It seemed like they were very lax in who could come. They seemed to let in just about anybody who wanted to come. We started having other smaller meetings in our house. Those were interesting because afterwards there were always noises in the house. It was like energy was left over. There were always creaks, like someone walking around. It was nice; it left a nice feeling in the house. Sometimes, before meetings would start, curtains would move, plants in our house would move, or a door would close. After the meetings ended and we went to bed, we could hear footsteps in different parts of the house. Many times there would be flashes of light above our bed or a tiny spot of light that would stay in one place for a few minutes. It became a regular schedule, the meetings on Friday, and it was a nice thing to look forward to. Sometimes it seemed like it would be nice to do something else, but we made a decision to go ahead and have the meetings so that people could learn from them. Marti started doing lectures on the material that she had put together and she was practicing with us. While people would have a private meeting with their entity, Marti would talk about the stages of development, natural emotions, the four quadrants, and anything else that interested people. So there was always something to be learned in there. I think a lot of the information they use today in psychodrama comes from that same material.

One incident I remember the most of the meetings at our house was what we called Black Monday. We had set aside a Monday for visitors' night, and held it at our house. Some strange things happened just before the meeting. I felt

363

almost compelled to leave the house and go to the library (I was in school at the time). As I was leaving Jay and Marti drove up, but I still felt I was being 'pushed' out of the house. I had to get out. I had to leave. Later on, when I found out about all the trouble that happened with the guy attacking the entity, maybe it was for the best I wasn't there. I know for the people that were there it was very hard. Looking back, it was important that I came back when I did that night and was as supportive as I could be. I tried to understand what happened. But that's one of the experiences that I will never forget. That situation in itself would have been enough proof to me to know that it wasn't Jay trying to be a fraud.

The groups kept getting bigger and bigger, more and more people coming in and taking it more and more for granted. Soon there were like 60 people at a meeting. Even as the meeting was in process, many were off into subgroups and doing their own things. There was no personal group support, no one was listening to the guitarist playing and singing, and no one was singing along like they should have been. I'm glad that when it got to that point the entities started to get much more strict on who could come. I felt much better after that. I wish the entities had done it sooner.

Other things that happened I could mention include a time a particular visitor came. She had decided, I guess, that the whole thing was a fraud and she was going to prove to her friend it was. I remember her asking me how many men were going to be there. That was interesting because it seemed like an odd question. I answered it and set it aside because I wasn't really that interested in what she was saying. The meeting was going along, and she had gone out with an entity and they had returned. All of a sudden she turned on the light. When I turned around from my seat, the entity I saw was certainly not Jay. What I saw was a very frail, pallid man who looked almost starved. He was very thin and looked very weak. She turned on the lights twice. I have always wondered why I never got up, why I never moved. It was almost like at the time there was no motivation to move. I had no energy to move. I think there must have been something going on with me because usually I would have done something.

People see different things. When we start talking about proof, many things come to mind. Entities I've been with have one week been one size and another week another size. It is amazing how different they can be and how different their voices are. They always explain it as being a change in the energy. I've always accepted that. When people start talking about doubts, I always have to look to myself. What have I seen? What have I experienced? I keep going back to that which I have seen and experienced is real. If it wasn't I wouldn't stay around one minute. If I thought there was fraud, I would leave.

Through my experience in the Darkroom meetings I have been around five different channels. Some were more experienced at what they were doing, so there was faster materialization. With more practice, the sooner materialization happened. To me, it also seemed [that] the more at peace the channel was with their own feelings, the faster [the] materialization took place. The mood of the people in the group also had an influence. In my experience the entity and the channel were of the same sex. I have heard there have been opposite sex entities but I have not been present at those meetings. I did see multiple entities from one channel.

The entities have given me a feeling I am loved, that I can love myself, and that I can trust. They will always be there; they will always be supportive for me. To be human is one of the greatest gifts that we have, and to experience it. I am learning to enjoy life. For that, I thank them. They have given me back hope in myself. I had lost it, buried it. I was just too afraid.

Brigette
About August or September of 1974, a friend shared with me an experience she had in a group. She explained about entities who had been visiting her. For some reason what she

told me just fit, I felt I had maybe found a piece of a puzzle that had been missing. I became very excited, and went with that friend to my first Darkroom in October of 1974. The room was darkened except for a luminous scarf, and I saw a pair of legs heading right toward me. I can remember thinking, "Where in the heck is the door? I want out of here." But I sat there, and this entity stood before me. I felt . . . no, not me the first one. I never experienced anything like this, and I don't even get a chance to see other people's experiences or hear other people's experiences?

The entity reached over and touched the person next to me, for which I was thankful. I didn't want to be the first one. I wanted to see and hear before I experienced it myself. This entity disappeared, and soon another pair of legs came heading right toward me. I had been told that entities do not invade your privacy or do anything without your permission. I gave him permission to touch me on the head if he was there for me, and I got a touch. I remember I was able to go out and visit with him that night. I found out his name was Charley and learned that we have shared many lives together.

I remember at the end of that meeting thinking, "My God, the love that radiated from him I have never in my life experienced from any human being." It just beamed from him, it was so strong. I swear, it could have knocked me over—in fact, I think it did. I can even remember thinking if I could learn this type of love and share it with the world it would be wonderful. That experience prompted me to begin working on myself, emotions and all. If I could learn to love myself then I could love others.

I remember sitting in the meetings many hours. A month later, on another guest night, I received another visit. A lot of anxiety was inside me. I can remember the people around me singing. Charley took me out of my chair and we danced in the middle of the room on the scarves until my anxiety ceased. I can remember asking him if he liked to dance, and he nodded yes, and I said, "I do, too." He shook his head to answer. They didn't speak in the room. They were there for you and not to share with everyone. I had a private visit with him that night also and again the love just radiated from him. I can remember later that evening sitting in the group room and becoming very ill. I had to get up and leave the room. I can remember leaving the room and going to an adjoining room where there was a fireplace I sat by. I remember walking out of the door and into this room and an entity was standing there. His hands were covering his face. They didn't like us to see their faces; I'm not exactly sure why. There was a sliding glass door in this other room and a light from down the street shone through the sliding glass door. He was standing in this light. I can remember his body being so luminous, almost like he glowed. As I walked toward the fireplace, the entity turned and walked back into the group room. As I was sitting there, I looked back at the door to the meeting room and out walks another entity who moved toward the sliding glass door. I swear he stuck his leg through the door.

In a few minutes I turned around again and there was an entity standing behind me. I tried to ask him questions, but he wouldn't answer. I found out many meetings later that he had been a guide of mine, checking to make sure I was all right. He stood nearby for a while. When I started feeling better he turned and walked back into the room.

Shortly after I joined the Darkroom, I shared my experience with some friends. These friends told some mutual acquaintances. I had specifically asked them not to share it with anybody, because there were a lot of people that weren't ready to hear about it yet. Weeks later we heard from mutual friends that we were being brainwashed, they knew it was a trick, and it wasn't any good. I can remember my husband and I being very upset with this. He was also a Darkroom member. We lied on the bed and held each other. We cried and asked for help. "God, if this is right, please let us know. You know what we are doing, and what we are getting ourselves into. Are we being so damn dumb that we'd just fall for anything?" I can remember going to sleep that night. As I often do when I'm ready to go to sleep I closed my eyes and then opened them for one last time. At the foot of my bed was Charley. He was standing there. I remember his moving closer to me, walking along my side of the bed. My hands were under the covers and I wanted so badly to hug him. I couldn't get my arms out; I couldn't have gotten them out to save my life. I remember blinking, and no sooner did I blink than he disappeared. I asked later why I couldn't get my arms out, and he said he was not in a solidly formed body and it would have frightened me to have touched him.

I've never really questioned after that night. If I ever wanted proof, that was it—that was the proof I needed. I wanted to get involved in the weekly group, and had been given permission to do that. I can remember sitting there one night when fingers appeared out of the curtains waving and wiggling back and forth. I saw them and let out a little screech of excitement. Everybody looked up, but by then the fingers were gone. I asked again, "Let the fingers come out again," and they did. Everybody saw them. The fingers were white—so illuminated they looked whiter than white.

I did much of my emotional work in the Darkroom. I had given the entities permission to do whatever was needed to help me grow. And they did. For a long time, probably close to a year, I worked on fear of the dark. I had a lot of anxiety about the dark. Evil lurks in the dark, bad things happen to you in the dark, that's the kind of stuff that was going through my mind. I can remember one night sitting in the chair, and from behind me came this hand touching me on the shoulder. I came unglued. If I could have, I would have run. I would have run that night. In my mind all I could picture was a hand and an arm up to about the elbow.

I remember after working with my fear for quite awhile, an entity took his hands and touched the top of my head and I can remember the love radiating out his hands helping to calm me down. It was like letting me know there isn't evil in the dark, there's love there. The same night

Aenka came out and told the group I had given the entities permission previously to help in any way that they could. They would usually not do things like that. I never saw them touch anyone unexpectedly again.

I learned later it was Mario that had come out and done that. Mario is a teacher to us all, and in one way or another has helped many of us through our emotional work a little faster. He is the one that comes in the brightest light. When he first started coming, he said, *"There are going to he some of you who love me and some of you who hate me."* I'll tell you, there have been many times I've hated him. At the same time, I also love him. I know sometimes I need a push, and he gives me that push. I don't always like it, but he gives me that push.

One night, we were all sitting and singing in the group, and the entity that comes to sing with us came. This is Willy. He told us to sit on the floor in a big circle close together. That night, I was upset about something. Everybody else was happy and singing. I felt because I was upset I would break the happiness, so I was trying to sit on my grief. The room was pitch black and nobody could see me. I scooted out of the circle, backed away to be by myself. Willy spoke up and said, *"The circle is not complete."* Someone asked aloud, "Who isn't here?" I didn't want to say anything, but pretty soon one of the other people said, "Brigette?" I responded, "What." My voice let them know I had moved away from the group. Willy got up, came to me, and danced with me. This helped me to let go of the grief.

It is interesting to me to watch the entities come out, cross the luminous scarf, and see their size. Usually about all you can see is up to about the knees. There are various sizes of legs, some huge, others small. I can remember visits with Charley when he would come at different heights. Sometimes I could rest my head on his shoulder, at other times only my nose would touch his shoulder. One time dancing with him, I had to stand on tiptoes to be able to lay my head there. They are never exactly the same size. I guess a lot depends on the energy. I

369

really kind of like it. To touch their bodies is like touching a baby's skin. Sometimes Charley's skin was damp and moist.

One night I was with Charley and I asked why we couldn't touch entities above the head or shoulders, or below the knees. He said that was true in the beginning, but that it was not so important now. He let me touch his head, I felt his eyes, and at one point he even took my hand and stuck it in his mouth and said, *"See, I even have teeth."* It was a beautiful head. They usually didn't materialize hair; they used turbans. I can remember feeling Charley's arms and he had very little hair on them. It was like they materialized enough for us to be happy with, but not use up a lot of energy.

Richard

When I first heard about the Darkroom somehow it fit into the scheme of the way I felt things should be. At the same time I was afraid to go and experience it. I thought about it. I finally decided that I would let myself challenge my fear, and experience it. At my first meeting at a guest night my fear lessened when I saw all the people. I was anxious for the session to start. When they turned out the lights and everyone started singing I could feel the fear in me rising. I wasn't sure what I was afraid of, but I was afraid.

As the group continued to sing an entity came out and walked over to where I was sitting. I could see his body shape illuminated by the scarves in the middle of the room. He walked very close to me, and I felt . . . now how in the hell am I going to get out of here? This guy's coming over by me. I wasn't quite sure who or what it was. All I knew was I was very afraid. I was glad when he moved over and stood before another group member.

As the evening progressed my fear lessened, and I could hardly wait until my turn came. When it did, the entity came and stood in front of me. My heart was pounding. I was so excited it was all I could do to ask a few yes and no questions which he answered by tapping me on the head. I can't describe the overwhelming feeling of love and acceptance that came through from just a tap on the head and his presence in front of me. I was afraid I wouldn't be able to go and have a personal visit with him, and I was afraid that I was going to have a visit with him. Later in the session Aenka came. I got the courage to ask him if there would be any more visits, if I would have a chance to go out with my friend. When Aenka told me I wouldn't be able to go out that night, I was relieved.

At the next visitors' night I was anxious and still scared, but not quite as scared. When my turn came, I did get to go out for a private visit. I re-experienced the total feeling of complete love and acceptance; that no matter what I did, it would be all right. We talked. I asked him a few questions about my past lives and other things, which at the time I found very interesting.

I don't remember at which visit he told me about my last life preceding this one. I was talking about different things, and asked him if he could tell me about the last physical life I had. I felt it wasn't long ago, and I'd had dreams or feelings about coming into this life. I asked what I had to experience in this life. The entity told me who I was in my last life. And I said, "Well that wasn't very long ago, was it?' He replied, *"No, it was'"t. You chose to come back very soon. Most people don't choose to come back in such a short time span. Your choosing to come back was very important."* *Little* did I realize at that time what all that was to involve.

I didn't realize starting these visits would eventually lead to changing my whole life, my whole lifestyle. I became aware of the feelings and emotions that I had hidden and which had lain dormant in me for a long period. When I became aware of these feelings, it just naturally led me into psychodrama work. My personal work was speeded up by my visits with my friend. In fact in the very beginning I believe if it hadn't been for my visits with my friend in the Darkroom, and seeing the work other people did, I probably wouldn't have continued with psychodrama. Drama was very painful for me in the beginning. It was very scary, and I could not see any changes coming about either in me or in those around me. As time progressed, I did more and more of my work in drama and less of it in the Darkroom. The Darkroom then became more a source of pleasure and enjoyment, and a source of verification of my intuitive hunches. I would have these during intervals between Darkrooms, and would ask the entity about as many of them as I could, or felt comfortable with. The answers I'd get would usually verify the hunches.

As time progressed, I could see the Darkroom as a valuable source of information. The entities didn't answer as many questions as I would have liked, but even so it was comforting to have someone there to check out as many hunches as possible. Doing this was a gradual process that erased the doubt from my mind. In the beginning there was a lot of doubt running through my mind about the authenticity of the Darkroom and the whole scope of the things that were involved with it. I can't really pinpoint anything specific that led to the removal of the doubt. There were a few minor things. Like during one session, the scarves were still fairly bright on the floor, and an entity walked across the room and I could clearly see him from the knees down. The part of the legs that I saw was entirely different from the channel's. Now, one could say, did someone else in the room get up and walk around, or someone come in? I'm here to tell you there's no way anybody else could have come in that room without me knowing it. And you'd better believe I would have heard somebody else getting up from their chair. There was just no way that could happen. And these legs were like a football player's legs. The calves were thick and muscular, and the channel's legs are not. They are slender and entirely different. At other times there would be two or three entities materialized in the room, and only one channel.

There were other incidents similar to these. Nothing major, and a lot of these might be explained away if you wanted to. But it was said once that people who believe will need no proof, and the people who don't believe, all the proof in the world will not convince them. I believe that. In conclusion, I'd like to mention Mario. He was an entity that came and started body acceptance workshops. During his groups, I learned much about myself, and did quite a bit of work that I'm still in the process of evaluating.

Evelyne

I first got involved in the Darkroom after hearing about it from my mother and my father. Both had been involved for a long time, and they told me some of the experiences they were having. I was very much afraid of what they were doing and they became careful what they would share with me. One day my father started talking about the Singer. I was interested in this because music was such an important part of my life. I asked him a lot of questions because to me my dad had always been very skeptical of any strange or unusual things. He was a very levelheaded person. As I listened to him, I suddenly felt compelled to ask if I could come sometime and hear the Singer. He said he would ask for permission for me to come. Permission was granted and I was given a date I could attend. However, I was unable to attend that particular date and I sort of forgot about it. One day a message was sent to me requesting I attend on a particular day in December of 1973. I said that I would go, providing I could hear the Singer and then leave immediately. I requested that the entity who sent for me be the only one who came near me. He was to deliver the message he had for me and he was not to touch me. The day came. I was introduced to everyone in the group, most of whom I had never met before. We sat in a room with lit-up [luminous] scarves and a trumpet. We all positioned ourselves in our seats, me very comfortably between two very trustworthy people. I was so scared I was shaking inside. I was too embarrassed to tell anyone I was terrified, because I had asked to come. The lights were turned off and we all began to sing. I love to sing, so this was somewhat soothing to me. An entity came into the room. Everyone was very excited and talked to him. No one was getting a response from the entity until finally I was told to ask if he was there to see me. I did ask, but I didn't get any response. Then I was reminded that one of the stipulations I had set when I agreed to come was that they would not touch me. I had to give my permission for them to touch me. When I asked the entity again if he was here for me and would he please touch me, I felt his toes touching my feet. Then very lightly there was a touch on the top of my head. I was sitting on the floor at the time and he reached down and stood me up. We walked out of the main room and into an adjoining room. We sat down for just a moment and I think I asked about 50 questions in a period of three seconds, never waiting for an answer. The entity said he would not harm me, that he was a friend and I had nothing to fear. That didn't help. I started to shake very badly, and he returned me to my seat and my comfortable safety. We sang again. My very first visit with an entity had been a total of three or four minutes. Suddenly, the trumpet went up and Aenka was there. He announced that he did not have time for questions because it was important to take a break because one of us was going to throw up all over the scarf if we didn't. Guess who that was?!! We took a short break and we returned to the dark again. Once again the entity came to visit me. We left the room again, only this time I think I lasted a total of five or six minutes. Again, Aenka came and stated that it was important to take a break. This occurred about eight times the first meeting I attended. I was terribly embarrassed and extremely frightened. At some point I was told the entity's name was Thomas. He said he was a very close friend of mine and he had been aware of my existence since I was born. On my first night I was too scared to ask too many questions. The funny part was I was given answers to questions that people had asked before and never been given answers to. I was given information and I didn't even ask. I realized later it was only because I wasn't the slightest bit interested in that kind of information. As a matter of fact, I didn't like to talk about those kinds of things. At first I didn't know what I wanted. I did, however, get to meet the Singer that day. He sang special songs for me, songs that were very meaningful.

My first meeting had ended, I had met Aenka several times, my friend Thomas at least eight times and the Singer who I really enjoyed. However, I left there still very frightened. My friend had told me he would not harm me, but there was something very strange about talking to someone you cannot see. At that time I lived alone, and I went home and straight to bed. Suddenly, I heard a lot of commotion in my living room. It sounded as if there were seven or eight people having a party. I was just terrified. I could hear footsteps going up and down the hallway and cupboard doors opening and closing. At one time I swore I heard the clink of two glasses as if they were having a toast. I was so frightened I didn't know what to do. Finally, I think I resigned myself to the fact that I was in for big trouble when whoever it was out there found out I was home. I really believed there were several people out there. They were the most real sounds I could ever imagine. Finally, after 10 or 15 minutes, I said aloud I was frightened. The moment I said I was scared, the noises stopped. There wasn't a sound, only a very calm feeling. This was all very alarming, and my reaction is a good example of the extent of my fears.

I still do not know what kept me going back each week. My fears were tremendous. I would literally get sick each time. There was something very strange about what I was doing, but there was also something that kept me going. In my third meeting I had a small breakthrough. My friend told me my purpose in coming to the Darkroom was to achieve self-growth and to learn to love and respect myself. That was my goal. I began to talk to him about my feelings on many different subjects, but mostly of my fears of men. I was confused about why I could talk to him and I was unable to talk to any other man. He laughed and said, *"Because I go poof when our meeting is over and you have no fear that I will ever repeat the information you share with me."* I just about fell on the floor. He was right. That thought had entered my mind during the week. The convenience of having someone to talk to that could not repeat what you told them because you had their word. But it seemed to be more than just their word. I can't explain it, but it's like a power of your own because they wouldn't be here in this Darkroom if there wasn't a you. I'm sure that doesn't make sense to you but for some strange reason it does to me. The really strange part of this philosophy for me is that my friend Thomas also later began to visit Lon (the man I married) when he came to the Darkroom. I never had a fear that he would tell Lon any of the things I said. There was also the convenience of knowing you might as well be honest, because they knew all about you anyway. There seemed no reason to not tell what you really meant. One example of their knowing was when I had been talking to my friend about many things but avoiding a certain question week after week. Finally, I made up my mind I was going to ask one very important question for sure. My friend came to see me and we talked about many subjects. Then out of the clear blue sky he said to me, *"I thought you were going to ask me your question this week."* I was amazed, so I tested him. I asked, "What question?" He said, *"The one you always come in here hoping to ask, always evade, and leave without asking."* Then he proceeded to answer my question in great detail. I know that doesn't seem so strange, but this particular thought I had never expressed to a single person in the entire world. It was something I had always wondered about for many years, but I never told anyone that I even thought that.

One particular Sunday I recall, we had a trust walk. That was a strange experience. There were several entities in the room at the same time. We were given instructions and told that we could not talk. We were led by the tops of our shoulders to different places. We were moved all around the room. You never knew if you were standing next to a person or an entity. We were shuffled around many times and eventually returned to our seats. I was so dizzy by the end of the exercise I couldn't even tell which room I was in. Suddenly, the trumpet went up and we were asked to take a break. I was dumbfounded to find we had all been returned to our original seats. It was amazing. I never did figure out how they knew who was who or where we were sitting. I get dizzy just being in a darkened room.

Regarding proof of the reality of the entities, one source for me was Black Monday. [See Chapt. 1, p. 60], I will talk mostly of how I think the entities prepared me for the experience. The day before I had gone home ahead of Lon. He was to be about 15 minutes behind me. We had planned to go out for the evening so I had gone home to wash my hair. I was in the house alone and in a nice tub of hot water when I heard someone in the house. I called to Lon and he did not respond. I called again and he still did not answer. This was very much unlike Lon. We had made an agreement that jokes like that were not funny and he would not have done that to me. Suddenly, I heard footsteps in my house. There were steps in the kitchen and steps in the living room, and then I heard someone standing at the bathroom door. I was very scared. The door handle to the bathroom jiggled. The footsteps began again all through the house. For approximately one hour I sat terrified in a bathtub of cold water just waiting for whoever it was to figure out I was in there and come in and get me. I prayed to the entities if it were they, to please stop, they were scaring me. The more I prayed, the more heavy breathing I heard at the door to the bathroom and the more the doorknob jiggled. Finally, after being trapped in the bathroom for about an hour, I decided to get out and see who the hell it was. I grabbed what appeared to me to be some form of protection and went out of the bathroom. No one was there, nor was there any evidence of anyone having been there. About five minutes later, Lon drove up explaining he had gotten tied up and wasn't able to get home any sooner. I fell apart emotionally and shared with him the fear that had paralyzed me.

The next night, Black Monday happened, and the meeting was at our house. Later I asked about my experience the night before. I stated I had been told if an entity was scaring you, all you needed to do was say so and they would not do it. It was explained to me that with the extreme fear that I had inside, had I not had the opportunity to express those fears, they would have turned Black Monday into a much more disastrous evening than it was. As it was, I was able to do all the appropriate things necessary to assure the safety of the other individuals in the room. I felt at ease asking everyone in the room to check the house if they too believed that there was another man in the house. The people looked about the house, but they didn't find anything. I knew there was no way for anyone to have gotten in or out of our windows in the back of the house. 1 knew that night for sure the channel and the entities were not one and the same. When I walked in the back room, my legs shaking from all the commotion, [I] turned on the lights and the channel got up, I knew he and the entity weren't the same. In some ways, the man that took it upon himself to try and prove the entity was a fraud actually proved the entities' existence beyond anything. I was told our house was chosen for Black Monday because the layout of our house insured the safety of the channel. He had his own little room there and was protected. I believe that.

My friend Thomas was not always the same size. Sometimes he would be shorter and sometimes heavier. I asked him once why he chose the body style he did and he said it was because it was familiar to me. Usually his body-build and arms were much like my father's. One thing that I always find fascinating is that their skin is always as smooth as a baby. I asked my friend one time, and his comment was, *"You must remember my dear, my skin is now only one-half hour old!"* I liked that.

Ninety percent of all my experiences were in doing my growth work. Thomas once told me they would do almost anything to help me grow no matter how painful it was. He proved it. You couldn't get away with much if you asked for their help. There were times when I really believed I hated the entities because they pushed me to really take a look at my behaviors, my personality, to begin to change the negative aspects. Sometimes it was extremely painful. I remember one particular guest night when I was feeling angry. It was not an appropriate evening to deal with feelings; it was a night to have a good time. Shortly after the meeting began an entity came to me, touched me on the foot, and left. He never returned. That night we went until 5:30 a.m. and everyone received a visit except me. By the next week my feelings were so hurt I had made up my mind to tell the entities to find another place other than my house to have their meetings. Thomas came and started in on me right away. He told me about my negative behavior, why he had come and touched me on the foot and left. He said he would continue to do such things as long as my goal in the Darkroom was self-growth. He said he would continue to help me no matter how painful it was. I didn't like it a bit but what could I do, he had me over a barrel. He knew my games.

One of my most memorable experiences of contact with the entities happened when I was away from the Darkroom. I was extremely upset one night about my beliefs. I was watching a movie on the life of Christ and I got even more nerved up. Finally I went to bed. I was very upset and unable to go to sleep. Suddenly, a very calm feeling came over me. I could feel hands going from my feet up my legs, and another pair of hands at my head. The hands at my feet were massaging me without really touching. The hands at my head were holding me. Suddenly, my physical body got very calm and very warm, and within seconds I was able to go to sleep. This was the first time I had ever recognized their presence on my own. I was able to distinguish the energy patterns and that was a really nice feeling. You can tell that by now I was much less afraid.

One other time there were three entities in our bedroom. This particular night they were fully materialized. It was the first time I had ever seen a fully materialized entity away from the Darkroom. One was definitely female and two were males. One of the males was my friend Thomas who was dancing in the room. He had something white on. The strange thing was the next morning there was a white towel on the floor in our front room. We didn't own a white towel. I do not know where it came from and it has since disappeared.

Sometimes at night when I feel and see entities, I try to wake Lon but I find myself in an immobile state. This has happened to me many times. If an entity stands in our room, I want Lon to see it to prove to me that I really see what I think I see. But when I try to awaken Lon, I'm not able. When I asked the entities about this, they told me it was for me to see. If it was meant for Lon, then I wouldn't be seeing it, he would.

Matthew

I am a retired Air Force Major and I've been in the Darkroom and associated with it since about 1973. In early July of 1976, I had the occasion in a meeting to go out with the entity named Ernest, with whom I have had many visits, and we were discussing various matters. Suddenly he said something like we wish you would be more attentive to your health and take your medication as prescribed. At that time I was on oral medication for diabetes. I acknowledged his warning but somehow I did not pay too much attention to it. I continued to have the sweets that I should not have had. About two weeks later on the morning of July 15th, 1976, as I went to the kitchen to get my morning orange juice, I had the distinct sensation of being on a ship and having to stagger to keep my balance with the roll of the ship. When I got back from the kitchen I laid down for about 15 minutes and when I felt something was happening to my right side, I knew then that I was having a stroke. I got a neighbor to come to my aid, and on the way to the hospital I began to see double. I was very happy that I had not attempted to do any driving myself. By the time I was admitted to a hospital room, after being checked in the emergency room, my right side was completely paralyzed. I could not move my arm or leg. My left eye was half out of its socket so that my vision was impaired and I was seeing double. I was unable to drink liquids because they would just drain down the side of my mouth and run down my chin. I felt pretty sorry for myself that night; I felt that my future days would be in some sort of a rest or convalescent home. In the morning after a very fitful night I noticed that the middle finger on my right hand could move about a half inch up and down. I tested the toe on my right foot and found that I could move it a little too. Then I took pad in hand and with my left hand I printed the following words: "I may be ill but I will persevere." I had the orderly tear that off and pasted it up where I could see it on my side chest of drawers, kind of a little night stand. In the ensuing days I was so determined I was going to get better that the physical therapist had to devise some exercises that would keep me slowed down a little bit. I graduated quickly from wheelchair to walker and then to cane and I was finally discharged.

Before the discharge I had to see the eye doctor about my eyes and double vision. There were two ophthalmologists who examined me quite thoroughly. When I asked what was the prognosis, their approach was, "Well, you may or may not get back your single vision, but you will probably have double vision that can be correctable by glasses." I left the hospital after 5 weeks and returned to my home trying to pick up the pieces. I could not do my work yet, but I could attend the Darkroom. The first available night I came to the Darkroom. Lily asked that the doctor come and attend to my ills. We went into session then and sure enough the doctor did come. He had me sit in the middle of the room facing a single candlelight in a red chimney similar to that you find in some restaurants. I saw two of them. He worked on my body and on my head for about 15 minutes. He pressed on the temples, on the cheekbone below the eye, and on the side of the forehead right by the eyelid. Then he pressed the eyeball through the closed lid and he pressed harder and harder and harder. I got this distinct feeling that he was pushing my eye to the back of my head. And then he released the pressure and there was a great feeling of relief. When I opened my eyes I then saw only one light. Three days later I was to have another examination by an ophthalmologist and these two same worthy gentlemen examined me and again shook their heads, but this time it was in amazement. They asked me what I did to overcome the double vision, and I said merely that if I told them they wouldn't believe it, and added that I was lucky. But I believe that it was the assistance, the healing that I got in the Darkroom.

Whenever I reflect on the Darkroom, this experience and one other especially, stand out for me. One night I saw an entity approach a door, which was sealed completely and locked so no one could come in or go out. As he approached it, his entire body began to glow and it looked like it was translucent. It seemed to change colors and he walked through the door. He came back through the door and then became solid-looking again. This convinced me of their reality once more time—if I had any doubts, they were dispelled. He was an entity and there was no question about his powers.

In summation, let me give you a few thoughts about the Darkroom, about the entities, about that which is the unknown. There are many, many people who doubt and they doubt for various reasons—religious, personal belief, the inability to accept that something they cannot see or hear exists. There are those who believe there is only one life and you're born, you live, you die and that's the end of it. There are always doubters. From my own experience I can only say that I have been very enriched. The late years of my life mean more to me now than they did before. If it were not for the Darkroom, the contacts with the entities, the understanding that has been brought to my life, I should probably have succumbed long ago. But they have taught me something about hope, about wanting to live. I think that the Darkroom, the ability to achieve a communion between ourselves and the spiritual world, is one of the greatest steps forward. And with each passing day there are more reports of people who have experienced being on the other side a short time and coming back. I wish that the media and newspapers and other periodicals that conduct interviews would do so in a strict sense of wanting to know facts, and not with any preconceived notions about what the Darkroom is. If you try to explain, most are unable to comprehend. Suffice it to say that I, for one, am not sorry about my contacts with the Darkroom or the entities and with the enlightenment that they have given to me.

Theresa

My first memory of the Darkroom was my sister sitting in her living room telling me about a trumpet, voice, and sitting in the dark. These phrases were all very foreign to me. I had to stop her and ask, "Wait, what are you talking about?" It was through my relationship with her I had my first experience in the Darkroom.

When I think about how I benefited from the Darkroom, it brings to mind why I stayed with it. It's hard to describe, but it's a feeling of being important which the entities conveyed. How can I describe this? I was told my entity would only materialize when I was there, and that made me feel very special. I was important enough that he'd only come when I was there. Many things I was told helped me realize and work through personal issues and feel better about myself. It has had extensive meaning in my life. I have a difficult time putting words to its meaning for me.

I don't remember ever asking for proof. However, if someone asked me, several instances come to mind. The first was early in my experience, before we were getting a lot of voice. An entity materialized, I forget what we called him, but for me he was the See-Through Man. We could see his bones—he was translucent. He wore boxing shorts. You could see the bones and the outline of his legs. The image might be compared to looking into a fluoroscopy machine. For me that was proof. Another time I asked to touch an entity's tongue and he made a tongue that felt like crumpled up cellophane and I touched it. Another I recall was when a young girl materialized through an adult male channel and stood in front of me. I could see her silhouette against the scarf on the floor. By the communication of taps she told me she was eight years old. There was no girl in the room the size of an eight year old. Another time we asked to see a face. I remember the entities always told us it took a lot more energy to make facial features. On one occasion we coaxed an entity to show his face, and his features were very distorted and unlike anybody's in the room. Another time I saw a ball of white energy appear on the scarf in the middle of the small room where we were seated. Out of that ball raised up first a hand, then arms, and then the trunk of a body extended upward until I saw a figure kneeling on the floor. Then he stood and I saw the fully materialized entity. That was a very moving experience to see that creation in front of me. Once after my visit with my entity I was returning to the room where everybody was seated. We passed through the hallway where the channel was on the floor. The entity was on my right-hand side and I was touching him, holding his arm, and the channel was on my left hand side. And as we passed the channel, my entity said, *"Do you want to touch the channel?"* It hadn't occurred to me, but I said, "Sure, ok."

I reached down and touched the channel's foot and leg. As I looked I could see his silhouette under the blanket as my eyes were accommodated to the light. At the time it didn't mean anything to me; I didn't have that curiosity. At this time it's a proof for me.

Monica

Initially, I did not doubt the entities, as they are for me a total source of acceptance and love. I was so busy taking in and indulging myself in their energy that doubt never entered my mind.

In general meetings and in private visits I have had with my guide, the entities' verbal and nonverbal communication and knowledge of the personality has astounded me. No human being possesses the amount of unconditional love and intimate knowledge of each person's psyche as is displayed by one of these entities. The personal warmth, strength of character, lack of negativity, and indescribable sense of humor they share with us is greater in intensity and duration than any human could attain. Each entity has a separate and distinct personality, but these rich qualities are present in all of them.

I know, without a doubt, this human form is no mortal man. Yet, the thought has crossed my mind that this figure before me who looks, feels, and talks like a man (although with a rather strange, foreign sounding accent) could be an importer, could be a fraud. I have noticed when this happens that it is the activity of thought, of a searching mind seeking the answers to the seemingly unexplainable that prods and pushes for proof. A careful check of my emotions and my judgment always puts my cynic mind to rest. There is no fraud here. There is only a human in the presence of a being of superior power, wrestling with the limits of her understanding.

I accept my curiosity and my discriminating intelligence that questions the possibility of this phenomenon before me. I swell with pride in my fine judgment and wisdom, which overrides any momentary doubt or demanding need I may have for proof of the existence of these entities. I feel nothing but unconditional love from them, and to ask for proof when there is total love is not only redundant but [also] extremely foolish. Thank God I am not a fool!

Another way of thinking of the entities is that they are real, but are not reality, just as a dream is real (you actually experience this phenomena) but it is not reality (a dream is not your everyday existence). In this sense, everyone has experienced something that is real but is not reality.

The love the entities exude has inspired my life and my positive jealousy has moved me to imitate their example and pursue a richer, stronger course in life. The entities love me more than I love myself. I had wasted a great deal of energy on unproductive and self-limiting doubt. When I was being honest with myself I could see my self-concept was negative, demeaning to the point of feeling I did not have the right to exist. The air that I breathed and the space I took up could be better used by someone else. This is fear and guilt at work.

I have worked with this paralyzing fear and guilt I learned as a child. I have moved away from that dark and rigid place. I have learned to trust myself, to recognize the truth when it is presented. I know it is an inward search that will allow me to use the knowledge and wisdom I possess. My authority for my life lies within myself. I have learned to trust my experience and my judgment in order to make my life work for me.

It is with this judgment and firmness of purpose I would say to the world the entities are indeed not of our physical existence. They are spirit guides who have committed themselves to teach us about our negativity, and of the love and happiness we so often deny ourselves.

Hank

When I was 20 years of age, due to impending circumstances, I was compelled to begin looking for answers to questions which forced themselves into my mind; questions which basically asked, "Who am I?" and, "What is the meaning of life?" I consider this to have been the beginning of my search to understand both myself and the world in which we live. It was a few years thereafter that I was introduced into the Darkroom with the entities and the teachings that they presented.

Because of my previous searching and learning, I felt I had at least developed my ability to discriminate enough to accurately and fairly assess the validity of this new teaching. I was particularly impressed by the means used to present the teaching—that is, via the Darkroom and the entities. I like to refer to this as the vehicle of the teaching. In answer to any misgivings some may have concerning the Darkroom and the entities, or, as I say, the vehicle of the teaching, I can only say if we really have a sincere wish to reach our homeland, does it make any difference if we travel by train, boat, plane or whatever? Isn't the most important thing to get there? In addition, I discovered the teachings appeal to my practical side. I believe that in order to change, we must first put forth work and effort in the here and now, rather than to believe we can discover ourselves by retreating to a mountaintop meditating, philosophizing, or exercising the intellect. This is not to say these things don't have their proper place. Certainly philosophy and theory are present in the teachings. However, it never exceeds the need for simple, practical work—work which calls for us to examine our emotional nature, work which requires us to begin to uncover our past emotional repressions.

I consider the teaching a means of emptying ourselves of what is useless and unnecessary. When that is accomplished, then we can begin to rebuild ourselves anew. We can allow ourselves to unfold rhythmically and harmoniously. As for me, because I see the soundness of the teaching, I wish to gather and learn from it all that I can. I believe this teaching has been introduced into our existence by a mind greater than our own, the greater mind being represented by the entities. I believe this teaching can assist us through this difficult period of time in which humankind now stands. This teaching can help us to begin to understand our true destiny.

Up to this point in this chapter, the personal accounts have been those of individuals who have participated in the Darkroom for several years. The following account is from one we might call a 'newcomer'. It is an account by the man who assisted in the preparation of this book. He uses his real name and shares with you some aspects of his recent involvement.

Tom
My unexpected entry into the Darkroom came months after I began to assist Marti with this book. My involvement with both is motivated by a desire to learn about and develop my own spiritual quadrant. I have benefited greatly from my contacts with Marti, Jay and Elisabeth as well as my Darkroom experiences. The effects are noticeable to my

family and friends, as well as to myself. I feel honored to be able to make what I hope might be a small contribution to interest in spiritual development for others. I would like to preface my account of my first experience in the Darkroom with some personal and professional background. I hope the reader will consider this.

I am 42 years old, and have been a licensed psychologist for 15 years. My Ph.D. degree in clinical psychology was earned in a university with a nationally approved training program. I have published research articles in reputable scientific journals, and have been in full time independent clinical practice for eight years. Before that I worked as a staff and supervising psychologist in in-patient, day treatment, and outpatient settings. For a year I was an administrator of a 42-bed in-patient psychiatric ward with multiple responsibilities.

Prior to my involvement with psychology I was majoring in physics and engineering. My background includes 20 years of skepticism regarding things psychic, mystical and spiritual. I have a hard-nosed insistence on verifiable data or at least consistent correlations with a sound theoretical basis. Since my Ph.D. 1 have invested considerable time and money in a variety of psychotherapeutic approaches as patient and as trainee. In these experiences and in my work with patients as a therapist I have learned to risk, to be very careful in assuming my interpretations are correct, and to allow myself to be as open as possible toward new learning. A significant amount of my post Ph.D. training has been in experiential psychotherapy. My graduate school training included some psychoanalytical focus, general psychodynamic therapy, and learning theory. Hopefully I will continue to learn to care for others, to pay attention to my limits, and to admit at least some of my ignorance. I do not consider myself naive, and am familiar with a variety of manipulations and con jobs. I am gladly married and have a son and stepson of whom I am very proud.

We sat in a pitch-black room. There were five of us

in the large room, Jay being in a small adjoining room where he laid down to "go to sleep" as he puts it. Now I wasn't as scared as I had been driving to the meeting place, when I had quite strong butterflies in my stomach, very tight breathing, and sweaty hands. As we sat singing in the dark, looking at the glowing scarf and tin trumpet, I reflected on my relative lack of fear.

I reminded myself that after all I had pretty extensive contact with Jay and Marti in talks over a period of a year. I had heard many anecdotal stories of phenomena in the Darkroom, and had been reassured whatever happened was usually not experienced as negative by the participants. There was never any forcing; there was always free choice and free will. A person could leave any time they wished. I had heard of the charges of fraud and deception, and was very impressed that in Jay and Marti's accounts their predominant feelings and attitudes toward their accusers were of sadness and pain, not anger or defensiveness. Also I had been experimenting with my own physical senses and mind, in what I guess would be described as inward and outward meditations for about a year. In some of these I experienced some fascinating perceptual shifts. Several experiences of abruptly becoming very frightened had offered me practice in dealing with my fear of both the unexpected and the dark. I had one experience of being 'guided' somewhere that had impressed me very much and which I simply could not explain. As I sat there looking at these glowing shapes in the dark, I felt somehow as ready as I could be for whatever was to happen. I was ready and willing to give up my hopes of genuineness if in my personal experience and judgment the stories simply could not be supported. The openness and acceptance of the regular members and Marti helped with my anxiety a tremendous amount. In no way did I feel alone.

After about 15 minutes or so, it began to happen. I was looking at the bands of light on the trumpet and all of a sudden they were gone. There was nothing but blackness. After a few moments they were back. The regular members

389

observed this also and seemed to become hopeful that something would develop. Nothing did until five minutes or so went by during which we sang (a bit more animated than before). Then I was stunned to see two black shadows in the shape of feet and ankles walk slowly over the scarf. Everyone was quite pleased and excited, saying an entity was with us. Then nothing for a few minutes, then the shapes moved back across the scarf and stood stock still in the middle of it.

I couldn't say very much at this time. I was simply too startled. As I looked at them, approximately eight to ten feet before me, the shapes looked crude; like someone had begun to sculpt feet from some substance and had completed only the block shape. I could not see any outline of individual toes, or the usual indentation behind the ankle just above the heel. After standing quite still for perhaps a minute, the shadow feet walked off the scarf and back into the darkness. Several participants spoke aloud asking for a sound, words, or a tap on the head that would indicate the entity was to talk with them. Sure enough, not three minutes later Susan (on my immediate left) squeals with delight and cries out, 'Cecil!' I hear a very low rumbling voice from her direction. After a confused minute or two, with most people (not including me) expressing their pleasure and delight, Susan announces that she and Cecil are going for a private visit. They leave and go to a small adjoining room, and for the next twenty minutes or so we who remain sit, sing, chat and generally amuse ourselves. We cannot move from our positions for it is said that would disturb the energy stabilization necessary to maintain materialization. Occasionally we shift weight, lean back or forward, etc., each time announcing any move or noise we are about to make or have just made. Although from time to time I can hear a low brief rumble of that deep voice, and a few sounds of crying or laughing coming from Susan, no words can be made out.

Susan comes back. Cecil walks into the dark and disappears. Susan shares with us some of what occurred and describes what she feels she has learned, complete with an announcement or commitment to work on a certain issue in her personal life.

Well, there I sit. An entity has apparently come and gone. The regular members take it like a sip of champagne on a very happy occasion. I feel confused, off balance. I can hear what the others say, I respond coherently, but I don't know what is happening. I continue to feel emotional support from the other people.

We are singing again by now, with vigor. The scarf suddenly flies high in the air, is moved about a bit as if waved briskly by one corner, and crumples to the floor. A brief shuffling sound is heard as if feet were quickly being rubbed on the thin carpet. Then, another pair of feet walk across the scarf. Expressions of pleasure from us. Laura says out loud she hopes it is Forest, she' hasn't seen him for a long time. Suddenly another scream of delight followed by quick tears of joy. Forest has tapped Laura on the head and they too go out for a visit. Again we sing and chat for about twenty minutes, Laura returns to her seat and Forest too withdraws into the darkness.

After another few minutes, two more feet. They stand in profile to me on the scarf, which somehow, once again lies flat on the floor. They turn, apparently in my direction. As I stare, sitting on the edge of my seat, I see the scarf light get narrower and the blackened areas get wider. Someone or something is coming my way! I announce this to the others, and finally the growing dark areas stop. I get excited advice from others, "Ask him for a tap on the head . . . ask him if he is here for you . . . tell him it is alright for him to touch you . . . ask him if you can touch him." I am very confused at this point. Still hearing and seeing ok, I manage to take the advice. There is no response until, after we stop chattering, I feel a very gentle tap right in the middle of my balding head. I report this. "He's here for you!" More advice, more talk. Nothing else occurs. He is gone.

Everyone by now is pleased. People would, I think,

have been satisfied if nothing more occurred. I would have. But the evening was far from over. We sing slower and gentler songs now, more softly. Then the trumpet rises straight up off the floor, makes a flourish or two, and ends up with its large end pointed at Marti who is on my immediate right. From its direction comes a heavily accented voice that sounds like it is coming through a cylinder or tube. *"Hello, Merit."* Merit was Marti's nickname as a child. This is Aenka, who has been the acknowledged coordinator of this Darkroom group for several years. Aenka says a couple of things I can't make out. His voice sounded garbled. One thing I did hear clearly was the statement, *"We are glad to see Isaac here tonight."* Then he suggests an intermission.

The trumpet goes down to its original position on the floor, and shortly after this we hear Jay cough. Marti asks him if he is awake, he answers yes, and the lights are turned on. Jay is half sitting and having the dry heaves. He is ok after a few minutes and stumbles out groggily. He looks like he has just wakened from a rather heavy nap.

We go outside, have coffee, chat among ourselves, etc. No one is familiar with Isaac. The general consensus is that Isaac is the name of the entity that touched me, and most people feel that he was 'there' for me. I have no opinion, just much curiosity. How could he/she find the exact center of my head in the pitch dark to give just one clear gentle tap? How could he/she even locate me that precisely? It was black in that room. I could not even see the outline of Marti or Susan on either side of me, and yet we were only about six inches from each other!

We resume after the intermission. Jay lay down again before the lights go out. I notice the small collapsible lamp beside Marti. It has a red bulb and a dimmer switch. If she has the opportunity she will ask an entity if she can turn the light on. This is never done without permission. While the light being turned on is not a frequent occurrence, apparently it happens enough for people to get adequate views. The only door leading out of the room is checked for security and the lights go out. We sing.

I really don't know how to describe what occurred next, but I will do my best. After a very few minutes a deep resonant voice comes out of the dark. Marti immediately recognizes this as Mario, and asks permission to turn on the light. This is given and when she turns it on I see a robed figure across the room. The long robe and cowl over the head looks white even though the light is a definite red. I cannot see hands or feet where they should or would be. I can only see the same shade of darkness as there is to either side of the figure. He gives Marti explicit directions with the light, *"Too bright . . . turn it down more toward the floor . . . up a little, etc."* He is finally satisfied. Marti wanted it as bright as possible. We had all been absolutely silent while the adjustments were being made. Mario pauses in speaking, then begins to move about in a slow, pacing manner. He talked as he moved, then would stop and talk, then pace again. I was totally absorbed by his deep voice. This voice as I heard it is very difficult to describe; very deep, strong, resonant, heavily accented with what sounded like a mixed European accent, yet soft. While I have heard many different voices of professional entertainers and announcers through the years, I have never heard a voice that had the timbre of gentle firmness this one had. The rate of speech was slow. The words were quite easy to make out, only once or twice was a repetition asked for. He would pause sometimes in his presentation. Mario stayed with us about 40 minutes. Part of the time he gave an informal talk or lecture, the remainder of the time was left open for dialogue between participants and himself. His lecture focused on simple, basic attitudes and truths yet there was such a freshness and impact in the way he said things. His simple statements came across to me as words of wisdom. I remember the awe of my total impression in reaction to both his voice and the content of his presentation. I can only describe his attitude as one of understanding and gentleness regarding the human condition and what we struggle with. His lecture, comments and dialogue with people were quite serious, but occasionally he would pause and abruptly shift to make a small joke.

During the dialogue time, the other participants were not filling the silences with questions. I rather selfishly interpreted this as an allowing of me as a newcomer to take time or initiative as I wanted or needed. I asked Mario if there was something he could do or say that would be helpful in two personal issues I was struggling with. He responded in a variety of ways, and I have found his responses quite helpful. Not wanting to hog all the time, and also not knowing what else at that time to ask or bring up I then took my turn at being silent. Someone else brought up an issue for themselves. Finally he said he had to leave. He had remained about twenty feet from us across the large room, and now asked Marti to lower the light. It was lowered to barely being on; he faded into the darkness, I could no longer see him. I could only see the outline of my own hand and knees. In a manner that sounded quite genuinely respectful, Mario asked aloud, *"May I have the honor of touching you?"* I didn't know who he was referring to, but others quickly said, "He's talking to you." I looked into the darkness, remembered his strong and gentle voice, his intellectual brilliance and perspective, his obvious caring. I replied, "Of course." He asked me to please stand. I stood, careful not to move from my space. Finally I could see the faint outline of the robed figure before me, and what I thought was an arm reaching my way. I tentatively put out my hand, and received a brief and quite unique handshake. He withdrew his hand and slowly I saw him kneel in front of me. No words, no sound. I said nothing. Just looked, and felt very honored.

Before he left us, we joined him as he said aloud three times, *"Thank you, O Spirit of Heaven, for providing us this day."*

The epilogue for the evening was a brief return by Aenka. He had a few words with Marti and they exchanged touches, which for Marti, is always very meaningful. Just before he left, the trumpet turned toward Richard. Richard has been a regular Darkroom member for years and in my personal experience is a very caring and patient man. He had not had a personal visit from his entity in over two years. And for those two years he had met whenever he was asked, singing and giving his support and energy for others to have their experiences. Two years of giving, and little direct getting. Aenka made a simple statement to him, something to the effect, *"We are aware of what you have accomplished in two years."* When Richard asked for clarification there was none.

This has been a descriptive account of the highlights for me of my first session in the Darkroom. I have had other experiences with similar impact. I have been in the Darkroom in five different physical locations with different people involved in three of them. In each there has been materialization. I have witnessed light phenomena, seen entities of different height and body build; received gentle and unique hugs from Mario. If there is fraud, in my opinion it would mean Jay or a confederate is able to do the following: have psychological knowledge at least equivalent to a Ph.D. and many years' experience; have knowledge of individuals' past and present experiences in detail with eidetic clarity; be able to produce different voice timbre and speech phrasing at high professional levels for lengthy periods with never a slip; somehow sneak into meetings on a few hours' notice at places where security of all entrances is extreme; in the silence of the room find their way about perfectly in pitch blackness without making any noise; have inordinate patience; show extreme compassion and understanding of the human condition—and do this all for free.

My doubts are resolved. Coming totally unexpectedly, I am being shown what I consider to be truths the extent of which I had vaguely hoped for but never allowed into full longing or even conscious awareness. I can now let go of my struggle to weed out hypocrisy, personal or doctrinal distortions that I was bothered by as a youth. In the darkness I have literally seen a light, and now follow it as my truth. We are not alone, and those usually unseen love us in a totally accepting and nonjudgmental way.

CHAPTER NINE
FREQUENTLY ASKED QUESTIONS

This chapter contains selected samples of direct teachings of the entities in our Darkroom meetings. They are verbatim quotations from dated transcripts of tape recordings. The selections are chosen as a sampler of the broad areas covered. They are included here to satisfy the curious reader and to share with you some of the revelations and information given. Growth and spiritual development must of necessity be by free will and free choice, using all four quadrants of the personality in evaluating our development.

Reality
"Reality is that which you experience with all of your faculties, meaning you are aware of the things about you, and that you are literally aware of your existence. It has little to do with your choice of existence. It is still reality. When an individual loses touch with reality their mind ceases to function. If you lose the capacity to reason, then you have lost the capacity to make choices. When you have lost your ability to make a choice you are no longer in touch with reality."

Growth
"Emotional growth is determined by our behavior in some positive way. Spiritual growth is to grow in our knowledge, understanding, wisdom and acceptance of oneself as a spiritual entity or being. Growth is the expansion of awareness of our existence and the purpose for that existence."

Natural Emotions
"Natural emotions are fear, jealousy, anger, love and grief. All are positive and rhythmic—like the ebb and flow of the

tide. They can become distorted only through the traumatic conditioning of the child from infancy to six years of age. The unnatural emotions or fears, which result are the cause of all the negativity within us. To be positive is natural and to be negative is unnatural."

Love

"Love is a combination of a million facets of your personality. Attempt to pinpoint it and it shall laugh at you. I shall attempt to guide you in what it is not. It is not selfishness; it is not suffering. It is not ecstasy. It is the desire to fulfill another. All erotic manifestations with feelings supposedly called love are associated with the desire for self-satisfaction. Selfishness is a desperate need to regress. The distorted interpretation of love is established by the awakening of all these desires. Often when one makes the statement, 'I love you' what they are saying is that you please me. Love in its truest sense is the feeling 'allow me to please you.

"Love is not a privilege, it is a God-given right. Love has no strings attached. I am loved by your acceptance of love from me. Such is unconditional love."

The Government of Life

"The government of life is a tentative plan we design for ourselves while in spiritual form prior to incarnation. This plan is a blueprint for achieving our destiny in our forthcoming life. The unobstructed universe and the Source play a part in maneuvering us through our physical destiny. We actually select our environment for each physical life, including the hemisphere, time, parents, and birth order."

The Gamble of Life

"The gamble of life is the design incorporated into the universe to offer us choices. There are many hazards in

physical life, which offer us the opportunity to grow in a positive way. If these challenges did not exist there would be no growth, no purpose to life. Free choice gives life meaning and differentiates man from being as a programmed robot."

Immutable Laws
The entities presented the following guidelines that they referred to as Immutable Laws. These guidelines apply only to the physical (obstructed) universe, i.e. that in which we presently live.

1.   HUMAN EQUALITY [All are subject to the gamble of life and the government of life.]
2.   SELF-ACCEPTANCE [Man accepts his total personality structure—physical, emotional, intellectual and spiritual facet.]
3.   INDEPENDENCE [Man bears within himself all the potential for self-fulfillment.]
4.   MAN HAS THE RIGHT OF FREE CHOICE.
5.   INTERDEPENDENCE [Man accepts that he has limitations.]
6.   RECOMPENSE [Man accepts the responsibility for his choices.]
7.   ALL TRUE BENEFITS MUST BE MUTUAL.
8.   EVERY MAN IS ENDOWED WITH A FACET OF DIVINITY, WHICH INSURES HIS HUMAN DIGNITY.
9.   EACH MAN IS UNIQUE AND HAS HIS INDIVIDUAL DESTINY TO FULFILL.
10. ALL TRUE BENEFITS MUST BE EARNED.

Universal Laws
"Universal laws govern the behavior of all entities. They apply to the unobstructed and do apply somewhat to the physical (obstructed) universe. They govern the behavior of all the universe, including the behavior of all molecular structure. There are thousands of such laws. An example is the first law, which is, 'No spiritual energy may behave in

a negative way.' Another universal law is, 'No entity can enter the body of a physical being once that body has been chosen by another entity.

"The universal laws are organized by function, rule and purpose. They are a part of the Archives of Knowledge, Center of Knowledge, or Akashic Records. All spirit forms have access to this knowledge. Those in the unobstructed cannot violate these laws. Only man has free choice. Accordingly, those in the physical have the option to choose to violate the universal laws and the immutable laws."

Leadership
"Leadership is a marvelous quality. It encompasses the ability to organize and to maintain a standard flow of energy toward a common interest. The inability to be a good leader derives from fears of rejection. Fear allows some individuals to be dominating. Instead of leading, they tend to dominate. The fear of giving orders is directly connected with your fear of rejection. Leadership is the full recognition of your own inner authority to manage your own affairs, but to manage the affairs of others you must be vested with the authority to do so. Otherwise you will undoubtedly be accused of being nosy. There should be no feeling of power with authority. Authority means you have a certain responsibility of position to direct or lead individuals to a common purpose."

Destiny
"Destiny is the completion of a physical and spiritual evolutionary cycle. We choose our physical destiny and our spiritual destiny. Our physical destiny concludes with death of the physical body and is always in furtherance of our spiritual destiny. Each life would be oriented toward development of your strongest potential whether it be art, science or religion [the study of Man]. To be fully developed you would gain sufficient knowledge of all three.

After birth from the Source all entities must progress through seven levels of growth before completing their chosen spiritual destiny and merging back with the Source. There are significant and unique features and requirements for each level."

Impingement
"A portion of the intuitive function of the personality receives spiritual energy and is the channel for impingement from entities in the unobstructed. Impingement is the signal or energy by which the entities transmit messages to the physical mind."

Intuition
"Intuition includes two channels or frequencies. One is physical or psychic; the other is spiritual. Each frequency has a separate transmitter and receiver. One allows us to communicate with spiritual energy, the other with physical energy. The intuition function is found in the spiritual quadrant. The development of this function allows us to communicate more readily on a psychic level with each other, and to open the channels for spiritual communications with the entities, with the Source of All Divinity, or Centers of Knowledge" [sometimes called Akashic Records].

Spiritual and Psychic Energy
"Spiritual energy has no potential for harm. Psychic energy does. When dealing with the psychic, the mind, there is always danger. It is so unpredictable. Your mind is capable of self-destruction but as long as your mind is pure in heart the effect of psychic energy shall never cause harm. Psychic power can be used destructively.

"Spiritual energy is any energy which is not of the physical. All the energy man experiences in his physical state is physical energy, including our atmosphere. An example of spiritual energy can be healing energy from the

Source. Spiritual energy emanates from the Source."

Auras

"An aura is a magnetic electronic field of energy produced by our physical body. I believe it has been photographed. The size and intensity reflects positive and negative behavior patterns. It is affected by many factors such as moods, physical health, illness, injury or trauma. Negative response as an emotion lessens the quality and strength of the aura. Positive emotions intensify and enlarge it. The basic aura reflects one's true nature or personality. There are four colors symbolizing the four quadrants of the personality structure, and like the personality structure the colors remain the same throughout our lifetime. Everyone has all four colors in their aura; however, two are predominant. Various blendings of these colors produce hues. In their basic essence they would reflect the personality types. The aura of a thinking/extrovert is primarily blue and green, supported by red and yellow. A thinking/introvert is blue and yellow, supported by red, then green. A feeling/extrovert aura is red and green, supported by blue and yellow. A feeling/introvert is red and yellow, supported by blue, then green. To those sensitive enough to distinguish them they appear somewhat as a diffused rainbow about the body."

Spiritual and Psychic Healing

"Psychic healing is the ability of an individual to create an energy pattern so devised that it would enhance or strengthen the molecular field, enabling that field to gain its balance in the fight for survival. Psychic healing is drawn from the physical mind. Psychic healers deal with their own mind in conjunction with the power of the mind of the individual who is ill. Spiritual healing is drawn from universal energy and is performed only by the Source of All Divinity. The results of psychic and spiritual healings are the same. They are correcting the imbalance of the chemistry of the body."

Miraculous Healing

"There are two types of miracles. A miracle from the Source is instant and involves spiritual energy. There is instant change or completeness. It is like perfect plastic surgery. The entire organ of the body is restored. Other miracles deal with impingement and work in conjunction with psychic energy. In such cases there is a gradual or slow cure as the body is assisted in healing itself—as in arresting an illness. "

Astral Travel or Projection

"Astral travel or soul travel is when the entity, spiritual body or the immortal part of us, chooses to temporarily leave the physical body and project itself to another location. This is also referred to as an out of-body experience.

"Such movement away from the body might be a few feet, or millions of miles reached at the speed of thought. To experience this phenomenon, the energy field or force within the body must be exact in size and quantity. It must be to the degree of stability sufficient to keep the physical body molecularly sound. It must be stable enough to keep the energy unchanged within its own energy pattern. When this vibration is reached, one can project oneself from the physical body. There is a 'Silver Cord' which ties you to your body. It is an imaginary cord, but it is an energy permanence. No one would leave their body unless the energy was so designed and so perfect that there would be no need for concern about the safety of the body. "

Possession by Devil or Evil Spirit

"There is no need for you to harbor fear. There is no chance of being possessed by a devil or demon. There is no such thing as possession by another spirit or being. I shall remind you only one soul possesses your body, and all the spirits respect this. Spiritual power or energy has no evil.

402

Psychic power or energy can be used for evil. Psychic power is managed only by the mind of man. Spiritual power is produced by our Facet of Divinity—that part of the Creator within us. Psychic forces can be called whatever you like. Psychic energy has the power not only to distort your mind but it could disfigure. Should you allow yourself to be involved with it, the mind could produce a monster or throw objects across the room. Psychic power can be used for good or evil. Man has the right of free choice; satan is a legend, a story, a fantasy which describes and gives substance to the negative powers of the mind."

Karma

"I only speak of karma as a word you have learned to be associated with punishment, purgatory or suffering. You shall never reincarnate to repay a debt for some misdeed committed in a prior life. However, during each lifetime, man must accept the responsibility for his choices arid the associated consequences for those choices."

Soul Mates

"Soul mates—a beautiful arrangement developed by the Source from the very beginning. The better to bear the journey of your destiny from the time you are born from the Source until you merge with the Source . . . you have a mate. Entities are born from the Source in pairs, threes and fives. Never one—never singular. Occasionally and more often than you imagine, triplets—three entities are born. Never four, but sometimes five are born together. There is always a combination of males and females within the group. You must live one successful life with your soulmate. And if soulmates incarnate within the same time frame, the government of life will maneuver them together even though they may be born on different continents. Every ten cycles of your earth around your sun those entities who have completed their destiny merge again with the Source, and the number of births of entities equals

403

those that merge."

Truth
"Truth can be the definition for behavior or anything which is positive or negative. For truth is nothing more than mutual understanding. Such as one person communicating with another, and both are in agreement; agreement which is in a positive way—mutually beneficial."

Death and the Transition
"Death occurs when physical consciousness ends and spiritual consciousness begins. Once your physical body loses consciousness in death you leave the body and have an awareness as a spiritual entity—not as a physical being. This transformation is from physical awareness to entity awareness. But you do not experience the transition physically or intellectually. You cannot compare it with the five senses. The awareness your physical body has differs from the awareness you have as an entity. Death itself is not painful. The body physically and psychologically prepares itself for death. At the moment of death the entity has an individual ethereal form shaped like the human form—only perfect in all respects. For example, a person with an amputation would be whole. Later the ethereal body changes to a unique and more condensed energy pattern. This form is in the shape of a sphere and can vary in dimension, generally the size of a large ball. The entities retain this form while in the unobstructed universe. At times, these energy patterns are visible to the sensitive human eye. The entities can alter the shape and density of their energy pattern at will. For example, when someone has a near death experience, it is common for them to be visited and greeted by departed loved ones or a familiar figure. The entity would take the form of the familiar person rather than a sphere, in order to be recognized."

Reincarnation

"Before incarnating, the entity chooses the environment and family he or she will join as a newborn infant, for a purpose. The purpose is to experience all harmonious rhythmic patterns in one lifetime. However, it would be likely impossible to do this. Subsequent incarnations may be necessary. In reincarnations, the entity would choose an environment, which would most likely offer the opportunity to experience a rhythmic pattern, which has not been experienced successfully in other physical lives. The ultimate objective is the fulfillment of the entity's chosen destiny."

The reader may notice similarities between material quoted here and information received through other channeling methods. In response to this the entities always reply, *"A rose is a rose is a rose"*.

CHAPTER TEN
SPIRITUALITY—DESTINY AND CHOICE

In a later publication an attempt will be made to organize the entities' many teachings regarding living and learning in the body, spiritual development both in and out of the body, and the purpose of life. In this chapter I would like to share some of the entities' comments on what might be called broader aspects of spirituality. I have selected quotations from Aenka that hold the greatest meaning for me.

"There have been many questions regarding spirituality and what it is. It is everything—everything combined with something else. It is a rhythmic combination of all the checks and balances of life. Every action, which occurs, shall be negative unless it has a quality of spirituality . . . a child before young adolescence is totally unaware of spirituality [except in the case of a dying child]. *You are not conscious of it until the awakening of the spiritual quality, and this usually happens in young adolescence. Then you*

become one with yourself and wonder what you are made of. The adolescent wonders about the universe and their position in it. They wonder about the universal energies, the Source of Divinity. They become aware of their strengths and their weaknesses, they realize there must be something more powerful, there must be some purpose for this life. They begin to search for and find the answers from within—the secret knowledge of spirituality. How harmonious it is and how truly life begins to blossom for them. Life begins to have meaning for them as their spiritual facet begins to unfold. They become more filled with humility. They become more understanding and of course, as they grow and learn, they begin to mellow and understand interdependence

"Interdependence is the true quality of spirituality—to give and receive, and a deep desire to give more than you receive. You have no fears of receiving, and as you grow you are so busy, so overwhelmed with sharing yourself with others, you do not need to be concerned about yourself. Because as you share, every facet is returned to you tenfold. Then you begin to feel your place in the universe, just like the grain of sand on the beach. Misplace one grain and it shall disturb the rhythm of the ocean. Let your spirituality be your rhythm. It is the catalyst of all there is, and all there shall ever be. Most of your thinking as you grow into adulthood, every positive thought you have, would have a quality of spirituality to reinforce it, to make it pure and strong.

"There is no fear, no guilt and no laziness - no inactivity in spirituality. Everything you do has a quality of greatness about it. Never in negative feeling - always the positive feeling of growth and progress—moving forward—never letting your mind dwell on a negative feeling. Anger is tempered by spirituality. You must be aggressive to live in a society. You must be submissive. You must be extroverted and introverted to live in a society. The strength of your

spiritual facet is determined by your ability to understand your fellowman, your ability to understand his needs—but most of all the ability to recognize your own needs and fulfill them—the courage to fulfill your own needs."

Question: How do you recognize true spirituality?

Aenka's response: *"Every time you find a part of the self which is not being expressed, you must understand this is a part of you. Spirituality is sharing your personality and learning about yourself. One of the greatest things is the love of your physical body. Children love the sensation of their body. They love the way they feel. Should this expression be allowed to develop in a natural way, they would begin to appreciate and love their body. All the steps of growth a child experiences lead them into the developing and awakening of their spirituality, and the marvel of knowing and learning. What am I? Who am I? What am I here for? What is my brother like? What is my fellowman like? The desire for expression—the desire to share your knowledge."*

Question: Would you comment on the feeling of a true spiritual experience? How might it be recognized? What is the difference between a spiritual experience and an ego trip?

Aenka's response: *"The birth of life occurs. Observe the growth of another individual. Have you ever observed an individual, young or old, attempting to master a problem, and watch him succeed? Of course, the ecstasy, the elated feeling overwhelms you. You become totally involved with feelings of spiritual enlightenment. Observe a child learning to walk. Observe your feelings. You shall become overwhelmed with the intent of nature. All of these small things an adolescent begins to observe helps the awakening of the spiritual development—not to compare, but to comprehend and observe."*

407

Aenka would respond to our many questions on spirituality in a variety of ways. Many of his teachings emphasized the importance of personal development in our four quadrants and its relationship to spiritual development. One December evening in 1974 Aenka told us a Christmas story in which he spoke of the extent of pain and suffering to which Christ subjected himself as illustrating the difficulty in teaching others regarding spirituality. As Aenka put it, *"Jesus observed changes in others being slow around Him, and He knew He must die to cause the multitude to believe Him."* He went on to say, *"So He died on the cross and they buried Him, and then the multitudes were hysterical. These mobs of individuals screaming, crying, shouting, 'You've taken our Lord, our Savior, our Healer; you have taken Him and given us nothing.' They began to organize and form committees. Each disciple chose committee leaders. Each leader of the committee would have the opportunity to witness a materialization of Christ. Christ would speak with them, and this to them was unbelievable. He appeared many times telling them they could love and they could rid themselves of their selfishness, of their fears. They began to live in rhythm. 'Let not your fears cause you to be selfish and greedy. But let your fears motivate you into kindness and understanding. Work together and love one another as 1 have loved you. Give to one another as I have chosen to do. But let it be your choice.' He knew His death would be the most effective way to burn in their minds what He had taught. That they may teach their offspring and their offspring may teach theirs until the people once again would realize equality among all men. No man, regardless of his wealth or position, is more superior than those who have nothing."*

On that same evening he went on to describe how some lessons learned during the Christ revolution have meaning and application to the problems of today's world. *"By now you are wondering what I am here for and where all I have said this evening is leading. All we ask of you is to have the courage to listen. I ask not of you to believe, only that I have the opportunity to say a few words that could possibly be very meaningful to this universe. It is time for change. People's fears and guilts are destroying them. Let not the fears and guilts of others destroy you. Let your destruction be your choice! Would it not be neighborly to try and convey some meaningful approaches to save yourself and to help your neighbor save himself?*

"It is not necessary for you to remain a pawn in a game of chess. It is necessary you carve your destiny in a world which could be peaceful and meaningful for you. How could this be done? It cannot be done like Christ did it because progress has changed mankind. The minds of the multitude have been educated. Fears are no less but it takes more to frighten . . . Christ taught become rhythmic—love yourself. Above all else, love yourself. How can you love yourself when you fear yourself? You fear your aggression. You fear your submission. You fear independence and you fear dependence. Fear. Afraid to act. But it is more than an act. Afraid to be. To be yourself. You cannot be yourself alone, and that is what so many are trying to do. When one speaks of freedom or independence they feel or think it must be at the expense of others. Arrogance and selfishness are not independence. Independence is the ability to give of oneself in an unselfish way . . . You must get back to rhythm—the quality of love. Everybody speaks of love and what love means to them. I'll tell you what love means to them. Love means to them how you can make them feel, what you can do for them. It is never in a true sense expressed 'what can I do for you.' What can I do for you, my friends? When a mind and body are psychologically and emotionally in rhythm; that is always foremost in your mind. 'What can I do for you?' Now I am asking you to change. I am asking you to devote your efforts to changing yourself to find this rhythmic pattern of life so that you may find the true

meaning of physical and spiritual destiny.

"Consider these thoughts for yourself and for all mankind. Allow me to say, with self-love there is no guilt, without guilt there is no greed, without greed there is no selfishness, without selfishness there can only be love.

"Continue to search for a better and more positive way of life. Although you may find dark pathways, continue to search for greater understanding of your destiny. This will necessitate great change within all individuals, and thus of all mankind. This is not philosophy; it is a fact. I have been blessed by your existence."

Although we had spoken with him many times, four years had passed since we had clearly seen the entity with ebony skin. Now, on a Saturday in December 1980, in a smaller group, he stood before us and said his familiar identifying words as he stepped forward into the light. *"Hello, Mert."* This was a nickname I was given as a child and the name the entities lovingly call me. Once again, Aenka was there to greet us and share another Christmas season.

He stood not as tall as before, a turban wrapped tightly about his head, and in a long white gown. His black skin glistened in the light as he paused, then walked about the room speaking, touching some of the members on the head and sharing with all of us his message for the Christmas season. The essence of his words were directed toward the importance of approaching those situations with seriousness that warranted it, but also taking time to have fun and enjoying pleasure to its greatest degree.

As I, and 18 others looked, touched, and hugged him, it was noteworthy to me that many changes which had occurred in the group were now evident. As I stared at Aenka his words of 1976 again echoed in my ears, *"Tonight there are over 60 of you. Next year there will be 200. I accept that many of you here this evening still have many doubts and suspicions. It is fair, because you must be fair with your mind. All of your life people will try to trick you. There will be a time when the few special words that I have spoken to you will be yours to keep. There will be a time that I will no longer be with you. For all of you that believe in self-love and the love of your fellowman, it is a time to come together. You are in numbers now, at least enough that you can speak and teach freely ... do not complicate life. Live it as it should be lived, simply and fully. Do not allow guilt and fear and negativity to spoil all the beauty that is here for you. Christ was one of the greatest teachers of self-love. The greatest decision that He made in His life was to share. He found sharing and loving very easy and very rewarding. It will not be long until the negativity about you is so great that I will not have an opportunity to visit with you. The group will be investigated and nearly destroyed because of the recognition. There will be those out there that will try to destroy you. You are strong enough to resist, to believe in yourself, to trust yourself ... Possibly the witnessing of materialization would prove to you our existence? No, it would not. So what would it take to prove, and what is proof? There is no way, and you will find this true in your personal life. There is no way that you can please negativity. There is no way that you can satisfy suspicion and doubt. So if I have taught you truth and you believed it to be true, let it be a part of you."*

The number that had been chosen to be invited to this 1980 Christmas meeting was fewer than in 1976. But perhaps those who met in the room, selected to see him and talk with him, had a special purpose. We asked why his visits with full visibility were not more frequent, and Aenka explained again about the amount of energy necessary to provide this experience. He also spoke of the importance of not living in the past. The past is a teacher, and must lay the foundation for what we are to experience in the future. The teachings, the experiences they've given us, have served to prepare us for our involvement in the revolution against negativity.

The purpose of this book has been to share with the reader those experiences I and others have had in what we call the Darkroom. Perhaps it would have been better to call it the Lightroom, because it certainly brought light into many people's lives and shed light on many experiences that might have otherwise lay dormant although still affecting behavior. Many participants, because of their experiences in the Darkroom, have begun to act on their lives rather than react.

I hope this journey has been a meaningful one for you, as it's been meaningful for me to share it with you. Our experiences have been duplicated and will continue to be duplicated. I have chosen to change all names except my own; that of the channel, my husband; that of the man who assisted in editing this book. This was done to ensure privacy. In view of the threats we have received, I preferred using aliases to ensure confidentiality. The entities have shared with us that the greatest meaning to all of the experiences is that it will provide an impetus for the struggle against negativity. No matter what path man chooses, hopefully he will understand that fear and guilt are his only enemies. Man bears within himself free choice and can at any time allow himself to use that choice to free himself from fear and guilt. He then may lay claim to his own gifts and abilities and find life a meaningful challenge rather than a threat.

The Darkroom will continue, and does continue. The times, the places of the meetings, are not shared except with those who are given permission to attend. I know there are those who will read this book who have had similar experiences. Experiences to be valued and held dear. As long as the entities continue to attempt to visit us, we will do our part to provide an environment that seems to best support those meetings. As time goes by, I believe they will be able to prolong their visits and someday, perhaps, the meetings will again be open to greater numbers. Even as I approach the closing of this book, I know there is a part of the Darkroom that also closes, and yet it moves forward. Hopefully I can also move forward, accepting in my heart a teaching the entities have shared with us many times. When we lose something, it is very painful. If we can grieve for it, then we can move on to greet the future, which may hold something even more meaningful for us.

Jay and I consider change a part of the growth process. Personal growth and development can at times be painful. Several years ago, Mario spoke at length about the pain that sometimes is present in the growth experience. In Mario's words, *"If you shield the canyons from the windstorms, you will never see the beauty of their carvings."*

CHAPTER ELEVEN
EPILOGUE

Although an epilogue usually refers to closure, this one involves disclosure. Elisabeth Kübler-Ross, M.D., a colleague and co-worker for four years, had written the original epilogue for this book. While the book was in the galley proof stage of printing she abruptly retracted her contribution. She did this in the form of a brief letter hand delivered to me by a third person on June 21, 1981, as I was conducting a workshop session in a psychodrama-training program. In this same letter she informed me she was now convinced my husband Jay had begun faking the entities in our Darkroom sessions and that accusations by others of sexual improprieties on his part were true.

Although the three of us had worked together in a five-day workshop in Canada the previous week, and just the night before had all participated in a Darkroom session, she had mentioned nothing to me or Jay, personally, regarding any suspicions, accusations, or conclusions. I learned later that only a few minutes prior to the delivery of this letter she had personally confronted Jay with the same conclusions. Jay states that in the brief confrontation at her home she presented no personal data as a basis for her conclusions.

Up to the time of the writing of this new epilogue Elisabeth has initiated neither questions nor dialogue with either Jay or myself regarding her accusations and conclusions. Within four days of the letter I received, Jay and I were both fired from Shanti Nilaya, the growth and healing center the three of us had been involved in full time since its opening in November of 1977. Jay was fired as a staff member on June 22, 1981, without benefit of any meeting or discussion with the board of directors or the executive director of Shanti Nilaya. On June 24, 1981, I was fired as a staff member and removed from my position as first vice-president on the executive board. I was given no reason verbally or in writing for termination or removal.

I could only speculate on possible factors involved in Elisabeth's decisions regarding her suspicions, accusations, and conclusions. However, at this point it seems more important to present some data for the readers' information. The three of us had worked together closely for about four years, had all been involved in the creation of Shanti Nilaya and its development, and Elisabeth had often referred to us as partners. Since June of 1977, Jay and I had assisted Elisabeth in her five-day workshops titled "Life, Death, and Transition." I had been first vice-president of Shanti Nilaya since its founding and in addition was regularly conducting psychodrama workshops and training workshops in psychodrama under the auspices of the center. Jay had been executive director of the center for some time before his resignation from that position at his initiative in January 1981. His primary interest was in psychic healing rather than administration, and as public interest in healing workshops increased he chose to focus his energy there.

During the last four years Jay and I have also sat in Darkroom meetings whenever Elisabeth requested, sometimes with others, sometimes just the three of us. There were many weeks when we would have a Darkroom session every day. Our calendars from these years are marked with S on those days she had asked us to be available for Darkroom.

At "Life, Death, and Transition" workshops, the three of us would frequently have a Darkroom after long hours of day and evening workshop sessions. Our workweek frequently was seven days, twelve to fifteen hours a day. In fact, to optimize Darkroom opportunity Elisabeth had asked us to buy a house as close to hers as possible. Shortly after she bought her own home in Valley Center, we asked the real estate agent who handled Elisabeth's house to find one for us. He did and it was adjacent to her property. In order to make this move we sold our home in San Diego.

Earlier in this book I have referred to doubts regarding the authenticity of Darkroom phenomena and materialization. I have pointed out that many people had difficulty resolving their doubts; some made accusations or conclusions of fraud. Since it appears a new round of rumor and accusations may occur it seems appropriate to present some documentable data for the readers' consideration. We are being accused once again of fraud, trickery, and manipulation. I will address what I consider some of the major issues from an historical point of view.

It has been rumored that Jay has lost his healing ability, yet he continues to share and experiment with healing energy and is still sought out for his unique abilities in these areas. It has been speculated the motivation for writing this book was to gain fame or fortune. What is fact is that until Elisabeth made her recent decision and Jay and I were fired, there was a contract drawn up by our attorney regarding disbursement of any profits from this book. The contract stipulated 50% of all net profit from "Bridging Two Worlds" was to be given to Shanti Nilaya. We considered this an additional contribution of our time and energy reflective of our commitment toward Shanti Nilaya and its purposes. This contract is now invalid. There was to be no financial investment on the part of Shanti Nilaya and should any incidental expenses be incurred by the center they were to be refunded from gross profits. Funds for the first printing of this book came entirely from a private loan negotiated by Jay and myself, neither Shanti Nilaya nor anyone associated with the center in even a remote manner were involved in any way with this loan. The Darkroom has never been a part of Shanti Nilaya; it has always been separate. It would have been inappropriate to seek their involvement in funding for this book.

We have been accused of gaining disproportionate financial benefits from our association with Shanti Nilaya. Financial facts are as follows. Since the inception of this center my salary has been $1500.00 per month, Jay's has been $1000.00 per month. We have never received any raise in salary. We have each been paid an additional $500.00 for every "Life, Death, and Transition" workshop in which we assisted. There were approximately ten to twelve of these a year for the last four years. Travel expenses for Jay and myself for business directly related to Shanti Nilaya were paid for by the center. Through the entirety of our working relationship Elisabeth has, at her initiative, given us personal gifts which total approximately $1700.00. Shanti Nilaya leased the facilities located on what we call our ranch property for workshops conducted there. Rental was $1750.00 a month initially and was progressively decreased to $1250.00 a month. All money accrued through workshops led by Jay or myself held at the ranch or elsewhere related to any type of classes, psychodrama, healing work, or teachings of any sort were paid directly to Shanti Nilaya. Often I would pay incidental expenses related to psychodrama supplies and workshop activities out of my own personal funds.

There have been accusations that Jay and I are emotionally disturbed in, one way or another. I do not believe this to be so. In our psychodrama and healing workshops as well as in "Life, Death, and Transition" workshops we have routinely worked with physicians, ministers, nurses, psychiatrists, psychologists, social workers, and other professionals as well as many intelligent lay people. To my knowledge none of these people have seen or described either of us as being emotionally disturbed. People do not always agree with us or share our beliefs, but differences in opinion have nothing to do with emotional disorder. It is true Jay and I had considerable elective personal counseling earlier in our adult lives, in working through some of our personal issues. To me, this means we are willing to practice what we preach and I believe such experience has been most beneficial in our work in helping others. If some want to view this otherwise, this is their choice and their value system. It is true Jay and I have some values, principles, and standards in our work and in our personal lives, which we stand for and refuse to deviate significantly from. While I see this, again, as practicing what we preach, those who disagree with our standards or values may see our behavior differently. We will not alter what we consider an important personal or professional position to please or placate someone who is displeased.

Some of the more highly emotionally charged types of accusations have revolved around alleged sexual activity both in and out of the Darkroom. We have been accused of leading sex orgies and manipulating people into sexual activities. Jay and I categorically deny we have ever engaged in any explicit sexual behavior of any type with any participant at any time, in our Darkroom experiments or while we were Shanti Nilaya employees. I cannot speak for anyone else regarding their sexual behavior. The reader is reminded our Darkroom meetings take place in a darkened room and once materialization became consistent, much of the time was taken up by private visits, which occurred apart from the group. Reports by participants of unrecorded experiences or conversations with entities in these personal visits can only be evaluated at face value. The essence of the validity of what is reported as having occurred in these personal visits is thus dependent on the credibility of the person reporting and the attitude of the listener. I do not know for a fact sexual behavior has occurred in private visits. I do know the entities have said this activity was possible. I do know the walls in our meeting places, while adequate for blocking conversation, would not have contained sounds of any type of forceful behavior. The entities have repeatedly stated that upon request any individual would be returned to the group. There have been, to my knowledge, only a very few people who have made direct accusations based on personal experience towards Jay regarding sexual behavior in the Darkroom. However a number of people, after assessing their own experiences and listening to the accusations of these few, have drawn the conclusion that something funny was going on. There is a difference between making an accusation based on alleged personal experience, and making up one's mind or reaching a conclusion regarding an experience reported by someone else.

Another of the consistent accusations has been that Jay posed as an entity. Jay's statement is, and always has been, that he has never faked being an entity nor tried to manipulate anyone into fraudulent or destructive behavior. I have been married to this man for 23 years and such deceptive behavior would be totally alien to my experience of him. What I have seen in his response to accusation is a non-threatening and non-defensive attempt to understand the issues. This is an impressive response from a person who is being accused of emotionally charged issues after giving literally hundreds of hours of free time in Darkroom activities. All group sessions in the Darkroom have always been free of any charge or fee, overt or covert, and this has been true from 1971 to the present. No one has ever been asked for any money in connection with these group sessions other than to chip in for coffee. At one time many people began asking if private Darkroom sessions were possible and/or available. Jay and I did experiment with these. We found when materialization was quite consistent and strong, it was possible for us to have a three or four person meeting, Jay channeling and one or two others forming a small group. Many people wanted to take advantage of such an opportunity, but Jay only had so much time available during non-work hours. This was before we became a part of Shanti Nilaya. In response to the many requests, Jay decided to reduce the number of hours he spent in his landscaping and gardening business to provide time for these small sessions. Our income dropped accordingly. To make up for this loss it is true we charged for these individual type sessions, $25 for a session lasting about an hour. If there was no materialization there was no charge. This period of individual sessions, lasting about a year, began and ended before our involvement with Shanti Nilaya.

Some have viewed our involvement with Shanti Nilaya, in any manner, as being motivated by self-gain of one sort or another. It seems pertinent to share a few brief facts about how Shanti Nilaya began and our involvement.

The concept of a growth and healing center was the result of shared interests of about ten people; all of whom were involved in our Darkroom sessions. As we discussed our dreams and interests a few of us became quite serious about making such a center a reality. When Elisabeth joined our Darkroom sessions in 1976, she shared and supported this dream and our efforts in that direction. In 1975 Jay had founded a church, the Facet of Divinity, to share and disseminate the teachings of the entities. This church was already chartered by the State of California and existed as a non-profit organization. We all decided this would be a practical short-term way to initially establish our center with a minimal amount of organizational effort and legal expense. This was a joint decision by all involved. In a few months several of our group felt this procedure was not appropriate and might represent a conflict of interest. By this time we were getting more organized in the function of the center, which we came to call Shanti Nilaya, and a total separation was made between the center and the church. Shanti Nilaya has since remained totally separate from the church with its own board of directors, articles of incorporation, etc. Each of the original founders of Shanti Nilaya offered what they could, regarding start up money, supplies, office equipment and volunteer service. Until the time Shanti Nilaya could afford salaries neither Jay nor I received any pay from the center. When revenues began to allow this we did go on salary. What I want to emphasize regarding the creation and development of Shanti Nilaya is that to my knowledge, there has never been any coercion by anyone; all decisions were strictly a joint effort based on free choice and mutual interests.

The last group of suspicions or accusations I wish to address involves complaints by some people regarding entities' verbal responses to their questions or issues. These complaints were that the responses from the entities were often ambiguous, unclear, inadequate in the sense of being too brief, or contradictory. In my own experience, and many others in the Darkroom agree, the entities have a unique approach in how they respond to issues and questions. Essentially they say they are not allowed to spoon-fed people and thus deprive them of personal learning at their own initiative, nor are they allowed to interfere with free choice and individual destiny. Those participants willing to do their part in their learning and personal destiny, which may be frustrating and difficult, accept the general assistance and guided learning opportunities the entities offer. Those who want to avoid struggling with their own issues are quite dissatisfied and seem to push for interpreting statements or behavior of entities rather than exploring possibilities. Any therapist can tell you how easy it is to misinterpret, particularly in emotionally charged areas.

The rumors, gossip, and speculation that arise seem to occur in a pattern which consists of a very few people actually making accusations claiming personal experience as a basis, a larger number of people who conclude the accusations are true, and an even larger number of people who apparently enjoy passing along rumors and hearsay as apparent fact. The entities themselves do not offer any assistance in such activities. They insist a person accept responsibility for their experience and emphasize free choice, both in behavior and in how verbal messages are heard and received. As stated previously in this book one of their bottom lines has always been that if a person does not believe in the authenticity of the Darkroom or they have negative experiences, they are free to leave and believe what they will. Those who remain are encouraged to deal with whatever issues or challenges of a personal growth nature they choose. For those people seeking easy answers, the entities are a poor choice. Spiritual energy cannot be manipulated by anyone. Anger directed toward the entities as the result of frustration is only met by acknowledgment and acceptance. I believe, know, and teach we are responsible for our choices of beliefs and behaviors. As people blame us for various things, I remind myself of free choice.

I am sure those people making accusations based on their own perceptions do believe their experiences to be true. Blaming someone else for one's own perceptions or experiences seems to me to somehow absolve one from the obvious responsibility of choosing or agreeing to engage in behaviors. This denies the necessity of involvement with one's own intellectual processes and conclusions. I firmly believe, regardless of the challenges life presents us, things will turn out for the best if we permit our experiences to be opportunities for learning rather than blaming.

Life and its vicissitudes have presented Jay and myself a change in our state of affairs. While we are both sad about our separation from Shanti Nilaya, and how this came about, we will persevere in our activities. We were involved in our own forms of helping others before we became a part of Shanti Nilaya and we will continue on our own once again. In general the direction of our work will be sharing the impact and purpose of the four quadrants of the personality structure as we all face the challenges of living. Jay is at this time scheduling classes on healing and spiritual awareness. I will present the Barham Method of Psychodrama and associated teachings in workshops held every few weeks. These activities will be conducted at our ranch site and hopefully at other places throughout the country. A book giving in-depth information about personality and methods of change is in process at this time. There are one or two other volumes planned on healing and spiritual teachings, which will elaborate on the steps of development and evolution as shared by the entities.

Marti Barham, R.N., Ph.D. is a licensed marriage and family counselor, who has studied and experimented with psychological and spiritual phenomena and processes for many years. She was a close associate and colleague of Elisabeth Kübler-Ross, M.D. and was first vice-president of Shanti Nilaya, a growth and healing center. For four years she assisted Dr. Kübler-Ross in residential workshops on the theme of life, death, and transition. Marti also conducts workshops on personal growth utilizing her own method of psychodrama. This book documents the challenges she and her husband experienced in their efforts toward total physical materialization of spirit guides. They succeeded and their contacts with these entities became teaching sessions directed toward the development of man's total personality—physical, emotional, intellectual and spiritual.

Appendix B

Summary of *The Silver Cord: Lifeline to the Unobstructed*
Elaine M. Heiby, Editor

M. J. Barham & J. T. Greene (1986). *The Silver Cord:
Lifeline to the Unobstructed*; DeVorss & Co., Pub: Marina
del Rey, CA.

This is a summary of *The Silver Cord: Lifeline to the
Unobstructed* and also contains additional information
obtained from two materialized entities who used the names
Aenka (pronounced ang-kah) and Mario. Redundancies in
this summary reflect redundancies in the *Silver Cord*. As
mentioned in the Editor's Preface of *47 Billion Years of
Evolution: A Case Report*, the reader who has not read *The
Silver Cord* is encouraged to review this Appendix in order
to put the book in context. *The Silver Cord* is part of a new
revelation that the Source deems is needed at this point in
the evolution of humankind. While humans were positively
affected by prior revelations, such as from the experiment of
endowment of humans 7 million years ago and the teachings
of highly influential mediums such as Moses, Buddha, and
Jesus, modern people have nevertheless devolved into highly
destructive behavior.

   Indicators of destructiveness include unnatural
behavior such as greed, materialism, destroying the
environment, and killing more people than ever before in the
history of humankind. This devolution is also evident in the
creation of corporations, who in the U.S. were given the
status of a human being by the 14th amendment to the
Constitution in 1868, an amendment ostensibly designed to
free slaves. Yet this same amendment also created
corporations that have no soul, no conscience, a reckless
disregard for the safety of others and the environment, an
incapacity to experience regret, a failure to conform to
social norms, and a lack of responsibility. Indeed, by law,
corporations are required to put profits first at the expense of

destroying the environment and harming people and other forms of life (http://en.wikipedia.org/wiki/The_Corporation_(film and http://www.filmsforaction.org/watch/the_corporation/).

Prior to corporations, businesses were people with responsibility and morals and a conscience. Prior to corporations, early capitalism with genuine humans in partnership was more collective and interdependent. In contrast, corporations are callous. This example of devolution of humankind from basic spiritual connections is only one reason that there has been a surge of communications from discarnate entities (spirits) worldwide with the intent of helping people become more rhythmic, understanding of an afterlife, and aware of their interconnectedness with all things, including the Source. This surge includes an increase in frequency of materializations, mediums, psychics, and impingements from spirit guides (e.g., intuition, gut feelings, premonitions, and dreams). This is a worldwide phenomenon and not limited to the U.S. by any means.

The process for experiencing materialized entities is described in author Barham and editor Greene's 1981 book *Bridging Two Worlds* (reproduced in Appendix A). The materialized entities provided 2+ hour-long lectures about twice a week over the course of approximately 30 years to present the material in *Bridging Two Worlds*, *The Silver Cord* and the current book on *Evolution*. Aenka and Mario noted that the material presented was a product of a committee of discarnate entities.

In brief and as mentioned in the Preface and Appendix A, a group of individuals who were seeking contact with discarnate entities met in a darkened room. The composition of the group varied each week but the authors of *Silver Cord* were regular participants. Over the decades of materializations, several hundred individuals attended the sessions, including many physicians and psychologists. Once the group gathered, the room was darkened, after which they prayed or said some unifying statement and sang upbeat songs. One group member would lay down in an adjoining closet or hallway and go into a trance, which is an altered state of consciousness, somewhat similar but not identical to sleep. The person in a trance would not voice channel and therefore might be called a physical channel or a physical medium. Presumably, the entities would use the energy of the channel and sitters to somehow produce materialization via what has been called ectoplasm. The entities would materialize what looked and felt like a full physical body, including operative vocal cords and larynx. It is unknown what other internal organs they materialized. They indicated that they used energy from the group members and the physical medium, which somehow provided a catalyst. The energy from singing and positive emotions also was utilized to create the ectoplasm. The ectoplasm first appeared like steam or white smoke that emitted from the medium's body and was seen to form into a physical body. The entities noted that materialization might be impeded if the entity engaged with a group was preoccupied; the group consists of people with negative thoughts and emotions (e.g., hostility); and lack of permission from a group member's main spirit guide. Therefore, sometimes the Darkroom meetings did not yield materialization or other physical phenomena. Regarding having an entity interested in materialization, Aenka and Mario noted that for some evolutionarily advanced discarnate entities, materialization is one way to obviate the need to obtain certain positive physical experiences otherwise obtained by reincarnation.

Barham and Greene noted that group members supplied clothing for the entities because some members were uncomfortable with the entities materializing nude. The materialized entities spoke with their own independent voices. Therefore, unlike voice channeling or automatic writing, distortions arising from the physical personality of the channel are circumvented.

Barham and Greene present both direct quotes and summaries of the entities' presentations in *Silver Cord*. Each session was tape recorded and transcribed. As Editor, I have listened to many of the tapes and read most of the

425

transcripts. I have also seen photographs of Aenka and Mario while materialized and clothed. Many of the photos also include the sitters. Aenka appears as an African male and Mario as an Italian male. The photos would not provide convincing evidence as they appear like an incarnated human being.

The Silver Cord contains an Introduction and seven chapters. A summary for each is provided below. The summaries are supplemented by information from unpublished transcripts of the teachings of the same entities.

Introduction

Commencing 7 million years ago, endowed humans adhered to beliefs in a meaning and purpose of life that extends beyond the physical. These beliefs are reflected in the world religions and involve some organizing consciousness, or God, as well as a soul that continues in an afterlife (i.e., a spirit or discarnate entity). God is referred to as the Source and the afterlife as the unobstructed universe in the books by Barham and Greene.

Modern scientists often dismiss such spiritual beliefs as figments of the imagination, such as wish fulfillment relating to fear of death or hallucinations created by some unspecified organic dysfunction of the brain. Nevertheless, these skeptical attitudes have not stifled an explosion of literature concerning the spiritual and psychic nature of the human being. This literature has developed outside of organized religion and university departments of theology, psychology, medicine, and related disciplines. It is as if people are seeking a spiritual framework that organized religion and classical science no longer satisfies and mainstream academia avoids. The major world religions have developed hierarchies that relegate the worshiper to a disempowered role. Their teachings emphasize guilt, sin, unnatural fear, and punishment by a vengeful Creator rather than teachings that leave one feeling uplifted and informed.

The authors contend that people are on a spiritual

quest because our souls are pushing us to be more connected to this aspect of our existence that much of modern science eschews and organized religions obfuscate. The entities assert that the human personality consists of not only physical, intellectual, and emotional aspects but also a spiritual one. They note that these four aspects used to be far more in balance than is now the case. Thus, the quest for a greater spiritual understanding is taking place worldwide.

While experiencing materialized entities may not be commonplace currently, it is by no means rare. Up until about a century ago, reports of materialization were anecdotal accounts, with the resurrection of Jesus being the most familiar one. But more recently, materialization has been studied more systematically and therefore scientifically. For one example of a more recent and more objectively documented demonstration of materialization, see *The Scole Report* by Keen, Ellison, and Fontana (2011) and *Witnessing the Impossible* (2008) by Robin Foy.

Chapter 1: The Soul, the Source, and the Three Universes

Each human being has a soul or incarnated entity, which is a spiritual energy pattern that consists of a high quantitative and qualitative degree of intelligence and consciousness along with emotions, intuition/psychic abilities, and instinctual concerns about protection of the physical body. Spiritual energy differs from physical energies in terms of its the frequency of its vibrations. Spiritual energy is pure energy, containing no matter. No other creature on the planet Earth is endowed with the degree and quality of consciousness that constitutes a human soul. Each soul has a unique energy pattern and thereby a unique personality. A soul is considered incarnate when it is within a human physical body and discarnate when it is not. Modern science has not yet learned to measure spiritual energy given its high frequency of vibration is beyond detection by current technology. In addition, spiritual energy cannot be measured by modern materialisitic science because it does not include atoms or cellular components. Just as some other widely accepted forms of energy, such as electricity and gravity, existed before humans learned to infer but not understand or directly observe them, eventually spiritual energy will be accepted and inferred.

The soul is created by the Source, also referred to as the Source of All Divinity or God. The Source is defined as an impenetrable field of energy that creates energy and designs universal laws. It is all there is and all there ever will be. It has caused everything to be.

The soul or entity is literally a Facet of the Source, which the entities also call *A Facet of Divinity*. Both a soul and the Source exist eternally. While one's physical body functionally dies, the soul or entity does not.

Each soul has a destiny. After being birthed by the Source, souls choose to specialize in the general and somewhat overlapping areas of art, science, or religion, and that specialty in part forms a specific destiny. The soul develops through a 7-Step (or level) evolutionary process, after which it merges back with the Source. All souls eventually return to the Source. Only upon completion of evolution and merging with the Source can an entity fully know It and understand the beginning of the Source. Given the entities providing these teachings have not merged with the Source, they indicate that they do not know the source of the Source or whether there are other Sources. As they put it *that will be the dessert of the efforts of evolution.* While the entities refused to indicate their own steps of evolution because they claimed incarnates will translate such information into status, they did suggest that they are on Steps 4 or 5 and that they were debating the need to reincarnate to further their evolution.

The purpose of life is to contribute to the growth of the Source. The Source evolves as a result of evolved souls merging with It. The Source is not static or all-knowing, but infinitely developing.

There are three universes that co-exist: (1) the obstructed universe (physical existence known to humans through the senses and technology; three-dimensional space and linear time); (2) the unobstructed universe (energy patterns of a frequency not commonly perceived by humans via the 5 physical senses but perceived by what some call the 6th sense) is where the soul (discarnate entity; spirit) resides between and after incarnations; space and time are relative/subjective, referred in quantum physics as being non-local with non-time; and (3) the Source's universe (energy that creates energy), which consists of everything. The entities describe the Source as the height of pleasure and heaven.

Co-existence of the three universes refers not to their being in different 'places' as space is understood in the obstructed universe. Each universe is both independent and interdependent but operating with different energies that do not interfere with one another. The term for this co-existence in quantum physics is entanglement or interconnectedness. The entities use the term interdependence.

There are also three types of energy that co-exist: physical energy of the obstructed universe, spiritual energy of the unobstructed universe and the Source, and psychic energy, which binds the three universes. Each type of energy differs in terms of the frequency within which it functions.

Physical energy of the obstructed is the type of energy with which humans are most familiar, and many forms of it (e.g., electromagnetic energy) have been measured by humans. The Source created physical energy, set it in motion, and developed its course of evolution, which continues eternally. Physical energy can be manipulated by humans. Types of physical energy that have not yet been measured by humans are thought energy, emotional energy, and psychic energy. See Appendix C for ways that physical, psychic, and spiritual energy can be used for healing.

Spiritual energy derives directly from the Source. It is a non-physical pure energy that suffuses all three universes and cannot be directly manipulated by humans. Humans can invoke the Source to use spiritual energies, such as praying for a miracle, but humans cannot control spiritual energy. All spiritual energy is positive energy, meaning the motive of the energy is for mutual benefit. There is no such thing as negative (destructive) energy such as in the form of a devil, demons, satan, or hell. Evil and negativity are products of humans, not the Source or discarnate entities. There are no evil spirits; only less evolved ones who may be misdirected by lack of experience.

Psychic energy is a "free energy" (an independent physical energy unimpeded by matter) that suffuses the obstructed universe. It is a "binding agent" for physical and spiritual energy and thus can be used as a communication link within and among the universes. Humans can harness and manipulate psychic energy. Examples of using psychic energy include telepathy, precognition, clairvoyance (remote viewing), clairaudience, healing, and other psychic abilities. While humans have learned to identify the effects of psychic energy, such as by demonstrating mind-to-mind communication, direct observation of psychic energy has not yet been attained. The entities state that one day, science will learn to measure psychic energy. For a review of research supporting psychic phenomena, see *The Conscious Universe* by Dean Radin, (1997).

All three types of energy are both independent and dependent, and therefore interdependent. Spiritual energy is 'replenished' by physical energy, permitting evolution. No energy including spiritual energy is perpetual on its own. Physical or psychic energy would serve no purpose without spiritual energy. Spiritual energy would not evolve without psychic and physical energy. In this very real sense, the Source is dependent upon the incarnate souls It created in order for Itself to expand and evolve. Similarly, an individual soul (incarnated entity), which is spiritual energy, depends upon physical energy in the form of a human body as a vehicle for learning experiences that promote its own evolution and as such empowers the Source.

Spiritual energy is dependent upon psychic energy given it is the connecting force between physical and spiritual energy. The "silver cord" in the title of this summarized book refers to a psychic energy permanence that connects the soul's spiritual energy with the body's physical energy as long as the body is alive. The silver cord maintains the relationship between body and soul. It detaches upon physical death and indeed it is this detachment that yields physical death. In addition, using the silver cord for the soul being too often detached from the physical body, such as via chronic out of body experiences (OBE's), can lead to neurological damage and psychosis.

In summary, each human has a unique soul or incarnated entity that consists of a spiritual energy pattern created by the Source and is part of the Source. The soul, like the Source of which it is a part, is consciousness that lives forever. The soul's purpose is to evolve, thereby permitting the Source to evolve. Each soul ultimately returns to the Source once its own 7 – Step (or level) evolution is completed. Upon merging with the Source, a soul retains its identity yet becomes part of the whole that is everything. All souls eventually merge with the Source—there is no hell or purgatory. There are no "lost souls" or "evil spirits".

Souls' Birth From and Merging With the Source

The Source gives birth to 2, 3, or 5 souls at a time. Each soul has a male or female energy pattern and at least one of each sex is included at a birthing. The sex of a discarnate entity is not anatomical but instead refers to a tendency to be more aggressive (male) or more cooperative (female). Souls birthed together are soulmates that also return together to the Source. Soulmates assist each other during their evolution while discarnate and while incarnate. Each soul must have a positive experience with each soulmate during at least one incarnation prior to merging with the Source. This positive experience can be as friends, siblings, partners, and other relationships.

Upon birth from the Source, the soul or entity enters the unobstructed universe where it exists as a unique

431

spiritual energy pattern. Entities communicate with each other via awareness or thought transference. Awareness is more expanded in the unobstructed than while in the obstructed with limitations imposed by the physical body—including sensory, emotional, and intellectual restraints. Indeed, the entities liken being incarnate to being imprisoned.

After birth from the Source, some choices are made regarding the entity's destiny. One choice is to select a major area of study (art, science, or religion). Each entity must master all three areas to some degree but specialize in one of them. The mastery of these areas of study reflects in part what one contributes to the Source upon merging with It.

Another choice after birth from the Source is to select the physical body for the first incarnation. A soul plans each incarnation in terms of its destiny in the physical and which aspect of that destiny one wants to challenge. The entity confers with other entities, including one's soulmate(s), in literally choosing one's parents-to-be and their geographic location. This planning for a particular incarnation is referred to as one's Government of Life (others call it a life plan or life blueprint). In the unobstructed, one can compute probabilities of characteristics of the newborn based upon genetic history and an understanding of the physical personalities of the parents.

The Government of Life also includes planning with entities who will remain in the unobstructed to influence one towards fulfilling the planned goals for that incarnation. These entities will serve as "spirit guides" or 'angels' to guide and influence the incarnate entity. While guides cannot interfere with an incarnate's free choice, they can yield influence through mechanisms such as impingements of thoughts and dreams as well as direct communication during out-of-body experiences.

The Government of Life is literally recorded in the Archives of Knowledge, which some have referred to as the

Akashic Records. This is a repository of all information. Every behavior, thought, feeling, and action, is recorded within the Archives of Knowledge from the beginning of creation. All entities may access the Archives, but doing so is limited by one's stage of evolution and interests.

The content of the Archives is public knowledge and thus there are no secrets. However, the more evolved an entity, the more comprehensible is some of the available information. Each entity has a 'cubicle' or 'folder' for its particular experiences and Governments of Life for each incarnation. However, there is more than one Archive—one for each of the three planets in the three galaxies created 47 billion years ago that supports life endowed with a soul. It is possible for the discarnate entity to access each of these Archives.

While incarnate, a person is nudged by one's soul and by discarnate entities who assist in reaching the goals of the Government of Life. Spirit guides may include but are not limited to one's soulmates. When a message comes from one's soul, it is referred to as intuition. When a message comes from discarnates, it is referred to as impingement. Psychic energy functions to transmit this information between spiritual energy of the soul, discarnates, and the physical body.

A Government of Life is based upon probabilities. Not all factors affecting one's chosen destiny for an incarnation can be predicted. While all events have a cause and effect, some experiences are not predictable or are not within one's personal control. Such factors are referred to as the Gamble of Life. The Source created what may seem like random events so that the soul in the physical body is challenged to learn.

In selecting a baby to endow, the discarnate entity is aware of the baby's genetic structure and probable physical personality structure. Physical personality structures differ in terms of introversion-extraversion and thinking-feeling dimensions. These differences affect the functioning of the spiritual, intellectual, emotional, and physical quadrants of the physical personality. An entity selects a particular physical personality structure in terms of considerations of what learning experiences are being sought in a particular incarnation. Different physical personalities are selected across incarnations.

After an entity has selected a physical body for the first incarnation, it monitors the fetus. After birth and about the time the infant takes its first breath, the entity enters the body through the upper forward quadrant of the medulla oblongata. This part of the brain is the locus of the soul and where impingement is received; it is also the source of intuition and other psychic abilities. The soul 'solidifies' with the physical body and intertwines with the physical, intellectual, and emotional aspects of the human personality. It is this intertwining that yields the spiritual aspect of the human personality—that aspect that motivates one to understand the purpose of life. The physical body therefore becomes a vehicle for the soul's learning experiences.

If the baby is aborted, miscarried, or dies upon birth, then the soul selects a different baby to endow. Only one soul endows each baby. There is a balance of newborns and souls that are ready to incarnate. The entities state that until an entity endows a baby, it is considered nothing but a growth and eliminating that growth does not violate any universal laws.

The physical personality undergoes stages of development that indicate when each of the 4 quadrants emerges as a primary influence. These stages are as follows. The physical quadrant is dominant upon birth as the infant learns about the 5 physical senses, which provides learning about the obstructed environment. From ages 8 months through 1 (one) year, the emotional quadrant consisting of the 5 natural emotions develop (fear of heights and loud noises, anger, unconditional love, grief, and jealousy, which is a desire to emulate. At about age 6, the intellectual quadrant and reasoning develops. Upon adolescence, the spiritual quadrant becomes more prominent and there is a greater sense of individuality and a purpose in life.

434

If children are raised with unconditional love, they are enlightened and uninhibited to challenge the basic attitudes they learned from their parents or caregivers. They will be free of unnatural fears and their derivatives, guilt and shame. Upon adolescence, when the spiritual quadrant dominates, they will be in tune with the Source's energy and will live rhythmic lives.

There is no possibility of being possessed by more than one soul or of having one's soul displaced by another. Reported incidents of possession involve the physical personality's distorted interpretations of positively intended impingements.

Upon stabilizing in the infant's physical body, a functional amnesia of life in the unobstructed occurs. In subsequent incarnations, the amnesia also applies to those former experiences in a physical body. Some refer to this loss of conscious awareness as a veil or curtain being drawn. The Source designed this amnesia in order to heighten the challenge to the soul's learning while in a physical body. Nevertheless, some people can access this information from the Archives of Knowledge via mediation, hypnosis, mediumship, and a highly sensitive intuition. However, while the soul can make contact with the unobstructed (via impingements, intuition, dreams, etc.) and 'nudge' the physical personality toward fulfillment of one's Government of Life, the soul cannot interfere with the physical personality's free choice in responding to the environment. The more sensitive one is to such pre-conscious plans, the more likely one's life will be in harmony with those plans.

The human physical body is designed to last about 70 years. Whether by natural deterioration, illness, or the Gamble of Life, when the physical body has served its purpose it dies. There is no pain involved in death itself. The silver cord is severed and the soul literally leaves the body and enters the unobstructed universe. The stages of death are described below under the summary of Chapter 6.

Re-entering the unobstructed entails a re-orientation phase. After adjustment to the unobstructed, the now discarnate entity undergoes a self-evaluation. This entails objectively comparing what one accomplished in the physical life to one's Government of Life. One outcome of this evaluation is whether the entity determines it is necessary to reincarnate. Choosing to reincarnate is not a result of being rewarded or punished for a prior incarnation, which is how 'karma' often is misinterpreted. Instead, an entity elects to reincarnate in order to obtain additional needed positive experiences in the physical body for its evolutionary progress. Reincarnation is one of the Source's "safety nets" for affording as many opportunities as needed to gather all of the positive experiences in the physical. It is these positive experiences in the physical that further individuates the entity in its evolutionary progression. And it is this further individuation that adds to the Source's evolution.

The Government of Life includes not only pursuing learning in art, science, or religion, but also living according to universal laws that yield a natural, balanced, rhythmic life while obstructed in the physical body. Human experience involves physical, intellectual, spiritual and emotional aspects of functioning that are a challenge to balance. A balanced or rhythmic life is not at all automatic owing to humans also having free choice. Only the endowed human has a large degree of free choice in the obstructed universe. Other animals operate primarily by instinct or simple conditioning, which afford little opportunity for the Source to expand and evolve.

The physical quadrant includes the physical apparatus interacting with the world and sustaining life. The intellectual quadrant provides the ability to reason. The spiritual involves ones sense of interdependence, having a purpose in life, and being connected with the Source. The spiritual quadrant also provides uniqueness, creativity, intuition, sensitivity to psychic energy, and a desire to evolve toward merging with the Source. The emotional quadrant includes 5 natural emotions. They are fear, love, anger, jealousy (desire to emulate), and grief. Each of these emotions serves their purpose by openly expressing them for about 15 seconds. The physical energy involved in each emotion stimulates positive coping behaviors when faced with challenges. How those behaviors are expressed are a function of the physical personality in terms of introversion-extraversion and the thinking-feeling dimensions. Repressed emotions are said to cause about 90% of physical illnesses (the other 10% being caused by genetics or accidents). For example, crying is a natural way to express grief. The entities do not endorse the use of psychoactive medication to avoid the expression of the basic emotions and to deal with the challenges they present. The basic emotions involve energy, and repression of that energy damages the physical body.

The 5 emotions can be expressed in a natural or a distorted unnatural manner. Maintaining the experience of natural emotions is part of the destiny for each entity.

Natural fear is protective of one's physical body and is essential for survival. Instinctually, humans fear only two things: falling and loud noises. Other healthy fears can be learned, such as avoiding touching the skin to fire. Distorted fear is not pertinent to physical survival and is learned. Examples of learned distorted fears include avoidance of exploring a new environment, concern over others' opinions, guilt, and shame.

Natural love is unconditional acceptance of and giving to both self and others. It is essential to the interdependent nature of the universes. Unconditional love is not the same as liking; it is the same as accepting and respecting. Distorted love is conditional and manipulative.

Natural anger pertains to being motivated to overcome an obstruction, such as refusing a request one does not want to fulfill. Simply saying "no thank you" involves natural anger. Distorted anger takes the form of hostility and destructive behaviors.

Natural jealousy involves a desire to emulate. It motivates individuals to imitate one another and be creative. Distorted jealousy involves envy and the motivation to do harm, such as for another to not have what one desires.

Natural grief is the sadness one feels when a loved person or object is lost. It is an indicator of interdependence and a desire to give. Distorted grief takes the form of depression and self-pity when the individual fails to replace the loss.

Living a balanced, rhythmic life in the physical involves mastering unconditional love. Given that each entity is a Facet of the Source, such unconditional love also involves loving oneself as well as the Source. Unconditional love is an acknowledgement of interdependence and a desire to serve others without judgment.

The entities identify at least 10 universal guidelines or immutable laws that will lead to a rhythmic life while incarnate. These laws differ from the 10 Commandments of the Old Testament in the Bible, but there is some overlap. The guidelines are not punitive but instead underscore the importance of equality of all souls as well as respect for self and others. They are listed in the summary of Chapter 4.

During its evolution, each entity at times resides in a physical body in the obstructed universe (incarnation and reincarnation) and at times resides in the unobstructed universe (dis-carnation and re-discarnation). Selection of a newborn during reincarnations is not necessarily linked genetically to prior incarnations. An entity can readily choose a different race, geographic location, and socioeconomic level of parents given the type of challenges sought in the Government of Life.

Each entity evolves through 7 steps prior to merging with the Source. These steps are described below in the summary of Chapter 2. In general, step 1 is fulfilled by living in the obstructed while steps 2—7 are fulfilled in the unobstructed. Steps 2—5 involve studying universal laws and serving as spirit guides. Steps 6—7 involve creating new universal laws. Step 1, living in the physical, is the most difficult step to master. Entities can work on Steps 2—5 in between incarnations, but cannot progress on to Step 6 without having mastered Step 1. Mastering Step 1 includes living a life in rhythm with the universal laws and having a positive relationship of some sort with each of one's soulmates while in the physical.

The importance of acquiring experiences while in the physical body may seem at odds with some approaches to religion/spirituality that emphasize "rising above" the physical. Examples include denying one's sexual needs, fasting, and seeking enlightenment. Such attitudes actually impede spiritual evolution as they involve avoidance of attaining a rhythmic life in the physical.

Once every 10 years of linear time as measured in the obstructed universe, souls who have completed all 7 steps return to the Source. The addition of new knowledge and discoveries to the Archives of Knowledge is evidenced on Earth by impingements that result in technological advances that tend to occur about every 10 years.

While incarnate, it is possible to access this data bank through intuition, impingement, and out-of-body experiences (while meditating, daydreaming, or while dreaming when asleep). All human-made inventions involve the inventor having accessed the Archives. Not all information in the Archives is accessible to all entities at all times. Ability to assimilate the information varies as a function of the step of evolution attained by a particular entity.

Chapter 2: The Unobstructed Universe

Upon birth from the Source, an entity is a fragment of the Source. It is a spherical pattern of pure spiritual energy of a unique configuration with colors of the entire spectrum that usually are not perceivable with physical eyes. The size of the pattern varies from about the size of a snowflake to about 12 linear inches. There are trillions of entities that have been birthed by the Source.

Entities communicate with awareness of frequencies and patterns of different energies in both the obstructed and unobstructed universes. Entities respond to communications by expanding and contracting. The transmission consists of "thought pictures" that travel instantaneously (i.e., faster than the speed of light).

Entities are never birthed alone from the Source. All entities have at least one soulmate with an inherent attraction to one another. Soulmates also return together to the Source upon completion of Step 7 in their evolutionary progression. If any entity among a pod of soulmates is not ready to merge with the Source, the other soulmate(s) wait until all of them have completed their destiny.

As mentioned earlier, there are 2, 3, or 5 entities born in each pod. At least one male and one female are represented in each pod. There are never 4 soulmates birthed together as this configuration could reduce challenges and learning by the same two routinely hooking up. Soulmates are an arrangement by the Source to ensure the learning of interdependence. A soulmate is not necessarily a partner or spouse. He/she may be a friend, relative, or acquaintance of the same or opposite sex. While sex in the physical is defined in terms of anatomical characteristics, sex in the unobstructed reflects an aggressive (male) vs. cooperative (female) aspect of the entity's personality.

Entities must experience at least one positive physical life with each soulmate, and failure to do so is one reason for reincarnation. If two soulmates choose to incarnate in the same time frame, each will have an unconscious spiritual yearning to be with and to experience interdependence with each other.

While in the unobstructed, soulmates plan incarnations together in pursuing their joint destiny plans. They each will draw up a Government of Life that will bring them together so they can love each other in the physical. This love can take many forms and need not be romantic love. During a joint incarnation, a soulmate cannot be a parent but can be a friend, lover, sibling, and other relative. It is noteworthy that many other spirit communicators, people who have undergone hypnosis or had a near-death or pre-death experience, and some reincarnation memories contradict Aenka's and Mario's assertion that a soulmate cannot be a parent. Indeed, the Editor has not seen the transcripts nor heard the audiotapes documenting this assertion. So it is possible that the information excluding a parent and child being soulmates is a distortion made by the authors of *Silver Cord*.

Upon birth in the unobstructed universe, work on Step 2 is not pursued until after the first incarnation (Step 1). Prior to the first incarnation, one's energy is focused upon selecting a major field of study (art, science, or religion) while minoring in the other two. The entities classify all evolutionary endeavors into these three categories, although there can be overlap among them.

Another focus after birth from the Source is upon selecting parents for the first incarnation. The soul or entity studies options in terms of the planned Government of Life. But such plans are only probabilities given that unknown factors come into play, such as accidents, free choice, and changes among individuals and society. These uncertainties are referred to as the Gamble of Life, which is part of the Source's design to assure evolutionary changes by creating challenges and a variety of learning experiences.

Contact Between Entities and the Source

On rare occasions, in the unobstructed universe an entity has direct contact with the Source. Such contact enhances and revitalizes an entity's energy. Because a discarnate entity does not have physical emotions, it is difficult for them to describe this experience other than *like falling in love every second.*

Direct contact with the Source serves other purposes in addition to enhancing energy of the entity. Contact permits the Source to monitor whether energies are functioning how they were designed and to evaluate evolutionary progress. The most common form of contact between entities in the unobstructed and the Source is an ongoing interaction of subtle influences with moments of peak experiences.

Unobstructed Time and Space

What constitutes 'rare' occasions of contact with the Source is difficult to specify given that time is a subjective quality of the unobstructed universe. Earth or linear time, measured in terms of the speed of light, does not govern the unobstructed. Instead, experiences are measured. There is only 'now' in the unobstructed. This is what quantum physics calls non-time. The quantity of experiences is what measures a entity's evolutionary progression. In the obstructed universe, one might catch a glimpse of unobstructed time by noticing that when one is interested and learning, time 'flies' but when one is bored, time 'drags'.

Similarly, space is linearly measured in the obstructed universe but is subjectively experienced in the unobstructed. This is what quantum physics calls non-locality. Travel is accomplished by consciously directing one's energy pattern to a different 'place'. Desire leads to 'movement' to a different 'location'. Such movement is faster than the speed of light as there are no obstructions by other energy, such as matter in the obstructed universe. Travel is almost instant.

Seven Steps of a Soul's Evolution

All souls, spirits, or entities are equal in their creation as a Facet of the Source. Each is subject to the same universal laws. Because spiritual energy is positive energy, there are only benign entities. This is inconsistent with some notions of higher versus lower spirits, including demons. Souls, spirits, or entities do differ in the quantity and quality of their experiences. Such differences reflect steps in their evolutionary progress.

Experience, rather than knowledge per se, yields

growth and evolutionary progress. Experience is necessary for true comprehension. Therefore, entities differ in terms of what experiences they have acquired. Greater experiences put an entity closer to completing its destiny and merging with the Source. However, there is no hierarchy or superiority or competitiveness in the unobstructed. Being closer to merging with the Source in no way makes one superior. All entities have access to all knowledge and all discarnate entities inherently conform to the universal laws.

While there are no hierarchical levels in the unobstructed, there are organizational working groups of entities that form a matrix. Each group has a coordinator. Any one entity could be a coordinator in one group and a member in another.

One example of a working group of discarnate entities is one focused on psychological development of incarnate entities via impingement. Such is the group that coordinated the lectures for *The Silver Cord* and the current volume *Evolution*. They are part of a more extensive group that is working on "the K plan", which is an effort to promote natural rhythmic living by awakening spirituality and potential for unconditional love in the obstructed universe. The entity K elected as a focus of its spiritual destiny the supervision of a coordinated effort in the unobstructed regarding psychological development on Earth. The K plan is evident in the surge of publications and other media in recent years that pertain to spirituality and the nature of the afterlife.

Working groups of discarnate entities have disagreements but they take the form of constructive discussions. Discarnate entities do not have the feelings experienced in the physical body. With no learned shame or guilt, there is no 'ego' to defend or offend. They do experience the five basic natural emotions of fear, love, anger, jealousy, and grief—but in a different form given they do not have a physical body. Discarnate entities cannot violate universal laws of unconditional love and mutually positive interdependence, and therefore cannot violate rhythmic patterns. However, they can differ in experiences, including the degree to which they have assimilated the Archives of Knowledge relevant to the three planets in three galaxies created 47 billion years ago with endowed life. Therefore, both the quality and the quantity of experiences are governed naturally by the universal law that ***all true benefits are earned.*** Benefits in this case, involve an inevitable evolutionary progression designed by the Source. Evolutionary progression is viewed as a natural process without value judgment and for which there is no choice.

Step One: First Incarnation

Upon birth from the Source, the evolutionary process that the Source set in motion was to place a facet of Itself in a physical human body as a vehicle for gaining experiences by being "not entirely Itself" and by being "separate from Itself". Therefore, based on a Government of Life, an entity enters a chosen infant's body to begin its first experiences in the physical. The soul or incarnate entity gradually solidifies within the physical body and that process involves an amnesia regarding all of its prior experiences in the unobstructed.

The entities Aenka and Mario indicate that an entity possesses a physical body but they are quick to clarify that the use of the term possession does not imply that the soul controls the body. They state that there is no such thing as being "possessed by an evil spirit" or "made to do things against one's will". The soul, which is a facet of the Source, cannot violate the universal law of an individual having freedom of choice. One, and only one, soul can possess a physical body at any point in time.

While souls or entities differ in terms of the particulars of their Government of Life (such as in pursuing experiences in art, science, or religion), there is the commonality of living a natural rhythmic life in accordance with the universal laws that govern physical life. As mentioned, doing so involves having a positive experience with one's soulmate(s). It is possible, but quite difficult, to accomplish this in one lifetime.

Many thousands of years ago, it was more common for an entity to develop a rhythmic life in one lifetime. At present, with humans estranged from their spiritual quadrant and overly involved in the material, doing so is unlikely and most entities live many lifetimes in order to complete Step One of evolution. Other spirit communicators have suggested 60 to 600 reincarnations may be required.

Upon death of the physical body (see summary of Chapter 6), the entity returns to the unobstructed universe and conducts an evaluation of the previous physical life. This evaluation is a nonjudgmental tally of what was accomplished in lieu of one's Government of Life. The record of this evaluation is placed in the Archives of Knowledge. The result is that the entity determines whether it is necessary to reincarnate in order to complete Step One.

Unlike the single-chance day-of-judgment described by some current religions, the Source designed as many opportunities for a Facet of Itself to live a rhythmic life in the physical as is needed. Positive experiences from each lifetime need not be repeated for evolutionary progression. Those missed will go into subsequent Governments of Life for future incarnations.

Each discarnate entity conducts its own evaluation. We are our own evaluators. The evaluation is strictly descriptive and objective. Because the evaluation is conducted in the unobstructed without a physical body, there are no distortions based upon intellectual defenses or distorted emotional concerns. There is no ego to defend. There are no experiences of guilt, sin, or shame. There are no rewards or honors. As such, 'karma' as the term is used to refer to punishment and reward in subsequent lives is a distortion of the physical personality.

The evaluation pertains to gaining an understanding of life in the physical body that follows universal laws. These involve not only living a rhythmic life, but also having had a positive relationship in the physical with one's soulmate(s) as well as developing a working knowledge in art, science, and religion and a specialty in one of these areas.

Step Two: Planning Reincarnation and Studies in the Unobstructed

If the evaluation outcome is that additional positive experiences are needed in the physical body, then the entity plans to reincarnate in order to further complete Step One. If so, the entity determines what additional experiences are needed and how to accomplish them. The entity once again searches for parents, culture, and growth potentials in the selection of another infant to endow. Some entities elect to reincarnate quite soon. Others choose to remain in the unobstructed universe for hundreds of earth years and work on Steps Two through Five. However, it is impossible to complete Step Five prior to completing Step One.

Upon selecting an infant for reincarnation, many factors may interfere with the Government of Life. The Gamble of Life may result in changes in the parents' behavior and the environment that the entity could not have predicted. Free choice of the incarnated soul can result in failure to pursue needed opportunities. Economic necessity for survival of the physical body may lead one to make decisions that fail to allow evolutionary progression. In such cases, it is possible that late in life the individual will develop a hobby or second career that affords the experiences needed and recorded in the Government of Life.

The entities' lectures make a clear distinction between the natural evolutionary choice to reincarnate and concepts of sin, punishment, hell, purgatory, and karma as defined in the world's major religions. There are only mistakes, not sins. There is no negativity in the unobstructed. Physical personality traits in one lifetime do not carry over into another lifetime. In each physical lifetime, the entity chooses an infant whose genetic structure dictates whether the physical personality will be introverted

446

vs. extraverted and thinking vs. feeling in orientation of the obstructed universe.

Electing to reincarnate is a natural part of seeking all the positive experiences needed for the evolutionary progression. Reincarnation is a natural consequence in accordance with the universal law of recompense. Reincarnation is not viewed as a punishment for past mistakes or a reward for past accomplishments. For example, if an individual went blind this would not indicate that he or she had blinded someone in a past life. This universal law of recompense states that when one makes a mistake, it is natural to apologize and make amends if possible, which, in turn, leads to self-forgiveness. Living in accordance with this law is part of living a rhythmic life.

There is an accumulation of knowledge about art, science, and religion across incarnations. While amnesia makes this knowledge vague during any one incarnation, the essence of it remains within the soul/entity. For example, if in a past life one mastered mathematics then learning math in subsequent lifetimes would be easier than it would for an individual who had not mastered it in prior lives.

When not involved in planning for the next physical incarnation or if reincarnation is not deemed necessary, then in Step Two souls begin to study the unobstructed universe. This study includes thousands of universal laws as they relate to our galaxy. For example, these include the formulae for all of the types of energies and learning how they operate. Another example is learning how the planets in our solar system are aligned and influence each other. This learning is done by observation and direct experience as well as by studying the Archives of Knowledge.

Another focus of study and research pertains to one's major field of study (art, science, or religion) both while in the obstructed and the unobstructed. Indeed, it is during Step Two when one finalizes the decision of one's major and two minor areas of study. The particular aspects and approach to the studies are determined. This is an irrevocable decision and involves a great deal of deliberation.

That the choice of major area of study cannot be changed reflects a difference of free choice between the obstructed and unobstructed universes. While in the physical, one is free to change their mind and to choose to violate universal laws (e.g., by making love conditional). While in the unobstructed, a soul cannot change its destiny. Behavior is directly governed by universal laws (e.g., all love is unconditional).

Selecting among art, science, and religion can be complicated given there are interrelationships among these areas of study. For example, social science can be both a science (e.g., biological bases of behavior) as well as a religion (e.g., developing rituals related to the continuity of life).

Just as one conducts an evaluation after a physical life (Step One), an objective tallying is done for a self-determination of whether to progress to subsequent Steps. Therefore, an entity chooses when to progress to Step Three. Again, Steps Two through Five can be worked upon simultaneously in the unobstructed while between incarnations (Step One).

Step Three: Universal Laws and Exceptions

Studies in Step Three are an extension of what was undertaken in Step Two. Topics of study include essential microscopic and macroscopic properties of energies in the universes. These include electrical, magnetic, chemical, and psychic energies. In addition, the organizing principles of these energies are studied, particularly in how physical energies interact with spiritual energy and yield evolutionary processes. Some of this learning is through direct study of the Archives of Knowledge and direct observation. Learning is also acquired by direct experience, such serving on committees.

There are at least two types of committees for entities in Step Three. One type is to consult with entities on

Step Two in their understanding of the universal laws that pertain to Earth's galaxy. Entities on Step Two are still learning to make decisions based on these universal laws. Entities on Step Three monitor these decisions to ensure universal laws are not unintentionally violated. No entity can violate a universal law without permission from the Source or a committee on Step Three. A greater universal law does not permit an entity to make the choice of unilaterally violating other universal laws. Such violation would be a negatively motivated act and there is no negativity in the unobstructed.

Another type of committee on Step Three functions to evaluate requests from entities on any Step to violate a universal law. While no entity can violate a universal law without permission, Step Three involves learning the wide variations in the thousands of universal laws and the huge responsibility involved in exceptions to these laws. For example, the universal law of free choice while in the physical may be given an exception in the case of an incarnated entity who is about to cross the road and step in front of a vehicle but instead feels compelled to stop and turn around. An entity may be given permission to impinge "look in the store window" if doing so does not interfere with the incarnate's learning needs for the Government of Life and needed challenges from the Gamble of Life. Some so-called miracles are due to entities receiving permission to violate free choice.

If permission to violate a universal law is not granted, then the requesting entity simply accepts this decision. Because discarnates do not experience physical emotions, it is not possible to be hostile.

By gaining more experience with the universal laws in Step Three, entities gain a better understanding of aspects of physical, psychic, and spiritual energies (see Appendix C for use of these energies in healing) as well as the function of entities in the Source's evolution. Is so doing, entities on Step Three also learn how to manipulate energies for spiritual purposes.

Step Four: Study of the Obstructed and Serving as Guides

During Step Four, discarnate entities focus their studies on learning about aspects of human life from the perspective of the unobstructed universe. This involves direct observation of incarnated entities, use of the Archives of Knowledge, and serving as a guide to one or more incarnates. Less commonly, it can include transient materialization to gain additional direct experience in the obstructed. Therefore, it is likely that Aenka and Mario had attained at least Step Four when they materialized and dictated the books by Barham and Greene as well as the current book *Evolution*.

Entities on Step Four select incarnate souls whose destiny or Government of Life has a special interest to them. Part of this interest is related to sharing a destiny involving art, science, or religion. When a discarnate entity formulates a Government of Life in the unobstructed, a number of other entities make a commitment to serve as helpers or guides during that incarnation. The sole purpose of a guide is to offer the incarnate information relevant to the archived Government of Life in order to facilitate one's individual destiny.

Guides volunteer and are not selected by the entity who is about to incarnate as a soul. The reason for this is to help maintain objectivity between the guide and the person in the physical. Also in order to maintain objectivity, guides are never one's soulmate(s). However, before an entity incarnates, it has some idea who the guides might be. Nevertheless, the amnesia upon incarnation helps maintain objectivity while in the physical.

Guides assist in pursuing the Government of Life by impingement, which can involve a nudge to attend to certain thoughts, feelings, desires, wishes, hunches, dreams, or aspects of the environment. At times guides might manipulate physical energy or free choice if given permission from the Source or a Step Three committee to do so. There are considerable and intricate responsibilities in taking on the commitment to serve as a guide for an incarnate.

Impingement involves spiritual energy in the unobstructed communicating with physical and spiritual energy in the obstructed. Doing so utilizes psychic energy. Guides send energy to the physical mind in the form of images, thoughts, urges, and words. This mental process is triggered by the use of psychic energy to transmit spiritual energy relevant to the thought process. However, the incarnate does not easily receive transmitted information or act upon it. The impingement is advice, and does not directly interfere with free choice. Therefore, guides' advice can be ineffectual.

There are three types of guides: main, secondary (auxiliary), and representative. A main guide remains a spiritual helper throughout a entity's entire incarnation. This commitment is made upon an entity's endowment of an infant. A person's main guide will not reincarnate until one's physical body dies and one's soul or entity leaves the physical body—although there are rare exceptions to this. In addition, a main guide coordinates secondary and representative guides.

A discarnate can serve as a secondary guide to a number of people and any one person may have numerous secondary guides. Secondary guides work as assistants or consultants to the main guide, and are unable to influence an incarnate without permission from that person's main guide. Secondary guides can represent the incarnate as well as the main guide in the unobstructed—again with permission of the main guide.

Unlike a main guide who commits to helping a person throughout an incarnation, a secondary guide may volunteer at any time during an individual's physical life. Volunteering is done in order to benefit both the discarnate entity and the one in the physical. Secondary guides find the incarnate's life to be fascinating, and therefore choose to be around that person's destiny in order to learn about behavior in the obstructed and how to effectively impinge. Over the course of an incarnation, there are likely to be many secondary guides interested in the person's life.

Being a representative of another guide is a third way to function as a guide. Representative guides have an interest in a particular individual in the physical, and volunteers to assist the main and secondary guides. Representative guides function on an ad hoc basis, whenever their services are needed. Main and secondary guides might invite a representative to ensure objectivity for both the discarnate guide and the incarnate. For example, if production of a physical materialization was deemed to be a positive influence, then a representative guide may be called upon to make the attempted contact and produce the phenomenon.

While guides are generally on Step Four, there have been entities on Step Two who choose to be a secondary guide or representative guide. They would do so because the incarnated entity holds a particular interest to the entity on Step Two.

With every incarnate being helped by multiple guides, the complication of the coordinator role of the main guide becomes apparent. The main guide is responsible for controlling what physical, psychic, and spiritual energies are imposed on an incarnate's body and external environment. The human physical structure's nervous system is influenced by its environment and an impingement involves energy that becomes part of that environment. Every interaction with a soul involves spiritual energy that remains in the environment and the Archives of Knowledge. This also holds true for interactions among incarnates as every thought, feeling, and action leaves energy in the environment. If one passes a stranger on the street who smiles, there is an influential effect. Therefore, the main guide monitors that the effects of impinged energies most likely have a positive effect.

The main guide should not be confused with what is called a 'gatekeeper' or 'control' in some of the spiritual literature. The gatekeeper concept reflects assumptions that there are good and evil spirits, sometimes called higher and lower entities. Given there is no negative or evil energy in the unobstructed universe this concept is viewed as a distortion of the physical personality. Incarnates who report experiencing demons are in fact projecting their own guilt and shame onto their experiences.

Step Five: Synthesis and Evaluation

Step Five involves integrating and evaluating what one has learned since being birthed by the Source. During this step, the entity determines if it has fully evolved through the first four steps. It is a phase of preparation for more advanced evolution during Steps Six and Seven. The entities likened Step Five to having completed college and proceeding through graduate school.

A critical part of Step Five is to ascertain whether Step One, existing in the obstructed, has been completed. Step One is the most difficult to complete of all the seven steps toward completing one's destiny. While Steps Two, Three, and Four can be worked on and completed while in the unobstructed between incarnations, Step Five cannot be completed until there is no longer a need to reincarnate. Evolving past Step Five indicates that all positive experiences relevant to one's Governments of Life in the physical have been completed. The remaining destiny of the entity will evolve in the unobstructed.

If the entity determines that it has no need to reincarnate and has mastered the tasks of Steps One, Two, Three, and Four, only then is finishing Step Five viable. Finishing involves integrating and synthesizing what has been learned up to that point of individual evolution and proceeding to Step Six.

Step Six: Study of the Galaxies and the Source

Step Six involves applying one's prior knowledge to

studying the other two planets in the two other galaxies with endowed, intelligent life. On Step Six, one also studies every life form and their systems in those galaxies. This studying involves communication with entities in the unobstructed environment of the other two planets, accessing the Archives of Knowledge pertinent to those planets, and using direct observation. The information derived from experiences in all three planets with endowed life is mastered. Laws that govern behavior in the physical on all planets with endowed life are understood. All three with endowed life are many light years apart, but travel in the unobstructed is as instantaneous as the thought and desire to be there.

The entities' lectures compare Step Six to a graduate level internship where individuals apply their knowledge. Applying this knowledge to different galaxies permits the entity to acquire a broader understanding of the potential contributions to the Source's evolution. The various ways in which the Source changes and expands in relation to how various energies function in different systems becomes better understood.

Another aspect of Step Six is to function as an overseer of committee's on Step Three, such as their decisions to violate universal laws. Souls or entities on Step Six maintain all of the laws created by the Source that govern the unobstructed. They are the 'governors' of other entities.

Step Seven: Original Research & Merge with the Source

During Step Seven, the overseer function of Step Six is continued. In addition, instructions from the Source to the unobstructed go to entities on Step Seven.

Step Seven also involves individual creativity and contributing new information to the Archives of Knowledge, such as the creation of new universal laws or a new synthesis of information in the Archives. Something is added to the unobstructed universe and knowledge expands in an interdependent fashion. The entities liken Step Seven to completing a dissertation in graduate school, the final formal step of a higher education, or publishing a book. Every entity has a unique identity and destiny, and makes unique contributions to the Archives of Knowledge. Additions to the Archives contribute to all other entities and to the Source. Such new information is shared with the obstructed or physical universe via impingement for advancement and discovery in art, science, and religion.

Once an entity has made an original contribution to the Archives of Knowledge, it then conducts a final evaluation. Each and every experience on the other six steps also is assessed. Everything the entity has gained is considered to ensure that all of the possible growth has been accomplished.

Once Step Seven is completed, the entity is ready to merge with the Source. Everything an entity has gained since its birth from the Source is returned to the Source. Every entity adds to that which is the Source and contributes to Its evolution.

This merging with the Source involves both maintaining individuality and becoming part of the whole. Entities merge with the Source not only with their soulmates but also with other pods of soulmates who have also completed Step Seven. Such merging occurs every 10 years in Earth's linear time. And it is about every 10 years on Earth that there is some major creative advancement. Indeed, all major discoveries on Earth are a result of impingement of what has already been discovered or created in the unobstructed.

Merging with the Source upon completion of Step Seven is described by the entities in a way that underscores the importance of having finished Step One (incarnating):

In completing Step One, you are to experience complete and total physical experiences of every positive quality to the fullest. When you go back to the Source, you return to the Source all of these experiences. This adds to the strength, to the power, and to the knowledge of the Source of all Divinity. The Source is then stronger, more intelligent to expand out to infinity, to other universes and set into motion other life forms, other ideas of phenomena.

Chapter 3: The Obstructed Universe: Physical/Spiritual Beings in Step One

Natural spirituality while incarnate is not some esoteric path of intense prayer, meditation, or some other ritual that escapes physical reality. It is not possible to return to the Source while in the physical body regardless of one's 'enlightenment' in the obstructed. Essential spiritual growth takes place in the fulfillment of positive experiences in the physical body. In the words of the entities:

do not separate the physical from the spiritual. They are inseparable in the first step of growth [incarnations]. *You cannot live in prayer. You cannot lose yourself in spirituality or religion. You cannot escape physical reality and physical responsibility by calling such avoidance spiritual, religious, or any contribution to the Source. Your responsibility in Step One is your physical being, your physical and psychological development . . .* [the Source] *would not have made all of the magnificent functions of this physical body had it not been intentional and for the purpose of full expression . . . .*

Step One of spiritual evolution occurs in the physical body and is the most difficult and thereby the most important. A great deal of unique learning takes place in the physical, and this learning becomes part of the Source. As noted earlier, spiritual evolution requires that an entity learn to exist in a natural rhythmic manner, i.e. in following with the universal laws of natural behavior while incarnate. The difficulty of doing so is reflected in the commonality of reincarnation.

What makes natural living in the physical so difficult? Why do incarnate entities need to try and try again? What about the physical body makes it so challenging to live life to the fullest?

First of all, the incarnated entity or soul has far more free choice than when discarnate, although free choice to some degree exists in all of the universes (obstructed, unobstructed, and the Source). Unlike when an entity is in the unobstructed, this free choice in the physical body includes the opportunity of violating the universal laws of natural behavior. Whenever an incarnated entity violates a universal law, he/she experiences discomfort yet is free to proceed. This discomfort might be experienced in the distorted emotions of guilt and shame, or repressed and then expressed in other unnatural emotions (e.g., projection) or physical disease.

A second reason Step One is so difficult is that the incarnate is challenged to use free choice with the limitations of a physical body that is exposed to the Gamble of Life. Awareness is obstructed by the 5 physical senses that perceive some forms of energy as matter. For example, only a limited portion of an object can be seen by the physical eye. Moreover, intellect is clouded with amnesia of former experiences and restricted by words. The 5 natural emotions (fear, love, anger, jealousy, and grief) have potent physical components that can readily be misunderstood and distorted in expression. Expressing these emotions in a natural rather than unnatural way is part of mastering Step One. Natural expression is done with constructive motives (e.g. love unconditionally) while unnatural expression is done with destructive motives (e.g., anxiety, conditional love, hostility, envy, and depression or self-pity).

A third reason Step One is difficult is that we must experience all positive experiences in a rhythmic fashion within our physical personality structure. Each infant's basic physical personality structure differs in terms of introversion, extroversion, feeling, and thinking dimensions that affect perceiving and reacting to the physical environment. These structures are genetically determined and the selection of a fetus to endow upon birth is based

457

partly upon the challenges inherent in its personality dimensions. Each physical personality is characterized as one of the following: thinking extrovert, thinking introvert, feeling extrovert, or feeling introvert. Different personality dimensions might be selected for different incarnations.

The aura, or light energy, around a human's body reflects its physical personality structure. Aura's have been captured in photographs (e.g., http://www.montcabirol.com/index.php/isabelle-psyhic-photographs) and are reportedly seen by some individuals via the 6th sense (intuitive sensitivity and psychic abilities). These colors include green for extraversion, red for emotional, yellow for introversion, and blue for thinking. A thinking extrovert would exhibit first blue and then green. A thinking introvert would exhibit first blue and then yellow. A feeling extravert would exhibit first red and then green. A feeling introvert would exhibit first red and then yellow.

Step One begins upon selection of a fetus and entering the physical body upon or shortly after birth. If the fetal body is miscarried, aborted, or stillborn, the entity selects a different physical body. About the time the infant takes its first breath, the entity infuses itself or possesses the body. The spiritual energy must be in the body for a certain period of time for the neurons and development of the brain to take the imprint for behavior and the potential for reasoning. The entity enters the physical body in the upper forward quadrant of the medulla oblongata and permeates the rest of the physical body. At that time, there is an amnesia of previous learning experiences in the unobstructed and memories of previous lifetimes. At times, some of these memories can be recalled, such as with memories of past incarnations, dreams, and intuition. However, the amnesia is designed to increase the challenges of living in a physical body.

The incarnate entity or soul is not experienced as separate from the physical body. Instead, it is experienced as one's preconscious or subconscious that nudges one to live in harmony and pursue one's Government of Life.

The entities emphasize that it is critical for parents/caregivers to support each child's unique personality structure. They emphasize that for growth there should be limits and fair, firm, and consistent discipline. Discipline involves natural consequences of mistakes, and not character assaults or corporal punishment. The basic physical personality structure of the child should be accepted and not punished.

There are four general developmental stages of the physical personality. These include: (1) autoerotic from birth to four years; (2) narcissistic from four to seven years; (3) homosexual from seven years to puberty; and (4) heterosexual from puberty to death.

In each of the four stages, one aspect of the physical personality is the focus of growth: (1) development of the physical quadrant during the autoerotic stage involves becoming familiar with and deriving pleasure from the physical body; (2) development of the emotional quadrant during the narcissistic stage involves accepting simple emotions that lead to more complex ones such as self-love, self-worth, and self-acceptance; (3) development of the intellectual quadrant during the homosexual stage involves abstract reasoning and acceptance of self in relation to others; and (4) development of the spiritual quadrant during the heterosexual stage leads one to sense a purpose in life, creativity, intuition, and developing rhythmic interpersonal relationships.

It is development during the first 7 years of life that determines one's basic attitudes toward life and the challenges entailed in living in accordance with universal laws. The nature of the physical personality is described in detail not only in *Silver Cord* but also in M. J. Barham and J.T. Greene's *Yesterday's Children*, Vantage Press, 1993.

Chapter 4: The Obstructed Universe: Struggling for Maturity

This chapter includes various topics related to the expression of the spiritual quadrant as the last stage of development of the physical personality (Step One). Spirituality in the physical is described by the entities as follows:

It is a rhythmic combination of all the checks and balances of life. Every action that occurs shall be negative unless it has the quality of spirituality, anything from singing to sexual intercourse . . . spirituality is learning about yourself and sharing your personality—the desire for expression, the desire to share your knowledge. Interdependence is a true quality of spirituality—to give, and a deep desire to give more than you receive. Have no fear of receiving, because as you share, every aspect is returned to you tenfold! Then you begin to feel your place in the universe . . . .

Expression of one's spiritual quadrant includes developing a sense of interdependence. While dependence is healthy as a child and independence is healthy as an adolescent, interdependence is the ability to be social. It involves acceptance of others as they are without comparing yourself with them. Unique differences from others are viewed with pride and courage.

Expression of interdependence also involves dealing with sex differences with a sense of pride and equality. The entities teach that one is born from the Source with either a male (i.e., aggressive) or female (i.e., cooperative) personality and an entity retains the same personality throughout incarnations. As mentioned above, it was not clearly documented from the entities' teachings whether the sex of an entity always matches the anatomical sex of a physical body it incarnates. Also as mentioned above, it is noteworthy that many psychics, mediums, and independent voice spirit communicators as well as many people who experienced reincarnation memories, hypnosis, pre-death communications, and near-death indicate that an entity chooses male, female, and inter-sexed physical bodies across reincarnations.

Regarding anatomical sex differences in the physical, the entities note the following:

The male is 49% female, and the female is 49% male. Male and female are equal in importance, and different . . . the male is no more intelligent than the female, or vice versa. Each have their destiny and as partners they have their destiny. Interdependence is the intent of each sex as they seek a rhythmic balance . . . .

The entities give specific advice regarding enjoyment of the sex drive and orgasms and the importance of allowing the body full physical expression. Orgasms include not only the genitalia, but also other sensory experiences such as tasting good food, sneezing, a bowel movement, and passing wind. Denial of these physical expressions, including expression of emotions, causes the body to deteriorate. The failure to experience these natural processes of the physical body not only causes illness but also becomes a reason to reincarnate.

Historically, women had been more sexually aggressive than men. This changed, however, as women became less openly accepting of their sexuality as a result of men trying to tame females. Women began to reject their true sexuality and instead used it as a weapon to influence men. Natural sexual relationships are monogamous ones that allow the experience of commitment and interdependence. When monogamy is violated, one will feel a sense of unrest, anxiety, or disappointment. This does not imply that divorce is unnatural and they define commitment as *so long as you choose to be together*. Therefore, serial monogamy is considered to be natural.

Differentiations between love and lust and between unconditional and conditional love are noted. Our society has distorted sexuality by equating it with conditional love. As the entities put it, *you begin to prostitute yourselves to gain what you want*. Conditional love is a manipulation. Unconditional love is a giving, not a taking. It is an affectionate feeling permitting an act of favor towards someone. Unconditional love is learned through the experience of being loved by another, which in turn leads to self-love. The entities point out Jesus demonstrated and taught unconditional love in phrases such as "love thy neighbor" and "love is everything". Unconditional love permeates the unobstructed universe but learning this sense of giving and acceptance in the obstructed is one of the great challenges of incarnations.

One measure of unconditional love for self and others is whether one has conquered criticism. *You are as critical of others as you are with yourself . . . for every fault you find in your fellowman you will find it in yourself or you will find the magnified fear of this fault in yourself.*

Ultimately, the indicators of spiritual maturity involve adhering to at least 10 universal laws of natural behavior designed by the Source. These laws are presented as being immutable in the pursuit of evolution. These laws differ from the thousands of universal laws that govern the obstructed and unobstructed universes.

The 10 major universal laws of natural behavior are presented as follows:
1. Every human is endowed with a Facet of Divinity (soul) that ensures dignity and equality.
2. Every human is unique and has an individual destiny to fulfill.
3. Self-acceptance of the physical, emotional, intellectual, and spiritual aspects of the personality structure.
4. Every human has free choice.
5. Recompense: acceptance of responsibility for the effects of one's choices. This acceptance involves owning a mistake, apologizing, making amends if possible, and then self-forgiveness. This is also referred to as the Universal Law of Confession.
6. Independence: each human has the potential for self-fulfillment.
7. Interdependence: each human has limitations and is

therefore social.

8. All true benefits are earned.
9. All true benefits are mutual.
10. Every human is equally subjected to the Gamble of Life (events one did not predict) and the Government of Life (one's plan for a particular incarnation).

Following the universal laws of natural behavior is the destiny of each individual and may take numerous incarnations. The entities mentioned several other universal laws that are involved in fulfilling one's destiny. There must be at least one incarnation with each soulmate that is mutually positive. Reincarnation is a natural response to needing further experience in the physical in order to evolve. Interdependence and monogamous commitment with a mate must be experienced in some lifetime, although the monogamy might be serial. Each entity must acquire a working knowledge of art, science, and religion, majoring in one and minoring in the other two. All entities have access to the Archives of Knowledge in accordance with their evolutionary development to comprehend the information. All entities evolve through the same 7 Steps. All entities are affected by physical, psychic, and spiritual energies. All incarnated entities have a "silver cord" or psychic energy permanence connecting the soul with the living physical body. All incarnated entities have spirit guides. Ultimately, all entities return to the Source.

Chapter 5: The Obstructed Universe: Psychic/Spiritual Influences

Fulfillment of one's destiny while incarnate is assisted by a system of influential factors. These include a Government of Life recorded in the Archives of Knowledge, guides in the unobstructed, some lifting of amnesia through impingement and intuition, and the use of psychic energy.

Impingement and Intuition

The primary methods by which an incarnate entity accesses contact with the unobstructed are by impingement and intuition via the spiritual quadrant. Contact is made possible by the use of psychic energy, which binds physical and spiritual energies.

Impingement refers to when a discarnate guide imparts messages using psychic energy as a means of communication. Intuition refers to when the incarnate initiates contact with the unobstructed, also using psychic energy.

Impingement and intuition are experienced similarly. They are experienced as insights, hunches, feelings, urges, and dreams. After receiving this information, it is often difficult to discriminate it from known information of the intellectual quadrant or some random thought. Yet one would have a feeling that the idea is 'right'.

Impingement and intuition may be aided by use of meditation and prayer. Meditation helps clear the mind so to be more receptive to information from the unobstructed. Prayer is simply an expressed desire for contact with the unobstructed. Both methods use psychic energy. Other uses of psychic energy include documented phenomena such as precognition, clairvoyance (remote viewing), clairaudience, telepathy, psychokinesis, and energy healing.

Some individuals who have a highly developed spiritual quadrant and thus are quite intuitive also can be quite sensitive to impingement and intuition. Some can perceive through the 5 physical senses an entity during an impingement. Some can perceive their guides in an ethereal forms or energy patterns. These abilities are often called the 6th sense.

Psychic Energy

As mentioned earlier, the entities discuss three types of energies (physical, spiritual, and psychic; see Appendix C).

Psychic energy, a form of physical energy, has not yet been directly measured by scientific instruments, but such a development is forthcoming. Psychic energy is distributed throughout the physical or obstructed universe for communication and healing purposes. It is the vehicle that connects physical energy in the obstructed and spiritual energy in the unobstructed. Meanwhile, effects of manipulating psychic energy have been measured, such as with demonstrations of telepathy, clairvoyance, clairaudience, psychokinesis, apparitions, after death communications, mediumship, and healing.

All incarnates can master the use of psychic energy. Doing so is a skill that requires practice. According to the entities: *what you must realize is the potential lies in every human being to understand and master these things; some master it, some do not.*

To use psychic energy requires a balance of the four personality quadrants (physical, intellectual, spiritual and emotional), placing a limitation on many individuals. While psychic energy is a free energy, there are certain universal laws and genetic laws that it cannot violate. Potential uses of psychic energy include attending to intuition, being open to impingement, increased awareness of the spiritual quadrant, healing, and direct access to the Archives of Knowledge.

Chapter 5 also describes multiple characteristics of psychic energy and a variety of ways in which one may learn to harness it. Topics include, among others, voice channeling or mediumship, precognition, poltergeist, Kirlian photography, electronically recorded communications, 'voodoo' (using psychic energy with a negative motive), voice channeling, and out-of-body experiences.

Chapter 6: Look Homeward, Angel Death

An entity lives for eternity. Death exists only for the physical body and the physical personality. The Gamble of Life notwithstanding, the physical body is designed to live about 70 years. Death itself is painless, although there may be pain leading up to death. Three types of death are described: lingering, relatively quick, and sudden.

In a lingering death, the frequency of out-of-body experiences (OBE's) increase as death approaches. The OBE's function is to assist the transition to the unobstructed. Such OBE's have been referred to as deathbed visions or pre-death experiences (PDE's). They are similar to near-death experiences (NDE's) when a physical body has been clinically dead but revives. OBE's in a lingering death can reassure the individual of the continued life of one's spiritual essence. One encounters other entities that appear in ethereal form. One is prevented from fully entering the unobstructed by a silver cord, which is a psychic energy permanence connecting the entity with the physical body.

In a quick death, such as falling from a tall building, the body goes into shock to prevent the experience of pain. There is also a life review that entails a slow-motion process of reliving one's physical life. This life review is a tranquil process and is not the same as the self-evaluation one undergoes in the unobstructed after physical death.

In a sudden death, such as being run over by an unseen vehicle, there is no awareness that one is about to die and therefore no need to prepare the physical personality. There is no need for assistance with one's emotions regarding death.

Regardless of the type of death, the actual moment of death is like going to sleep. When one enters sleep, there is no awareness of becoming unconscious. Then the entity becomes aware that the physical body is dead.

Transition to the Unobstructed

Upon physical death and realizing one is an entity, the consciousness changes from physical to spiritual awareness. There are 3 stages of this transition to a pure energy pattern that can take from several hours to several days in linear time. These phases create a gradual re-familiarization with the unobstructed.

466

In the first stage, the entity (i.e., spiritual energy) is released from the physical body but is still connected to it via psychic energy called the silver cord. The psychic energy permits the entity to assume an ethereal form, which is a perfected version of the physical body. The ethereal body can sometimes be seen by highly sensitive and intuitive incarnates, but is invisible usually. The ethereal body can exist for seconds to days in linear time, depending on the individual's needs. During this phase, the entity is greeted by other entities that also assume an ethereal form. The greeters include one's guides as well as any loved ones in the unobstructed. The guides help prepare for the later phase of becoming a pure energy pattern.

During the ethereal phase, the entity is in a dense energy form that sometimes can be seen by the physical eye. One can see through the ethereal form but detect its outline. Prior to the ethereal form, often there are collections of ectoplasm, which can appear like smoke, clouds, or fog.

Materialization of an entity entails the reverse process. The pure energy form of the entity becomes ethereal, which then develops ectoplasm, and then solidification of matter in the form of a physical body.

While in an ethereal form, there is an initial celebration with affiliated entities. There is also an orientation for the return to the unobstructed.

In the second stage of the transition, there is a shift in shape from an ethereal form to a pure energy pattern. Initially, one is still bound to psychic energy by the silver cord. The purpose of this is to 'buffer' the enormous sense of beauty and expanded awareness of the entity upon assuming an unobstructed form. Those who greeted the entity upon death remain and assist with this transformation.

In the third and final stage of the transition, the silver cord is severed, which breaks the connection to psychic energy. A life evaluation is then conducted by the entity itself. No other entity or energy source assists with the evaluation. This self-evaluation entails correlating the recent physical life experiences with the experiences of all prior incarnations and one's Government of Life for the most recent incarnation. This self-evaluation yields the determination as to whether additional incarnations are necessary in order to obtain all of the possible positive experiences while in a physical body (Step One).

The entity is now fully back into the unobstructed and proceeds with Steps Two through Seven of the evolutionary process. Following completion of Step Seven, the entity merges with the Source.

Merging with the Source

When the entity is ready to merge with the Source, its energy pattern transforms to allow penetration of an invisible barrier of the Source. The entity becomes one with the Source yet retains its unique identity. The merging process has been referred to as 'heaven'. It is the height of ecstasy. There is a celebration of this rebirth back into the Source, which takes place at 10-year intervals in terms of linear time. This aspect of the evolutionary process is described by the entities as follows:

It is difficult at times for an individual to understand the purpose of the evolutionary process from the source and back to the Source. Why do we accumulate our knowledge? The very purpose is the expanded growth and knowledge that is returned to the Source. With the birth of new entities and eventual mergence with the source there is a continual adding to the Source's strength, knowledge, and power. So the Source Itself continues to grow. That is why the aspects of reincarnation and evolution were designed. As evolution continues, the Source becomes greater, stronger, and there is no limitation to the expansion. You have gone to the moon in your lifetime. A thousand years from now you will be traveling to other galaxies. It all has to do with progress, evolutionary studies, and the progress of the universe.

Chapter Seven: Authors' Postscript

Each individual has a unique destiny. It is common to ask oneself about the meaning and purpose of life. Modern society involves many mis-directions—such as an emphasis on material gain and status as measures of success in life. Yet, unconsciously, we all have an inner wisdom that nudges us toward the spiritual truth.

APPENDIX C

PHYSICAL, PSYCHIC, AND SPIRITUAL ENERGY HEALING

Transcript of Audio Tape of Jay Barham on 8-18-1981
Tom Greene, Ph.D., Interviewer

This is the transcript of an interview with Reverend Jay Barham on the dynamics of energy healing. The interviewer is Tom Greene, a clinical psychologist from Honolulu, Hawaii. Therefore, this transcript is in conversation style and is not edited except for punctuation. Comments by Jay Barham are in quotation marks. Comments by the Editor are indicated as an Editor's Note.

Jay, you have been involved in healing for many years now and lately you have been conducting workshops and teaching people healing processes. If I were to come to one of your workshops what would I learn, what is your approach?

Healing with Physical Energy

"Tom, the first day in the workshop we get involved in identifying energy, how it behaves and how it affects our physical body. To identify energy there is a physical energy that flows through our body, a vital energy that keeps and maintains the health of the body organs, the body tissue. If this energy becomes blocked in any way then there is a deterioration of the physical body that causes it to be susceptible to disease.

"Now we want to understand how this energy behaves and how a person can be a healer and how you can assist your fellow man in keeping their energy flowing. So we have to backup and identify energy—what is it, how does it behave? To me it behaves very similar to that of a magnetic field. It has a negative and positive polarity as it flows through the body. Energy in our body, the vital energy

470

that keeps our body healthy, has a basic tendency to flow down our body as it flows up and down and pulsates through the tissue and the organs and the fiber.

"Now, basically, every person's energy behaves identically, or the same, even though it is unique. So having the quality of a magnetic field then we can understand how each person's energy will influence another person's energy. So if energy becomes blocked in the body then you can use your physical energy to push and influence an unhealthy person's energy. Once you get the energy flowing then the body will begin to heal itself"

So then in healing processes with physical energy what you would be doing with your energy would be unblocking mine, so to speak?

"Yes, every time that I touch your body or anybody's body I know that my energy, my physical energy is going to influence your energy and push it to get it flowing again."

Okay, how do you know where to push? You mentioned something about polarities?

"Yes. The body energy behaves very similarly to a magnetic field. It has a negative and positive polarity. So what we have to do is recognize or identify the process that is going on, which we have identified. The right side of our body creates a positive energy field. The left side of our body creates a negative field. So, just like magnets, if you put two magnets together like poles they will repel, push against. If you put opposite poles together they attract.

"Now, in the healing process you want to give that pushing effect rather than attracting or pulling. And it seems to be more effective and stronger if you can push against a person's energy that is blocked and you can get it moving and get it flowing through the tissue or the damaged organ and then the body will take over and begin to heal itself."

Okay, what else do we need to establish about how energy works and its relationship to disease before we actually get into other healing processes. Is there more that you would like to say on that?

"Yes, to be a healer with nothing but your physical energy there are simple processes that you have to understand and how to influence, and how the influence on another person's body begins. So, we have identified the negative and positive polarity and the fact that the right side of us creates a positive field and the left side a negative field, as the two magnets we want to push against the energy to get it moving. Now at this time I would share how energy becomes blocked in the body.

"What blocks our energy to become blocked in the body? What blocks our energy to cause our body to begin to deteriorate and cause it to be susceptible to diseases? There are three traumas that I refer to that damage the body."

And interfere with the energy flow?

"Yes. And those three traumas are genetic, physical, and emotional trauma. Now genetic trauma is nothing more than the strength and the vitality that a body is put together genetically. You have heard people talk about their systems being more vulnerable or weaker than others. So, that causes some of us to be more susceptible to our environment. But if you are genetically very healthy the body can usually tolerate or has a higher level of immunity . . . ."

Resistance?

"Resistance to most diseases. But if you are genetically weak then you have to be aware of this in your body and you would protect yourself against certain exposures, whereas someone that is very healthy and strong—they have a high resistance to certain things and they can become exposed to many elements of the environment and not seem to be affected by it."

So if you and I have different constitutional resistance levels, we might be exposed to the same virus and one of us might get sick and the other not?

"Yes. So that is what I am referring to as genetic trauma. Now, physical traumas are those that happen to the body in a physical way. Like breaking your leg or cutting yourself. "

Tissue damage?

"Yes, wounds, tissue damage, bone damage and even organ damage. Many people are in accidents and they break a rib and then they rupture a lung or a kidney or whatever. So those are physical traumas. And these physical traumas sometime block the energy and the energy can't flow through the tissue, so consequently the tissue begins to weaken and deteriorate to the point that it becomes very susceptible to infection. Now if you can help a person and keep the energy flowing through that tissue then the body will very quickly mend itself and heal itself."

So our bodies need healthy tissue for the energy to flow freely. Any damage to the physical tissue will retard the flow of the energy?

"Yes. And the lack of energy flow through tissue causes the tissue to deteriorate very quickly and in many cases, die. That is part of the process of infection. If you can keep that energy flowing through that tissue it will heal very quickly. We have demonstrated this in experiential processes where surgeons, immediately after closing the incision, we would have a healer place their hands in certain ways over the incision causing a high energy flow rate through that wound and the body would begin to knit and heal itself many times faster than it would in a normal process."

This is something that people could do with members of their own family if they were injured. You could cup your hands or place your hands around the wound, or the sutures and that might speed up the recovery?

"Yes. And that is where the old wives' tale comes from where mother kisses the bruised knee or the fingers? And it is that body, that physical contact, that causes the energy to flow through that wound very rapidly and the body begins to heal itself very quickly."

Okay. How about the third what you call trauma, emotional?

"Emotional trauma is probably the most devastating to the body. I think that majority of illness is caused by emotional trauma. The reason for that is that of our attitude and our learning about being an emotional creature. There

473

are natural emotions that have been identified and there are five of them.

"We have anger, fear, grief, jealousy and love. Now out of those five natural emotions many of us are taught that they are unacceptable."

Before you go any further, Jay, when you say five natural emotions I assume you are referring to these being part of our basic equipment that we all have, these five basic emotions?

"Yes. They are basic emotions that are built in to the personality structure. We are emotional creatures. These five natural emotions as they are referred to, are the behaviors and responses that we have to our exposure and our relationship with people that we deal with loss, and we deal with the challenges of life."

These are built in natural responses, is that you mean?

"Yes they are. They become distorted because we are taught that anger is a no-no and fear is a no-no. Grief, it's not manly or even womanly to cry after you are a certain age. You are called a sissy or a baby. So we are deprived of that natural process to deal with grief or fear. If you are above the age of one year old and you express any type of fear you are usually laughed at or ridiculed about being so afraid, you are a scaredy-cat. So we learn very quickly to deny and to rationalize and to refuse to admit and to let happen these natural responses, so we begin to when we feel them, whether it is anger, fear, grief, or jealousy, we begin to suppress or repress them."

What is the difference? Between suppression and repression to you? To me suppression is a conscious process, while repression can be totally out of awareness.

"Yes, and that is what is the most dangerous, the most effective. In a repressed state you are consciously denying or refusing to openly admit that you are afraid so you just suppress your fear. But it goes even farther than that because we build up such a guilt complex for having these emotions and we think that no matter what the qualitative or quantitative process of the emotion when it is felt or expressed is always out of proportion. So we minimize, if we are angry we begin to deny it and we set up a process of where we can totally repress any conscious response to the feeling of anger."

You say totally repress, like it is not there?

"It is not consciously. You are not consciously aware of this rage and anger, because you have denied it so long that it becomes below the conscious memory. You are not really conscious of how angry you have been or how angry you are."

Well, what happens with the effect on a person when these natural emotions are distorted and we push them inside or push them down. What happens?

"We have identified that especially two of the five natural emotions which are anger and fear in a repressed state is very devastating to the health of a physical body (Editor's note: see Appendix B on the five natural emotions and how they can be conditioned to be unnatural).

"Let's take anger in a repressed state over a long period of time. It sets up a muscular armor in our body that blocks our vital energy flow. Now, anger in a repressed state it sets up a positive field of energy. Fear repressed over a long period of time sets up a negative field of energy."

When you say, 'sets up' a positive field, how do you mean?

"Well, it creates a positive . . . you body energy behaves . . . you know we were talking about that magnetic behavior . . . so anger creates a positive field of energy and fear creates a negative field of energy."

So, the picture I have is like a disproportionate build up of energy? Okay?

"Yes. And so what we have determined is that anger repressed over a long period of time will usually affect such vital organs of the body—the heart, liver, kidney, spleen, bone, bone marrow, the blood in the vein and the muscle tissue. Fear, which creates a negative field of energy repressed over a long period of time usually affects the vital organs such as the respiratory system, upper and lower, the digestive system, the derma (the skin) and various other organs of the body."

Editor's Note: In an audiotape of one of Jay's workshops in 1980, he explicated the relation between repressed emotions and their deteriorating effects on different body parts. He indicated that anger is a positive pole and healing should involve touching with the right hand and catharsis. Repressed anger can deteriorate the body in terms of the heart, liver, kidney, spleen, bone, bone marrow, blood system, deep muscle tissue, parts of the reproductive organs, blood supply to brain tissue, adrenal glands, and the basis of migraine headaches. He indicated that fear and grief have a negative polarity and healing should involve touching with the left hand and catharsis. Repressed fear and grief can adversely affect the respiratory system, asthma, digestive system, pancreas, as well as other parts of reproductive organs, grey matter in the brain, spinal canal/fluid, smooth muscles, and skin (e.g., eczema). Catharsis of grief can include crying, of fear by screaming, and of anger by overt physical behavior toward an object that has benign consequences for others (e.g. pounding a pillow). Some individuals are afraid of expressing anger overtly, so both emotions would be involved in catharsis. Because of the interconnectedness of the physical body, physical energy healing should involve experimentation of touch with both the right and left hands. Because of the interdependence of humans, any touch can be healing. Jay did not address the effects of repressed jealousy or love upon the physical body. In addition to physical touch and catharsis, Jay indicated that for long-term healing of physical problems related to repressed emotions, the individual must learn to make the repressed emotions conscious, learn to accept their cause including self-responsibility for one's reaction to the precipitant of the emotion, and learn to express these emotions in a natural manner.

And these occur as relatively specific effects on different parts of the body so that's another dimension then to the right-left, positive-negative?

"Yes. When you identify the repression process and the type of energy blockage or the field, you can identify the polarity (the negative and positive polarity). Then you can begin your healing approach more effectively to get that energy moving. So, let's say that someone has a stomach ache. Now, not all stomachaches are directly related to the digestive system, but if you had a medical workup and you have determined that you have a digestive process (or there's something going on in the digestive system that is ailing you) or if you can just identify it with the pain. Most of the time where the pain is where the problem is. There are such things as referred pain. Certainly there can be no damage done by approaching a healing process and being wrong. You can't damage the body by being wrong. So, if the person comes to you and they say 'well, I have a problem with my stomach. I have had a stomachache' and so the two of you determine that it is in the digestive tract. What you realize is that the digestive system is affected by repressed fear unless it is a physical trauma. And so there is a negative field involved, or the . . . . "

Some build-up or blockage?

"There is a blockage. So you want to get the person's energy flowing. Now back to the magnets again. Like poles repel each other, so we want to push against that person's energy to get it flowing. So what we have to remember is that the left side of our body—the left hemisphere and side of our body—is a negative field. So we have a negative field condition in the body (which is the digestive system) so we merely place our left hand, which is a negative field on the pained area over the abdomen and touch the skin preferably and then take the opposite pole or the right hand and put it somewhere down the lower extremities, just to make contact with the body."

You would place the right hand lower than the pushing hand?

"Yes."

Always?

"Always. As long as the opposite pole, or the opposite hand is somewhere down the lower extremity. Now if you have something going on in your foot or your hand where there are no extremities left, then you would merely cup your hands around that area. But we find to get the opposite pole or field of your body somewhere down lower down the body, then what happens is that your energy, in your healthy body, pushes against that person's energy in that area that you are touching and you will influence their energy and push it and get it moving through that organ or through that damaged or diseased or weakened area and the energy will begin to flow. Now the moment that you make contact with the body you will notice a sensation (a physical sensation) under each hand. Don't get terribly involved with the sensation you are feeling, just recognize the difference. There may be a warm feeling under one hand, a cool feeling under the other. But just recognize that difference, when you first touch the body. Now, it takes anywhere from seven seconds to three minutes for your energy to get the person's energy flowing. Once their energy begins to flow you will feel that under your hands. You will begin to identify a balance, meaning that you will feel the same sensation under one hand as you do the other."

And this is not just a physical accommodation effect of the skin temperatures balancing.

"No, it is not."

I know that you and some people have the ability to detect the energy level by not touching the body you can feel it by just being close to the body, with your own hands.

"Yes, body energy can be felt by the physical hand and it is very faint and very slight but you can teach yourself how to feel this energy and you can begin to identify and actually begin to diagnose in the body the blocked areas. When the energy is not flowing then you can detect that just by your naked hand."

Would this relate to the aura of the body in any way?

"Well, there is some relation because it is the same

478

energy that produces the aura around the body. But the aura will not necessarily be affected by a blocked area of the body. But the aura is an emission of energy from that physical energy that we are talking about. And as I was saying, it takes anywhere from seven seconds to three minutes for the energy to start flowing. And I have never had to hold my hand on a person for longer than seven minutes in order to get their energy flowing. Once that energy starts flowing then naturally the body is going to begin to mend itself."

So, up to three minutes is the usual range, but there are occasions where you need to stay in contact longer?

"Yes. Many people ask me, 'what if you don't get a balance under your hands, are you hooked up wrong?' Not necessarily, but if you are holding your hand and you feel that the energy is not flowing you can always reverse them, because it may be some organ in the body that is causing the pain that is not related to the digestive tract and so what you are doing is attracting the energy or pulling it and you are not getting the energy flowing."

So, even though in your experience you notice some general correlations between symptoms, organs, positive and negative polarities, sometimes it is still quite necessary to experiment with balancing the energy or the placement of the hands?

"Yes, there is no danger in it. You can experiment with it and adapt your own technique and your own expertise in it."

I believe that that is important to point out, that there is no danger. Some people are concerned about their energy being negatively affected in one way or another. Things like energies mixing or taking on bad energy. Could you comment on that?

"Yes. That is a fallacy. It is impossible to take on bad energy or negative energy from another person because even though physical energy behaves the same in each individual person, one person's energy does not mix with another person's energy. It is like oil and water."

They influence it but they don't intermix?

"Yes. You cannot drain a person of their energy. Take it away from them. You can influence it and move it around but you do not take energy from them."

Is there more to say about how the energy operates in the body, Jay, before we get to . . . more about the healing processes physically and then to psychic and spiritual healing processes?

"Well, what we usually do is discuss these energies and their behaviors and how to identify the energy and even feel it with your hands and when we move into the experiential process of how to identify energies then I explain to persons how to start from the beginning, if you are not familiar with energy flow, and the feel of the energy. We have a session where the people pair off and scan each other's body and putting your hand about three inches from the body you can usually feel the energy flow, quite well."

So in your workshops you lead people through experiments and exercises acquainting them with that sensitivity. And demonstrating how it can be identified and felt and people learn very quickly how to feel this energy flow. And also how to recognize when they are moving their hand across the body, they identify where the energy is blocked.

What comes next in your workshop?

Healing with Psychic Energy

"Well, before we get into too much of the experiential stuff I go on to share the stronger of the energies, one of the energies that can be used to be more effective in the healing process. And that is psychic energy.

"Psychic energy is much stronger and you can harness it and use it in a healing process to push physical energy, to get it moving."

Before you go any further, Jay, is psychic energy totally different from the physical energy you have been talking about? What is psychic energy?

480

"Psychic energy is a free energy that is outside of our body and we have the capability of harnessing that energy with our mind and using it in a positive therapeutic way. I describe and explain how the mind, the processes of the mind, can harness this energy and then project it into the body to move energy and to unblock energy flow."

I must interrupt you again. I am having a hard time getting a picture of what psychic energy is. Before you go on is there more you could say to give me a picture of what is this psychic energy that is all over the place?

"Well, psychic energy is a physical energy, it is a physical substance. But it is a separate energy from other types of physical energy."

Can I see it?

"You can't see it with your physical eyes. You can feel it with your hands and to know that it is out there and that it exists then you can use it in a positive way."

Now the picture I have is of psychic energy something like a different frequency of light rays, it's a form of energy that permeates the air, so to, speak.

"Well, it does, but it functions on a different frequency than other types of physical energy. And even though you can't see it with your physical eyes, it is just like the air you breath. It is an energy, but you can't see it with your physical eye."

You say you can feel the difference with your hands between psychic and physical energy?

"Yes, you can learn to be sensitive and recognize the difference between the two energies."

I have heard you before today use the phrase, 'laying claim to psychic energy' Jay, and 'harnessing' it. Could you speak some of how you use psychic energy and how you apply it and how you teach that in your workshops?

"Well, Tom, I say that we are all sensitive to this energy and we can lay claim to it. Now, what I mean by laying claim to it is that it is a free energy out there that can be harnessed by the mind and projected by the mind."

How do you do that?

481

"You do that by recognizing the part of the mind that you can use as tools to harness the energy. Those three functions of the mind are visualization, imagination and projection. Now: the function of the mind that we refer to as visualization. Visualization is the mind's ability to lay claim to reality or to something that exists. Say that I ask you to visualize or to mentally go to your home in Hawaii and seek out an object, mentally, that you are familiar with, you could visualize what it looks like and you could describe it to me, you could tell me its texture, dimensions and the color. Now that is visualization. Visualization is laying claim to something that exists. Imagination is the ability of the mind to create something non-existent. You can imagine . . . and in your imagination . . . you can create something that you have never seen before. You can give it its own dimensions, its own color, its own size. That's imagination. Projection is the function of the mind that manages the energy. It is like the hammer that drives the nail. The paintbrush that puts the paint on the canvas. When an artist is creating a masterpiece, an original, they are not using visualization, they are using imagination and they are creating something that has never been created before, so they capture and create it with their imagination and then they use projection—just like tracing paper—and projection of the mind is the ability to trace the paper. To put on paper, bring to reality what the mind has created. So as I say, again, projection is the hammer that drives the nail. So you can bring into your mind psychic energy and with projection you make it behave the way you want it to behave. You can project it. That's the way psychic healers heal in long distance. They project the energy with their mind, any distance that they choose and they can be . . . effective with it. So projection is a tool, it is a means of communication. Projection is used in mental telepathy. Like you are sending thought processes to another individual. Projection is that process of the mind that sends psychic energy to be used as a just like a telephone wire."

Could you give an example, Jay, in your healing work? Could you describe how you might use these processes with psychic energy?

"Yes, I can. Knowing that I can harness this energy and knowing the effect of it on the body, say that someone came to me that had hypoglycemia. That is a common problem with many people. And so immediately what I do is check the energy of the body and we determine what areas of the body is very sluggish. Usually the organs that are malfunctioning and causing this symptom or problem of the body are the pancreas, the adrenal glands and the pituitary gland. So what I do is, I draw in energy in my mind and then I mentally project . . . ."

Psychic energy?

"Yes, I draw in psychic energy and then I project it into the pancreas and what I do with the psychic emery is I stimulate and massage the inner lining of the pancreas. And then I massage the adrenal gland."

Now when you are projecting psychic energy in the example you are giving, do you create a picture in your mind of the energy taking on a certain shape or color or form? How do you imagine it as you project it?

"Well, then you have to rely on visualitization until you can learn to psychically perceive or 'see' the organ. So what you could do is create in your mind what an organ looks like, or a certain part of the body and then with visualization you hold that picture of what it looks like and where it is located in the body and then with the process of projection you project the energy into that area or organ of the body. Now as you continue to work with this and develop psychically, you can learn to 'see' the organ of the body. What I would like to say now, Tom, is what I haven't shared with you is the part of the brain that helps you bring in and store this energy. And that organ in the brain is the medulla oblongata. Now that is the part of the brain that receives and transmits psychic energy. So the way you bring the energy into your mind and store it, is the process of nothing more than thought or will or desire. And if you have the desire and the thought process to bring energy in, there is what I call a valve or a gate that opens in the medulla

483

[oblongata], and then the psychic energy flows in and you can bring it in to whatever strength that you are capable of, to be able to harness. And then with the process of projection to hurl it out and make it behave the way you want it to."

When you project the psychic energy out, Jay, do you visualize that coming out any certain part of your body or how do you, what is your own imagination or visualization process of the energy going out?

"Okay, we have discussed the difference between visualization and imagination. Now, both processes are involved whenever you are projecting energy. Energy exists. So you can learn to visualize what it looks like. But what you want it to do and what you make it do with projection, a part of imagination is involved in that, because you are creating. You are creating a process that hasn't existed yet, or doesn't exist. So you are creating something, bringing something to reality. So you imagine . . . most of the process is the imaginative part of it. You are projecting the energy in and making it do what you wanted it to do."

Okay, to go back to your example of hypoglycemia. If you were using psychic energy to affect a person's pancreas, do you have any most productive visualization or imagination in hurling the energy out?

"When I am doing it, visualization is a part of the process because I know what the pancreas looks like, but I don't rely on visualization at this point in my practice, because I have learned to perceive or see the organ psychically. So I can psychically go in and project energy in and so I am literally experiencing the pancreas in a psychic way, as I project the energy in there. So I can see psychically the pancreas."

Okay. So if you are looking at the pancreas psychically as you use psychic energy, can you see the psychic energy you are putting in?

"Sometimes you can, yes."

What does that look like when you put it in, when you can see it?

"It looks anyway that you are managing it or you are creating it."

Do you have a favorite way for the pancreas?

"Well, I use it in many different ways. If you project a beam of energy, then it would like a thread of energy and the texture and color of it is kind of a bluish silver color And so you can learn to recognize it. But when I am making it do what I want it to, say I go into the pancreas and I want to comb the little follicles that protrude from the inner lining of the pancreas, then I would create a beam of energy and then psychically create a deflector at the end of the beam (you know like a garden spray that you spray your roses with and you adjust that little valve—you can put a straight stream or you can make a mist), so what I do psychically is I create a little rake, a little spray effect and that spreads the energy out so when I gently or psychically comb or move it down the inner lining of the pancreas, then I am gently stimulating those little tentacles (as I call them). And in stimulating those with psychic energy it causes the pancreas to function at a higher level. It pushes the physical energy and causes the energy to flow through the pancreas and it begins to function at a higher rate."

You mentioned earlier, if I heard you correctly, that psychic energy is the stronger of the two, as compared to physical energy.

"Yes."

What else could you say about your use of psychic energy in healing work or how you bring this into your workshops and training?

"In psychic energy?"

Yes.

"What we do in the workshop is that we have sessions where people learn to visualize and learn to use their imagination and learn to project. And then, experientially we work on each other, where we can identify the energy and learn to understand what it feels like."

Is there any danger in using psychic energy? You said that in physical energy there is no danger; it is quite

485

safe. How about with psychic energy?

"Psychic energy is much different than the physical energy of the body. Your physical energy, when you are healing with your physical energy, there is no danger whatsoever. But when you get involved with psychic energy, it is a very powerful energy and there is no such thing as negative energy, but psychic energy is very powerful, and depending on your ability to harness it you can either use it in a destructive way or in a positive way. Just like atomic energy. Atomic energy is a very positive, powerful energy. It can be used destructively or it can be used positively."

Well, if I were in one of your workshops and I developed some ability to channel and direct psychic energy could I harm someone by accident?

"You could not harm someone by accident because any harm that can be done psychically has to be done with the motive, to harm and then you have to learn how to project it and to do harm."

It comes up only in intentionality, awareness . . . ?

"Yes. Because you could conceivably and intentionally stop somebody's heart by projecting energy in and slowing down the pulse rate or the heart beat and this is conceivable. So, what I am saying, it is like any other talent, when you are learning a powerful skill if you are learning how to run a skill saw, you have to learn to dangers of it so you can be more effective with it in a positive way."

Is there more you could say again, about the general use or application of psychic energy in healing? One question I have, as you bring in psychic energy and store it, before you project it outwardly, do you have any sensory experience? How do you know how much you are storing?

"This comes through experience in learning how to store psychic energy, if you work with psychic energy, or psychically for long periods of time and bringing in large amounts of energy and storing it, to project it, there is sometimes a sensation of the mind or the head—the brain— you will feel a fullness or a little pressure, like a stuffy feeling, in your head, and so these are some of the sensations that you learn to understand when you begin to familiarize yourself with psychic energy. I would suggest to people, and I do in the workshop, that they can be a very effective healer just sticking with physical application and using their physical energy until they learn more about psychic energy. They can learn very quickly . . . ."

You advise caution with trying to develop psychically?

"Yes. Examine your motive for wanting to get involved with psychic energy and how to manage it. A little description of using psychic energy indiscriminately is that of poltergeist. A lot of people think that is some spiritual phenomena, but in a literal sense what it is and it usually happens in teenagers—irate teenagers. Now what they have come upon is that someway they have learned to, unconsciously without really knowing what they are doing, is open the valve in the medulla [oblongata] and a tremendous amount of psychic energy is drawn into the mind and in their anxiety and frustration they project this energy out indiscriminately. And what you find, is that mirrors break, bottles break, bottles fall off shelves. And it usually happens in the home where there is a disturbed or irate teenager."

Jay, in using psychic energy in healing, is that totally separate in applying that energy from the polarities of the physical energy, or is there some overplay there?

"There's really no correlation at all in using psychic energy because when you are using psychic energy you are not involved with the polarity at all. The polarity is important in using physical energy to heal, to push the person's energy but when you are using psychic energy to push another person's energy and get it flowing you don't really have to be concerned about polarity whatsoever."

And in using psychic energy you are affecting their physical energy and their energy flow?

"Yes."

And I also heard that sometimes you will do something like sewing inside a person with psychic energy or creating something, could you comment on that?

"Well, some people refer to it as psychic surgery. What I think that you are asking me, Tom, is that some of the things that I have done with neurological or nerve problems. It is conceivable to create a nerve fiber or a psychic fiber like a cobweb (if you could relate it to a cobweb). What you do is create with your mind a psychic thread and then you find the damaged nerve and you attach it to the existing nerve and then you 'jumper' (just like a jumper wire) over the damaged part and pick up the nerve on the other side and when you rake across that psychically you will get a flicker of a muscle movement or whatever you are trying to repair. Then you attach that psychic thread to that nerve and you will find that a person that is paralyzed can move that muscle. Now they can move that muscle if the muscle hasn't been so damaged or so atrophied, if there have been years of inactivity in a muscle it becomes so atrophied that it has no strength whatsoever, then you have a lot of problems. But if a person has just had an injury or is recovering from an injury, the sooner you can get to the healthy muscle and put that psychic thread in the easier it is to recognize the function of it. And through experiential processes we have shown that this is possible."

The impression that I have is that with psychic energy—with your ability with it—you can literally do a number of things inside the body.

"Yes you can and my hope is that eventually, or someday, that psychic energy will be used for sutures in operations."

Oh, okay. I would assume, Jay, that it is safe to say that the psychic—the ability to channel psychic energy in healing—is not something one gains overnight. Physical energy sounds like part of our natural equipment while channeling psychic energy may be a part of our natural equipment. Could you comment on how long it has taken you to learn how to use it?

"Well, Tom it has taken me over twenty years to use it and I consider myself just in the infancy of really understanding it. But what I find is that when I share these processes with others they seem to pick it up very quickly and they too can use it. Many people after a five-day workshop can be very effective in harnessing psychic energy. The way they do that is I teach them that doubt is the only factor, the only interfering factor, in one's ability to harness this energy and use it."

Believing you can do it is important?

"Yes. You have to believe it and you have to just accept that it is there to be used and use the processes of the mind, and go ahead and do it. And it really works for you. The more practice you get in doing that, naturally the more successes. Success is very good for the ego and what you can't allow to happen is self-doubt. Many times when you work on a person you don't get an immediate result."

Yes, I was going to ask you about the time element in healing processes.

"Well, what we have to remember, Tom, is that the body heals itself and you as a psychic healer will get the energy flowing in the appropriate place and then the body gets to heal itself. Many times a person will feel relieved, you can alleviate pain and they will feel better and walk away from you saying, 'gee, I feel so much better that was really great.' Some people will get up off of the table (if you are working on a table) and say 'I don't feel any different than I did before you started.' So that could set up a doubt in you, you want instant success. So if you allow those comments to cause question or doubt in your ability to be a healer then the next time you try it you are going to be less effective because you are doubting your ability to do it. I try to tell people that you have to be a little bit like the bumblebee. That story goes that scientifically it has been proven that it is impossible for a bumblebee to fly, but the bumblebee doesn't know that so he does a good job of it. So what you have to accept is that you can do this; it is a God-given tool and gift that we all have. We just somewhere in the past have lost these talents so we can learn them over again and begin to use them in a very effective way."

Healing with Spiritual Energy

Okay! Jay, could we move now to spiritual intervention, or spiritual aspects of healing, I am a little concerned about time here.

"Tom, spiritual energy is the most powerful energy there is. It is the energy that created all things. Many people think and believe that they can become faith healers. What I am saying is that I believe that to be a cop out. They are blaming God for something that they are doing themselves. You cannot bring into your body spiritual energy. It is a separate all powerful energy outside your body and you have no manipulative power or control over spiritual energy whatsoever."

Spiritual energy is not channeled through the body like psychic energy is?

"It is not. The only gift that we have to be a part of spiritual energy in a healing process is that of invoking [from the Source]. We can invoke spiritual energy and ask us to do things for us, assist us, or we can literally say 'heal that body for me,' and if It [the Source] sees fit It will, but you have no manipulative power, you cannot control it, project it or manage it in any way."

It is totally unpredictable then for the healer?

"Yes, it is and that is why that since spiritual energy is all-powerful it is the only energy that can create a miracle. It is the only energy that can violate the universal laws or the genetic laws. Meaning that with psychic and physical energy you can help the body heal itself. Spiritual energy can transform, it can make whole something that has literally been destroyed. You cannot do that with psychic energy or physical energy."

That is a true miracle?

"That is a true miracle."

Does the healer's attitude in invoking spiritual energy make any difference do you think, Jay?

"I think it does because being a ritualistic creature,

490

our sincerity in what we project or desire has a great deal to do in whether or not spiritual energy is going to command itself to yield the request or answer the prayer. And prayer meaning sincere desire, it is a request."

If there is nothing more that you would like to add about spiritual energy I have a few other questions for you.

"That would be fine, unfortunately that is about all I can share with spiritual energy. What you have to understand is that I have witnessed many miracles and I never go into a healing session without that sincere desire or silent prayer, as I call it, in asking spiritual energy from the Source (and some people may refer to It as God) to assist me in every way possible."

Attitude and Intention of the Healer

This was going to be my next question, if you would speak of the attitude and intentionality of a healer, or the person wanting to do healing? How much difference does that make?

"It makes a considerable amount of difference because when you go into this you have to be in a positive frame of mind, you have to be sincere desire to help your fellow man and the more positive you can feel, and the sincerity that you project in it, the more effective you are going to be."

Going in for an ego trip, that won't do it?

"No, it won't."

Would that get in the way?

"It would because if you approach healing from an ego standpoint, you are not going to get the immediate response or a response that your ego expects, so you are going to meet with disillusionment and discouragement."

So you need to believe, you need to hope, you need to respect, but you don't need an ego trip?

"That is true and it is very important that you have high regard and respect for your fellow man's body and also your own body."

491

Could you say something now about the factors in the recipient of the healing processes? Does their attitude make any difference, does how they handle their feelings make any difference, does their belief make any difference?

"Yes, it does, and particularly when you are working with psychic energy because you cannot affect or influence another person psychically without permission because they can block you with their own psychic energy. Now that differs slightly when you are working with physical energy because any time you touch another person's body your energy is going to influence their energy in some way."

Jay, regarding the influence of the recipient's attitude: could you say something about conscious and unconscious factors of the recipient and how that might affect?

"Yes, Tom. Many times a person will come with a conscious desire to have a healing but occasionally we find people that have an unconscious fear that comes in and what this fear or unconscious rejection of the healing process does is that it blocks any attempt to be successful with them psychically."

So that can undermine conscious desire or intentionality at times?

"Yes, it can."

Okay, I know in awhile we'll get to more of the role of emotions in interaction with healing so I have no difficulty in understanding that, as a psychologist. Could I direct you back to the time element in the healing process? You have commented that sometimes people feel better immediately but you emphasized that what the healer does is set into process or set into motion the person's own self-healing process. Could you say more about length of time in healing and perhaps at this point get into the involvement of the emotions?

"Yes, Tom, when a person comes to me with a problem we determine what the problem is, what the ailment is. Then I give them what we call a healing session. Now sometimes there is an immediate response (like feeling better or pain has been alleviated)."

They come to you with a symptom and sometimes the symptom is relieved on the spot?

"Yes. Then the reports usually come like . . . say that I have worked with someone and they have not responded in what we could call a positive or favorable way immediately. I know from experience that I have influenced their energy. So they will leave me not feeling much better and they would indicate this, most people are honest. So what I tell them to do is to report back to me in about three (3) days. Usually after a session when you get the energy flowing in the body there is a period of time that the body has to adjust to this, and as we know, the body heals itself. So if you get the energy moving and you stimulate the tissue where it can start its healing process some minor ailments will heal up in about three days. More serious problems it takes the body about ten (10) days to heal itself. So that is the time period that I have experienced with people's response to this. They call me back in a couple of weeks and say that they have no more symptoms and they feel much better."

That makes sense since this is a process. It would make sense that the person's body would take time for its own healing process with your assistance in setting it in motion and that is no different from conventional medicine in many cases—as I understand it. How about other factors involved in response to healing processes and I will ask again about the involvement of the emotions, if you are ready to get into that?

"Yes. The emotional factor involved in healing is that what I understand and I accept thoroughly, is that when a person comes to me I am only treating the symptom. And what I am saying by that is that I am treating the body in its condition. Now the cause for this condition could be undetermined. There are ways of determining what is causing it whether it is depression or physical trauma."

And I know that you prefer that people you work

with have medical evaluations and that is another way of determining the cause.

"Yes. If a person comes to me and they have had a medical workup and they have been diagnosed, I will still give for my own satisfaction a psychic diagnostic process, to determine for myself what is wrong with the body and to see if that correlates with the medical examination. And it usually does. But what I am referring to at this point and the reason that I say I am treating the symptom is that the greater majority of problems (physical problems) correlates to the pool of repressed emotions. And it is usually this trauma that causes most of our illness. I am not in a habit of suggesting therapy to a person, some people just don't want to become involved with therapy."

By therapy do you mean psychotherapy?

"Yes. Some therapeutic process in which they can become involved to empty and clear up the pool of repressed emotions. So in that way they will be treating the cause. I can have a healing session with someone and they will . . . their body will get better . . . it may correct the problem temporarily. But if they don't do something about the cause they find themselves under the same stressful situation and so then their energy blocks again and the system, the same area of the body that has been weakened, that those emotions correlate to, then they will wind up with the same problem. So I just tell them in a gentle way that I suggest that they do something about the cause. And until they do, they're coming back to me for what I call a 'fix.' I get their energy flowing and their body heals temporarily, adjusts itself, and then they block again and they have to come back to me for a fix."

That is a little similar to someone who would want to take painkillers rather than investigate the source of their chronic headaches.

What is your attitude about doing 'fixes' on a repetitive basis when a person doesn't seem to be interested or willing to look at causes?

"Well, I used to have a problem with that but I don't

anymore, because I accept that that is their choice, to do what they want to but it is my choice and my responsibility to try to help them keep their body healthy and if a body is deteriorating and I can do something to change that condition (even if it is temporarily) we can keep patching it up and keep them going. And if they don't make the choice to do something about the cause they know that they are going to have to come back to me and get their energy flowing again so their body can stay healthy or at least limp along and keep it functioning. But, I make it very clear to individuals that I work with and many of them don't have a problem with that."

With accepting the suggestion of therapy or . . . ?

"Yes. They listen without seeming to be too insulted about the suggestion that there is an emotional problem there. And you have to be diplomatic; you can't suggest to a person that they are maladjusted. It is just one of those things that we are all afflicted with."

Yes.

"And so . . . but they still have to make the choice to do something about the cause. Because I know from experience that if they don't clear up that fear and guilt and shame and so something with the acceptance of those natural emotions and they continue to repress it and deny it that they are going or move out of their environment, someway to get away from that stressful process, they are going to be caught right back up into it and their energy is going to block. They will continue to suffer the consequences."

Right. Jay, your attitude towards recommending therapy (psychotherapy) to people seems to reflect similar type of respect that you referred to in the healer's attitude in general. That is, as I hear you, you seem to read between your lines—it seems important that to use healing processes optimally you can't force . . . you can't push the person, and you can't be on an ego trip. Is that an accurate interpretation?

"Yes Tom, in my experience in working with people (counseling and working with psychic healing) it is that it must be the individual's choice. You just can't force or make a person be well. You start treading on an ego trip with psychoanalytic processes that you think you know what is good for that person you are going to set up a rebellion or defense in that person."

Umhmm, you are setting yourself up as an authority.

"Yes, and I refuse to do that because I respect where the person is coming from and what they project and what they share with me their needs are. And I do not violate or go beyond those limits. I will share my experience and my expertise with them but I do not try to cram it down their throat. I share with them what I have to offer and then if they move toward that then I accept that. So I have a high regard and a respect for a person and where they are at and that is all right with me."

Umhmmm . . . okay. Jay, I would like to shift here and ask you if you would speak some of your experience in general or maybe some specific highlights through the years. For example I know that you worked for four years or more with Elisabeth Kübler-Ross, M.D. You haven't mentioned that. And I know that you did some healing work in assisting her in her workshops. Could you say a bit about some of your experiences during that period?

"Yes, the four years that I was involved with Elisabeth I had some very positive experiences with people in the healing process. One day of her five-day Dying and Transition workshop was set aside for the teaching of the healing—and also in that day I would also work with people. There were many people in her workshops that were in need of some particular attention in the healing process.

"Throughout the week of the five days, in between the sessions (her regular sessions), I was constantly working in small groups or one to one with people that had specific physical problems and I experienced many miracles through that four years . . . ."

When you say miracles you are referring to, experiences with which you were working with something and apparently some spiritual energy lent a hand, is that correct?

"Yes, indeed, and the reason that I know that it was a miracle or spiritual energy at work, there would be things of immediate cures or transformations in people's bodies that do not happen with physical or psychic energy."

Immediate?

"Yes, immediate changes."

Could you give an example or two if you could pull one out of your memory?

"Yes, there is one person (and I'll mention no names) in particular that I remember. She was severely ridden with arthritis and had been in pain for some years with this problem. Now I have been effective with the healing process in alleviating pain and even causing the clearing of this disease . . . ."

Arthritis?

"Yes . . . but this particular person I had two sessions with her during that workshop and she contacted me several months later and said that she was completely cured. The swelling in the joints, the inflammation and the pain had disappeared and she had total freedom in joint movement and motion. My experience teaches me that it would not have been that rapid of progress, so spiritual energy had to have been working in that process."

I know you could probably give other examples, Jay, but I am a little concerned about time. Let me ask you this, when you are conducting a healing session you said earlier that you usually invoke spiritual assistance. Do you have any way, any feeling or any way of knowing when that is happening?

"Sometimes Tom you can be aware of spiritual energy in its . . . ."

Sometimes not?

"Not all the time. Because it is a very difficult energy to be aware of."

Umhmm . . . now just to be clear here, spiritual energy you are referring to is God or the Source, some energy from the Almighty so to speak?

"Yes, that is true. Now I have had occasions to be working psychically or physically with someone's body and when spiritual energy chooses to be involved with that sometimes you can psychically perceive it or be aware of it. It is a beautiful experience when that energy comes in and assists you or begins a healing right there before your eyes."

Could you describe what that is like, or how it feels, or what your experience is?

"It affects you physically and emotionally when it happens. And you can also experience a reaction in the person that you are working with much differently than you can when you are getting results with psychic energy."

Jay, I know that you have been willing to work with some people with very severe neurological problems, uncontrolled seizure disorders for example, and you have met with some success with some of these people. Could you briefly describe what you do when you attempt to do that? I'm talking about people that the physicians have done all they can for regarding medication, but they are still having seizures, large or small. What do you do to these people?

"Basically we get involved with the neurological process. We try to identify the neurological problem (the damaged area in the brain) that is causing this seizure activity and the stray energy or the energy that is emitted by the lesion travels through the brain and reaches area of the brain that causes seizure."

Umhmm.

"What we have attempted to do is close off and barricade with psychic energy to abort the seizure by blocking the energy traveling through the brain. And repairing or influencing the brain process."

I know that you locate or attempt to locate the lesion with your ability to see psychically. Do you ever use any of the psychic 'threads'; ever do any sewing inside there, or shunting of electrical connections?

"Yes, we have experimented with this. We feel that we have had some results such as locating a lesion and surrounding it or encapsulating it with a psychic shield so that the energy cannot travel through the brain. We isolate that part."

You attempt to build a barricade around the lesion with psychic energy?

"Yes. And those that I have worked with that have seizure problems we have been able to influence the process to where they can reduce their medication or seizure control medication down to a very minimal dosage that they can tolerate."

I respect your interest and willingness to work with people with such severe difficulties and your goals certainly seem quite reasonable and I know you are pleased when you can assist whatever the difficulty is.

Origin of Healing Information

Jay, to shift once again. Your wife is a registered nurse and a Ph.D. psychologist, she has developed her own form of psychodrama—a form of psychotherapy—to deal with people with repressed feelings. I know you are very familiar with that work. She was also involved with Elisabeth Kübler-Ross during the period that you were. Now, I heard you say that some of the information you have received, and your wife in her work, comes from what you call entities in the unobstructed. Would you speak some of that?

"Yes, Tom, it is true that most of the information, in fact all of the information that I share . . . everything that I teach and believe . . . I have been taught by spirit guides or entities as we refer to them. Because eleven years ago I was involved with a process that we achieved materialization."

When you say materialization, what do you mean?

"What I mean by materialization is that you create a condition of energy whereby spirit guides can come to you and clone or materialize a physical body and then sit down with you and you can discuss any subject that you choose. And I have spent thousands of hours with materialized entities, discussing the art of healing and many therapeutic processes."

Your wife's book *Bridging Two Worlds* documents I believe, the history of your experiments in this (see Appendix A).

"Yes, Marti has just written a book that has been named *Bridging Two Worlds* and in this she shares our eleven years experience with materialization, how it came about and many, many teachings that we have received."

Jay, you were involved with voice channeling and other psychic abilities prior to this rather enormous expenditure of time in looking for materialization. Why weren't you satisfied with voice channeling?

"Tom, because the intellect has a tendency to cheat and to distort many things that one receives through voice channeling and the maximum accuracy as far as I am concerned is about 80 per cent."

Maximum?

"Yes, on your information received. And the average I would say would be about 60 per cent. So you see there is a broad range of distortion because the conscious mind or the intellect or even the ego will come in and the material that you are receiving psychically or spiritually, whatever you want to call it, will take that information and very quickly the mind can distort it, shape it, form it, in the way you think it should be."

And you believe that that occurs even though the voice channel may be in a trance or an altered state of consciousness, you believe that distortion still occurs?

"Yes. I definitely . . . I believe it 100 per cent. I know it happens. And I know that it happens in all voice channeling."

Okay, so part of your motivation in going for materialization was accuracy?

"Well, yes. To improve the accuracy. I thought that if we could get the information from the "horse's mouth" so to speak then our truths and our concepts of teaching and the accuracy of it, would be much more valid than constantly fighting that mental process that was always distorting. And even when I was working as a voice channel, no matter how honest, with how much humility you approach the subject the mental process will come in the struggle. And the way that happens, it happens in a very subtle way."

So when you speak of distortions in voice channeling you are not speaking of conscious intentionality so much as you are—it happens?

"It just happens. It seems that the voice channel will almost, without a conscious knowing, begin to manipulate and to use . . . you can receive a message and if it isn't to your liking and you have an argument with your wife or friend . . . then you are going to form and manipulate that message to get your message across."

Okay. Well, Jay, how do you know these materialized entities . . . how do you know they are not lower spirits, evil spirits. Many people believe in that sort of thing. How do you know these beings you speak to are accurate?

"Because Tom, I have visited with them so much in the last fifteen or twenty years in my psychic and spiritual research and experience—with many, many out of body experiences that I have had—and that is well over a thousand. That you can achieve a relationship with the entities that offers you that knowledge that is beyond question."

And you have sat with them when they are in materialized physical form and they speak to you and you speak to them?

"Yes. You can carry on a conversation just like I am talking to you and you ask them a question and if the universal laws permit them to answer it . . . they will."

Jay, just to be clear . . . you do not believe in evil spirits? Or lower or higher spirits? Is that correct?

"That's true, Tom, my experience has proven to me that there is no such thing as evil or negative energy. There is no such thing as higher and lower entities."

So the beings, or the entities that you relate to (either in out of body experiences or in materialized form) you trust?

"Yes. I trust it because it is consistent. The know that the entities are in touch with all knowledge in spirit form so there is no hierarchy of superiority in knowledge."

How are you handling all the controversy about the Darkroom (as you call it) and the entities?

"I handle it very well, I think, Tom. Because I leave people with the freedom to believe what they believe and I make no judgment on that."

And you are firm in your beliefs?

"Yes. Very firm."

Thank you very much, Jay, it has been a delightful interview, for me.

"Thank you very much, Tom, it has been a privilege spending the day with you and as our friends would say upon parting, 'I have been blessed by your existence'."

REFERENCES

Arcangel, D. (2005). *Afterlife Encounters: Ordinary People, Extraordinary Experiences*. Charlottesville, VA: Hampton Roads Pub. Co.

Atwater, P.M.H. (2007). *The Big Book of Near-Death Experiences: The Ultimate Guide to What Happens When We Die*. Charlottesville, VA: Hampton Roads Pub. Co.

Bainton, R. H. (2000). *Christianity*. New York: First Mariner Books.

Barham, M. & Greene, T. (Ed.) (1981). *Bridging Two Worlds*. Valley Center, CA: MJB Books.

Barham, M.J. & Greene, J.T. (1986) *The Silver Cord: Lifeline to the Unobstructed*. Los Angeles, CA: DeVorss Publications.

Barham, M. & Greene, J.T. (1993). *Yesterday's Children*. New York: Vantage Press.

Botkin, A.L. & Hogan, R.C. (2005). *Induced After Death Communication: A New Therapy for Healing Grief and Trauma*. Charlottesville, VA: Hampton Roads Pub. Co.

Cavendish, R. (1980). *Mythology, An Illustrated Encyclopedia*. New York, Rizzoli.

Collins, F.A. (2006). *The Language of God: A Scientist Presents Evidence for Belief*. New York: The Free Press.

Cremo, M.A. & Thompson, R.L. (1996). *Hidden History of the Human Race: The Condensed Edition of Forbidden Archeology*. Adger, CA: Bhaktivedanta Book Pub. Co.

Cummings, N., O'Donohue, W., & Cummings, J. (Eds.)

(2009). *Psychology's War on Religion*. Phoenix, AZ: Zeig, Tucker & Theisen, Inc.

Dossey, L. (1999) *Reinventing Medicine: Beyond Mind-Body to a New Era of Healing*. New York: HarperCollins e-books.

Dossey, L. (2009). *The Power of Premonitions: How Knowing the Future Can Shape Our Lives*. New York: Penguin Group.

Fenwick, P. & Fenwick, E. (1999). *Past Lives: An Investigation into Reincarnation Memories*. New York: Berkley Books.

Fontana, D. (2003). *Psychology, Religion, and Spirituality*. Oxford, UK: BPS Blackwell.

Fontana, D. (2005). *Is There an Afterlife?: A Comprehensive Overview of the Evidence*. O Books: United Kingdom.

Fox, M. (1983). *Original Blessing: A Primer in Creation Spirituality*. New York: Putnam.

Foy, R. P. (2008). *Witnessing the Impossible*. Kings Lynn, Norfolk, UK: Torcal Publications.

Furst, J. (1968). *Edgar Cayce's Story of Jesus*. New York: Berkeley Publishing Group.

Goldberg, B. (2004). *Past Lives, Future Lives Revealed*. Franklin Lakes, NJ: New Page Books.

Goswami, A. (2001) *Physics of the Soul: The Quantum Book of Living, Dying, Reincarnation, and Immortality*. Charlottesville, VA: Hamptom Roads Publishing Co. Inc.

Goswami, A. (1995). *The Self-Aware Universe: How Consciousness Creates the Material World*. New York:

Penguin Putnam, Inc.

Goswami, A. (2008). *God Is Not Dead: What Quantum Physics Tells Us about Our Origins and How We Should Live*. Charlottesville, VA: Hamptom Roads Publishing Co. Inc.

Greene, T. & Barham, M. (1994). *Our Spiritual Connection*. Los Angeles, CA: DeVorss Publications.

Greer, J. (2003). *The Afterlife Connection: A Therapist Reveals How To Communicate With Departed Loved Ones*. New York: St. Martins Press.

Guggenheim, B. & Guggenheim, J. (1995). *Hello From Heaven!* Bantam Books: New York.

Haag, H. (1969). *Is Original Sin in the Scriptures?* New York: Sheed and Ward.

Haisch, G. (2006). *The God Theory: Universes, Zero-Point Field, and What's Behind it All*. San Francisco, CA: WeiserBooks.

Haisch, B. (2010). *The Purpose-Guided Universe: Believing in Einstein, Darwin, and God*. Franklin Lakes, NJ: Career Press. WeiserBooks.

Kapuscinski, A.N. & Masters, K.S. (2010). The current status of measures of spirituality: A critical review of scale development. *Psychology of Religion and Spirituality, 2,* 191-205.

Kardec, A. (n.d.). *The Spirits' Book*. http://www.spiritwritings.com/kardecspiritstoc.html

Keen, M., Ellison, A., & Fontana, D. (2011). *The Scole Report*. (no location): Saturday Night Press Publications.

Kenyon, J.D. (2005). *Forbidden History: Prehistoric Technologies, Extraterrestrial Intervention, and the Suppressed Origins of Civilization.* Rochester, Vermont: Bear & Company.

Koszycki, D., Raab, K., Aldosary, F., & Bradwejn, J. (2010). A Multi-faith Spiritually Based Intervention for Generalized Anxiety Disorder: A Pilot Randomized Trial. *Journal of Clinical Psychology, 66,* 430 – 441.

Krauss, L. M. (2012). *A Universe from Nothing: Why There Is Something Rather than Nothing.* New York: Simon & Schuster.

Kübler-Ross, E. (1997). *The Wheel of Life: A Memoir of Living and Dying.* New York: Simon & Schuster.

Kuhn, T.S. (1970). *The Structure of Scientific Revolutions* (2nd. Ed.) Chicago, IL: University of Chicago Press.

Lapple, A. (1986). *The Catholic Church: A Brief History.* New York: Paulist Press.

Leakey, R. (1994) *The Origin of Humankind.* New York: Basic Books.

LeShan, L. (2003). *The Medium, the Mystic, and the Physicist: Toward a General Theory of the Paranormal.* New York: Allworth Press.

Lermer, J. (2007). *Into the Light: Real Life Stories about Angelic Visits, Visions of the Afterlife, and Other Pre-death Experiences.* Franklin Lakes: New Page Books.

Levin, J. (2001). *God, Faith, and Health: Exploring the Spirituality-Healing Connection.* New York: John Wiley & Sons, Inc.

McDannell, C. & Lang, B. (2001). *Heaven: A History*. New Haven, CT: Yale University Press.

Milliken, M. (2012). *The Afterlife Survey: A Rabbi, a CEO, a Dog Walker, and Others on the Universal Question WHAT COMES NEXT?* Avon, Massachusetts: Aadamsmedia.

Newton, M. (2001). *Destiny of Souls: New Case Studies of Life Between Lives*. St. Paul, MN: Llewellyn Publications.

Newton, M. (2003). *Journey of Souls: Case Studies of Life between Lives*. St.Paul, MN: Llewellyn Publications.

Playfair, G. L. (2011). *The Flying Cow: Exploring the Psychic World of Brazil*. Guilford: UK: White Crow Books.

Radin, D. I. (1997). *The Conscious Universe: The Scientific Truth of Psychic Phenomena*. New York: HarperOne.

Radin, D.I. (2006). *Entangled Minds: Extrasensory experiences in a Quantum Reality*. New York: Paraview Pocket Books.

Ricouer, P. (1984). (quoted in Henri Blocher, *In the Beginning: The Opening Chapters of Genesis*, Leicester, England: Inter-Varsity Press, 1984, pp. 157, 158).

Roberts, J. (1970). *The Seth Material*. New York: Bantum Books.

Roberts, J. (1972). *Seth Speaks*. San Rafael, CA: Amber-Allen Pub. And New World Library.

Rosenblum, B. & Kuttner, F. (2006). *Quantum Enigma: Physics Encounters Consciousness*. New York: Oxford University Press.

Schroeder, G. (1997). *The Science of God: The Convergence of Scientific and Biblical Wisdom*. New York: The Free Press.

Schwartz, G.E. & Russek, L.G. (1999). *The Living Energy Universe*. Charlottesville, VA: Hampton Roads Pub. Co.

Schwartz, G.E. & Simon, W.L. (2005). *The Truth about Medium*. Charlottesville, VA: Hampton Roads Pub. Co.

Schwartz, G.E. & Simon, W.L. (2006). *The G.O.D. Experiments*. New York: Atria Books.

Schwartz, G.E., Simon, W.L., & Russek, L.G. (2002). *The Afterlife Experiments: Breakthrough Scientific Evidence of Life After Death*. New York: Pocket Books.

Schwartz, R. (2009). *Your Soul's Plan: Discovering the Real Meaning of the Life You Planned Before You Were Born*. Frog Books: Berkeley, CA.

Stevenson, I. (1997). *Where Reincarnation and Biology Intersect*. West Port, CT: Praeger.

Targ, R. & Katra, J. (1999). *Miracles of Mind: Exploring Nonlocal Consciousness and Spiritual Healing*. Novato, CA: New World Library.

Tart, C.T. (2009). *The End of Materialism: How Evidence of the Paranormal is Bringing Science and Spirit Together*. New Harbinger Pub. Inc.: Oakland, CA.

The Lost Tomb of Jesus. Dir. Simcha Jacobovici. Discovery Channel, 2007. DVD.

Todeschi, K.J. (1998). *Edgar Cayce on the Akashic Records*. Virginia Beach, VA: A.R.E. Press.

Tucker, J.B. (2005). *Life Before Life: A Scientific Investigation of Children's Memories of Previous Lives.* New York: St. Martin's Press.

Turner, J.L. (2009). *Medicine, Miracles, and Manifestations: A Doctor's Journey Through the Worlds of Divine Intervention, Near-Death Experiences, and Universal Energy.* Franklin Lakes, NJ: Career Press Inc.

Tymn, M.E. (2008). *The Articulate Dead: They Brought the Spirit World Alive.* Lakeville, MN: Galde Press.

Tymn, M.E. (2011). *The Afterlife Revealed: What Happens After We Die.* Guildford, UK: While Crow Books.

Van Lommel, P. (2010). *Consciousness Beyond Life: The Science of the Near Death Experience.* HarperCollins e-books.

Vandersande, J. W. (2008). *Life After Death: Some of the Best Evidence.* Denver, CO: Outskirts Press, Inc.

Vandersande, J.W. (2012). Three materialization séances with David Thompson. *The Journal of Spirituality and Paranormal Studies, 35,* 136-143.

Walsch, N.D. (1995). *Conversations with God: An Uncommon Dialogue Book 1.* New York: G.P. Putnam's Sons.

Weiss, B. L. (2004). *Same Soul, Many Bodies: Discover the Healing Power of Future Lives Through Progression Therapy.* New York: Free Press.

Worthington, E.L., Hook, J.N., Davis, D.E. & McDaniel, M.C. (2011). Religion and Spirituality, *Journal of Clinical Psychology: In Session, 67,* 204 – 214.

Additional Suggested Readings

Adler, M.J. (1982). *The Angels and Us*. eISBN 978-1-43910-578-8.

Allen, M.E. (2007). *The Survival Files: The Most Convincing Evidence Yet Compiled for the Survival of Your Soul*. Hanover, PA: Momentpoint Media.

Anderson, G. & Barone, A. (2012). *Ask George Anderson What Souls in the Afterlife Can Teach Us About Life*. New York: Berkley Books.

Atwater, P.M.H. (2005). *Beyond the Indigo Children: The New Children and the Coming of the Fifth World*. Rochester, VT: Bear & Company.

Barker, E. (2009). *Letters from a Living Dead Man*. LaVerge, TN: White Crow Books.

Barrett, S.W. (2011). *Deathbed Visions*. Guildford, UK: White Crow Books.

Borgia, A. (1954). *Life in the Unseen World*. London: Odhams Press. Retrieved from http://anthony3741.tripod.com/

Bragdon, E. (2012). *Spiritism and Mental Health: Practices from Spiritist Centers and Spiritist Psychiatric Hospitals in Brazil*. London: Singing Dragon.

Chopra, D. (2000). *How to Know God: The Soul's Journey into the Mystery of Mysteries*. New York: Three Rivers Press.

Crookall, R. (1974). *The Supreme Adventure: Analyses of Psychic Communications*. Cambridge, UK: James Clarke & Co. Ltd.

Cusick, A. (2012). *The Psychology of the Soul.* (no location): www.angelville.net.

Dalzell, G. E. (2002). *Messages: Evidence for Life After Death.* Charlottesville, VA: Hampton Roads Pub. Co.

Feather, S.R. & Schmicker, M. (2005). *The Gift: ESP, the Extraordinary Experiences of Ordinary People.* New York: St. Martins Paperbacks.

Fontana, D. (2003). *Psychology, Religion, and Spirituality.* Malden, MA: Blackwell Publishing.

Friedlander, J. & Hemsher, G. (2011). *Psychic Psychology: Energy Skills for Life and Relationships.* Berkeley, CA: North Atlantic Books.

Goforth, A. & Gray, T. (2009). *The Risen: Dialogues of Love, Grief, & Survival-Beyond Death-.* New York: Tempestina Teapot Books.

Kardec, A. & Blackwell, A. (2010). *The Gospel According to Spiritism.* London: The Headquarters Publishing Co. Ltd. Retrieved from http://www.geae.inf.br/en/books/codification/gospel.pdf (Original work published 1866)

Kardec, A. (2010). *The Book on Mediums.* LaVergne, TN: White Crow Books.

Klimo, J. (1998). *Channeling: Investigations on Receiving Information from Paranormal Sources.* Berkeley, CA: North Atlantic Books.

Koenig, H.G. (2007). *Spirituality in Patient Care: Why, How, When, and What.* Philadelphia: Templeton Foundation Press.

Krajenke, R.W. (2012). *Edgar Cayce's Story of the Bible.* Virginia Beach, VA: A.R.E. Press.

Kribbe, P. (2008). *The Jeshua Channelings: Christ Consciousness in a New Era.* (no location): Booklocker.com, Inc.

Laddon, J. (1987). *Beyond the Veil.* Spokane, WA: The Printed Word.

Laddon, J. (1988/2001). *A Further Step Beyond the Veil.* Spokane, WA: The Printed Word.

Laddon, J. (1988). *Another Look at Life Beyond the Veil.* Spokane, WA: The Printed Word.

Lazarus (1987). *The Sacred Journey: You and Your Higher Self.* Beverley Hills, CA: Concept: Synergy Publishing.

Little, G.L., Little, L., & Van Auken, J. (2006). *Edgar Cayce's Atlantis.* Virginia Beach: A.R.E. Press.

Multiple Authors (1996-2010). *The Urantia Book.* New York: Uversa Press.

Parry, J., Robinson, S., Watson, N.J., & Nesti, M. (2007). *Sport and Spirituality: An Introduction.* London: Routledge Taylor & Francis Group.

Playfair, G.L. (2008). *Twin Telepathy.* Guilford, UK: White Crow Books.

Roberts, J. (1988). *Seth, Dreams and Projections of Consciousness.* Manhasset, NY: New Awareness Network.

Roberts, J. (1997). *Dreams," Evolution," and Value Fulfillment.* Volume One. San Rafael, CA: Amber-Allen

Pub. Co.

Roberts, J. (1997). *Dreams," Evolution," and Value Fulfillment*. Volume Two. San Rafael, CA: Amber-Allen Pub. Co.

Roberts, J. (2001). *The Afterdeath Journal of an American Philosopher: The World View of William James*. Manhasset, NY: New Awareness Network, Inc.

Schmicker, M. (2002). *Best Evidence 2nd Edition: An Investigative Reporter's Three Year Quest to Uncover the Best Scientific Evidence for ESP, Psychokinesis, Mental Healing, Ghosts and Poltergeists, Dowsing, Medius, Near Death Experiences, Reincarnation, and Other Impossible Phenomena That Refuse to Disappear*. San Jose, CA: Writers Club Press.

Schwartz, G.E. (2011). *The Sacred Promise: How Science is Discovering Spirit's Collaboration with Us in Our Daily Lives*. New York: Atria Books.

Schwartz, R. (2012). *Your Soul's Gift: The Healing Power of the Life You Planned Before You Were Born*. (no location): Whispering Winds Press.

Scranton, L. (2006). *The Science of the Dogon: Decoding the African Mystery Tradition*. Rochester, VT: Inner Traditions.

Sheldrake, R. (2009). *Morphic Resonance: The Nature of Formative Causation*. Rochester, VT: Park Street Press.

Smith, S. (1999). *Life Is Forever: Evidence for Survival After Death*. Lincoln, NE: toExcel.

Smith.S. (2000). *The Book of James (William James, That Is)*. Lincoln, NE: toExcel.

Solomon, G. & Solomon, J. ((1999). *The Scole Experiment: Scientific Evidence for Life After Death*. Essex, UK: Campion Books.

Thurston, M. (2004). *The Essential Edgar Cayce*. New York: Penguin Group.

Tymn, M. (2012). *Transcending the Titanic: Beyond Death's Door*. Guilford, UK: White Crow Books.

Tymn, M. (2013. *Resurrecting Leonora Piper: How Science Discovered the Afterlife*. Guilford, UK: White Crow Books.

Van Praagh, J. (1997). *Talking to Heaven: A Medium's Message of Life After Death*. New York: Penguin Putnam, Inc.

Varghese, R.A. (2010). *There Is Life After Death: Compelling Reports From Those Who Have Glimpsed the Afterlife*. Franklin Lakes, NJ: New Page Books.

Virtue, D. (1997). *Angel Therapy: Healing Messages for Every Area of Your Life*. Carlsbad, CA: Hay House, Inc.

Walsch, N.D. (1995). *Conversations with God: An Uncommon Dialogue Book 1*. New York: G.P. Putnam's Sons.

Walsch, N.D. (1997). *Conversations with God Book 2: Living in the World With Honesty, Courage, and Love*. Charlottesville, VA: Hampton Roads Pub.

Walsch, N.D. (2002). *The New Revelations: A Conversation With God*. New York: Atria Boods.

Walsch, N.D. (2006). *Home With God: In a Life that Never Ends: A Wondrous Message of Love in a Final Conversation*

With God. New York: Atria Books.

Wands, J.A. (n.d.). *Another Door Opens: A Psychic Explains How Those in the World of Spirit Continue to Impact Our Lives*. New York: Atria Books. ISBN 0-7432-9367-3

Weiss, B.L. (1988). *Many Lives, Many Masters: The True Story of a Prominent Psychiatrist, His Young Patient, and the Past-Life Therapy That Changed Both Their Lives*. New York: A Touchstone Book.

Weiss, B.L. (1992). Through Time Into Healing: Discovering the Power of Regression Therapy to Erase Trauma and Transform Mind, Body, and Relationships. New York: A Touchstone Book.

Wells, H.G. (1993-2013). *A Short History of the World*. Retrieved from http://www.bartleby.com/86/ (Original work published 1922)

White, S.E. (2003). *The Unobstructed Universe*. Retrieved from http://gutenberg.not.au/ebooks03/0301131txt (Original work published 1941)

Xavier, F.C. (2009). *And Life Goes On: Life in the Spirit World*. Brasilia(DF), Brazil: Federacao Espirita Brasileira.

Xavier, F.C. (2009). *Missionaries of the Light: Life in the Spirit World*. Brasilia(DF), Brazil: Federacao Espirita Brasileira.

Acknowledgement to Annette Priesman, M.A.

The Editor wishes to deeply thank Annette for her help with this manuscript. She assisted with copyediting and with clarifying the content by asking incisive questions and making clarifying contributions. Working with her has been a delight. I am sure we are kindred spirits and I am grateful that she agreed to work with me on converting the original manuscript into an updated book suitable for the world literature. Annette, I am blessed by your existence.

Cover by David Iwamoto

The cover is symbolic of the contents of this book. David explains the cover as follows:

"Because the amoeba arose from the ocean, I have the atom representing the building blocks of the physical body, rising or floating above flowing water. The water is a bit abstract; however, if you use your imagination, it represents water or ocean waves. The electrons on the atom are green, red, yellow, and blue. Marti says those are the colors of the four quadrants. The two blue triangles represent the letter 'K' named after " . . . the entity 'K' who supervised the teachings of the materialized entities Aenka and Mario.

As mentioned in Chapter Six of this book, "aura's can be used for identifying the physical personality structure. There are four colors in the aura that make up the basic personality structure with which one is born and these never change during a particular incarnation. Indeed, when electing to incarnate, a discarnate considers the basic personality structure of the newborn before deciding to endow it. The four colors are green, red, yellow, and blue. Green reflects the physical function/quadrant of extraversion. Red reflects the emotional/feeling quadrant. Yellow reflects the intuitive/spiritual quadrant of introversion. Blue reflects the intellectual/thinking quadrant. The two bands of color closest to the body indicate the personality structure. There are four basic personality structures of the physical body: (1) thinking extravert (blue first, then green); (2) thinking introvert (blue first, then yellow); (3) feeling extravert (red first, then green); and (4) feeling introvert (red first, then yellow). Perceiving one's personality structure is informative in how to approach an individual and oneself."

The Author and Editor are deeply grateful to David for his creation of the cover for this book. David is a close comrade of the Author and has assisted her with the illustrations for a number of books she uses in her private practice when working with children and families. These include books about assisting children about drug abuse, grief, deployment of a parent, anger and frustration, shame, and parental divorce. David is a true and humble friend.

Printed in Poland
by Amazon Fulfillment
Poland Sp. z o.o., Wrocław

60441705R00295